Cori spezzati

VOLUME I

Cori spezzati deals with polychoral church music from its beginnings in the first few decades of the sixteenth century to its climax in the work of Giovanni Gabrieli and Heinrich Schütz. In polychoral music the singers, sometimes with instrumentalists also, were split into two (or more) groups which often engaged in lively dialogue and joined in majestic tutti climaxes. The book draws on contemporary descriptions of the idiom, especially from the writings of Vicentino and Zarlino, but concentrates in the main on musical analysis, showing how antiphonal chanting (such as that of the psalms), dialogue and canon influenced the phenomenon. Polychoral music has often been considered synonymous not only with Venetian music, but with impressive pomp. Anthony Carver's study shows that it was cultivated by many composers outside Venice – in Rome, all over Northern Italy, in Catholic and Protestant areas of Germany, in Spain and the New World – and that it was as capable of quiet devotion or mannerist expressionism as of outgoing pomp. Perhaps most important, music by several major composers about which there is still surprisingly little in the literature is treated in depth: the Gabrielis, Lasso, Palestrina, Victoria, and several German masters. The book is illustrated with many musical examples.

A companion volume offers an anthology of seventeen complete pieces, most of which are analysed in the text of Volume I.

Cori spezzati

VOLUME I
THE DEVELOPMENT OF
SACRED POLYCHORAL MUSIC
TO THE TIME OF SCHÜTZ

ANTHONY F. CARVER

Senior Lecturer in Music
The Queen's University of Belfast

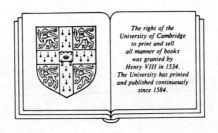

The right of the
University of Cambridge
to print and sell
all manner of books
was granted by
Henry VIII in 1534.
The University has printed
and published continuously
since 1584.

CAMBRIDGE UNIVERSITY PRESS

Cambridge
New York   New Rochelle   Melbourne   Sydney

Published by the Press Syndicate of the University of Cambridge
The Pitt Building, Trumpington Street, Cambridge CB2 1RP
32 East 57th Street, New York, NY 10022, USA
10 Stamford Road, Oakleigh, Melbourne 3166, Australia

First published 1988

Printed in Great Britain at
the University Press, Cambridge

British Library cataloguing in publication data
Carver, Anthony F.
Cori spezzati.
Vol. I: The development of sacred
polychoral music to the time of Schütz.
1. Cori spezzati – History and criticism
I. Title
783.4   ML1554

Library of Congress cataloguing in publication data
Carver, Anthony F.
The development of sacred polychoral music to the
time of Schütz.
(Cori spezzati; v. I)
Bibliography.
Includes index.
1. Choral music. 2. Church music. I. Title.
II. Series.
M1.C79   1987   vol. I   784.1 s   87–24904
[783.4′09′032]

ISBN 0 521 30398 2 Volume I
ISBN 0 521 30399 0 Volume II
ISBN 0 521 36172 9 the set

For my wife

CONTENTS

PREFACE

With the continuing interest of contemporary composers in the compositional possibilities of space and the acceptance of stereophony as the norm in the reproduction of music, it seems an appropriate time to celebrate one of the glories of the late Renaissance and early Baroque music – the polychoral style. By the late sixteenth century music for two and sometimes more choirs was cultivated over much of Italy, Spain and both Catholic and Protestant areas of German-speaking lands. The primacy traditionally assigned to Venice in the origins of this style must be questioned both in the light of the sheer volume of polychoral music produced elsewhere and through an examination of the probable origins of the technique in its earliest manifestations. We shall find its roots in formal and stylistic tendencies of the music of Josquin and his generation, in composers' responses to the demands of their texts, and in the age-old liturgical practice of antiphony. The achievements of the Gabrielis will be given due attention as great music without exaggerating their historical significance.

This study makes no claim to completeness as a history of polychoral music. This is ruled out by the sheer quantity of extant sources dating from the 1570s onwards. I have tried to give as comprehensive an account as possible of the formative years of the style, to about 1570, and then to select composers whose outputs in this area seem significant: Lasso; the Gabrielis and their Venetian contemporaries; the most prolific of late sixteenth-century composers active elsewhere in Northern Italy; Palestrina, Victoria and some of their Roman and Spanish contemporaries, and the most important German masters. The discussion of German music will range further into the seventeenth century because of the continued popularity there of the Gabrielian brand of polychoral music after its star had waned in Italy, and also because two other scholars have dealt with developments in Italy in the first half of the seventeenth century: Jerome Roche in his study of church music in Northern Italy (1984), and Graham Dixon in his thesis on church music in Rome (1981). Although I have tried to incorporate where appropriate the latest findings of those involved in archival research, this book is primarily about the music itself, the glorious sonority and fascinating formal patterns which first drew me to the subject.

The companion anthology to this book has been compiled both to facilitate analysis and to provide as representative a collection as the space available allows. In the selection of musical examples within the present volume, priority has been given to music unavailable or less accessible in modern edition. Enjoyment of the book will be enhanced by reference to the complete editions of, especially, Willaert, Lasso, Palestrina, Victoria and Schütz.

ACKNOWLEDGMENTS

First I must thank Professor David Greer for suggesting that this book be written. My grateful thanks are due also to the late Professor Denis Arnold, Professor Paul Doe and Dr Nigel Fortune for their help and supervision during the earlier stages of my research. I should like to thank the following scholars for sharing their thoughts and in some cases materials freely: David Bryant, Frank Carey, Roger Jacob, David Nutter, Noel O'Regan, Victor Ravizza, and Bojan Bujič for his help with Höfler's article in Serbo-Croat.

My work on this subject was begun with the aid of a Major State Studentship from the Department of Education and Science, and I am also grateful to that body for financing an extended visit to Europe. My thanks also to the University of Birmingham and the Queen's University of Belfast for assistance in the acquisition of microfilms, and to Queen's University and the British Academy for grants enabling me to visit Treviso and Bologna respectively. This book could not have been written without the generous granting by Queen's of a year's study leave.

Thanks are due also to the staff of many libraries for their courteous and efficient service. I acknowledge with thanks permission to quote from manuscripts in the possession of the following: Bayerische Staatsbibliothek, Munich (Ex. 29); Biblioteca Della Curia Vescovile, Padua (Exx. 7–10); Biblioteca Apostolica Vaticana, Rome (Ex. 15); Biblioteca Capitolare, Treviso (Exx. 6, 11); Accademia Filarmonica, Verona (Exx. 2–5); Österreichische Nationalbibliothek, Vienna (Exx. 21, 60). I would also like to thank the following: Queen's University Library, Belfast; Biblioteca Civica, Bergamo; Library of the Barber Institute, Birmingham; Civico Museo Bibliografico Musicale, Bologna; Pendlebury Library, Cambridge; British Library, London; Library of the University of London; Biblioteca Capitolare, Modena; Biblioteca Estense, Modena; Library of the Hispanic Society of America, New York; Library of the University of North Carolina; Bibliothèque Nationale, Paris; Bibliothèque Sainte-Geneviève, Paris; Ratsschulbibliothek, Zwickau.

Finally, I wish to thank the following publishers for permission to quote from copyright material:

Akademische Druck- und Verlagsanstalt (Exx. 70, 71 & 72, from DDT 2, rev. edn by C. Russell Crosby, © Copyright 1961 by Akademische Druck- und Verlagsanstalt; Ex. 69, from DTÖ 12, Ex. 68, from DTÖ 24, Exx. 65 & 67, from DTÖ 40, Ex. 66, from DTÖ 48, all ed. E. Bezecny & J. Mantuani,

ABBREVIATIONS

General

c.f.	*cantus firmus*	ch.	choir
diss.	dissertation	mod. edn	modern edition
R	reprint	suppl.	supplement
trans.	translation		
transcr.	unpublished transcription		
U.	University	v.	verse
vol.	volume		

Voice names

D: discantus
S: soprano
Tr: treble
A: alto or contralto
Ct: contratenor
T: tenor
Bar: baritone
B: bass
8: octava pars

Clef notation

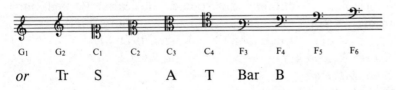

G₁	G₂	C₁	C₂	C₃	C₄	F₃	F₄	F₅	F₆

or   Tr   S   A   T   Bar   B

Bibliographical references

In general a modified form of the author–date system has been used. Books, articles and original publications of music by a single composer are referred to by surname and year of publication. Where reference is made to two distinct publications of the same year by an author or composer, they are distinguished as, for example, 1596a, 1596b. Articles in *The New Grove* are cited in the text but not listed in the Bibliography unless of particular importance.

Modern editions of music by a single composer are listed under the composer's surname, by year of publication unless part of a collected edition or publication of the *Denkmäler* type, in which case abbreviations like 'Werke', 'Opera' or 'DDT' are used. Sixteenth- and seventeenth-century anthologies are cited by RISM number (e.g. 1564[(1)]), modern anthologies by editor and year of publication. Latin psalms are numbered as in the Vulgate, those in German according to the normal Protestant order.

Bibliographical abbreviations

AcM	*Acta Musicologica*
AMw	*Archiv für Musikwissenschaft*
CMM	Corpus mensurabilis musicae
DTÖ	Denkmäler der Tonkunst in Österreich
DDT	Denkmäler deutscher Tonkunst
EDM	Das Erbe deutscher Musik
EM	*Early Music*
EMH	*Early Music History*
HAM	*Historical Anthology of Music*, ed. W. Apel & A. T. Davison. 2 vols., Cambridge, Mass., 1950.
JAMS	*Journal of the American Musicological Society*
JRBM	*Journal of Renaissance and Baroque Music*
LU	Liber usualis
Mf	*Die Musikforschung*
ML	*Music and Letters*
MQ	*Musical Quarterly*
NA	*Note d'archivio*
NGr	*The New Grove Dictionary of Music and Musicians*, ed. Stanley Sadie. London, 1980.
PRMA	*Proceedings of the Royal Musical Association*
RdM	*Revue de Musicologie*
RISM	Répertoire international des sources musicales: Recueils imprimés, XVIe–XVIIe siècles. Munich & Duisburg, 1960. Series A: Einzeldrucke vor 1800. Kassel, 1971–81.
RRMR	*Recent Researches in the Music of the Renaissance*
SM	*Studi Musicali*
ZMw	*Zeitschrift für Musikwissenschaft*

Libraries

A-Wn	Vienna, Österreichische Nationalbibliothek
D-Mbs	Munich, Bayerische Staatsbibliothek
I-Bc	Bologna, Civico Museo Bibliografico Musicale
I-MOd	Modena, Biblioteca Capitolare
I-Rn	Rome, Biblioteca Nazionale Centrale
I-VEaf	Verona, Accademia Filarmonica

Musical examples and analysis

In musical examples, except for Exx. 1, 54 (G. Gabrieli), 55 and 76–9, note values are halved in duple-time sections (signatures ¢ and ¢). Those in triple-time sections are sometimes halved, sometimes quartered, the signatures 3/2 and 3/4 respectively being employed. The Helmholtz system of pitch identification has been used whereby c' = middle C.

a	A minor (chord, cadence or key, depending on the context); cadences ending with a major chord are indicated a(♯), g(♮) etc.
A	A major
à 2, 3 etc.	for two, three etc. voices
Ch. 1 → 2	antiphonal repetition by Choir 2 of a phrase stated by Choir 1
Ch. 1 ↔ 2	Choirs 1 & 2 exchange material when a passage is repeated

A DEFINITION

It is essential to be clear exactly what is meant by 'polychoral'. The following definition is suggested as being consistent with sixteenth-century theory and practice: *a polychoral work or passage is one in which the ensemble is consistently split into two or more groups, each retaining its own identity, which sing separately and together within a through-composed framework in which antiphony is a fundamental compositional resource; in tutti passages all voice-parts should normally remain independent, with the possible exception of the bass parts.* Thus most Anglican *cantoris–decani* practice does not come within the definition, being more of a kind of antiphonal *divisi* technique. Poly-choralism usually lies within the realm of technique or style rather than genre, though there are exceptions to this where the liturgical format of, for example, psalms or canticles is strictly adhered to. My approach to the phenomenon is primarily as a compositional technique; the question of performing locations and spatial separation will be treated mainly in terms of its reflection in the technique of individual pieces.

1

THE ORIGINS AND DEVELOPMENT OF *CORI SPEZZATI*

Early references in archival and other documents

Evidence for the cultivation of polychoral music is to be found in several types of source material: archival records, other documents and books, theoretical treatises and musical sources. Analysis of the surviving music will form the main part of this study, but it will be helpful first to assemble a summary of the evidence available from other sources. Most of the material presented here has been gleaned from secondary sources; important exceptions are the extracts from Massimo Troiano (1568), his famous description of the 1568 Munich wedding celebrations, and the treatises of Vicentino and Zarlino, whose discussions are analysed in some detail.

References to polychoral music in the Renaissance aside from musical sources are not particularly numerous. Many are circumstantial or imprecise in some respect, and some only appear to refer to polychoral performances. Thus when we read (Sandberger 1894–5, vol. 1: 104) that the singers at Antwerp Cathedral in 1482 were divided into two groups of 29 and 31, undoubtedly this represents a continuation of the *alternatim* practice described by Reese (1954: 118) whereby at Our Lady of Antwerp during Ockeghem's time there in 1443–4 the 25 *cantoris* singers sang the polyphony, the *decani* singers the chant.

Similarly circumstantial for much of the sixteenth century is the evidence of more than one organ in some churches. A second organist was appointed at St Mark's, Venice, from 1490 (Caffi 1854–5: 54), which would have made it feasible to perform double-choir music with one choir in each of the organ galleries, each with support from its own organ. However, there is no direct evidence of such an accompanimental rôle for the organ until the appearance of organ parts in some late sixteenth-century prints; the most we can say is that the latter might represent a codification of an existing practice. (In actual fact composers were as likely to provide a single organ bass following the lowest sounding note at any moment as a separate organ bass for each choir.) The tests given to candidates applying for vacant organists' posts at St Mark's (Benvenuti 1931: xlv) are not particularly illuminating on this point; they stress improvisation on given *cantus firmi* and *alternatim* between choir and organ. St Mark's was not unique in possessing two organs. St Antony's in Padua also had two from about 1490 (Tebaldini 1895: 2) and in 1539 the authorities decided to have two new organs positioned on columns on either side of the choir (ibid.: 3). Milan Cathedral had two organs from about 1466 (Muoni 1883: 8, 11 & 17), and the Santa Casa in Loreto commissioned a second organ in 1563 (Alfieri 1970: 38). The Archiconfraternità della Santissima Trinità in Rome possessed a small portable organ in addition to a permanent instrument. Further circumstantial evidence pre-dating precise reference to polychoral music in the confraternity concerns the construction in 1572 of access doors to two *cantori di sopra*, i.e. choir galleries or balconies (O'Regan 1985).

Several accounts, some very well known, describe a division of musical forces without specifying the nature of the music. At Pesaro in 1475, for example, at the wedding of Costanzo Sforza with Camilla di Aragona,

Mass was celebrated triumphantly with organs, shawms, and trumpets and countless drums, there being two choirs [*capelle*] and many singers, which sang now one, now the other, and there were about sixteen singers in each choir.   (Gamba 1836: 17, my translation)

The presence of two *capelle* reminds us of the famous meeting of Henry VIII and Francis I on the Field of the Cloth of Gold in 1520 (Godefroy 1649, vol. 2: 745). At Mass the English singers sang one introit, the French (under Mouton) a second, and thereafter they alternated separate portions of the Ordinary, without performing anything together.

When the Queen of Cyprus visited Brescia in 1497 we read that instrumentalists were divided into two groups, fourteen 'tamborini, stafeti, violete e lauti' and ten 'tromboni et piferi' (Kimmel 1942, vol. 1: 17). Three-quarters of a century later, in 1570, Philip II entered Seville Cathedral:

In opposite niches of this floral archway, thirteen instrumentalists are stationed: on one side six shawmers and sackbut players wearing blue robes and hats bordered with gold; on the other side seven specially hired viol players wearing crimson and gold. The procession includes sixteen cathedral boys. . .eight singing and the other eight dancing. After Philip has sworn to observe the ancient privileges of the Cathedral, all the singers and instrumentalists stationed in the various parts of the huge edifice burst into a hymn of acclamation.   (Stevenson 1961: 29)

Clearly a resplendent tutti, but was there any antiphony?

All these cases concern performances of music of an unknown type. One account tells us of the performance of a known monochoral piece by divided forces. When in 1539 Eleonora of Toledo arrived at the gate of the city of Florence prior to her wedding with Cosimo I de' Medici, Corteccia's *Ingredere* was sung on top of a specially constructed archway by 'twenty-four voices in one group, and in the other four trombones and four cornetti' (1539[25]: contents page). The motet (Minor and Mitchell 1968: 104) is for an undivided eight-part ensemble. The scoring described strongly suggests that all eight parts were to be heard sung on one side and played on the other.

Indubitable references to polychoral music seem to date from the 1520s. In Treviso in the years 1521, 1522 and 1523 at the annual commemoration of deceased members of the Confraternità del Santissimo Sacramento, Vespers and Requiem Mass were sung by the Cappella of Treviso Cathedral under the direction of Francesco Santacroce with music for two choirs (D'Alessi 1954: 71). The vesper psalms might have been Santacroce's own double-choir settings, some of which are preserved in the archive of the Cathedral (see Chapter 2). In Ferrara in 1529 Don Ercole d'Este gave a banquet during the third course of which *dialoghi* were performed with 'four voices, one lute, one viola, one transverse flute and one trombone in each group' (Anthon 1943: 122; Nutter 1977: 167–9). If these were genuine double-choir dialogues, 1529 is quite an early date for them.

In Bergamo in 1536 Pietro Aaron was admitted to the *Crociferi* at the monastery of S. Leonardo; Gasparo Alberti and twenty-two singers performed psalms and a magnificat with *cori spezzati* (Jeppesen 1941: 38; D'Alessi 1954: 78). The music for one choir of double-choir psalm-settings by Ruffino and by Alberti himself has been preserved in a Bergamo manuscript (see Chapter 2). Our first reference from outside Italy is Spanish: at the time of Morales's application for the post of *maestro de capilla* at Toledo Cathedral in 1545 prospective candidates were required to write an *Asperges* for double choir (Stevenson 1961: 29). Confirmation of double-choir practice at the Santa Casa in Loreto comes in a reference in 1552 to the purchase of two choir-books of *psalmi spezzati* 'to be sung with two choirs' (Alfieri 1970: 37).

Lavish court celebrations, particularly those with political significance, were sometimes adorned with polychoral music, and accounts of such events tend to furnish more details of the works performed. Florentine *intermedii* included polychoral madrigals as early as 1565; in that year, on the occasion of the wedding of Francesco de' Medici and Joanna of Austria, Striggio's eight-part *A me, che fatta son negletta* was performed as part of the *Intermedii* for Francesco d'Ambra's *La Cofanaria*. It was sung by eight voices onstage (Venus, three Graces and four Seasons), accompanied from offstage by two harpsichords, four violas da gamba, alto lute, mute cornetto, trombone and two recorders (Brown 1973: 97; the music: Osthoff 1967: suppl. no. 15). The most sumptuous *intermedii* of all, those of 1589, contained much polychoral music, described in detail by Howard Brown (1973) and edited from the original 1591 publication by D. P. Walker (1963). In Ferrara in 1565, at the wedding of Alfonso II d'Este and Barbara of Austria, Wert's *Cara Germania mia*, a double-choir dialogue, was performed antiphonally from two balconies (Mac-Clintock 1966: 92).

The Bavarian Royal Wedding, 1568

This celebration, one of the most lavish events in the entire sixteenth century, was described in some detail by Massimo Troiano in his famous dialogue (1568). Troiano was one of the court musicians and his book is of great value for its descriptions of the musical personnel and their performances. The original versions of the passages which follow will be found in Appendix 1. He gives details of the scoring of some unspecified music in twelve parts divided into three choirs:

[the] first Choir with four viola [sic] da Gamba, [the] second, four bass recorders, and [the] third, four different instruments: that is a Dulzaine, a Cornamuse, a Flute,[1] and a Mute corn[ett]o.   (Troiano 1568: 102)

Similar principles of scoring were apparently applied in the performance of a 'concerto' for twenty-four voices, three choirs à 8:

Eight violas da Gamba, eight Violas, da braccio, & eight different instruments: that is a Bassoon, a Cornamuse, a mute Cornetto: an alto Cornetto: a large curved Cornetto, a Flute, a dulzaine, & a Trombone, bass: the first and second parts were played once without voices: and afterwards, with parts for eight Sonorous voices by Messer Orlando, it was given once more.
                                                                                                (ibid.: 150)

Our last quotation concerns two identifiable polychoral works on a huge scale:

FORTUNIO: On Sunday [7 March], was sung with solemnity, a Mass à 24 by the excellent Messer Aniballe Paduano, Organist, of the Most Ser. Archduke Carl of Austria. And during dinner the excellent Messere Orlando di Lasso, amongst the other pieces, which he performed, caused to be sung and played a Motet in forty parts which was worthy of all honour and praise.
   MARINIO: Tell me in what way were the parts arranged?
   FOR: Eight Trombones, eight Violas da gamba, eight bass recorders, a harpsichord, and a large Lute; all the rest the voices supplied, and it was given three times, with the greatest attention.
   MAR: And who was the author of this superb, and not displeasing composition?
   FOR: Signore Alesandro striggio [a] gentleman from Mantua. . .   (ibid.: 182)

We can be reasonably certain that the Mass à 24 by Annibale is that preserved in a Vienna manuscript (Nationalbibliothek, Ms. 16702: f. 240v), whilst the forty-part motet by Striggio is doubtless *Ecce beatam lucem*, which survives in a Zwickau copy dated 1587 (Ratsschulbibliothek, Ms. 732). Both works will be discussed in Chapter 4.

The first reference to the performance of a known polychoral work in Venice appears to be from 1574, in which year Andrea Gabrieli composed two double-choir madrigals, *Hor che nel suo bel seno* à 8 and *Ecco Vineggia bella* à 12 (Gabrieli, A., CM, vol. 12: viii). Such references are in fact quite rare, rendering the dating of multi-part music by the Gabrielis very difficult, a problem we shall return to in Chapter 7. Prior to the Gabrielis – Andrea's first polychoral work appeared in 1568 – the only evidence of polychoral sacred music in Venice is the existence of Willaert's *Salmi spezzati* of 1550, though, as we shall see, the actual manner in which such pieces were sung in St Mark's was probably to be found nowhere else. Documentation of polychoral performances in Rome also begins in the 1570s. In 1573 Victoria's *Super flumina Babylonis* à 8 was performed at a ceremony marking the separation of the Collegium Romanum and the Collegium Germanicum (Collet 1914: 56–7). From 1576 at the Seminario Romano Vespers and Compline were sung 'a due Chori' on principal feasts; extra singers were brought in from outside for the purpose

(Casimiri 1935: 12–14). Recent research by Noel O'Regan and Graham Dixon shows that polychoral music became popular in Rome from the late sixteenth century onwards, particularly with confraternities.

Accounts such as the preceding give only a partial picture of the gradual rise in importance of the polychoral technique in sixteenth-century church music. Most of the above material concerns festive occasions, in some cases purely secular ones. This is to be expected, since by its very nature the medium is ideally suited to adding pomp and splendour to an important ceremony. However, the large volume of polychoral music preserved leads one to conclude that quite a few establishments must have been able to muster the forces to perform such music on a regular basis. To begin to assess the everyday importance of the medium let us explore the work of those who attempt to codify standard practice: the musical theorists.

Vicentino and Zarlino

Until the discovery of earlier sources containing double-choir music by Ruffino, Santacroce and other North Italian composers (D'Alessi 1952) it was thought that Willaert invented the *coro spezzato*. It is probably still widely assumed that the famous 1550 publication was the chief inspiration for subsequent cultivation of the medium. And yet those strictly liturgical psalms, so lacking in the outgoing pomp that was surely one of the chief attractions of the style, were preceded in print by Phinot's more overtly progressive double-choir motets, contained in his *Liber secundus mutetarum* (1548a). It is surely significant also that in the 1550s two of the most important theorists of the time, Zarlino and Vicentino, each devoted passages to the technique of writing for two or even three choirs. The implication is that by their time of writing polychoral music was already well established. The passages to be discussed from Zarlino's *Le istitutioni harmoniche* (1558) and Vicentino's *L'antica musica ridotta alla moderna prattica* (1555) are given in full in Appendix 1. A comparison of the points made by the two authors will yield considerable information. First, however, it will be instructive to look at Zarlino alone.

Le istitutioni harmoniche went through four editions: 1558, 1562, 1573 and 1589, the last as part of an *Opera omnia*. In each the most extended discussion of '*choro spezzato*', Zarlino's own term, comes just before the end of Part 3: Chapter 66, a long chapter dealing with composition for more than three voices, including the use of *cantus firmus*. The precise significance of the term '*choro spezzato*' is not clear; it seems meaningless in the singular if given the usual connotation of spacing in performance. Gerstenberg suggested (Willaert, Opera, vol. 8: x–xi) that the spacing referred to might be the rests on the page of a choir's music.

There are some interesting variations between the various editions (effectively three since 1558 and 1562 are almost identical). In 1558: 268 we read that the forces may be divided 'into two Choirs, or even into three'; in 1573: 329 the corresponding passage reads 'into two or more Choirs'. Similarly we are told in 1558: 268 that four voices sing in each choir; 1573: 329 reads 'four or more voices'. In other words Zarlino in his revisions took cognisance of a trend towards larger forces. We have already taken note of the 1568 Munich performances of music in twenty-four and forty parts, and in the same year Andrea Gabrieli's *Deus misereatur nostri* à 12 became the first three-choir piece to be printed (in 1568[6]). The 1589 edition retains such revisions. Its version of Chapter 66 (p. 346) contains a further insertion suggesting that

when the number of choirs is more than two, and also when there are only two, the Basses of one Choir should sing also the [bass] part of the other [choir].

This idea of common bass parts will come to the fore again below. Artusi (1589: 46) also indicated a growth in the performance of multi-part music when he referred to

concertos, which these days are performed with three, or four choirs, with many instruments; Organs, Bass Viols, Lutes, Trombones, Cornetti, Cornamuses, and others.

Zarlino, then, devotes a fairly substantial passage of Part 3, Chapter 66 to polychoral music. In addition there is a shorter section in Part 4, Chapter 15 dealing with the various methods of setting the psalms, including 'à choro spezzato'. Vicentino devotes a separate chapter to composition 'à due chori' (Book 4, Chapter 28), treating it before the more time-honoured techniques of canon and *cantus firmus*, and there are a few sporadic references elsewhere. As Zarlino's contribution is complicated by the various editions, the following series of points has been compiled in the order in which they are presented by Vicentino in Book 4, Chapter 28, 'Ordine di comporre à due chori Psalmi e dialoghi, et altre fantasie', save points 11 and 12 which are made solely by Zarlino.

1. Sonority

In churches, and in other broad and spacious places, music composed for four voices makes little impression, even [though] there might be many singing each part. However, for variety, and for the necessity of making a big sound in such places, one can compose [? for two choirs] Masses, Psalms, and Dialogues, and other things to be performed with various instruments mixed with [the] voices.

It seems from his chapter heading that Vicentino is talking about double-choir music and has omitted the words 'for two choirs'. If so, he has realised the basic principle of stereophony: i.e. that to fill a hall with sound it is not necessary to fill it with musicians but to use two or more separated sound sources.

2. Genre

Masses, Psalms, and Dialogues, and other things. . .

Zarlino (1558, Part 3, Chapter 66) mentions only psalms, which may be set 'a Choro spezzato'; such pieces are often sung in Venice at Vespers, and [at] other hours of solemn feasts.

He cites as examples compositions by Willaert: *Confitebor tibi**, *Laudate pueri**, *Lauda Ierusalem**, *De profundis**, *Memento Domine David** 'and many others'. In 1573 the 'many others' are said to include *Dixit Dominus*, *Laudate pueri**, *Laudate Dominum*, *Lauda anima mea Dominum*, *Laudate Dominum quoniam bonus est Psalmus* and *Lauda Ierusalem**. It is puzzling that two psalms are repeated in the supplementary list of 1573 until we realise that, omitting *Dixit Dominus*, the latter consists of the *Cinque Laudate*, a sequence of Vesper psalms proper to certain feasts in the Venetian rite and some other pre-Tridentine rites, including Sarum (Moore 1981a: 129–32; 1981b). Those titles asterisked correspond with *salmi spezzati* by Willaert in 1550[1]. In 1558 Zarlino says that many years before he had composed a Magnificat for three choirs; in 1589 he claims to have written it for use at St Mark's. If this is true, it must have been written after he left his native Chioggia for Venice in 1541. The piece is now lost.

The psalmodic basis of Zarlino's conception of *coro spezzato* is further reinforced in Part 4 of *Le istitutioni*, much of which is concerned with psalm-singing. In Chapter 15 (1558: 316) he sets out three methods of psalm composition:

[a] in [such a] way, that its verses might be sung with another choir alternately, as Iachetto has composed, and many others [i.e. alternate closed verses for two choirs];
[b] or also they might be all [set] complete, as Lupo composed the Psalms In convertendo. . .and Beati omnes. . .for Four voices. [i.e. all the verses set for one choir];
[c] or indeed they might be composed for two choirs, like the Psalms of Adriano *Laudate pueri Dominum*: Lauda Hierusalem Dominum**, and many others, which [method] is known as *a choro spezzato*.

Zarlino's criterion for the use of the term '*choro spezzato*' is that the choirs should sometimes sing together.

With regard to the other categories of composition mentioned by Vicentino we may observe that double-choir writing had, by 1555, been applied to the mass ordinary, the motet and the madrigal dialogue as well as to psalmody.

3. The use of instruments

with various instruments, mixed with [the] voices.

Zarlino does not mention this practice specifically in connection with *coro spezzato*, but he alludes to it elsewhere, e.g. in Part 4, Chapter 17, whilst discussing modal transposition. Such evidence as we have does not associate it with liturgical psalm-singing.

4. More than two choirs

To make [the] greatest sound one could even compose for three choirs.

See Zarlino's references to three or more choirs already cited.

5. *Observation of the mode*

The Composer will first notice, and select the tone which he wishes to place above the words, and then he will compose and observe the tone, or the mode, of the composition, [whether] made on the *canto fermo*, or of his own invention, with fugue, or without.

Zarlino relates this more specifically to the use of psalm-tones in polyphonic settings, writing in Part 4, Chapter 15:

It is necessary, that he follow the mode and the Intonation, [to] which the said canticle is sung in plainchant [*ne i Canti fermi*].

He goes a stage further in Chapter 18, recommending that the cadences of the psalm-tone should normally be preserved in the tenor part:

We must also take care, to make the Cadences principally in the Tenor, conscious that this part is the principal guide to the Modes in which the song is composed; and from it the Composer must take the invention of the other parts. But such Cadences may be made in the other parts of the Composition, when they turn out well.

6. *A secure beginning*

When the first choir sings the opening, one must make sure that the intonation of the first voices is secure in pitch.

7. *Trouble-free exchanging of choirs*

When one wishes to pause, and to finish the first phrase of the first choir, one arranges that the second choir takes over in the middle of the final note of the aforementioned first choir, in unisons or octaves with all the parts; (for example) as it might be that the Tenor takes the unison with the other Tenor, and the Contralto the unison with the other Contralto; and the Soprano *a voce mutata* [see point 8], which is like a Contralto, enters at the unison, or at the consonance of a third, or fifth, below the said Soprano: and the Bass enters at the unison with the other Bass, or at the octave, as is most convenient; and when a choir does not take over the notes from the other choir, in unisons, or octaves, it is not good to hear, and the takeover of the voices will be false; and this transference of notes must always be in the middle of the last note [of the previous choir] which will be just after a sigh, or a rest, or several rests, so that the note sounding might be a secure guide, to the other which must [now] intone and maintain the mode.

It seems that composers did not always do all that they could to help singers to pick up their notes at choral exchanges. In reality, of course, although Vicentino does not express it in these terms, a certain minimal overlapping between the choirs is also essential to musical continuity. He is also reminding the composer that the vertical sound where the second choir enters must obey the usual rules of consonance and dissonance.

8. *Differently-scored choirs*

For variety the second choir is composed with the Soprano *a voce mutata*, and the other *a voce piena*.

This important point is made solely by Vicentino. It implies that the concept of a colour contrast between the choirs was present very early in the history of polychoral music, as is confirmed by an examination of the psalm repertory to be discussed in the next chapter. Identical clef combinations for the two choirs are in a minority. The most usual difference is a lower clef for the highest one or two voices of one of the choirs. This may only mean a third or fourth in terms of the total range of that choir, but the close chord spacing produced gives it a distinctive colour. Willaert's *Salmi spezzati*, often described as for equal choirs (e.g. Arnold 1955–6: 47), in fact contrast a choir containing both highest and lowest voices with a more closely-spaced one.

The term *a voce mutata* is defined by both Vicentino and Zarlino as the substitution of a lower voice for the soprano. Vicentino (Book 4, Chapter 38) describes a trick of writing pieces for SATB which can be sung, without any ambiguities, with the soprano part transposed down an octave to become another tenor part in what is then an *a voce mutata* piece scored ATTB. Zarlino (1558, Part 3, Chapter 65; Part 4, Chapter 31) implies the additional possibility of AATB scoring, and brings in the term *a voci pari* in connection with ensembles consisting entirely of tenor and bass voices. The precise meaning of the term *mutata* is not clear. Vicentino uses it to describe changing the register of a voice part. It may also refer to the type of voice employed in the lower choir. Such choirs might have consisted entirely of 'broken' voices, i.e. adult tenors and basses, whereas the top line of the higher choir would require boys or falsettists. Typical clef combinations found in the 'lower' choir are $C_3C_3C_4F_4$ and $C_3C_4C_4F_4$ instead of the standard $C_1C_3C_4F_4$. Vicentino uses the term *a voce piena* to denote an ordinary SATB choir (Book 4, Chapters 28 & 38). This meaning should not be confused with *a piena voce* (Vicentino Book 2, Chapter 23; Zarlino Part 3, Chapter 45), which denotes a style of singing suited to large buildings rather than to private chambers.

9. Treatment of the bass parts/spacing of the choirs

[The composer] is warned that when he wishes to cause two or three choirs to sing together, he must make the Basses of the two, or of all three choirs consonant, and never one Bass a fifth below the other. . .because [one or more of the upper voices of] the other choir would have the fourth above [the bass of that choir], and [it] would be discordant in all its parts, because these [the singers] would not hear the fifth below, if the choir were some distance from the other choir; and if he wishes to make all the Basses concordant, they will always make a unison, or an octave, or sometimes a major third, but this should not be sustained for more than a minim, because [the] said major third is weak for sustaining so many voices. And by this method the parts will not be discordant, and the choirs will also be able to sing separately one from the other, if they are [composed] in accordance with the above scheme, and likewise if the parts are distant [from each other].

Thus the choirs may be spaced from each other, and because of the consequent danger of the singers not perceiving the true bass of the harmony Vicentino wishes to guard against the occurrence of 6/4 chords in any choir in tuttis. He appends an example (Ex. 1) which appears to contradict his recommendation that the major third should not be held for longer than a minim.

Zarlino makes the same points in a slightly different manner in Part 3, Chapter 66:

Ex. 1   Essempi de due Bassi, che s'accorderanno, quando si canterà a due Chori.

[Barlines are editorial.]

Because such Choirs are placed at some distance from each other, the Composer should be warned (so that he is not displeased by dissonance amongst the parts of any of them) to compose the piece in this manner, that each Choir be consonant; that is that the parts of one Choir be ordered in such a way as if they were composed simply for Four voices without considering the other Choirs, having nevertheless regard in the placing of the parts, that they accord with one another, and there be no dissonance. So that [with] the Choirs composed in such a manner, each one would be able to sing separately, and one would not hear anything which might offend the hearer. This advice is not to be despised, because it is very useful; and it was discovered by the Most Excellent Adriano.

Thus Zarlino credits Willaert not with the invention of *coro spezzato* itself; as was once believed, but with the formulation of a method of handling the bass parts. The tuttis in the master's *Salmi spezzati*, admittedly not extensive, do illustrate the procedure outlined by his pupil. Zarlino goes on to recommend octaves, unisons and thirds between the bass parts. He prohibits fifths, though in 1589 he adds a rider covering the possibility of the tenor temporarily functioning as the real bass, the bass voice crossing above it. 1589 contains a longer insertion on this subject later in Chapter 66, part of which has already been referred to:

When the number of choirs is more than two, and also when there are only two, the Basses of one Choir should sing also the [bass] part of the other [choir]. . .for that part [which] is doubled is more likely to be heard than if it were to be sung simply by one voice. . .Apart from this the Composer would be able to vary the Harmony more than if he does not [double the bass parts] for in giving the Basses different notes, one cannot achieve much variety of Harmony in Compositions. . .Also it would not be necessary in *capelle*, in choirs, that there be other than one voice to a part in the singing of the compositions which are sung there.

Zarlino seems to advocate here a bass line common to all the choirs. This recommendation is made still more forcefully by Artusi (1589: 47):

I should commend greatly, that in conjunctions of the Choirs, those parts which are lowest, that is all the Basses, should move together in unison, so that, besides, the whole fabric might come to have sufficient support.

Zarlino's emphasis on spatial separation does not seem to apply, paradoxically, to the performance of *salmi spezzati* in St Mark's as it is now understood. Both James Moore (1981a: 98, 106; 1981b: 276–7) and David Bryant (1981a: 168–75), after long overdue study of ceremonial books from St Mark's, agree that in that church *salmi spezzati* were performed 'responsorially' with four singers in one choir and the rest (between two and three to a part) in the other. These groups were not spatially separated but grouped together in one of several possible locations, including the hexagonal *pergolo* (a pulpit-like structure just outside the choir at the south end of the iconostasis), the *pulpitum novum lectionum*, positioned in the corresponding place on the north side, and the choir itself, by the high altar (Bryant 1981a: 170–5). There is no reason to suppose that such psalms were not performed spatially elsewhere. Zarlino's apparent reference to the singing of large-scale music one-to-a-part in 1589 is extremely interesting; if this happened even occasionally it would go a long way towards explaining the surprisingly large volume of surviving polychoral music. It has been suggested that the practice was customary in Venetian *scuole* (Glixon 1983: 400), and it seems to have been so also in the Papal choir from the late sixteenth century (Lionnet 1987).

10. Bass parts in dialogues

Then in the composition of Dialogues, one will arrange that all the parts sing in a circle; then one may compose fifths in Bass parts, arranging however that they are always close to each other, having regard to the fact that one of the Basses will have the fourth [fifth?] above the other, so that [a voice] might not be discordant if it be some distance from the Bass part; and the same instruction holds where voices take over from each other, as I have given above.

Zarlino does not make this point, of course, since his treatment is concerned only with psalms. The expression *in circulo* seems to preclude spatially separated groups. In all probability Vicentino is talking about domestic performance of madrigal dialogues in which the singers would be close enough together to discern the true bass at any given moment in the normal manner. It is however interesting in this connection that, quite apart from what we have learned about St Mark's, Venice, several North Italian churches (e.g. Verona Cathedral, St Antony's in Padua) have semi-circular choir stalls behind the high altar in which, for instance, double-choir psalms could have been performed without the choirs being unduly separated. Some composers never employ 'spatial' bass parts in their sacred polychoral music; others are inconsistent.

The last two points, 11 and 12, are made solely by Zarlino (Part 3, Chapter 66).

11. Antiphony and tutti

The Choirs sing now one, now the other in turn; and sometimes (depending on the intention) all together, especially at the end, which is very good.

12. A difficult art

And although it presents some difficulty, one must not on that account avoid the labour, because it is a very praiseworthy and virtuosic thing.

Sixteenth-century musicians are often referred to as *virtuosi*, and the praise-worthiness of achieving something 'difficult' was well established in the arts in general in the late Renaissance. If polychoral music was considered a difficult art, it is not surprising that it played such an important part on ceremonial occasions, especially those with a political significance.

One thing which has not emerged in our discussion so far is the pre-eminence of Venice itself as a centre for polychoral music. The evidence embraces other cities in Northern Italy, as well as Munich, and specifically polychoral performances are documented in Treviso before Willaert's appointment to St Mark's in 1527. Although Zarlino treats *coro spezzato* as a Venetian phenomenon he may be referring to the Veneto as a whole, and Vicentino, although a pupil of Willaert, does not even mention Venice and widens his discussion far beyond psalmody, giving the impression that at his time of writing the idiom was not limited by geographical area or genre. His treatise was printed in Rome, and his career was spent mainly in Ferrara and Rome in the service of Cardinal Ippolito d'Este. In the next part of this chapter we shall attempt to chart the beginnings of polychoral music from another angle.

Dialogue, psalmody and voice-pairing

The dialogue in madrigal and motet

Under the influence of humanism, or for that matter both Reformation and Counter-reformation, sixteenth-century composers became ever more pre-occupied with the relationship betweeen words and music. Whilst mass settings were still regarded to some extent as either utilitarian or as vehicles for compositional virtuosity, the motet and madrigal of the period may exhibit a close, indeed inseparable bond between speech and song; the music is bound up with the rhetoric and meaning of the text as well as with its patterns of syllables. It seems logical, therefore, to consider in what specific ways the polychoral idea itself might have derived from the nature of the texts being set.

The most obvious category is the dialogue, in setting which the composer might seek to represent the protagonists in contrasting voice-groups. This type of piece commonly rounded off collections of Italian madrigals, and has been the subject of a comprehensive survey by David Nutter (1977). He has shown that the term *dialogo* was applied first to settings of dialogue texts. Often, as in the four à 7 dialogues in Willaert's *Musica nova* collection (1559), the texture is not split into consistent, self-contained groupings; in *Quando nascesti, Amore?* (Willaert, Opera, vol. 13: 103) for instance the top three voices always belong to Cupid but are reinforced by a different fourth voice in each speech. Thus the composer may create the illusion of eight-part double-choir writing with only six or seven voices. In other cases, such as Perissone Cambio's version of *Quando nascesti* (1550), also à 7, successive exchanges are set with ever-changing combinations of voices (Nutter 1977: 104).

Real double-choir writing is also found in the madrigal dialogue, especially when there are eight or more voices. The first printed secular dialogue with a consistently split choir appears to have been Novello's *Dite a me – Il tuo foco*, published in 1546 but dated before 1525 by Einstein (1949: 345) on stylistic grounds. There are later examples by Cambio, Nasco and Portinaro. Double-choir writing was used in the setting of non-dialogic secular texts at least as early as 1548, the year in which Phinot published four such chansons (1548b: nos. 36 & 37; 1548c: nos. 2 & 26); the first piece, *A dieu, Loyse*, is a canon 8 in 4. Tudino 1554 contains two double-choir Petrarch settings, and three years later Portinaro published a setting of Petrarch's *Dolce ire*, again not a dialogue, in an à 8, two-choir setting which he described as a *dialogo*. Sonnets, particularly those of Petrarch, were favoured for such treatment (Nutter 1977: 149, 268–70). Such pieces are the secular equivalents of polychoral motets, and are perhaps best described as polychoral chansons or polychoral madrigals rather than dialogues. Sixteenth-century usage did not restrict the last term to textual dialogues, but it would be advantageous for us to do so.

In sacred music the dialogue is much rarer in the earlier years. The first printed examples seem to date from 1564. Bonardo's *Quem vidistis* and *Laeta quid nunc* in 1564[1], of which more in Chapter 4, are influenced by the dialogue principle, and Claude Le Jeune's *Dix pseaumes* of the same year contains a seven-part dialogue, *Mais qui es tu, dy moy* (Expert 1928: 77), whose text is an allegorical conversation between the poet and religion. The poet's enquiries are given throughout to the four lowest voices ($C_3C_4C_4F_4$), religion's replies to the three highest ($C_1C_2C_3$). These groups remain distinct, despite dovetailing at intersections, until religion's final reply, in which all seven voices join.

The liturgy contains very few suitable dialogue texts. *Quem vidistis*, occurring in both antiphon and responsory form on the Feast of the Nativity, is exceptional. Even so, at least four later double-choir settings of this text, by Andrea Gabrieli (antiphon, 1587[16]: no. 27), Asola (centonised text, 1584: no. 1), Bendinelli (antiphon, 1585: no. 14) and Ingegneri (responsory, 1590[5]: no. 1), do not use choral exchanges to reflect the textual dialogue. When sacred dialogues appear later in the century their texts are generally either allegorical or taken from the Gospels. Franz Sales's extraordinary *Dialogismus de amore Christi* (1598) is an example of the first type; there are contributions from all three members of the Trinity, the Church and a chorus of angels and archangels, though Sales uses only two four-part choirs, one high and one low. Lasso's *Dixit Martha* (1577b) and Wert's *Egressus Jesus* (1581) are gospel dialogues; such texts enjoyed a considerable vogue by the early seventeenth century (Smither 1967).

In this context we might have expected to encounter polychoral dialogue techniques in settings of the Passion. In fact polyphonic settings almost always have a purely sectional structure. A partial exception is Jacob Handl's *Passio Domini. . .secundum Ioannem* (1587a: no. 2; DTÖ vol. 24: 123), whose text is actually a conflation of the narratives of Matthew, Luke and John with an appended prayer and amen. The words of Jesus are always given to Choir 2 (low) except for one tutti. Other single characters are represented by Choir 1 (high) and groups and crowds are always tutti. The narration is set in a variety of ways: one choir, antiphonal and tutti.

A phenomenon which might be considered a special case of the dialogue is the echo. Frederick Sternfeld (1980) has drawn attention to echo ideas in frottola poetry, and Alexander Silbiger (1977) discovered the altus part of what appears to be a secular Latin echo piece, *Que celebrat thermas*, in a Vatican manuscript which he dates in the 1520s. Repeated phrases are separated off by a vertical stroke. The same text was set much later by Le Jeune (1585) (Sternfeld 1980), but probably the most famous echo-piece of the period is Lasso's *O la, o che bon eccho!* (1581; Werke 1, vol. 10: 140). Such pieces fall loosely into the 'imitation of nature' concept; when echoes are found in sacred music at the end of the century, the texts are sometimes constructed in the form of a punning dialogue. Such is the case with the echoes of Handl (see Chapter 8), Anerio's *Jam de somno* (1588[(2)]: no. 56), Croce's *Virgo decus* (1594: 14) and Donato's setting of the same text (1599: no. 49); subsequently the idea was transferred to monody, as in Monteverdi's *Audi coelum* in his 1610 *Vespers*.

Antiphonal psalmody

There is another textual category which is of even greater importance to our subject: those texts associated in the liturgy with ritual antiphonal performance. Antiphony, like responsory, is one of the pillars of Western chant; antiphonal performance of psalms and canticles makes up a large proportion of the Latin Office. Normally when polyphony was applied to antiphonal chants the result was an *alternatim* composition, with one choir singing polyphony, the other plainchant (a purely liturgical approach), or a through-composed or sectionalised setting of the whole text for a single choir (sometimes less tied to a liturgical context). More rarely we encounter settings with two choirs alternating closed polyphonic verses, or through-composed settings for double choir with some tutti writing (cf. Zarlino's categories, p. 7 above). The last two are probably rarer because they require a greater number of singers, and *salmi spezzati* also present problems of ensemble and continuity. There is, however, a geographically limited yet significant corpus of double-choir psalms written in Northern Italy during the first half of the sixteenth century, representing another important strand in the development of polychoral music; this will be dealt with in the next chapter.

The Flemish influence

Although certain kinds of text may well have inspired polychoral writing, much more significant is the purely musical impulse to split the texture. Already in the *salmo spezzato* repertory we find composers departing from strictly liturgical antiphony; even the austere Willaert does this in the doxology. The concept of applying polychoral technique in pieces where its use is not suggested at all by extra-musical considerations is but a step away. The antiphony in pure dialogue and in Willaert's psalms (if not always in those of his contemporaries) is of a kind we may call 'non-repetitive'. Each choir answers the other with new text to new music. The mainstay of later polychoral music is, however, antiphonal repetition or variation, representing a much more dynamic relationship between the choirs. It is here that the Franco-Flemish tradition seems to have provided a vital input. Hertzmann (1929–30) posited a connection between polychoral writing and such typically Flemish procedures as voice-pairing and canon, a fruitful idea which we shall explore in Chapter 3. A seminal figure who seems to sum up this stage in the development of the idiom is Dominique Phinot. Indeed, we might see Phinot and Willaert as representing the twin poles of polychoral writing up to 1550. Between them, in only a handful of pieces, they summed up the origins of *coro spezzato* and laid the foundations for later exponents.

Developments after 1550

In the second half of the sixteenth century and especially after 1570, polychoral music was printed in surprisingly large, and growing, quantities. The statistics given in Table 1, though they should not be taken too literally, give an idea of the growth in the volume of polychoral music between 1550 and 1610. Included are all publications that I have come across which contain at least one sacred piece à 8, including those in the vernacular. I have tried to exclude reprints of entire collections though not reprints of individual pieces.

The figures suggest that the vast majority of publications not surveyed would turn out to contain polychoral music. The technique was applied to sacred genres of all kinds, including mass ordinary (rarely the proper), psalm, magnificat and other canticles, litany, motet, German sacred song (liturgical and non-liturgical) and occasional music (wedding songs and the like). Polychoral music was produced in most important Italian centres, especially in the North but also in Rome and Naples, and in Spain, and it became especially popular in Germany and the Habsburg lands. There, as is well known, a vogue developed for the Venetian style as represented by the Gabrielis, but this is predated by some indigenous activity, and by the polychoral works of Lasso, whose influence on composers in Germany was immense. Moreover there is a large quantity of polychoral music by composers for whom a direct Vene-

Table 1

	Polychoral	Not polychoral	Not surveyed	Total
1551–1555	3	5	1	9
1556–1560	1	4	0	5
1561–1565	4	0	3	7
1566–1570	12	4	1	17
1571–1575	13	6	6	25
1576–1580	19	2	12	33
1581–1585	29	1	17	47
1586–1590	44	0	27	71
1591–1595	29	0	20	49
1596–1600	49	0	42	91
1601–1605	62	0	61	123
1606–1610	82	3	64	149

tian connection cannot be proven, such as Jacob Handl and Hieronymus Praetorius. Curiously, especially when we remember that a good deal of Lasso's polychoral music was published in Paris, the style did not catch on in France until the seventeenth century (Launay 1957).

The basic medium remained double choir. Some three- and four-choir music was published, but it is likely that more did not reach the presses because the market for it was smaller. The very biggest works of the period are represented only in manuscripts, such as the wonderful series of choirbooks from the turn of the century preserved in the Nationalbibliothek in Vienna, some regrettably incomplete, testifying to the richness of music-making in the court at Graz in particular. It is difficult to believe that some of these works, particularly the masses for sixteen or more voices in Ms. 16702, could have been performed anywhere else (see Appendix 2).

Performances in the Habsburg lands, as in Munich and Venice, were characterised by the use of instruments with the voices. Increasingly, wealthier Italian churches and confraternities began to hire instrumentalists for special occasions where they could not afford to employ them permanently. The use of instruments in polychoral music adds a new dimension of colour, but for much of our period composers continued to notate the music as if it were purely vocal, leaving the decisions concerning scoring to the *maestro di cappella*. Eventually they felt obliged, even where flexibility was still allowed, to make concrete suggestions (e.g. Viadana 1612: preface) and ultimately to 'score' pieces in the sense in which we would understand the term (e.g. some pieces in Gabrieli, G., 1615). The Germans in particular, if Michael Praetorius is to be believed, became especially fond of using instruments of diverse families. By this time the 'classical' phase in polychoral music was over in Italy. Increasingly composers were drawn both to smaller media and to greater diversification in the use of larger forces; in the emerging *concertato* idioms the polychoral element became one among many possibilities and ceased to be the driving force of the music.

2

THE EARLY ITALIAN
CONTRIBUTION

With one important exception, Ruffino's Mass, this chapter is concerned with *salmi spezzati*, most of them coming from the Veneto region of Northern Italy. It is not intended to be an exhaustive study of psalm-singing in that region, for which we would need also to consider works employing *alternatim* and closed-verse polyphonic antiphony. Rather we shall be concerned with antiphonal psalmody as a source of inspiration for double-choir technique. The earliest source containing psalms with polyphony for both sides of the choir appears to be a pair of late fifteenth-century choirbooks in the Estense library in Modena (cod. lat. 454 & 455), to which attention was drawn by Bukofzer (1950) and which may have come originally from Verona (Kanazawa 1975: 159). Each choir has music for three voices, the middle one sometimes needing to be supplied by the application of *fauxbourdon*. In the sixteenth century closed-verse and *alternatim* settings occur alongside *salmi spezzati*, chiefly in manuscript sources but also in the 1550[1] collection. The earliest examples of *salmi spezzati*, i.e. continuous settings for double choir, were written in Northern Italy during the two or three decades preceding 1550, the year in which Willaert's famous examples were published. As with the madrigal Willaert was cultivating a genre which had emerged first in the work of native Italians.

The sources

The Treviso manuscripts

A central place in our discussion must be occupied by a group of manuscripts surviving in the archive of Treviso Cathedral. Some of them are interrelated and also have concordances with manuscripts at Bergamo and Verona and with the prints 1550[1] and 1554[17]. Of at least four complete pairs of choirbooks containing double-choir psalmody two pairs have survived complete (Mss. 12a & 12b, 24a & 24b), whilst two other books (Mss. 11b, 22) have lost their companions. A catalogue of 1574 indicates that the church once possessed copies of psalms for three choirs (d'Alessi 1954: 181–2).

The oldest source in the group would appear to be Ms. 24. There are no dates in the body of the manuscript; d'Alessi (1954: 85–6) assigned it to about 1550, Leeman Perkins (Census-catalogue vol. 3: 247) to 1535–50. The contents are summarised below.[1]

21 *salmi spezzati* for vespers:
3 liturgical sequences of 5 psalms, 1 sequence (24a: f. 67v, 24b: f. 63v) ascribed to 'Fran. Pat.' (Francesco Santacroce), 2 psalms of another sequence (ff. 12v, 16v; 15v, 13v) anon. but = Willaert in 1550[(1)], 2 of the third (ff. 45v, 44v; 51v, 50v), found in Bergamo (Ms. 1209D: f. 125v, 127v; one choir lost), where one, *Dixit Dominus*, is ascribed to Ruffino.
6 further psalms, anon., but 2 (ff. 1v; 40v, 39v) = Willaert in 1550[(1)].
4 *salmi spezzati* and *Nunc dimittis* for compline (ff. 59v, 55v): ascribed to 'Fran. Pat.'. The psalms also in Verona Ms. 218 (discantus f. 33r).
12 closed-verse settings of vesper psalms, music for all verses: 2 liturgical sequences, 2 further psalms, all anon. Partial concordances with 1550[(1)] and 1554[(17)]; in most cases one choir's music is by Jachet.[2]

The possibility of the manuscript's having been compiled before 1550 is intriguing since it may mean that some at least of Willaert's psalms circulated in manuscript before they were printed. One, *Laudate pueri* (f. 12v, 16v), is a fourth lower than in the print. The absence of ascription to Willaert raises the possibility that other 'anonymous' settings may be his.

The other three Treviso sources have internal dates as follows:

Ms. 11b   1556–60   music for vespers
Ms. 12   1562–68   music for vespers
Ms. 22   1561–69   music for terce & compline

The contents of Ms. 11b are summarised below.

26 *salmi spezzati*:
they include 3 liturgical sequences of 5 and 2 incomplete sequences of 3 and 4 respectively. Ascriptions: *Laudate pueri* (f. 11v) to 'Adrianus W', *Beatus vir* (f. 30v) to 'Nicolaus Oliveto'.
12 closed-verse psalm-settings:
including 1 liturgical sequence of 5
1 closed-verse *Te Deum*

Ms. 11b has many concordances with both Ms. 24 and 1550[(1)], and evidence I have assembled more fully elsewhere (Carver 1980: 39–42) suggests that it may have been compiled in part from one or both of them. It includes material from Ms. 24 in sequence, including (f. 27v) the first three psalms of the vesper sequence ascribed there to Santacroce; the first four of the sequence of five closed-verse psalms in Ms. 11b (f. 31v) are present in the same order in Ms. 24b (f. 33v). All eight of Willaert's *salmi spezzati* are present; *Laudate pueri* is given twice (f. 11v; f. 38v), once (f. 11v, with ascription) a fourth lower than the print, as in Ms. 24. Two of Willaert's psalms, *Laudate pueri* (f. 38v) and *Lauda Jerusalem* (f. 41v), appear with settings of the remaining three *Cinque Laudate* psalms; as we know from Zarlino that these were set by Willaert, we shall consider the possibility of his authorship below.

Ms. 12 contains twenty vesper psalms and two magnificats, all for double choir. Two liturgical sets of psalms are discernible; one set (f. 48v, 49v), although one psalm is missing, is followed by a Magnificat (f. 64v) which has a concordance in Chamaterò 1575. One group of three psalms is by Asola (printed in 1574). The only ascription in the manuscript is of a *Dixit Dominus* to Portinaro. There are no concordances betweeen Ms. 12 and the other Treviso manuscripts.

The contents of Ms. 22 are summarised below.

3 *salmi spezzati* forming a set for Sunday terce.
3 sets of *spezzato* settings of the 4 psalms for Sunday compline:
    1 (f. 25v) is followed by an à 4 setting of v. 2 of the hymn *Te lucis* and double-choir
    settings of the Nunc dimittis and *Salve regina*; another (f. 35v) is Santacroce's, also
    with the Nunc and seemingly copied from Ms. 24a. No ascription in Ms. 22.
1 further *spezzato* setting of the compline psalm *In te Domine speravi*.
1 set of closed-verse settings of the Sunday compline psalms: these are followed by 4 à 4
    hymn verses, 3 (ff. 23v, 24v & 24bv) ascribed to 'Nicolaus Olivetus'.
1 closed-verse Credo marked 'F. P. [Santacroce?] Secundus Chorus'.

The lack of concordances between Mss. 11b, 12 and 22 is perhaps not surprising in view of their proximity in date of compilation. We know that the musical repertory of Treviso Cathedral underwent a great expansion during the Fleming Jan Nasco's tenure as *maestro di cappella* from 1551 to 1561 (d'Alessi 1954: 106–7). Ms. 11b allows vespers material from an older repertory to continue in use, whilst Ms. 12 provides new music, all for *cori spezzati*. Ms. 22 provides evidence for a new prominence of the office of compline.

There was also a modest expansion in the resources of the Cappella. At the end of Santacroce's first period as *maestro* (1520–27) there were eleven singers (four boys, three contraltos, two tenors and two basses), the *maestro di cappella*, the *maestro di canto fermo* and the organist (d'Alessi 1954: 69–70). In 1532, during the tenure of Nicolò Oliveto (1529–37), the canons reduced the size of the Cappella from fifteen (excluding the *maestro di cappella*) to twelve (ibid.: 93). In 1536 instrumentalists ('sonatores') began to take part in services on feasts. Later figures, such as 17 for 1541, 19 for 1544, *c*22 for 1551, include all musical personnel; the instrumentalists in the last figure comprised four cornetto and sackbut players, and they may also have doubled as singers (ibid.: 101, 106). Bearing in mind that the boys probably all sang the same part, it seems likely that at Treviso double-choir performances, especially early on, took place with one singer on all or some of the lower parts. Even in 1565, it was impossible on one occasion to sing vespers in polyphony because of the absence of two singers! (ibid.: 120–1).

Verona Ms. 218

Ms. 218 of the Accademia Filarmonica in Verona has been described by Böker-Heil (1969), who dates it in the mid-1530s. An inventory quoted by Turrini (1941) suggests that the manuscript may have been in the possession of the Accademia as early as 1544, the year after its foundation. The main body of the manuscript, which consists of eight partbooks, contains an anthology of multi-voiced motets, many by Flemish composers but including some by Giordano Passetto of Padua. In a self-contained section at the end are two substantial double-choir works, both by composers of Paduan origin: a Mass by Ruffino, and a Compline setting by Santacroce. Böker-Heil speculates that the manuscript may be of Paduan provenance, especially as Passetto is referred to familiarly as 'Jordam' in the index. Verona 218 has Santacroce's compline psalms in common with Treviso 24, but one is unlikely to have been copied from the other. Treviso has the Nunc dimittis, absent in Verona, whilst Verona has the opening versicle and response, the short lesson and the short responsory, all absent in Treviso.

The Bergamo manuscripts

The Biblioteca Civica in Bergamo contains three large choirbooks, Mss. 1207D, 1208D and 1209D. They were copied by Gasparo Alberti around 1541-2, according to dates in the first two. Inventories are given by Jeppesen (1958) and Ravizza (1972b). Of interest to us are two eight-part Magnificats by Alberti himself, laid out as if for double choir in Mss. 1207D and 1208D, and the second choir of eleven psalms for *cori spezzati* in Ms. 1209D, of which eight are ascribed to Ruffino, two to Alberti and one is anonymous. Ruffino's *Dixit Dominus* (f. 125v) and the anonymous *Laudate pueri* (f. 127v) are found complete in Treviso Ms. 24, as noted above. D'Alessi (1954: 76, 78–80) accepted the latter as the work of Ruffino, which is plausible on stylistic grounds.

The Padua manuscripts

A pair of choirbooks in the Cathedral Library in Padua, Mss. D25 and D26, would appear to contain a sequence of psalm settings by successive *maestri di cappella* bound together later. (For an inventory, see Carver 1980: 46–7.) The first section, headed in both books 'Frater iordanus a 8', is probably an auto-graph of Giordano Passetto[3] and contains ten *salmi spezzati* for vespers. This portion of the manuscript has been rebound, possibly more than once, with portions of capital letters having sometimes been cut off. This has not hap-pened with the remaining leaves, which contain double-choir psalms by Giovanni Battista Mosto (6), Pietr'Antonio Guainaro (1) and Costanzo Porta (2, of which one is closed-verse). Mosto and Porta both served the Cathedral in the 1580s and 1590s, and Guainaro (*d* 1576) was active both there and at San Antonio.

The archive of San Petronio in Bologna

One pair of choirbooks at San Petronio containing double-choir psalms appears to belong to the mid-sixteenth century (Census-catalogue vol. 1: 84): Mss. A36 and A37. Both contain eight vesper psalms and a magnificat for double choir, and A36 has a second magnificat for four voices only. All are anonymous.

Printed sources

The full contents of 1550[1], which contains many closed-verse settings by Willaert and others, are given in vol. 8 of Willaert's *Opera omnia*; we are primarily concerned with the eight *Salmi spezzati* at the end. The *Thesaurus musicus* of Montanus and Neuber (Nuremberg, 1564[1]) will be discussed in more detail in Chapter 4; it contains a cycle of compline psalms ascribed to 'Adrianus W', an anonymous Magnificat and a Magnificat by Antonio Scandello from Bergamo.

In the following list I have assembled statistics from the above sources of *spezzato* psalm and canticle settings written by Willaert, his predecessors and his contemporaries in Northern Italy, including those for which only one choir has survived.

Vesper psalms: 81
  2 by Gasparo Alberti (*c*1480–1560)
  3 by Giammateo Asola (?1532–1609)
  1 by Nicolò Oliveto (*fl* 1528–38)
 10 by Giordano Passetto (*d* 1557)
  1 by Francesco Portinaro (*c*1520 – after
    1578)
  9 by Ruffino d'Assisi (*fl* 1510–32)
  5 by Francesco Santacroce (1488–1556)
  1 by Claudio Veggio (*fl* 1540–4)[4]
  8 by Adriano Willaert (*b c*1490, *d* 1562)
 41 anonymous
Magnificats: 8
  2 by Alberti
  1 by Ippolito Chamaterò (*b c*1535–40,
    d after 1592)[5]
  1 by Antonio Scandello (1517–1580)
  4 anonymous

Matins psalms: 1
  1 by Pietr'Antonio Guainaro (*d* 1576)
Terce psalms: 3
  3 anonymous
Compline psalms: 17
  4 by Santacroce
  4 ascribed to Willaert
  9 anonymous
Nunc dimittis: 2
  1 by Santacroce
  1 anonymous

The links through concordances between some of these sources and the patterns of the careers of the named composers enable us to regard these pieces as an interlinked corpus representative of a significant local tradition. Fra Ruffino Bartolucci d'Assisi was active in Padua, both at the Cathedral (where he was succeeded in 1520 by Passetto, one of whose successors was Guainaro) and the Basilica del Santo. Santacroce sang under Ruffino at Padua Cathedral before leaving his home city for Treviso, where he introduced *cori spezzati* in (or before) 1521. Oliveto was one of Santacroce's successors as *maestro di cappella* at Treviso Cathedral (1530–8), whilst Portinaro was born in Padua and was active in the area. The link with Alberti, who spent all his working life at Santa Maria Maggiore in Bergamo, lies in the above-noted concordances between Bergamo and Treviso manuscripts. Willaert's stature, the proximity of Venice to Padua and Treviso and the presence of his psalms in Treviso sources more than justify his inclusion here. Veggio was active in Venice and Piacenza; two eight-part canonic madrigals by him were printed in Doni's *Dialogo* (1544). The psalms of Willaert, then, which have too often been regarded as the fountainhead of polychoral music, are part of a tradition; their fame should derive not from a spurious pioneer status but from their intrinsic value as the work of one of the sixteenth century's greatest composers.

The music

The pieces which conform most strictly to liturgical antiphony suggest the following 'blueprint' against which we may consider the whims of individual composers:

1 Strict alternation of the choirs verse by verse.
2 Freer treatment of the doxology, common to all the psalms in liturgical usage, with more rapid alternation of the choirs, text repetition and eight-part writing for at least the closing bars.
3 Use of the melodic outline of the psalm-tone, usually in the tenor part.
4 Derivation of the cadential structure from the psalm-tone.

Ruffino d'Assisi

Probably the earliest of this group of composers, Fra Ruffino came from the Convento dei Frari in Venice to take up the post of *maestro di cappella* at Padua Cathedral in 1510. From 1520 to 1525 he held the corresponding post at Padua's Basilica of St Antony, and in the latter year moved to Vicenza Cathedral. He was back at the 'Santo' around 1531 or 1532. Paradoxically, Ruffino treats the double-choir medium with great freedom and flexibility, especially in *Laudate pueri* (substantial musical examples in d'Alessi 1952: 193–7) and the *Missa verbum bonum*. The other psalm surviving complete, *Dixit Dominus*, is less avant-garde, maintaining a balance between liturgical and imaginative considerations; the antiphony includes lively choral exchanges with text repetition:

             v. 1: Ch. 1
             v. 2: Ch. 2
             v. 3a: Ch. 1;   v. 3b: antiphony
             v. 4a: Ch. 2;   v. 4b: Ch. 1
             v. 5a: Ch. 2+antiphony/tutti;   v. 5b: antiphony
             v. 6a: Ch. 1;   v. 6b: antiphony
             vv. 7, 8: antiphony
doxology   v. 9a: tutti;   v. 9b: antiphony
             v. 10a: Ch. 1+antiphony/tutti;   v. 10b: antiphony+tutti

There is no plainchant incipit, but tone 8 is paraphrased imitatively in the first verse. Subsequently, regardless of the antiphonal interaction of the choirs, C and G are used as cadential finals at respectively the mediant and ending of each verse, and the psalm-tone returns melodically in the doxology to point the words 'Sicut erat in principio'.

It is perhaps not surprising that Ruffino, so adventurous in his exploration of the at that time almost uncharted territory of double-choir writing in his psalms, should have been seemingly the first composer to apply through-composed antiphony to the mass, in his *Missa verbum bonum* (Verona Ms. 218: discantus f. 45r; transcr. Carver 1980, vol. 2: 187). It is loosely based on the old sequence melody, and is a lengthy affair since its main structural resource is repetition, most often by one choir of text and music stated by the other. Repetition in the sequence melody operates at two levels, line and stanza, and it may be that Ruffino derived the idea of repetition from it, though he hardly employs more than the first few notes of the chant.

Ruffino's technique has affinities with Mouton's in the latter's eight-part setting of *Verbum bonum*, published in 1564[1] and, perhaps significantly, present in the same manuscript as Ruffino's Mass (discantus f. 20r).[6] Hertzmann (1929–30: 140) cited a passage from the Mouton as an early example of antiphony resulting from the temporary splitting into four-part groups of an eight-part ensemble. The passage concerned is actually a homophonic application of a principle applied by Mouton throughout the piece, i.e. a very free canonic treatment of successive phrases of the sequence melody and various counterpoints. It seems possible that Ruffino knew the work and used Mouton's technique in a systematically antiphonal fashion in his Mass. There is no question of parody, and Ruffino's Mass does not employ the repetition of material between different movements characteristic of the parody mass. It appears to have no connection other than title with Willaert's six-part *Verbum bonum* (Opera vol. 4: 16), Mouton's *Missa verbum bonum* (Opera vol. 4: 79) or the model for the latter by Therache (Mouton, Opera vol. 4: 126). The Flemish antecedents of polychoral writing will be discussed fully in the next chapter; their relevance here warns us against postulating a single origin or indeed two or more completely independent sources of the technique.

In his Mass Ruffino varies the amount of overlap between the choirs considerably, from leisurely antiphony through close-knit quasi-canonic textures (as in Ex. 5 below) to eight-part writing. The phrases exchanged by the choirs vary in length from less than a bar (Ex. 2) to four bars or more; the longer the phrase the less likely is its exact repetition (Ex. 3). In shorter phrases the bass or soprano is often imitated with new counterpoint. The small difference between the clefs ($C_1C_3C_4F_4/C_2C_3C_4F_4$) belies an often greater pitch contrast at intersections; one bass part is often a fifth above or below the other. Although homophony predominates to the point of monotony, imitation of a rather pedestrian kind occurs sporadically (e.g. Ex. 4), usually at the beginning of a section. This appears to be 'lip-service' to convention of a type still paid by the Gabrielis at the beginning of many works.

Ex. 2   R<small>UFFINO</small>, Missa 'Verbum bonum'

Ex. 3   R<small>UFFINO</small>, Missa 'Verbum bonum'

Unfortunately Ruffino does not find the right balance between antiphony and tutti. The repetition is wearisome and the tuttis are rendered ineffective by lack of control over the build-up towards them, quite apart from the poor quality of the part-writing. There is a high incidence of parallel octave and unison writing in tuttis and choral overlaps. In the latter it might be argued that Ruffino is attempting to aid the entry of a choir after rests, as in Ex. 4 where the 7–8 cadential resolution is doubled. There is a great deal of unconventional dissonance treatment which is sometimes convincing enough to suggest deliberate experimentation. Some sharp dissonances seem impossible to remove with any sensible application of *musica ficta* and countless suspen-

Ex. 4   RUFFINO, Missa 'Verbum bonum'

sions are sounded harshly against their note of resolution or resolved by leap. The Gloria contains a twice-heard quasi-canonic passage (Ex. 5) which presents us with stark choices: either we accept a simultaneous false relation between B and B flat (no editorial accidentals required), or we flatten the Bs in the third bar of Ex. 5 and allow a B flat – E tritone in the top part of Choir 2, or, with all the accidentals given above the notes, we accept that the piece slips down a semitone in terms of absolute pitch and remains there. Recent research by Margaret Bent (1984) suggests that the latter possibility might have been acceptable to Renaissance musicians if the vertical and horizontal relationships were correct progression by progression. *Ficta* problems of a similar kind arise with some of the strict canons dealt with in Chapter 3.

Ruffino uses several times a technique which might be termed suspension of one choir against the other (see Ex. 3), by analogy with the suspension of one part against the other(s) in ordinary counterpoint. A device which echoes down the years as a standard trick is the dramatic tutti after a rest. Ruffino uses it to emphasise the traditional climax-word 'Gratias' in the Gloria; unfortunately he goes on to use it so often that its impact is weakened. It is impossible when studying this Mass not to admire its audacious originality whilst

Ex. 5   RUFFINO, Missa 'Verbum bonum'

fervently wishing that it were by a better composer with a greater sense of proportion.

Francesco Santacroce

In comparison with Ruffino, Santacroce's music, as seen in his psalms and Nunc dimittis for compline and psalms for vespers, possesses great harmonic clarity. (The music for compline is transcribed in Carver 1980, vol. 2: 1.) While he does occasionally enliven the texture contrapuntally he does not always avoid the monotony inherent in so much reliance on homophony. He treats the half-verse as the antiphonal unit, almost invariably exchanging choirs at flex, mediant and ending, and occasionally elsewhere. However, his varying of the speed of choral interchange is more restrained than Ruffino's, and there is less text-repetition except in the doxology and less disruption to the verse structure. The latter is preserved, as in Ruffino's *Dixit*, by an alternating cadence pattern.

The third compline psalm, *Qui habitat* (Ps. 90), is especially interesting since its long text (sixteen verses plus doxology) challenges the composer to employ his skill in providing variety to sustain the interest. After the opening intonation, the second half of verse 1 is set to unusually florid imitative polyphony for Choir 1, whilst Choir 2 enters with verse 2 in Santacroce's more typical homophonic manner (quoted in Carver 1975: 276–8). The contrast is further pointed by the lower, closer chording of the second choir. The more polyphonic vein is given full rein in verses 4 and 5 where each half-verse is a duet sung by like voices from both choirs in the order cantus, altus, bassus, tenor. Metrical contrast occurs in verses 9, 14, 16 and 18, where triple time is introduced in the form of *sesquialtera* notated by coloration. Such variety co-exists with the unity provided by the cadential structure. The mediant cadences are on C, those at the ends of verses on G, corresponding to tone 8. There are also two instances of long-range repetition of material. The music of the tutti for the second half of verse 10 is repeated for verse 13; its massiveness derives from its progress in semibreves and minims in contrast to the prevailing minims and crotchets. The other re-use of material is, appropriately enough, at 'Sicut erat' in the doxology, where the music of Choir 2's first entry recurs with adjustments to fit the new text.

The fourth compline psalm, *Ecce nunc benedicite* (Ps. 133), is given in the Anthology (no. 1) as a sample of Santacroce's style. It also contains musical repetition: 'et Spiritui Sancto' in the doxology quotes the last phrase of verse 3. In the Nunc dimittis the first verse of the doxology is lifted from verse 2 and the close from the second half of verse 3, the tutti being equally appropriate for 'omnium populorum' and the final 'saeculorum. Amen'.

Verona Ms. 218, whilst not containing the Nunc dimittis, contains uniquely (1) the opening versicle 'Jube domne', the response 'Qui fecit caelum et terra' and the short lesson, all set à 4 for Choir 2, (2) the short responsory, divided between the choirs in closed antiphony, and (3) an untexted four-part setting of verse 2 of the compline hymn *Te lucis ante terminum* ((1) and (2) are given in Carver 1980, vol. 2). Joan Long (1971: 163) is therefore not strictly correct when she asserts that Willaert (1555) provided the earliest setting of this office; his is entirely *alternatim*.

The first three of Santacroce's vesper psalms, *Dixit Dominus, Confitebor* and *Beatus vir*,[7] are even more restrained than those for compline. There are no tuttis outside the doxology, and choral interchange is almost invariably restricted to flex, mediant or ending, with some verses set for one choir throughout. There is no text repetition. The doxologies of all three begin dramatically with a tutti following a rest, as may be seen in Ex. 6 from *Dixit*; at 'Sicut erat' the tenor has the first half of the psalm-tone as a *cantus firmus*. Our assumption that the ascription in Treviso Ms. 24a applies to the succeeding psalms as well as to *Dixit* is borne out by the curious fact that in *Confitebor* the 'Gloria Patri' tutti from *Dixit* is quoted at the words 'et Spiritui Sancto', complete with parallel unisons (Ex. 6: bars 4–5).

Ex. 6 SANTACROCE, Dixit Dominus

Multi-part cadences

Presumably those unisons are an accident. However, in another area it is interesting to ponder the effect on the harmony of multi-part writing: I refer to the treatment of leading notes. I generally assume that, throughout the period under consideration, leading notes at clear-cut cadences will be sharpened (see Zarlino 1558, part 3: chapter 53), with the important exception of phrygian progressions. However, passages like Ex. 6: bars 4–6 contain, in a way that four-part cadences hardly ever do, voice-leading which seems to indicate that the leading note should not be sharpened, despite the stylised cadential outline of the top part. As we shall see, some composers allow, in the manner of the so-called 'English' cadence, a clash between the leading note (sharpened or flattened) and its suspension. The difference is that the whole thrust of the English cadence is the false relation, whereas in Continental examples there is sometimes real doubt as to the raising or not of the leading note. What I shall tend to call the 'clash' cadence seems not to appeal to Santacroce, though in *Qui habitat*, bars 137–8 (repeated at 167–8), he sustains the unraised leading-note against a (from the dominant bass) 3–4–3 progression.

Clefs

Ruffino's *Dixit Dominus* is for equal choirs ($2 \times C_1C_2C_3F_3$), but his Mass and *Laudate pueri* both employ the subtle register contrast referred to by Vicentino, having respectively $C_1C_2C_3F_4/C_2C_3C_4F_4$ and $C_1C_3C_4F_4/C_2C_3C_4F_4$. Santacroce's psalms all have contrasting choirs, the biggest difference occurring in *Laudate Dominum* (Treviso Ms. 24: ff. 76v, 70v) ($G_2C_2C_3F_3/C_2C_3C_4F_4$); the Nunc dimittis has an equally wide total range. The minimum difference occurs in *Cum invocarem*, which has the same clefs as Ruffino's Mass. It will be apparent that in polychoral music *chiavette* are even more problematic than usual if we postulate that they imply a downward transposition, since they often occur in combination with 'normal' clef systems in another choir. In fact of course clef combinations are usually dependent on the mode (Powers 1981), though such an assertion is not incompatible with the transposition theory.

Giordano Passetto

In the ten psalms of Giordano Passetto preserved in Padua Cathedral Mss. D25 and D26 similar contrasts are found, with a predominance of the $C_1C_3C_4F_4/C_3C_3C_4F_4$ combination. An outstanding exception is the first *Beatus vir* setting (f. 2v; transcr. Carver 1980, vol. 2: 64), which has the rich low scoring $C_3C_4C_4F_4/C_4F_3F_3F_4$. This *Beatus vir* is exceptional in other ways. There are distinct echoes of *fauxbourdon* at certain points (Ex. 7). The influence of

Ex. 7   Passetto, *Beatus vir* no. 1

fauxbourdon is actually conspicuously absent from the psalms in this repertory that I have examined. Its presence here might indicate the influence of Flemish composers, in keeping with Böker-Heil's hypothesis concerning the Paduan origin of Verona Ms. 218, with its large Flemish content.

This psalm stands by itself at the beginning of the Padua manuscript. (A liturgical sequence begins on f. 5v with the succeeding *Dixit*.) It is stylistically the most elaborate, with occasional imitation or other contrapuntal enlivening of the texture. Nevertheless, it shares many features with the other nine psalms, which are best described as workaday settings with much tedious homophony and rather four-square exchanges of the choirs at almost every flex, mediant and ending, and elsewhere, often with no overlapping. Single-choir passages and even tuttis may be punctuated by rests, and these are sometimes followed by word-repetition which does not motivate choral imitation.

Some of Passetto's psalms stick more rigidly to the cadential pattern of the psalm-tone (e.g. *In exitu Israel*, f. 15v, based on the *tonus peregrinus*) than others. The opening of *In exitu* is à 2 instead of being intoned, and a curious switch of choirs occurs during the second half of the first verse (Ex. 8). This passage also illustrates Passetto's rather stiff antiphonal manner. This psalm (113) is very long in the Vulgate (twenty-seven verses plus doxology), far longer than *Qui habitat*, but Passetto shows little inclination to introduce strong contrasts of scoring or texture to create variety, apart from two excursions into triple time. *In exitu* and *Beatus vir* no. 1 are the only psalms to introduce a tutti outside the doxology, in the former to mock the heathen at 'non clamabant in gutture suo' and in the latter to dispatch the enemies of the man who fears the Lord at 'donec dispiciat inimicos suos'. These two psalms also contain some attempt to vary the harmonic rhythm; it is virtually double towards the end of

Ex. 8   PASSETTO, In exitu Israel

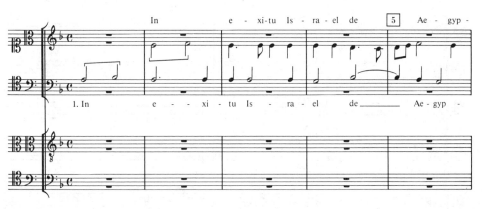

In exitu and in the *doxology* of *Beatus vir*, at 'Sicut erat'. These are single-choir passages, not tuttis where such a broadening-out is more to be expected.

In the doxologies we find occasional use of varied antiphonal repetition, for a definition of which see Chapter 3. In *Laudate pueri* (f. 10v) the result at the close is uncannily like Phinot (Ex. 9). At such points Passetto can rise above mediocrity, as in the harmonic thrust at the close of *Laudate Dominum* (f. 11v; Ex. 10). His psalms appear to have remained in use at least until 1574, when the *maestro di canto* was paid for copying two books of them (Casimiri 1941–2: 152–3, 156).

Bass parts

We might at this point compare our three Paduan composers with regard to *spezzato* in its other connotation – i.e. whether or not the choirs might have been spaced. Ruffino and Passetto, apart from a few anomalies, generally adhere in tuttis to the principle of avoiding 6/4 chords in individual choirs by

Ex. 9   PASSETTO, Laudate pueri

Ex. 10   Passetto, Laudate Dominum

means of contrary-motion octave and unison doubling and occasional thirds between the bass parts. Santacroce, on the other hand, makes no attempt to do so, so perhaps he did not envisage undue spacing between the choirs. As he seems the most competent of the three composers in other respects, it is hard to believe that he was oblivious to the technical problems posed by singers who could not perceive the harmony. Spaced performance of Passetto's pieces would produce a rather disjointed effect, though, given the frequent lack of overlapping at choral interchanges.

Gasparo Alberti

Ruffino's psalms were clearly known to Alberti, who copied several of them into what is now Ms. 1209D of the Biblioteca Civica in Bergamo. Alberti's two psalms in the same source are unfortunately also lacking the first choir, though we can tell a great deal about their structure from the surviving music of Choir 2. *Laudate pueri* (f. 117v) is clearly an antiphonal piece of the type we have been considering, with exchanges between the choirs at the rate of one or two per half-verse. The first half of the doxology appears to be à 8, freely imitative, the choirs splitting again in the second half. *Confitebor* (f. 113v), on the other hand, begins antiphonally but begins to blur the division after what looks like a tutti for the second half of verse 4. The primary choral division returns in verse 8, but disappears again in the doxology, which probably begins with a homophonic tutti.

Alberti's two magnificats for eight voices hardly merit the designation polychoral at all, despite the fact that the openings in the Bergamo choirbooks are clearly labelled 'first. . .' and 'second choir'. After opening passages for the specified choirs the *octavi toni* (mod. edn, 1983: 7) reverts to the common sixteenth-century practice in non-polychoral many-voiced works whereby various voice-groupings are drawn from the ensemble. The *sexti toni* (ibid.: 23) bears scarcely any trace of double-choir writing.

Bologna, San Petronio Mss. A36 and A37

The eight psalms and magnificat for double choir in this source, all anonymous, are very similar to the examples we have been considering from Treviso and Padua, to judge by the samples I have transcribed. Changes of choir occur fairly frequently, but there is no antiphonal repetition in the body of the psalm. The cadential pitches of the psalm-tone are employed for the most part, but others are introduced judiciously to create variety. The style is predominantly homophonic, with a little decorative melisma, though at least one psalm, *Nisi Dominus* (f. 24v, 23v) opens with imitation after the chant incipit, and both that psalm and *Dixit Dominus* contain a brief tutti in addition to that at the end. The bass parts, with some anomalies, are spatially conceived.

Francesco Portinaro

One more psalm surviving complete which we might consider before moving on to Willaert[8] is the *Dixit Dominus* of Portinaro (Treviso Ms. 12: f. 17v; transcr. Carver 1980, vol. 2: 101), copied in 1565. Its later date of composition probably accounts for its richer and more flexible style, richer and grander than anything we have yet encountered, especially in its exuberant use of tuttis. The bass parts are not spatial, and in verses 6–8 Portinaro's four- and five-part textures sometimes draw voices from both choirs. He is not unduly concerned with retaining psalm-tone 8, quoted imitatively at the beginning; in the first two verses Choir 2 cadences on G at the end of the verse but Choir 1 then repeats the second half cadencing on C. Thereafter the pattern is abandoned, despite frequent cadences on C. The texture is at times quite polyphonic, but not usually imitative. Portinaro published multi-voiced motets in 1568 (one à 8 and one à 10) and 1572 (two à 8); those in 1568 are not polychoral, but I have not seen 1572.

Adriano Willaert

We are inclined to think of the 1550[(1)] collection, *I salmi appertinenti alli vesperi. . .*, as Willaert's, but in actual fact the lion's share of the twenty-three closed-verse and *alternatim* psalms is by Jachet. It has been suggested (Lewis 1979: 260–1) that the initiative came from Gardane, the publisher, rather than Willaert. Be that as it may, our concern is with the eight *Salmi spezzati*, the first to be printed, which are all by Willaert: *Laudate pueri, Confitebor tibi, Lauda Jerusalem, De profundis, Memento Domine David, Domine probasti me, Credidi* and *In convertendo* (Willaert, Opera, vol. 8: nos. 24–31). They do not provide for a whole sequence of vespers psalms to be sung with *cori spezzati*, but each is proper to one or more of the feasts on which vespers is known to have been sung in St Mark's with double-choir music (Bryant 1981a: 165), occasions on which the fabulous *pala d'oro* was opened (Moore 1981b: 268–9).

As we noted in Chapter 1, in St Mark's double-choir psalm performance did not require large numbers of singers, one choir was one-to-a-part, and the choirs were not spaced. Whilst the same works may not have been performed the same way if they were performed by other establishments, these circumstances do to some extent explain the quality they possess in comparison with those we have already studied: austerity. Yet that word must not obscure the extraordinary variety that Willaert achieves within his strict framework. The character of each psalm, as to some extent in the whole repertory, derives as much from the character of the psalm-tone as from any desire on Willaert's part to portray the mood of the text. Thus *Laudate pueri* and *Confitebor*, both psalms of praise built on tone 1, are alike in mood. *Credidi*, the most subjectively expressive text ('I was greatly afflicted'), gains a sombre colouring from the persistent phrygian cadences appropriate to tone 4. On the other hand *De profundis*, whose text also opens in a mood of darkness, is relatively tranquil owing to the strong (as we would term it) 'F major' tendencies of tone 5. Sensitive as Willaert the madrigalist is to the text, Willaert the composer for the liturgy must observe the strong element of objectivity inherent in the system of psalm-tones.

The psalm-tone also influences the melodic writing, particularly at cadences; the characteristic cadential shape of the tone may be retained even where the harmony is deflected to another modal centre, as in *Memento* at bars 109–10, where the psalm-tone ending is harmonised in C rather than G, or where the cadence is overlapped or avoided, as in the same psalm at bars 126–7, where a cadence figure of C in the tenor precedes a cadence on G. In this respect Willaert is less strict than Santacroce and avoids absolute regularity of cadential structure.

As well as often appearing paraphrased, usually in a tenor part, the psalm-tone also provides melodic material for all the voices to use in imitation, or for the top voice in block chords. Hardly a verse of *Laudate pueri* is free from the three rising notes of the incipit of tone 1. This psalm is a good illustration of the textural variety of these works. The predominant texture is syllabic, mainly note-against-note counterpoint of the kind explored by Willaert elsewhere, notably in the motets and madrigals of *Musica nova* (Opera, vols. 5 & 13). The opposite poles are block chords (e.g. *Laudate*: bars 100–2) and decorative melisma, usually at a cadence (ibid.: 34–8). Between these extremes the variety is astonishing. The little imitative points, often employing only a four- or five-note rhythmic shape, exploit all the possible voice-combinations, including voice-pairing (ibid.: 1–3), four-fold entries (ibid.: 15–18), 2+1+1 schemes (ibid.: 38–40), and what became a Venetian mannerism, the syncopation of one voice against the rest (ibid.: 32–4).

Voice-pairing on a larger scale, i.e. for whole verses, occurs as one would expect in the two longest psalms, *Memento* and *Domine probasti*. Unlike Santacroce Willaert always draws the two voices from the same choir, in keeping with the spaced performance implied by his treatment of the bass parts in tuttis. Four psalms employ triple-time sections as an additional device for contrast. In three cases music from earlier in the psalm is brought back in the doxology: in *Confitebor* the music of 'Sicut erat' is taken from bars 12ff, and similarly in *Lauda Jerusalem* 'Gloria' is from bars 28ff and in *De profundis* 'Sicut erat' from bars 6ff.

There is no striving for effect in these pieces – simply continuous small-scale subtlety of line and texture. Direct portrayal of the text occurs occasionally where the ideas are sufficiently pictorial. Gerstenberg (Willaert, Opera, vol. 8: xiii) cites a couple of striking examples of word-painting, to which we might add bars 8–11 of *Lauda Jerusalem*, where the word 'confortavit' is portrayed by sustained B flat harmony. The most lavish resources available – the rapid interchange of choirs and the eight-part tutti – Willaert reserves for the doxology, where it matters little if the words are less audible and where a musical climax seems also liturgically appropriate. In the body of the psalm Willaert changes choirs only at the end of a verse. *Credidi* is unique in its introduction of a tutti for the words 'O Domine ego servus tuus' in verse 6, an act of faith amidst prevailing despair. The final tuttis are more substantial than the merely cadential affairs found often in Passetto and sometimes in Santacroce. They may function as a thematic summing-up; a good illustration of this is the significance acquired by a conventional little dotted figure in *Lauda Jerusalem* (bars 6–7, 11–13, 28–32, 45–9, 100, 103, 107–9, 117–19, 134, 136 and 138–end). In this rôle they may contain a climactic, *cantus firmus*-like setting of the psalm-tone, as at the close of *De profundis*.

The tuttis are preceded by shorter choral exchanges which may involve (for the first time in the piece) repetition of text which has just been sung by the opposite choir. Even here Willaert is noticeably restrained compared with his predecessors, particularly Ruffino. There are no 'trick' effects, and the final tutti is only in two cases (the long psalms *Memento* and *Domine probasti*) interrupted by antiphony once it has begun. The choral exchanges prior to the tutti do not involve straightforward repetition of music, though usually the answering choir will exploit the same rhythmic and melodic ideas, as in *Lauda Jerusalem*, which has two exchanges before the tutti, one long phrase and one short. The tenor of Choir 1 (bar 120) is given a 'real answer' a fifth higher by the alto of Choir 2 (bar 125), the material being the first part of the psalm-tone. The effect is of a modulation to the dominant at bars 130–1. Transposition of material and cadences of this sort becomes a more fundamental device in polychoral music, particularly where the pitch contrast between choirs is wider, and may ultimately have contributed to composers' awareness of tonal as opposed to modal progressions. In Willaert's psalms the pitch contrast is not large, and indeed is more a question of chord-spacing, since Choir 1 always contains the highest and lowest voices, giving Choir 2 a closer spacing. One might speculate that it was the latter to which the four solo singers were assigned in St Mark's; certainly closer spacing makes the blending of solo voices easier to obtain.

Four of Willaert's tuttis contain 'clash' cadences. In two cases (*Lauda*: bar 139; *Memento*: bar 230) the suspension of the leading note is sounded against the minor seventh of the scale, whilst in *Domine probasti*: bar 297 it clashes with the major seventh. Dissonance of a slightly different type occurs in *De profundis*: bar 134 where a double 6/4 suspension is sounded against the fifth of the chord. Such dissonances do seem to be an especially Venetian phenomenon. We shall encounter them again in the Gabrielis but not in Lasso.

The presence without ascription of Willaert's *salmi spezzati* in Treviso manuscripts makes one wonder whether some of the anonymous settings could be his. Particular interest attaches to a group of five psalms in Ms. 11b (ff. 37v–42r); they are settings of the *Cinque laudate*, with the first two psalms reversed: *Laudate Dominum omnes gentes, Laudate pueri, Lauda anima mea Dominum, Laudate Dominum quoniam bonus est psalmus* and *Lauda Jerusa-*

lem. The second and the last are indubitably Willaert's, but although Zarlino testified (1573) that Willaert had set all five (see above, p. 7), only these two were printed in 1550[(1)]. The first of the group is not in the style of Willaert so far as we can determine – it is largely homophonic and hangs fire on long notes in a way that Willaert does not. It also contains choral exchanges and probably antiphonal repetition in the second verse, i.e. the last before the doxology, though one hesitates to apply normal judgments to such a uniquely short psalm. The other two, sandwiched between those known to be his in Ms. 11b, are stylistically much closer to Willaert's work. The choral alternation is strictly by verses except for one place in *Lauda anima mea* where vv. 6–7 seem to be split into half-verses. In this psalm the alternating cadence pattern of tone 3 may be discerned but with some striking and masterly shifts to other areas, notably in v. 9 where the C–a alternation is replaced by F–g (Ex. 11);

Ex. 11   ?WILLAERT, Lauda anima mea Dominum

such modal shifts involving the addition of B flat are found in Willaert's psalms (e.g. *Credidi*, the tutti at bars 47–52), though perhaps not as dramatically as here. The long notes in the soprano on 'in eternum' are a Willaertian madrigalism. Both the incipit and ending of the psalm-tone are to be found melodically, notably in the tenor at the close, where the ending is used as a *cantus firmus*, as in several Willaert psalms. *Laudate Dominum quoniam. . .* begins with a harmonisation of tone 7 in the tenor, and its cadential pattern is sometimes retained, though with the E at the mediant often harmonised with C harmony. In vv. 8 and 10 the first half of the verse is given to a pair of voices (cf. *Confitebor*: bars 62ff and 77ff).

Many of the stylistic fingerprints we isolated in the above discussion are found in these two psalms: homophony contrasted with note-against-note polyphony, concise imitative points, syllabic writing with controlled melisma towards the cadence. The harmony remains 'correct' in the concluding sections; since in all probability the lowest (C_4) part is the higher of the two bass parts, we are probably dealing with spatial writing in tuttis. It is unfortunate that there remains just one choir of these pieces; I think they are very likely to be Willaert's – perhaps written later than 1550 as Zarlino does not mention them until 1573 – but even if they are not, they are by a very good composer.

There is only one other double-choir piece which is ascribed to Willaert – a setting of the compline psalm *Cum invocarem* which appeared after his death in 1564[1]. By implication the ascription applies also to the three succeeding psalms since the music of the doxology is identical with that of the third psalm *Qui habitat*, the remaining two forming a similar pair (all transcr. in Carver 1980, vol. 2: 115). The authenticity of these works is open to doubt. They do not contain the wealth of textural detail found in Willaert's eight vesper psalms, and the bass parts in tuttis show no sign of conforming to Zarlino's rules for spaced performance. Moreover, though the alternating cadence pattern of the psalm-tone may be discerned, the choral exchanges are more frequent than in Willaert, dictated more by the meaning and syntax of the text than its versification. Unlike the compline psalms of Santacroce this set appears to be based entirely on one psalm-tone (8; cf. LU: 264–6) which facilitates the borrowing of doxology music. Of the music we have discussed, it is Santacroce's which seems most akin to these psalms.

The sensitivity to the text which they reveal is illustrated by Ex. 12, in which the words 'A fructu frumenti, vini et olei' are set to marvellous 'floating' chords which reveal a consummate grasp of the expressive possibilities of simple triads alternated by groups of subtly differing composition. This device is nowhere exploited in Willaert's 1550 psalms. *Qui habitat* has (bar 129) a highly dramatic interjection from Choir 2 of the word 'non' into a phrase sung by Choir 1; it also contains, like Santacroce's setting, duet sections, but in this case both voices are always drawn from the same choir. The only tutti section outside the doxologies is that found, appropriately, for the words 'Omnes servi. . .' immediately after the intonation of *Ecce nunc benedicite*.

Ex. 12   ?WILLAERT, Cum invocarem

Outside Italy

The liturgical double-choir psalm seems to be virtually unknown outside Italy.
Composers like Claudin de Sermisy treat psalms in a motet-like manner. His
Inclina Domine (Ps. 86) (1553[7]: tenor f. 20; Sermisy, *Opera*, vol. 2: 39), despite the modern editor's division into two choirs, does not stick to a fixed
choral division. Settings of French translations of the psalms can hardly be
called liturgical, and are rarely in as many as eight parts. Goudimel's setting of
Psalm 18, *Je t'aymeray en toute obéissance* (1566: superius p. 19), is divided
into eight sections of which only the last is à 8; it begins with a suggestion of
two choirs and these occasionally re-emerge, in a manner not unlike the Viennese motet style (see Chapter 4). Le Jeune, whose seven-voice dialogue we
discussed in Chapter 1, did later write a real eight-part double-choir setting

of Psalm 136, *Loué'-tous ce Dieu qui est dous* (1606: no. 7; Expert 1905–6, vol. 22: 53). It is a stiff piece in *musique mesurée* style with no overlapping of voices between choirs or even between single-choir and tutti sections.

Conclusion

The early sources of Italian sacred polychoral music consist, then, almost entirely of psalms. Yet, whilst antiphonal psalmody may have been the germinal force, only Willaert remains substantially true to liturgical antiphony by verses. Other composers alternate the choirs more freely, though most pay attention to the cadential structure of the psalm-tone. The adventurous Ruffino, very early on, applied double-choir writing to the ordinary of the mass. Whilst the psalmody of the Office may have invited *cori spezzati*, as we shall see in the next chapter, the technical musical resources, except for spatial bass parts, are inherent in the syntax of Flemish polyphony.

3
THE FRANCO-FLEMISH TRADITION

In this chapter we shall explore how polychoral writing seems to have arisen within the mainstream of Franco-Flemish polyphony in the first half of the sixteenth century. This happened in two main ways: firstly through the employment of a particular type of canon, and secondly through the projection of the common device of voice-pairing onto ensembles of eight or more voices. In reality, since voice-pairing is often imitative, these two possibilities might be thought of as strict and free facets of the same fundamental idea.

Double-choir canon

It was Theodor Kroyer (1909: 14, 26) and subsequently Erich Hertzmann (1929–30: 138–40) who drew attention to a possible connection between polychoral music and a type of canonic writing in the works of composers of the generation after Josquin, i.e. Mouton and his contemporaries. Neither of them cited any examples of canon which are actually polychoral. Zarlino writes as follows of the type of canon concerned:

One might also compose pieces with the parts doubled up, that is to say moving the parts two by two in consequence or imitation, as Mouton did in the motet *Nesciens mater*, and Gombert in *Inviolata, integra et casta*, both for eight voices, and Adriano Willaert in the above-mentioned motet *Salve sancte parens*, and the chanson *Sur l'herbe brunette*, both of which are for six voices. (1558, Part 3: Chapter 66)

In this type of canon each voice gives rise to another; it is easy to see that if the canonic voices were all to commence after the same time interval and if also simultaneous rests were to occur between phrases in the notated voices, an antiphonal texture would result. This possibility is not explicitly mentioned by Zarlino, who does not link his above remarks with his discussion of polychoral music in the same chapter, nor is any reference made to it by Vicentino. Indeed, antiphony does not result in the two pieces cited by Zarlino which we can identify: Mouton's *Nesciens mater* (1534[(5)]: no. 6; mod. edn, Smijers & Merritt 1934–64, vol. 3: no. 6), an eight-in-four canon, and Willaert's *Salve sancte parens* (1559: no. 15; Opera vol. 5: 127), which has two canonic pairs of voices and two free voices. The latter's chanson is no longer known; nor is an eight-part setting by Gombert of *Inviolata*.[1] However, it is alongside pieces like Mouton's *Nesciens* in the repertory of the French Royal Chapel as printed by Attaingnant that we find the first indications of double-choir canon.

Book 3 of Attaingnant's motets contains an anonymous *Salve mater pietas* (Smijers & Merritt vol. 3: no. 19) in which the two notated voices give two canonic voices at the upper octave. The placing of the rests produces almost continuous voice-pairing. The six-part *Ave sanctissima Maria* from the same volume is usually attributed to Verdelot but is probably by Pierre de la Rue (Slim, *NGr* vol. 19: 632), who used it as the basis of a parody mass (mod. edn: 1950). The motet employs six-in-three canon, with the rests disposed so as to produce a double-choir texture for the most part. Rather than have the piece consist entirely of leisurely antiphony with a tutti at the end, the composer mitigates the inflexibility of canonic procedure by setting the opening salute as a close canon at one breve's distance, giving the effect of a tutti. A pause then allows the time interval to be changed to four breves. The *comes* (i.e. canonic) voices are a fourth above the *dux* (i.e. notated) voices, which offers both register contrast and an interesting layout of cadential pitches; those following the pause are as follows:

comes	F		C		g	F		C		d		G		d	g
dux		C		g		d		C		g	a		d	a	d	g

Pierre de la Rue's preoccupation in his *Missa 'Ave sanctissima'* is with canon rather than double-choir textures. Wholesale polyphonic quotation is rare, and little of the Mass is in any sense antiphonal.

The earliest surviving example of an eight-in-four double-choir canon seems to be a chanson, Gombert's *Qui ne l'aymeroit*, printed in an Augsburg anthology of canons, the *Selectissimae necnon cantiones* (1540[7]; Gombert, Opera vol. 3: 241). It appeared again as *O Jesu Christe*, a rather unsatisfactory contrafactum in the Nuremberg *Cantiones triginta* (1568[7]). Musically it is very fine, and as with *Ave sanctissima* the composer utilises the canonic interval (here the lower fifth) to produce a satisfying sequence of cadential pitches:

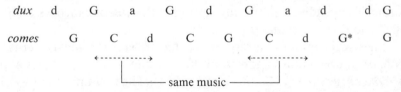

Structural coherence is further enhanced by the repetition of music indicated, and from * free close imitation of a descending scale figure blurs the choral division and produces an effective climax. The texture of this closing passage seems to anticipate the motivic complexity of final tuttis in Andrea Gabrieli or Lasso.

Another canon eight-in-four in the chanson repertory was Phinot's *A dieu, Loyse* (1548b: no. 1; Opera vol. 3, pars 1: 92); the pitch interval here is the unison and double-choir textures are only intermittently suggested. In the rather unlikely area of the Italian madrigal Claudio Veggio's *Madonna il mio dolor* (Doni 1544; mod. edn Malipiero & Fagotto 1965: 266), again a canon eight-in-four at the unison, retains double-choir textures throughout its two *parti*.

The first surviving example in sacred music of a motet in eight-in-four double-choir canon may well be a setting of *Inviolata, integra et casta es* by Costanzo Festa (*b* c1490, *d* 1545) preserved in Vatican Cappella Sistina Cod. 20 (f. 121v; the second section: Anthology no. 2). The sequence melody (cf. LU: 1861–2) is employed throughout as a *cantus firmus* in the second highest voice of each group. The three sections have different, progressively contracting pitch and time intervals: (1) the upper octave after four breves, (2) the upper fifth after three breves, and (3) the upper fourth after one breve. The first two sections have a clear double-choir texture and are non-imitative apart from the canon itself. The third section acts as a huge tutti climax with a full pseudo-imitative texture predominating.

Phinot also left a motet in double-choir canon, *Ecce sacerdos* (1554; mod. edn Opera vol. 2: 159), ten voices in five at the unison. If this sounds a little alarming, its musical effect is straightforward. After stately antiphony at the beginning the rests gradually become shorter and staggered entries of the voices merge into the final tutti. The last quarter of the piece is a slightly varied repeat of the third quarter and this added to the unison canon means that the piece homes rather too often on G.

Stephani's *Cantiones triginta selectissimae*, 1568[7], consists entirely of canons, of which three fall into the double-choir category, all eight-in-four. Two are reprints: Gombert's *O Jesu Christe*, already discussed, and Kugelmann's *Nun lob mein Seel*, about which see below. The third is Bonmarché's *Constitues eos*, a setting of the response of the gradual at Mass on the Feast of St Peter and St Paul (transcr. Carver 1980, vol. 2: 238). It is the only known printed work by this composer, a Fleming who held positions at Cambrai and Madrid. Continuously overlapped cadences give the effect of imitation by choirs with short enlivening snatches of imitation by voices. A certain stolid monotony is engendered by the alternation in the *dux* of cadences on F and g, giving C and d in the *comes* (upper fifth).

Johannes Kugelmann's eight-part setting of *Nun lob mein Seel* is a rare example of double-choir canon from the German repertory. It first appeared in his *Concentus novi* (1540; mod. edn, 1955). The volume actually contains four settings of the melody, for three, four, five and eight voices. In all cases the melody is in the tenor. The three- and four-part settings are homophonic harmonisations, that in five parts in motet style. The eight-part setting is an eight-in-four canon at the lower fourth. The version of the melody in the eight-part setting differs slightly from that in the others, sometimes, it seems, perversely and not for the better, but sometimes to facilitate the canon. This is particularly apparent in the middle where the phrases are longer than the four breves of the canonic time interval, causing the melody to overlap itself (Ex. 13). Far less competent is Leonhard Paminger's handling of an optional canon at the unison in his *Ach Gott wem soll ichs klagen* bearing the legend

Ex. 13   KUGELMANN, Nun lob mein Seel

* Eb in 1568[(7)]

melody as in settings à 3, à 4, à 5

'without the rests, 5 voices, with the rests, 10 voices'[2] (1556[(29)]: no. 52). A ten-voice realisation reveals none-too-satisfactory joins between the choirs, particularly where a change of cadential pitch is implied by the notated voices alone, as at bar 6 of Ex. 14.

Ex. 14 PAMINGER, Ach Gott wem soll ichs klagen

Musica ficta in double-choir canon

Consideration of *musica ficta* is essential in order to arrive at a performing realisation of one of these works. I am not only thinking of the accidentals which may need to be applied to the notated voices (*dux*), a problem which has to be grappled with in the same way as in any other music of the period. There is the additional question of whether, having established the intervallic structure of the *dux* we can retain it in the *comes*. In a strict canon, as we use the term today, the *comes* must imitate the *dux* note-for-note; rhythmic values and direction of melodic movement will correspond exactly, and of course often in the sixteenth century the *comes* was not separately notated. If the canon is at the unison or octave, exact intervallic correspondence also results. With canons at other intervals important questions arise: should the *comes* singers attempt to reproduce the exact sequence of intervals in the *dux*, i.e. effectively transpose the mode by adding or subtracting from the key signature and/or applying *ficta* accidentals, or should they regard the *overall* mode as paramount, tempering the intervals accordingly? In canons with an open antiphonal texture the harmonic context does not really help us to apply the correct accidentals.

At this point it is extremely helpful to turn to Zarlino.[3] Almost alone among theorists he divides what we should call canon into two types: strict *fuga* or *consequenza* on the one hand, and strict *imitatione* on the other. In both cases the rhythm is followed exactly but only in *fuga* are the precise intervals retained. As he expresses it, the *comes* voices in an example of *fuga*

whether in similar or contrary motion contain the same intervals as their Guide. . .but Imitation. . .does not proceed by the same intervals in the following parts.

(1558, Part 3: Chapter 52)

Canons at the second, third, sixth and seventh always result in *imitatione*, but Zarlino implies that canons at the fourth or fifth *may* or *may not* retain the intervallic structure in the *comes*.

Zarlino's classification may of course be over-systematic, but it has the merit of giving us some criteria on which to make decisions. When only a couple of voices in the texture are involved in canonic procedure it is easier to ascertain the correct accidentals in the *comes*. It would seem that the Credo of Josquin's *Missa de Beata Virgine* (Werken vol. 3: 125) is a *fuga*, since it is possible, without creating impossible clashes, to flatten all the Bs in the *comes*, which is at the fifth below. On the other hand in the Sanctus, which has a one flat signature, the canon is at the fifth above but it is necessary to retain many B flats in the *comes*. The Sanctus seems therefore to employ *imitatione*. In the Agnus Dei the subject avoids the troublesome B and therefore the possibility of F sharps in the *comes*.

It seems reasonable to suppose that if a passage works as *fuga*, i.e. no faulty progressions appear, then it is meant to in the absence of contra-indications in the source. Verdelot's (or la Rue's) *Ave sanctissima Maria*, as printed by Attaingnant, allows *fuga* for much of its length. The B flat of the signature is imitated as E flat, and editorial B naturals (whether to avoid the tritone or provide the raised leading note) are imitated as E naturals. At 'in quo non dubito', however, *fuga* breaks down in the middle voice; a B flat in the *dux* at bar 51 must be answered by an E natural (bar 55) to avoid its clashing with an A–E chord. Strangely Schering (1931: 93) chooses to render the B flat in bar 51 as B natural, which seems to me to be approaching the puzzle from the wrong end. I prefer to pass into *imitatione* from this point until the end of the piece.[4]

One would expect Kugelmann's *Nun lob mein Seel* to preserve the intervallic structure of the *dux* in the *comes* in view of the presence of a pre-existing melody – Kugelmann adapted it from a secular song.[5] As we have seen, he has to alter the melody in at least one place to make it work as a canon at all! The piece does make sense as an example of *fuga*, even allowing for slight variants between the versions provided by 1540[8] and 1568[7].

Gombert's *Qui ne l'aymeroit* seems to be an example of *imitatione*, Bonmarché's *Constitues eos* of *fuga* if we accept in the latter case a couple of oblique false relations. The *secunda pars* of Festa's *Inviolata* (Anthology no. 2) works intermittently as *fuga*, but there are a number of places (bars 14, 28, 47(?), 66) where B flats are necessary in the *resolutio*. The *tertia pars* is fascinating for two reasons. First, the second highest voice of the *dux* contains precautionary natural signs which refer not to the Bs in the *dux* near which they stand but to the Es in the *comes* which in *fuga* would be rendered as E flats. There are three of these signs, occurring in three successive, slightly varied statements of the same melodic idea; Ex. 15 is taken from the first of these. The context rules out B naturals in the *dux* but requires E naturals in the *comes*. Second, at the words 'qui sola inviolata', a situation arises comparable with that in the Gloria of Ruffino's Mass (Ex. 5). *Fuga* added to the normal rules of *musica ficta* leads to a permanent shift down a semitone. Other

Ex. 15   FESTA, Inviolata, integra et casta es

attempts at a solution produce varying combinations of tritonal intervals and chords, false relations and awkward chordal shifts. The source provides no precautionary accidentals to aid us here. If Festa's precautionary accidentals show indirectly that *fuga* is a possible method of realising such a canon, Guerrero seems to specify *imitatione* for his Pater noster (1555: tenor, p. 36), which only intermittently suggests double-choir textures. The print gives clefs and signatures of both *dux* and *comes* of the eight-in-four arrangement. Although the canonic interval is the upper fifth, all the signatures have one flat. The issues raised here need to be considered not just in applying *musica ficta* to canons but in all cases involving imitation, whether by voices or choirs.

As I have already implied, canonic procedures are rather inflexible when the whole texture is involved. A piece may become monotonous once it is realised that in the *comes* not just melodic lines but complete harmonies are predetermined, especially when the canon is at the unison, as in Phinot's two examples. Doubtless for this reason as well as for its compositional difficulty double-choir canon remained relatively rare. It could still provide Victoria with a technical *tour de force* with which to end his four-part Mass on Guerrero's motet *Simile est regnum coelorum* (1576; mod. edn, Opera vol. 2: 21), the third Agnus of which is an eight-in-four double-choir canon at the unison. Even a Venetian could employ snatches of canon in the course of a work, as Andrea Gabrieli did in *Egredimini et videte* (1587[16]: no. 22; mod. edn, 1965: 9), recalling the style of Ruffino. Only Jacob Handl seems to have composed a complete Mass in double-choir canon, again at the unison, his *Missa canonica* (1580: no. 16; mod. edn, DTÖ 94–5: 42), and it has to be admitted that the result is rather tedious.[6]

The origin of flexible antiphony

Voice-pairing: Josquin

Voice-pairing, a compositional device close to the heart of the style of Josquin's generation, was probably, with its flexibility, more influential in the long run in the evolution of polychoral writing than strict canon. It is such a well-known ingredient of sixteenth-century style that an exhaustive account of it is not necessary here. There are fundamentally two kinds of paired imitation – that in which all the voices have the same theme:

type 1

and that in which each voice of the pair has a distinct idea:

———————

xxxxxxxx

type 2

———————

xxxxxxxx

Reese (1954: 257–8) drew attention to the variety of treatment Josquin may give to the answering pair, by means of inversion, reversal of order of entry, and double counterpoint. We shall be especially interested in the concept of projecting type 2 onto a larger ensemble, the effect of which, if the voice-groupings are consistently maintained, is double-choir writing.

We are not concerned here merely with the derivation of double-choir textures but also with the formal structure which can arise from successive splitting and re-uniting of the ensemble. Josquin's *In principio erat verbum* (mod. edn, 1933: 4) begins with a point of type 1, the choir dividing discantus + tenor, altus + bassus, the latter pair entering at the fifth below. The point is then repeated in a slightly decorated version. D+T then state a related theme a fourth higher, imitated again by A + B at the lower fifth but with T still sounding to give a three-voice texture. D+T continue with a further point at the new pitch, A + B following this time at the lower octave. Close imitation of a five-note figure by all the voices, almost ostinato-fashion, culminates in the first four-part cadence of the piece. The diagram below summarises these opening bars, omitting the thematic aspect.

```
                                                          à 4 cadence in d
                                                               ↓
    D  C   C     C  C      F   d     F    a        __ ____

    T ——    ——         ————   ————         —— —— — —{
                                                      
    A     F   F     F  F     Bb   d      F    F   __ ____

    B      ——     ——      ——      —— —— — —— —{
```

(each pair of letters indicates the pitch of the point and its cadence respectively)

Josquin is not of course thinking in terms of a permanent division of the choir. The remainder of the *prima pars* tends to pair D with A and T with B, if not as consistently. However, the procedure adopted in the opening passage contains in its essentials a fundamental form-building process of polychoral music: the succession of antiphony, progressive integration of the forces, and tutti. Unlike strict canon, imitative procedures of this kind allow plasticity of phrase length, variety in pitch of entries and cadences, and diversity of contrapuntal detail. Register contrast is implicit unless the piece is *a voci pari*. The opening of *In principio* is essentially linear, though later Josquin makes use of homophonic writing in four parts. His *Tu pauperum refugium*, easily accessible in *HAM* (vol. 1: 92), contains at bars 46ff a striking example of voice-pairing made emphatically antiphonal by rests separating the phrases, a homophonic texture, and the succeeding à 4 tutti.

The splitting of larger ensembles

It is not surprising that such stock devices of four-part writing should have been applied to pieces scored for more voices. Hertzmann (1929–30: 139–40) quoted passages from two eight-part works, Josquin's *Lugebat David / Tulerunt Dominum*[7] and Mouton's *Verbum bonum*, which contrast two SATB groups. In neither work are these combinations permanent, and the same is true of many sixteenth-century multi-voiced pieces.[8]

A piece on an exceptionally large scale which makes use of split textures is Brumel's *Missa 'Et ecce terrae motus'* à 12 (Opera vol. 3: 1), one of the first really massive works of the late Renaissance. It is surprising that it does not seem to have been generally recognised as an important precursor of poly-choral music;[9] it contains striking antiphonal effects which are reiterated in a way that draws attention, temporarily, to a particular choral division. The divisions favour high–low contrast and involve groupings of 6+6, 5+4, 4+4 and 4+4+4 voices. In most cases the antiphony is followed by a tutti, either suddenly or via telescoped imitation. There is considerable flexibility in the antiphonal repetition. Some is almost exact, recalling canon or imitative voice-pairing, and some is varied. Ex. 16 from the Gloria shows antiphony between two four-part groups leading via a six-part phrase to a tutti. The opening phrase is varied by the second group, the next two repeated literally except for register contrast. The six-part group is made up of one voice from each of these groups added to the four voices which have not hitherto sounded in this section. I have laid out the voices in an order which reveals the antiphony; Hudson's edition naturally arranges the voices in the usual pitch order.

In the Benedictus four-part groups, one low and one high, alternate at first with independent, freely-evolving material, after which the high group begins to imitate the lower at the upper octave, the section ending with a short à 8 'tutti'. Instances also occur where such imitation is at an interval other than the unison or octave, as in the second Kyrie, where imitation at the lower fifth occurs between the first two of the three four-part groups; to be more precise, the second highest voice is imitated with new counterpoint. Variation in the antiphonal repetition sometimes goes beyond mere decoration or new coun-terpoint, involving a shift in tonal level; in Ex. 17 from the Credo the effect is of *ouvert–clos*. Immediately after the extract given the first group re-states its opening phrase unaltered.

For completeness it is worth mentioning a twelve-part setting of *Inviolata, integra et casta es*, doubtfully attributed to Josquin (Werken, suppl.: 45). The entire piece consists of a passage for each of three distinct groups, à 3, à 4 and à 4, culminating in a tutti in which the twelfth voice, tenor I, bears the *cantus firmus* 'O Maria flos virginum'.

It is interesting at this point to glance sideways at another strand of tradition – the seemingly isolated florid style of English church music in the two or three decades after 1500. Block-like layout of forces was common in large-scale

Ex. 16   BRUMEL, Missa 'Et ecce terrae motus'

Ex. 16 (cont.)

Ex. 17   Brumel, Missa 'Et ecce terrae motus'

festal works, with sections for smaller groups punctuated by tuttis. In the more syllabic, 'progressive' and perhaps later music of Taverner his general compression of the structure does begin to produce antiphonal textures, as between high and low sections of the choir in his Masses '*Small devotion*' and '*Mater Christi*' (mod. edns, 1923: 70, 99). The only work in the English repertory which reveals the full, albeit *a cappella* possibilities of the polychoral style is Tallis's famous *Spem in alium* (mod. edn, 1966), whose forty voices subdivide into eight five-part choirs.[10] The quietly liturgical *cantoris–decani* music of the Anglican church does not normally require a composer to write for more than four or five voices, since like voices from both sides usually double up in full sections.

The emergence of the double-choir motet

Jean Rousée

There seems to be every reason to suppose that polychoral writing arose within the Franco-Flemish tradition through the two techniques discussed above – the 2*x*-in-*x* type of canon, and the antiphonal juxtaposition of groups of voices as in voice-pairing. If we return to Attaingnant's motets, we find in the twelfth book (1535[(4)]) a setting by Jean Rousée of *Regina caeli* (Anthology no. 3) which very effectively plugs a gap in our evolutionist argument. A significant step must have been taken towards the polychoral motet, and even if it was not Rousée who took that step, his piece represents an important stage in the development of the genre. Rousée, who later sang in the French Royal Chapel from 1547 to 1559, based his setting on the marvellous *Regina* plainchant, which, simplified, provides the melodic material for each section. For much of the piece each choir ($C_1C_3C_4F_4$) establishes its identity clearly, with long passages for each choir alone and thematic repetition between them. Paired imitation takes place within each choir. Answering antiphonal phrases involve both exact and varied repetition, though primitive technique reveals itself in the lack of overlap at some choral exchanges.

We are not dealing with a spaced-choir piece, since the choral division is blurred at times, particularly at the close of each *pars* and the opening of the *secunda pars*. In such places there is a certain tendency for parts of like range to imitate each other, as in double-choir canon but without the synchronisation, as it were. The style of the piece is restrained and dignified. Antiphonal repetition is limited to long phrases, and the texture varies from note-against-note to a more polyphonic, broadly imitative vein. The melismata arise from the brevity of the text; in contrapuntal terms the style is not far removed from that of the North Italian psalms. This is particularly true of the 'alleluia' sections with their clear-cut cadences.

It would be foolish to make the highest claims for Rousée's piece, intrinsically or as a vital seminal force. We do not know how wide its circulation was – I have encountered no sources other than Attaingnant. It certainly did not lead directly to widespread cultivation of polychoral music in France. It does seem, however, to represent a transitional stage in the evolution of polychoral style from basic principles of Franco-Flemish polyphony, and is early enough to have been largely independent of developments in the Veneto.

Dominique Phinot

The composer whose work above all seems to indicate that before 1550 polychoral techniques were highly developed and not restricted to Italy is Dominique Phinot, probably a Frenchman who was active also in Italy but whose life remains largely obscure (Jacob, *NGr* vol. 14: 662). He had connections with the Duke of Urbino and with Lyons, where much of his extant music was published in two books of motets (1547 and 1548a) and two books of chansons (1548b and c). His music was quite widely dispersed, and particularly noteworthy are the reprints in German anthologies. Two of the *salmi a versi con le sue risposte* in 1550[1] are by Jachet and Phinot jointly.

We have already come across Phinot's double-choir canons *Ecce sacerdos* and *A Dieu Loyse*, but his really significant contribution to the development of polychoral writing lies in a group of five eight-part motets in his *Liber secundus mutetarum* (1548a; Opera vol. 4: nos. 13–17), each for two equal four-part choirs: *O sacrum convivium, Tanto tempore, Jam non dicam, Sancta Trinitas* and *Incipit oratio Jeremiae prophetae*. All use normal SATB clefs except *Tanto tempore*, which has *chiavette*. Whether these works take their inspiration wholly from the Franco-Flemish strand of development or owe something also to the Italian tradition is impossible to answer. What is certain is that they exerted a considerable fascination, perhaps greater than Willaert's psalms, particularly in Germany, as is clear from their being reprinted in several important German anthologies: Montanus and Neuber's *Evangeliorum* (Nuremberg, 1555[10] & [11]; all except the Lamentations), the same firm's *Thesaurus musicus* (1564[1]; all five) and Wyriot's *Selectae cantiones*, printed in Strasbourg (1578[1]; all five). *Jam non dicam* appeared also in both editions of Bodenschatz's *Florilegium* (1603[1] and 1618[1]). Many manuscript copies survive in Germany and a few elsewhere (Höfler in Phinot, Opera vol. 4: xi–xiii & xv–xvi).

Right from the outset of any of these five pieces we are aware that the interaction between the choirs is the primary structural force, and the subtlety of Phinot's manipulation of that interaction is considerable.[11] His plasticity of approach is apparent in the overwhelming predominance of varied repetition over exact repetition. The whole structure depends on such antiphony, with virtually none of the non-repetitive antiphony typical of the *salmo spezzato*. Antiphonal phrases may be of shorter or longer duration: as little as one bar or as much as three bars or more. The answering phrase may be at a different pitch; it may be varied in melodic, harmonic and rhythmic detail; it may begin differently but end the same, like a musical rhyme; the answering choir may extend the phrase by adding further text.

Eight-part textures assume importance as musical punctuation marks, as ways of emphasising particular phrases, and of course as all-embracing conclusions. They usually arise from an overlapped choral exchange in which the leading choir continues sounding whilst the other choir imitates, or from the merging of multiple exchanges. Sometimes a phrase set à 4 is repeated à 8, or the last half of a phrase begun à 4 is emphasised by the addition of the other choir. Phinot's antiphonal phrases are usually homophonic, the tuttis more polyphonic in the Flemish style, with no attempt to retain harmonic completeness in each choir. Further illustration of Phinot's non-spatial concept of the idiom occurs in the Lamentations, where two self-contained four-part sections mix voices from both choirs to give in one case a high group, in the other a low group.

Sancta Trinitas (Anthology no. 4) will serve to illustrate Phinot's style. In the very first phrase Phinot eschews exact repetition: Choir 2's reiteration of 'Sancta Trinitas' takes us to the dominant where Choir 1 had remained in the tonic. The succeeding phrase 'unus Deus' shows how overlapping echoes can produce a tutti. Towards the end of the piece it is instructive to compare the delightful variants of the three chords of 'ex hoc nunc' as they pass from choir to choir. Structural cohesion on a larger scale is provided by the repetition of the 'miserere nobis' cadence figure (bars 18–22) at 'o beata trinitas' (49–54, slightly expanded) and at the end for 'et usque in saeculum'. This purely musical 'refrain' is interesting in view of the striking textual and musical refrain found in *Jam non dicam*, whose three 'alleluia' sections share the same forthright material, anticipating the refrain structures of Giovanni Gabrieli.

Another formal characteristic of these motets which anticipates many a Venetian piece is the repetition of the final section as a crowning climax. When this happens in *Tanto tempore*, like voices from each choir, except for the basses, are exchanged with some minor variants. In *Sancta Trinitas*, in which the texture remains more antiphonal, the choirs are not swapped. In both cases the start of the repeat is dovetailed in with great subtlety, as may be seen by comparing bars 79–82 of *Sancta Trinitas* with bars 73–5.

Whilst such formal devices seem to anticipate later Venetian practices, the character of Phinot's music in general is more in the line of development towards Palestrina. His treatment of dissonance is on the whole in accord with all that that implies (Jeppesen 1946). An interesting exception is his treatment of 4–3 suspension cadences in eight parts. In all the double-choir motets except the Lamentations instances may be found of the suspension's clashing with its resolution, producing in G and D modes a form of the so-called 'English cadence', and in F and B flat modes a sharp dissonance with the *subsemitonum*. These clashes are generally found more often in Venetian music but are anathema to Palestrina and Lasso.

Two of Phinot's double-choir motets became models for parody masses. In 1563 Michele Varotto published his *Missa 'Sancta Trinitas'*. Only four part-books of the print are known,[12] but the Mass in question survives without ascription and lacking its Agnus Dei in a Zwickau manuscript (Ratsschulbibliothek Ms. 325).[13] A thoroughgoing polychoral style was certainly cultivated by Varotto later,[14] but here he sometimes relaxes the choral division, adding or subtracting voices at will; this happens in parts of the Gloria and Credo, especially in passages not based on the model. The Sanctus dispenses with the polychoral texture almost entirely. The Kyrie draws more on Phinot than any other movement, though all except the Sanctus use the opening phrase as a head motif in various guises. In Kyrie, Gloria and Credo the final plagal cadence is preceded by a remarkable non-antiphonal ostinato passage, seemingly independent of the model (quoted in Carver 1980, vol. 1: 147–8). *Jam non dicam* apparently enjoyed the longest fame of any of these works and it received two late parody treatments: a Mass by Jacob Handl, of which only the Kyrie and Gloria survive in Wrocław manuscripts (mod. edn, DTÖ 94–5: 95), and one by Bartholomäus Gesius (cited by Höfler in Phinot, Opera vol. 4: x).

Phinot's polychoral works are really the first mature examples of the style. If one cannot quite agree with Höfler's estimate that they 'rank among the finest sacred compositions of the late [sic] sixteenth century' (ibid.: ix), it is nevertheless far more likely that they, rather than Willaert's psalms, produced most of the impetus which created the vogue. Phinot's choirs were probably not spaced, but then nor usually were the choirs in the large polychoral output of Lasso whose development Phinot's motets made possible.

4

DISSEMINATION AND
AGGRANDISEMENT

The 1560s were years which saw a gradual spread and expansion in the scale of polychoral music. Three events stand out, and significantly all have strong German or Austrian connections. Two were important publications of multi-voiced music, the third a magnificent wedding celebration in which polychoral music on the most lavish scale played an important part.

The three strands in the *Thesaurus musicus*

The first volume of the *Thesaurus musicus*, printed by Montanus and Neuber in Nuremberg (1564[(1)]), represents, after Willaert's psalms and Phinot's motets, the third landmark in the establishment of the polychoral style as a standard idiom. It contains sixty-three pieces for eight voices of which the first forty-eight are for undivided choir. They are fairly representative of the à 8 repertory of the time and include Mouton's *Verbum bonum* and *Nesciens mater*, Corteccia's *Ingredere*, Arcadelt's *Pater noster*, Scandello's *Noe, noe*, Senfl's *Veni sancte Spiritus*, Josquin's *Lugebat David*, Gombert's and Clemens's independent settings of the Credo, and Jachet's *Sancta Trinitas*. Gombert's Credo (Opera vol. 3: 103) is another piece which exemplifies the connection between polychoral writing and Flemish voice-pairing techniques – it proceeds chiefly by antiphonal repetition between variously constituted SATB groups.

After the single-choir pieces follow a smaller group headed 'per duos choros', perhaps placed at the end because of their novelty. They are listed in the index as follows:

49. Confitebor tibi Domine   ORLANDUS DI LASSUS
50. Jam lucis orto   ORLANDUS DI LASSUS
51. Cum invocarem   ADRIANUS W
52. In te Domine speravi
53. Qui habitat
54. Ecce nunc benedicite
55. Magnificat
56. Magnificat   ANTHONIUS SCANDELLUS
57. Quem vidistis pastores   FRANCISCUS BONARDI
58. Laeta quid nunc tantum   FRANCISCUS BONARDI
59. Incipit oratio Ieremiae   DOMINICUS PHINOT
60. O sacrum convivium   DOMINICUS PHINOT
61. Tanto tempore vobiscum sum   DOMINICUS PHINOT

62. Iam non dicam vos servos   DOMINICUS PHINOT
63. Sancta Trinitas   DOMINICUS PHINOT

It will be seen that both Franco-Flemish (Lasso and Phinot) and Italian composers (Scandello and Bonardo[?]) are represented here, and behind the compline psalms and the first Magnificat may well lie another Italian or two. (Despite the attribution to Willaert I argued in Chapter 2 that *Cum invocarem* is probably not by him.) More strikingly, when we examine the pieces it becomes apparent that the three strands of the polychoral idea, viz. dialogic (Bonardo), psalmodic (the psalms and magnificats) and purely musical (Lasso and Phinot), are all present.

Bonardo's *Quem vidistis, pastores?* (Anthology no. 5) reflects the opening dialogue of the antiphon, and the piece falls into three sections:

1. 'Quem vidistis. . .'   Ch. 1 ($C_2C_3C_3C_4$): the shepherds are questioned
2. 'Natum vidimus. . .'   Ch. 2 ($G_2C_2C_3F_3$): their reply
3. 'Gloria in altissimis. . .'   tutti+antiphony: the song of the angels

The opening is imitative, with triadic themes and static harmony; at 'dicite' (bars 13–21) the note-against-note texture gives way to overlapping melismata portraying the eagerness of the questioners. Each new phrase receives its own theme. The shepherd's reply returns to the opening triadic idea, beginning now on the tonic rather than the dominant, the piece being unequivocally in C major. Voice-pairing occurs between high and low voices of Choir 2 at 'et choros angelorum' (bars 43–52), the second pair recalling the melismata that the first choir had at 'dicite'.

The text has only this single question and answer, and from 'Gloria' Bonardo employs *spezzato* as a purely compositional device:

'Gloria in altissimis Deo'   tutti
'et in terra pax'   Ch. 1
'hominibus bonae voluntatis'   Ch. 2
       'bonae voluntatis'   Ch. 1
'Alleluia'   tutti
      (freely imitative)

No use is made of antiphonal repetition of music at 'bonae voluntatis', the only instance of antiphonal repetition of text. The return to four-part textures at 'et in terra pax' is highly appropriate to the text and creates balance in the overall structure.

Laeta quid nunc tantum (transcr. Carver 1980, vol. 2: 252) is an allegorical dialogue between the poet and his soul. Its structure is similar to that of *Quem vidistis* except that there are two lengthy dialogue exchanges before the integrating '*finale*' begins at 'Grates ergo'. As in its companion piece Bonardo returns to antiphony after a tutti, and this time antiphonal repetition is employed: Choir 2 echoes the words 'ut regna' (bars 80ff) before Choir 1 continues with the rest of the phrase. Another tutti follows and then the whole '*finale*' is repeated.

Bonardo is an obscure personality, though revealing in these two pieces a high degree of competence as a composer. Van den Borren (1946: 36, 43–4) considered him Italian; Casimiri (1941: 37–9) equated him with Francesco Perisson, *maestro di cappella* at Padua Cathedral from 1565 to 1571, but asserts that the surname indicates French origin. Once again, though, Padua crops up as a possible centre of polychoral activity.

The four compline psalms were discussed in Chapter 2. The Magnificats apply double-choir writing to liturgical antiphony in a way that we have not so far encountered. They are *alternatim* settings in which the polyphony for double choir is applied to the even verses. This method, employed also by Lasso in his *Magnificat septimi toni* (1576), provides a paradox: strict verse-by-verse antiphony with motet-style polychoral writing within it. Curiously Scandello through-composes the remainder of verse 1 after the incipit with verse 2 (transcr. Carver 1980, vol. 2: 262). In this his only known polychoral work he seeks to impose some unity on the polyphonic verses not so much by means of the psalm-tone, though tone 8 is paraphrased sporadically in the earlier verses, as by a formal procedure which may be summarised as free antiphony followed by a twice-stated tutti, sometimes varied on its repeat. There is much text repetition, some of it within the same choir, some of it antiphonal, and some between single-choir phrases and a succeeding tutti. The phrases are often separated by dramatic rests, giving the piece a rather disjointed air. This impression is reinforced by the pervading homophonic textures, enlivened by syncopation and occasionally by syllabic pseudo-imitation. The last two polyphonic verses are slightly more complex, with tuttis before the end and further choral exchanges following.

Scandello could have been an early populariser of the polychoral style in Lutheran circles, though this is the only piece of this kind by him that we have. He came originally from Bergamo, where he was born in 1517 and where he was employed in Santa Maria Maggiore, one of the centres of the double-choir psalm tradition. After a short stay in Trent he moved in 1549 to Dresden as a cornetto player in the Hofkantorei, eventually becoming *Kapellmeister* and embracing Protestantism (Kade 1913–14). Montanus and Neuber's *Thesaurus* contains more music by him than by any other Italian composer.

The anonymous Magnificat (no. 55) was unaccountably printed by Commer (1844–58: vol. 2: 60) as the work of Willaert. This attribution seems quite ludicrous from a stylistic point of view. Both single-choir and tutti passages consist of unrelieved homophony with restricted and monotonous melodic lines – Willaert's note-against-note writing always contains a modicum of polyphonic voice-leading. More persuasive still is the incompetent harmony in the tuttis: parallel unisons and octaves (not just in the bass parts) and other peculiarities which may or may not be copyist's errors, though these are not a notable feature elsewhere in the *Thesaurus musicus*. Such features are certainly not explicable in terms of a hypothetical change in Willaert's style.

What does come to mind is Ruffino's Mass. In fact, quite a strong case could be made on stylistic grounds for Ruffino's authorship of this Magnificat, taking into account the above factors and also the obsessive and in the end highly monotonous use of antiphonal repetition. Structurally it has much in common with the more concise Scandello. As so often, what is really a rather incompetent work provides us with surprises. The setting of verse 6 is appropriately dramatic. At the beginning, 'Fecit potentiam', each tenor part in turn states the psalm-tone unaccompanied, answered on each occasion with almost Baroque drama by the full ensemble, and the succeeding short exchanges are appropriate to 'dispersit superbos' (Ex. 18).

Ex. 18 ANONYMOUS, Magnificat octavi toni

The two motets by Lasso (nos. 49 & 50) are the first double-choir works by him to be printed, predating by four years the earliest appearance of a polychoral work by Andrea Gabrieli. We shall return to them in Chapter 5.

Pomp and splendour: the *Novus thesaurus musicus*

In 1568 Pietro Giovanelli, a native of Gandino near Bergamo, published at his own expense a huge collection containing much multi-voiced music, the five-volume *Novus thesaurus musicus* (1568$^{(2-6)}$). It was printed in Venice, but all but a handful of its contents are by composers in Habsburg employ. Much of this repertory belongs to the period of Ferdinand I; by the time of his death in 1564 the numbers of the Imperial *Kapelle* had increased to eighty-three.

The significance of the *Novus thesaurus* repertory for our study lies not so much in the amount of polychoral music it contains, which is by our strict definition quite small. Rather it is a question of style. The psalms of Willaert, Santacroce and others are restrained in their antiphonal effects and clear but not emphatic in their declamation; Ruffino alone seems to point forward aggressively to the future. In his polychoral motets Phinot, whilst greatly widening the range of antiphonal techniques, is thoroughly Flemish in his avoidance of jagged dramatic utterance. We may well ask, whence the power and colour of Venetian polychoral music? Part of the answer may well lie in Habsburg music and in Andrea Gabrieli's probable acquaintance with it.

We have already looked at much music which is to a greater or lesser degree homophonic, but in Willaert for example the treatment of syllabic word-setting is usually gentle and subtle. The increasing pressure for verbal intelligibility through syllabic word-setting, favoured by reformer and counter-reformer alike, influenced the motet repertoire in general, and probably the rhythmic directness of the chanson/canzona was also a factor. It is possible for a composer to use syllabic stress in a strictly homophonic context in such a way as to produce declamation of a strikingly pompous kind. Such pomposity, the result of shifting emphasis rather than an intrinsically new technical resource, is found in many works in Giovanelli's collection. Such a style is highly appropriate to music with political overtones; this is state as well as church music, and indeed some of the texts are overtly political.

The division of the ensemble into sub-groups may be seen as providing variety in the absence of any great polyphonic interest. In the majority of cases the sub-groups do not remain constant, as they must in true polychoral writing. Thus in this collection polychoral pieces may be considered special cases of a broader compositional type. Only three are unequivocally polychoral: Utendal's *Jubilate Deo* (vol. 2: cantus, 223), Lasso's *In convertendo* (vol. 4: 353) and Hollander's *Austria virtutes* (vol. 5: 441), all à 8. It will be objected that Andrea Gabriel's *Deux misereatur nostri* à 12 (vol. 5: 457) is actually labelled polychoral – indeed is the only one to be so designated – but paradoxically it fails to satisfy our strict definition because at 'laetentur et exultent gentes' a triple-time passage occurs in which the texture splits into two six-part groups, drawing two voices from each of the previously-defined four-part choirs; the phrase immediately preceding is an incomplete tutti à 9. There are other momentary inter-choral mixings, such as at 'salutare tuum', where the composer's wish for five- and six-part textures overrides other considerations.

The fact remains that it would be pedantic to exclude such pieces from our discussion when such passages form a relatively small proportion of the whole. If we therefore include pieces in which each choir maintains its identity most if not all of the time, we may add, as well as *Deus misereatur*, Henri De la Court's *Cesaris ad bustum* (vol. 5: 442) and, with more reservation, Vaet's Te Deum (vol. 5: 463).

It has become customary for any polychoral manifestations of this period to be described as 'Venetian' by historians (e.g. Redlich, *New Oxford History*, vol. 4: 267; Osthoff 1967: 212); this is the result of an assumption that polychoral music is a unitary phenomenon stemming from Venice. If the works by Habsburg musicians in the *Novus thesaurus* are 'Venetian', they are presumably supposed to be in imitation of an established Venetian repertory. Such a repertory cannot be proved to have existed before 1568. We must regard Andrea Gabrieli as the founder of the colourful Venetian school of the late sixteenth and early seventeenth centuries. He had at least three models to draw on: North Italian psalmody, Phinot's motets and these Habsburg pieces. The presence of his own music in the *Novus thesaurus* is indicative of his Habsburg connections – see the opening of Chapter 7.

The pieces by Lasso, Andrea Gabrieli and Utendal are settings of complete psalms (respectively Pss. 125, 66 and 99), though without the incipit and doxology of liturgical usage. Those by De la Court and Hollander have political texts, whilst Vaet sets the familiar matins hymn. Detailed discussion of Lasso and Gabrieli belongs in later chapters; here we shall consider the remaining four composers in order of seniority.

The eldest would seem to be Christian Hollander, born around 1510–15 in Dordrecht. He entered the chapel of Ferdinand I in 1557 and saw Habsburg service in Prague, Vienna and Innsbruck, where he died in 1568 or 1569 (Wagner, *NGr* vol. 8: 647–8). Like Ivo de Vento he applied double-choir techniques to the polyphonic lied (Osthoff 1967: 245, 255, 266). *Austria virtutes,*[1] 'in praise of the glorious House of Austria', illustrates the energetic pomposity of which we have spoken (Ex. 19). It proceeds almost entirely in exact or varied antiphonal repetition punctuated by tuttis. The homorhythmic single-choir sections develop a fanfare-like thrust in contrast to the broader and more polyrhythmic tuttis. A forward-looking feature is the liberal supply of accidentals, including the shift from F to F sharp in bar 8.

Henri De la Court sang at Soissons Cathedral from 1547, and was in Imperial service as an alto from 1563 until his death in 1577. His only published works would appear to be those in the *Novus thesaurus. Cesaris ad bustum*,[2] 'in praise of the most illustrious prince Alphonso d'Este, Duke of Ferrara', is similar to *Austria virtutes* in texture and in its use of varied antiphonal repetition, but De la Court prefers to build his tuttis with overlapped echoes rather than to treat them as self-contained blocks. When he does this in the final tutti there is a strong canonic element (Ex. 20). Note, though, the six-part textures and the à 6, à 7, à 8 terraced *crescendo* leading

Ex. 19   HOLLANDER, Austria virtutes

into the final cadence. Earlier, at 'Ecce tibi assurgunt', De la Court mixes
voices from both choirs for a delightful register contrast. There is a conspicuous lack of accidentals in comparison with Hollander's piece. Both are ostensibly in the same transposed dorian; Hollander's opening B naturals are
characteristic of the Gabrielis. Johannes de Cleve, represented in the *Novus
thesaurus* but not by polychoral music, provided a later example of this political double-choir style in his *Veni maxime Dux* (1579: no. 30) for Rudolf II.

Jacobus Vaet (*b* c1529, *d* 1567) is quite well represented in the *Novus thesaurus*, with seven pieces in Book 5 alone. Probably a native of Courtrai, he
entered Habsburg service in 1553, serving under Maximilian in Prague until
1564, when he became *Kapellmeister* at the Imperial Court in Vienna. He
was fairly prolific as a writer of motets (Steinhardt 1951), but his Te Deum
(mod. edn, Dunning 1974: 268) is the only work of his which is in any sense
polychoral. It is actually a rather curious example of polychoralism, but a fine,
eloquent setting of a difficult and rambling text. Unlike the political works
examined above it has a second choir which is considerably lower than the
first: $C_1C_3C_4F_4/C_2C_3C_4F_5$. It begins with a long 'solo' for each choir in turn,
each singing two lines of text, with occasional hints at the plainchant. The full
ensemble is brought in for 'Sanctus. . .gloriae tuae'. The choirs alternate twice
more, the bass of Choir 1 joining with Choir 2 in the first of these 'couplets',
and the *prima pars* ends with another tutti at 'Sanctum quoque paraclitum

Ex. 20   LA COURT, Cesaris ad bustum

Spiritum'. There is no antiphonal repetition, and just once, at 'Venerandum tuum verum', text is transferred from one choir to the other.

The *secunda pars*, from 'Tu Rex gloriae', is scored for the first choir only. Its first section is imitative, using the top three voices only; when the bass enters at 'Tu devicto mortis' the texture becomes declamatory and madrigalian. The opening line of the *tertia pars* is given to Choir 2 in solemn homophony, but oddly such antiphony as develops later in the piece, similar though it is to the rhythmically forthright style of De la Court and Hollander, cuts across the previous choral division.

The full impact of the political style on the setting of a non-political text is shown in Utendal's *Jubilate Deo* (Anthology no. 6). Alexander Utendal was born around 1543–5 in the Netherlands (Bossuyt 1983: 22–5), and apparently served the house of Austria from his youth, attaining the post of *Vizekapellmeister* at Innsbruck, where he died in 1581. His first published works appear to be those in the *Noves thesaurus*; three books of motets, other sacred music and a volume of lieder followed in the 1570s. *Jubilate Deo* also appears in his motet collection of 1573 (as no. 18); it contains three further eight-part pieces, of which *Inclina Domine* (no. 19; also in 1568[(3)]) is not polychoral, whilst *Cantate Domine* and *Haec dicit Dominus* (nos. 17 & 20) are of the quasi-polychoral type common in the *Novus thesaurus*.

Jubilate Deo combines psalmodic antiphony with Phinot's plastic interaction between the choirs and the forthright declamation of the *Novus thesaurus* repertory. Verse 1 is given to Choir 1, verse 2 to Choir 2, recalling Santacroce's *Qui habitat* in the way polyphony in Choir 1 is contrasted with homophony in Choir 2. Here, though, no psalm-tone is present and the homophony is of the energetic type of De la Court and Hollander. Verse 3 builds through antiphonal repetition to a tutti, returning to choral imitation after the mediant. The remainder of the piece revolves structurally around the tuttis without special regard for the verse divisions. The antiphonal devices employed are very similar to those of Phinot. We have reached the final stage in the stylistic evolution of the mature polychoral motet.

Utendal wrote one other, more ambitious polychoral work, *Angelus Domini* à 23, which survives in a Vienna manuscript (Nationalbibliothek Ms. 9814) copied for a performance of 1617. According to Bossuyt (1983: 120–2) it has a curiously asymmetrical arrangement of choirs; Choirs 1–3, each of four voices but with contrasting registers, are often put together against Choir 4, which is à 11, and when both are sounding the bass of Choir 3 doubles that of Choir 4, a 'spatial' arrangement not utilised in *Jubilate Deo*.

Music for the 1568 Munich wedding

Before 1568 we have no evidence of any sacred polychoral works for more than eight voices, with the sole exception of Phinot's ten-in-five canonic setting of *Ecce sacerdos* (1554). Nor apparently were any secular dialogues for more than eight voices published until 1567 (Nutter 1977: 395). In 1568, as well as Giovanelli's publication of Andrea Gabrieli's *Deus misereatur* à 12, we have from Troiano (1568: 150 & 182) documentation of the performance in Munich of two works à 24 and one à 40, performances which by themselves would have caused the musical part of the celebrations for Duke Wilhelm's wedding to exceed in opulence just about any other sixteenth-century musical event save the 1589 *Intermedii* for *La Pellegrina* in Florence. The first twenty-four-part work is not named, though some details about its scoring are recorded by Troiano (see p. 3). By good fortune the other two *magna opera* have survived in later manuscripts.

It seems reasonable to equate the Mass à 24 described by Troiano with that ascribed to 'Hannibal Patavinus' in Vienna Nationalbibliothek Ms. 16702: f. 240v; it is the last of a series of mass settings copied into four large choir-books. All are for four choirs except Annibale's, which is for three and is copied into the first three books only. The other composers represented are Giovanni Croce (*b c*1557, *d* 1609), Francesco Stivori (*b c*1550, *d* 1605), Gregorio Zucchini (*c*1540 – after 1616), Lambert de Sayve (1548 or 1549 – 1614), Alessandro Tadei (*b c*1585, *d* 1667), Georg Poss (*b c*1570, *d* after 1633), Giovanni Priuli (*b c*1575, *d* 1629) and Reimundo Ballestra (*d* 1634).[3] These composers were all associated with the Austrian royal house and/or Venice;

most served at Vienna or Graz or both, the exceptions being Zucchini and Croce.

Annibale's Mass would appear to be the earliest, perhaps the germinal piece in this Austro-Venetian repertory. The probable birth-date of the youngest composer, Tadei, fixes the compilation of the manuscript as no earlier than about 1605. Annibale left Venice in 1566 and subsequently entered the service of Archduke Karl in Graz, where he died in 1575. His Mass must have been retained in what was clearly a very sumptuous repertory in Graz around the turn of the century, a repertory documented in other manuscripts of the period.[4]

It is far from being a purely occasional piece – it is a work of power as well as pomp (the Kyrie and Credo: Carver 1980, vol. 2: 288; the Agnus Dei: Anthology no. 7). Let us first note a few stylistic traits which are typical of the work as a whole. There is no formal imitation by voices at all; this is partly a function of the large number of voices, with which it would be a lengthy process. Tallis in *Spem in alium* showed that it can be done, but it does not seem to interest Annibale here. More surprising is the very restricted use of choral imitation. Annibale's syntax admits of antiphonal repetition of text, but musically such antiphony is made up of balancing rather than closely-related phrases.

Annibale's techniques for coping with the large number of voices are principally the syncopation of part movement across chord changes where the chords have a note or two in common, and close imitation of simple scale and/or arpeggio figures which fit in with the slow-moving harmony of full sections. There is no room for linear expansion in individual voices; when lyrical moments occur they are due to the momentary heightening of a tiny phrase or even a single note by the colour of a judicious harmonic change. Harmonic movement and harmonic colour are thus the chief compositional parameters in this work next to the antiphonal manipulation of the choirs. Tuttis are employed sparingly, and the following sections are given to one choir only: Christe eleison (Ch. 2), *Et incarnatus est* (Ch. 2), *Crucifixus* (Ch. 3) and Sanctus (Ch. 1).

Kyrie I is a classic polychoral statement, building into a tutti through a shortening of the choral phrases and a quickening of harmonic rhythm (Table 2 & Ex. 21). Kyrie II begins by partially reversing the procedure of Kyrie I; an opening tutti is wound down through successive exits of the choirs. Antiphony in phrases of intermediate length leads to a tutti interrupted by a perfect cadence in G for Ch. 3 alone. The cadence is repeated tutti and followed by a plagal close. Tonally the whole Kyrie forms a unity in G mixolydian. Each section defines the G mode at the start and proceeds to the following cadential tonalities:

Kyrie I : G–a–G–D–G
Christe : d–G–C
Kyrie II : d–a–G–C–G–G

Table 2

Phrase length	Choir	Harmonic rhythm
7	1	𝅝
7	2	𝅗𝅥
9	3	𝅗𝅥
2	1	𝅝
3	2	𝅝
3½	3	𝅝
1	2	♩
1	3	♩
3½	Tutti	𝅝

The Gloria is divided into two sections, the break occurring before the second 'Dominus Deus'.[5] Annibale's deployment of the forces in this movement is extremely economical. The *Et in terra pax* contains only two tuttis, 'unigenite' and the final 'Jesu Christe', whilst the only tutti in the *Domine Deus* is the closing 'Cum sancto Spiritu'. There are however in the first section semi-tuttis involving two choirs at a time and overlapped phrases between the choirs which have a tutti effect. There is a certain amount of textual repetition, and unlike in the Kyrie there is a suggestion of varied antiphonal repetition. The second section contains much of interest. The opening epithets addressed to Christ are set to three variants of a bass progression, one for each choir. At two solemn moments the texture drops to four voices: 'peccata mundi' (lowest four of Ch. 3), 'qui sedes' (Ch. 1, voices 4–7; this passage ends à 6 at 'miserere nobis'). The final tutti begins after a dramatic rest, Choir 3 having cadenced in five parts only. The block of sound then gradually loosens as a triadic 'in gloria' figure invades more and more parts. The tonal orbit is wider than in the Kyrie, with an at times breathtaking introduction of the B flat triad. Annibale continues to vary the harmonic rhythm; at 'qui sedes', for instance, Choir 1 has chord changes which shorten in length from minim to crotchet to quaver.

The Credo splits into four sections: *Patrem, Et incarnatus est* (Ch. 2), *Crucifixus* (Ch. 3) and *Et in Spiritum*. In the first two sections the chief points of interest are tonal. The *Patrem* has no textual repetition until 'et propter nostram salutem', where Choir 2's statement is varied by Choir 3. 'Descendit' is also echoed, with overlapping of Choirs 1 and 2, and from its third statement (Choir 3) quasi-canonic treatment of a falling fourth figure in the bass parts of successive choral entries leads to a remarkable circle-of-fifths movement: F–C–G–d– a–e. The *Et incarnatus est*, a mere eighteen bars for Choir 2 alone, is one of the most beautiful and intimate parts of the work, and certainly har-

Ex. 21 ANNIBALE PADOVANO, Mass à 24

Ex. 21 (*cont.*)

monically the most interesting. It begins in G, proceeding via a and d to D. The effect of the A major chords following G minor harmony in bars 66 and 70 is striking; a subsequent move even further to the sharp side (E major) for 'ex Maria virgine' is balanced by a ravishing move through the flat side (as far as B flat) during the words 'et homo factus est'. The warmth of the harmony is lent further subtle colour by delicate contrasts of scoring.

In the *Crucifixus* the subdivision of Choir 3 approaches a secondary poly-choral division. Indeed, the opening two phrases for the two four-part groups are reminiscent of double-choir canon except that the interval of imitation changes from the octave to the fifth. In the last section, at 'Et unam sanctam. . .', there is a rare instance of thorough imitation; a lively triadic motif is taken through all the voices, one choir at a time.

The Sanctus (there is no Benedictus) is again à 8, this time for Choir 1. It is laid out consistently for two four-part groups, $G_2C_2C_3F_3/C_1C_3C_4F_4$. The Agnus Dei (Anthology no. 7) begins with a massive tutti, shot through with imitation in a few voices of a rising figure on the word 'Agnus', sometimes inconsistently dotted, adding a touch of fantasy. This tutti fades to a few voices from each choir – a written-in *diminuendo* – with a cadence in six parts as Choir 3 enters with a basically chordal but rhythmically lively setting of 'qui tollis. . .'. When this is imitated by Choir 1 the rhythms (derived from the verbal accents) remain but the tonality is completely changed. The lively short note-values given to 'dona nobis pacem' give this movement a festive rather than penitential air. It is the only complete movement which does not begin and end in G – it opens on C, and an unequivocal cadence on G is not heard until bars 33–4 (Choir 3). This is followed by a rest and then the simultaneous attack of the brief final tutti which is harmonically just a plagal cadence.

We may wonder whether the 1568 performance of this Mass utilised the same forces as Striggio's forty-part motet performed on the same day (see above, p. 3, and below). It was, of course, quite common for musicians to be proficient on one or more instruments as well as in singing, and some may have been silent during one or other of the works. Curiously, though, the list of instruments given by Troiano for Striggio's piece does include twenty-four melody instruments. A straightforward assignation of one instrumental family to each of Annibale's eight-part choirs is not possible, since trombones could not manage the higher voices of any choir; only viols could have played the parts of a whole choir as a consort. The Vienna source, as may be seen in Ex. 21, has only partial texting for the highest (G_2) parts of Choirs 1 and 3, suggesting the participation of cornetti. There is of course no reason at all to suppose that Austrian performances employed precisely the same methods of scoring as those in Munich in 1568.

Annibale's treatment of the bass parts is interesting. Curiously, octave doubling by contrary motion is found quite often between the lowest two parts of a single choir. Its prime use, however, is to fulfil the recommendations made by Zarlino, Vicentino and Artusi for the bass parts in tuttis where the choirs are spaced. It is always applied in two-choir semi-tuttis. In full à 24 passages it is scrupulously and almost exclusively applied to the bass parts of Choirs 1 and 3, leaving Choir 2's bass line to fit in where it may; Choir 2 considered by itself, therefore, has many incidental 6/4 chords. These usually occur when the Choir 2 bass either delays a falling fifth root progression or anticipates a rising fifth one. All the bass parts always end on the root of the final chord. The Agnus Dei is freest in its treatment of the bass lines because they participate in the imitation. Generally, though, Choirs 1 and 3 would seem to be self-supporting at a distance; perhaps Choir 2 was placed between them.

Three eight-part sacred works by Annibale survive in collections printed after his death: *O altitudo divitiarum* and a Kyrie (1590[4]: 10 & 12) and *Domine a lingua dolosa* (1598[2]: no. 58). I have seen only the latter, in the incomplete British Library copy. Its outer sections maintain a consistent high/low choral division, though it is relaxed in the middle of the piece. Recall of a striking triple-time section at the end gives it a responsorial aBcB outline, and stylistically it relates very closely to the music of Andrea Gabrieli, with subtle use of varied antiphonal repetition and strikingly rhythmic homophony.

Striggio's forty-part *Ecce beatam lucem* has been cited more on account of the 'bassone' part (the forty-first 'voice' in the Zwickau source Ratsschulbib-liothek Ms. 732, dated 1587) and its importance to the history of the continuo than as a remarkable predecessor of Tallis's *Spem in alium*. This situation can be remedied, especially now that the work is available in a modern edition (1980). Recently it has been plausibly suggested (Fenlon & Keyte 1980: 333–4) that the work was originally written in 1561 in honour of Cardinal Ippolito d'Este, who was passing through Florence on his way to France on a mission to quell Protestantism, an occasion for which the text is more suitable than for a wedding, and if so that Striggio *could* have had the piece with him when he visited London in 1567. This raises the intriguing possibility of its having given Tallis the idea for his forty-part motet (ibid.: 334).

The forty parts are notated separately, generally occupying two sides apiece, and the number of mistakes and the general appearance of the source suggest that it was copied rather hastily for performance. There are two numbering systems: each voice bears a number from 1 to 40, and consecutively-numbered voices are grouped asymmetrically into four choirs:

Ch. 1 à 8	voices 1–8	$G_2C_2C_3F_3/C_1C_2C_4F_4$
Ch. 3 à 16	voices 9–24	$G_2C_2C_3F_3/G_2C_2C_3F_3/G_2C_2C_3F_3/C_1C_3C_4F_4$
Ch. 4 à 6	voices 25–30	$G_2C_2C_3F_3/G_2C_2$
Ch. 2 à 10	voices 31–40	$C_3F_3/G_2C_2C_3F_3/C_1C_3C_4F_4$

It will be seen that the voice-ranges fall into ten conventional four-voice patterns: seven with *chiavette*, one of which is divided between Choirs 2 and 4, and three with standard SATB clefs. In fact, it is the voice-numbering which has more bearing on the structure of the work than the division into choirs. As Keyte points out in the preface to his edition, the German scribe derived his choral numbering from the first three groups to enter; the remaining six voices are present in the fourth entry, but they never sound alone. Striggio's principal compositional parameter is the contrasting of various voice-groups which are almost invariably made up of consecutively-numbered voices. Since voices 1 and 40 never sing together, except in forty-part tuttis, performance with the forces in an arc or semi-circle is an attractive possibility consonant with a phrase in the heading to the continuo part which should probably read 'per sonar in mezzo del circolo' (Keyte, preface to the 1980 edition). This seems to relate to Vicentino's remark about the performance of dialogues cited in Chapter 1 (p. 11).

The 'antiphony' involves much repetition, usually with variation. An especially effective series of entries occurs at 'Haec voluptas...' (bars 96–100), the bass progressions outlining a series of thirds falling from C to B flat. The most dramatic use of the tutti is to be found in the two cries of 'O', bars 53 and 88, preceded by rests in all the voices. At 'Hic David' (bars 73–5) a phrase sung by voices 1–10 is reiterated by the whole ensemble.

Two substantial à 40 passages provide us with instructive examples as to how Striggio copes with counterpoint for such an ensemble. At 'Cantans sonans' (bars 78ff) virtually all the voices in turn sing, over slow-moving harmonies, a dotted scalic figure or its inversion. This technical trick is essentially the same as that of the 'harmonic triad' canon of J. S. Bach (David & Mendel 1945: 175, 403–4), and indeed of many simple popular canons. Here the dotted rhythm permits the staggering of part-movement by a time interval as small as the quaver in transcription (Ex. 22). This device is undeniably effective, but wisely

Ex. 22 Striggio, Ecce beatam lucem

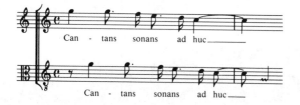

Striggio does not over-employ it. In the final tutti he begins at the other extreme with forty-part homorhythmic declamation on a single chord, loosening into fanfare-like repeated-note figures which come and go in various groups of voices, with just the occasional scalic flourish emerging. This entire section is repeated to crown the whole. It is not the only instance of repetition of music: the passage immediately following the first 'O' is set to different words after the second. As in Annibale's Mass there are instances of voices dropping out to create written-in *diminuendi* (e.g. bars 39–4 and 85–7).

It is not possible to be certain how this piece was scored in 1568, even given Troiano's description. The principles of sixteenth-century scoring as applied to polychoral works normally seem to have involved associating one family or blended mixed consort of instruments with each choir, or such was the practice at any rate in Florence with which Striggio would have been familiar (Brown 1973). The difficulties of this particular piece together with some suggestions for realisation are given in Keyte (ibid.) and Carver 1980 (vol. 1: 326–31). An entirely vocal performance, with perhaps some kind of continuo, is a possibility as an alternative to the sumptuous blend of instruments and voices which so astonished the hearers at Munich.

5

THE POLYCHORAL WORKS
OF ORLANDO DI LASSO

Much of Lasso's polychoral output – i.e. the vast majority of those pieces which might be loosely termed motets – has been available for decades in the old 'complete' edition (Werke 1), compiled from the posthumous *Magnum opus musicum* of 1604. Although allotted space in Boetticher's monumental study of the composer (1958), and more recently in an article by Denis Arnold (1978), they have never been considered in detail. It is possible to compile a rough chronology of Lasso's works for eight or more voices, using date of first publication, date of copying or, in the absence of either, Boetticher's stylistic criteria:

[Publications are referred to by RISM numbers – anthologies by year with superscript in brackets and prints devoted to Lasso by year with Series A listing in parentheses.]

Confitebor tibi à 8 \
Jam lucis orto à 8 $\Big\}$ 1564[1]

In convertendo à 8[1] \
Quo properas facunde à 10 $\Big\}$ 1565 (L 784)

Alma redemptoris mater à 8 \
Bone Jesu à 8 \
Domine, quid multiplicati sunt à 12 \
Ecce quam bonum à 8 \
Ergo rex vivat à 8 $\Big\}$ c1565 (Boetticher; first pr. 1604 (L 1019)) \
Inclina Domine à 9 \
Laudabit usque à 8 \
Quid vulgo memorant à 8 \
Tui sunt caeli à 8

Deus misereatur nostri à 8 \
Levavi oculos à 8 $\Big\}$ 1566 (L 796)[1]

Edite Caesareo Boiorum à 8 1568 (L 815) \
Dixit Dominus à 8 1570 (L 833) \
Vinum bonum à 8 1570 (L 833 & 834) \
Dic mihi à 8 1570 (L 834) \
Benedic Domine à 8 c1570 (Arnold; first pr. 1588 (L 985)) \
Laudate Dominum à 12 1573 (L 858) \
Unde revertimini à 8 1573 (L 860)

Magnificat sexti toni à 8 \
Magnificat septimi toni à 8 $\Big\}$ 1576 (L 885)

Beatus Nicolaus à 8 \
Mira loquor à 10 $\Big\}$ 1577 (Munich Ms. Maier 45)

Dixi custodiam à 8 \
Dixit Martha à 9 $\Big\}$ 1577 (L 904)

Missa super Vinum bonum à 8 1577 (L 900)

Magnificat octavi toni à 8 c1573–9 (Boetticher; Augsburg Ms. Ton. Schl. 14 (1583–4))
Vive, pater patriae à 8 c1579 (Boetticher; first pr. 1604 (L 1019);=pars 9 of Princeps
  morte potens à 4)
Osculetur me osculo à 8 1582 (L 937)
Missa super Osculetur me osculo à 8 (Ljubljana Ms. La 339)
Magnificat quarti toni à 8 }
Magnificat septimi toni à 8 } 1582 (Munich Ms. Maier 49)
Aurora lucis rutilat à 10 1582 or later[2] (first pr. 1604 (L 1019))
Magnificat octavi toni à 8 1583 (Munich Ms. Maier 49)
Missa super Bell'Amfitrit'altera à 8 c1583 (Munich Ms. Maier 29)
Salve regina à 8 c1584–5 (Munich Ms. Maier 50)
Stabat mater à 8 1585 (L 955)
Omnia tempus habent à 8 1585 (L 956)
Omnes de Saba veniunt à 8 1590[5]
Litania de gloriosissima Dei genetrice à 9 c1590–2 (Munich Ms. Maier 50)
Magnificat octavi toni super Aurora lucis rutilat à 10 1592 (Munich Ms. Maier 51)

Late works, precise date unknown:
Benedictus Dominus Deus Israel primi toni à 9   )
Benedictus Dominus Deus Israel tertii toni à 9 }
Benedictus Dominus Deus Israel quarti toni à 9 } Munich Ms. Maier 98
Miserere mei Deus à 9   )
Litania de glorissima Dei genetrice à 10   Munich Ms. Maier 100
Litania de glorissima Dei genetrice à 8 }
Litania de glorissima Dei genetrice à 9 } 1596[2]
Providebam Dominum à 7[3]   1604 (L 1019)

The vast majority of these works are for double choir. Four have inconsistent
choral divisions in the manner of the Habsburg composers: *Domine quid
multiplicati sunt, Laudate Dominum, Edite Caesareo* and *Beatus Nicolaus*
(Werke 1, vol. 21: 135, 152; vol. 19: 146; vol. 21: 23). The first two, for twelve
voices, are the only works in which Lasso approaches three-choir writing.
Princeps morte potens (ibid., vol. 1: 61) is a curiosity; its first eight *partes* are
scored for an exceptionally high $C_1C_1C_1C_3$ choir, to which a choir of wide
range ($G_2C_4C_4F_4$) is added for the final *pars, Vive pater patriae.* Lasso's polychoral output, then, though never employing more than two choirs, covers all
the genres we have met so far – dialogue, psalm, canticle, motet and parody
mass – as well as the litany.

Double-choir music at the Munich Court

Music for double choir must have occupied a conspicuous part of festal
music-making at Munich during Lasso's tenure as *Kapellmeister* (1563–94).
We may well wonder whether he was responsible for its introduction. All the
sixteenth-century polychoral music in manuscript contained in the Bavarian
State Library is either by Lasso or is found also in printed sources from which
it is probably copied[4] and which date mostly from after Lasso's arrival in
1556. It is possible that the *Kapelle* was already familiar with Phinot's motets,
which survive in the State Library in copies both of the original 1548 edition
and the reprints in Montanus and Neuber's *Evangeliorum* (1555[10] & [11]).

Despite Denis Arnold's claim (1978: 181, n. 3), the Munich Mss. Maier 18, 23 and 127 do not contain polychoral music. Of the ten motets à 8 in Ms. 127 the first nine (including compositions by Mouton, Senfl, Vaet and Crecquillon) are for undivided choir. The tenth, Ludwig Daser's *Benedictus Dominus Deus meus* (f. 138v; mod. edn, 1964: 33) is described by Maier (1879: 88) as double-choir, but it is not. This interesting piece combines a written-out four-in-one canon with four free voices. The canonic voices, in longer notes, begin to enter after fifteen breves; they also have a brief rest later, but there is no meaningful interaction between the two groups of voices as choirs. Daser was Lasso's predecessor as *Kapellmeister.* A Protestant, he was pensioned off in 1563 but remained in Munich until 1572, when he took up the post of *Kapellmeister* at Stuttgart, where the court was Protestant. Two double-choir pieces survive from his Stuttgart days. *Fratres, sobrii estote* (1964: 52), an eight-part setting of a compline text, is unremarkable in polychoral technique, though interesting for its adoption at times of an almost 'instrumental', sequential style. *Ecce quam bonum* (ibid.: 84) dates from 1578, though it survives only in organ tablature in Paix's *Thesaurus motetarum* (1589[17]). This setting of Psalm 133 is short on counterpoint, aiming at a deliberately massive effect with a good deal of tutti writing, though also some fairly subtle choral imitation. Neither of the two pieces has spatial bass-parts.

Ms. 18 has the eight-part *Missa 'Amour au cueur'* by Guyot (Castileti), which, whilst having a double-choir motto which opens the Kyrie, Gloria, Credo and Agnus (the last à 12), continues with ensembles of varying composition in the usual Habsburg manner.[5] There are three eight-part masses in Ms. 23, two ascribed to 'Janetto Palestrino' and one to 'Francesco Londariti', and all are for undivided choir.

The dialogues

Lasso left six double-choir Latin dialogues: *Quid vulgo memorant* (Werke 1, vol. 19: 122), *Quo properas* (ibid., vol. 21: 112), *Dic mihi* (ibid., vol. 19: 133) and *Unde revertimini* (ibid.: 138) have political texts and date from around 1565–73, whilst *Mira loquor* (Anthology no. 9) and *Dixit Martha* (Werke 1, vol. 21: 98) are sacred dialogues of around 1577. The political dialogues round off somewhat dry exchanges with resplendent tuttis. In *Quid vulgo* close canon merges into a tutti, re-emerging in a more continuous texture. *Quo properas* and *Dic mihi* have less interest as polychoral structures, since each comprises a longer dialogue crowned by a massive tutti with no antiphonal content. *Unde revertimini* is perhaps the finest of the political dialogues, with superb declamation in the single-choir sections animated considerably by rhythmic displacement of individual voices and on occasion by polyphonic elaboration of the texture. The tutti begins dramatically with a vocative 'O' and loosens later into antiphonal repetition which reflects the pitch difference between the choirs ($G_2C_2C_3F_3/C_1C_3C_4F_4$) in what are effectively tonal

answers. These lead into an impressive final tutti which progresses up the circle
of fifths from B flat to E.

The two slightly later sacred dialogues have texts which allow much more
scope to the composer of expressive motets and madrigals. *Mira loquor* por-
trays a mystical conversation with St Bernard, represented by a five-part choir
whose range is slightly wider than that representing the amazed worshipper.
This is the most subtle of all the dialogues, with real 'cut and thrust' between
the parties. It would present considerable ensemble problems even if sung *in
circulo* since not only do the choirs rarely overlap, but one will sometimes
enter on a chord a tone away from the last chord of the previous phrase (see
bars 35–6, 38, 47–8, 97–8, 102–3) and even at one point on a chord containing
a false relation with the previous one (bars 89–90). There is no antiphonal
repetition, but the masterly use of rising and falling scale patterns in the final
tutti renders it one of Lasso's most splendid.

In *Dixit Martha*, Martha is characterised by a standard SATB choir, Jesus
by a five-part choir with an extra tenor. The dialogue (John 11: 21–7) is non-
dramatic in the sense that the narrative portions of the text such as the opening
'Dixit Martha ad Jesum' are given to the same choir as the ensuing direct
speech, imparting a somewhat detached, formal air. However, the chief
interest of the piece lies in the intense madrigalian imagery of the speeches
themselves. Some of this is conventional (a B flat chord for 'mortuos', animated rhythm and texture for 'resurrectione'), but only a master could have
conceived the wonderful setting of Jesus's urgent appeal to Martha to confess
her faith, with its upward surges culminating in a breathtaking stepwise
progression from B flat via C to D (Ex. 23). Martha's affirmation itself forms
the closing tutti which begins, like that of *Quid vulgo*, with canonic overlapping of the choirs.

Ex. 23 Lasso, Dixit Martha

Psalms and psalm-motets

Psalms occupy a significant proportion of the sources for the texts of Lasso's many-voiced motets. Six psalms are set complete, all for eight voices except the last: *In convertendo* (Ps. 125), *Deus misereatur nostri* (Ps. 66), *Levavi oculos* (Ps. 120), *Ecce quam bonum* (Ps. 132), *Dixit Dominus* (Ps. 109) and *Miserere mei, Deus* à 9 (Ps. 50). The first four form a stylistic group, and a number of features distinguish them from the psalms in the North Italian repertory. They lack doxology, plainsong incipit and, usually, any perceptible influence of the psalm-tone. The interaction between the choirs is handled in a confident Phinot-like manner to which is added at times more than a trace of the forthright homophony found in the *Novus thesaurus musicus* repertory. There is a large ratio of tutti to single-choir music. Lasso's madrigalian attitude to text-setting is apparent, though his harmonic palette has yet to exhibit the subtlety of later style which we have already encountered in the sacred dialogues.

It is inevitable that, even leaving aside liturgical considerations, a composer of Lasso's sensitivity to the syntax of the text will in some way reflect the verse divisions in his setting. In *In convertendo* (Anthology no. 8) for instance each of the two *partes* opens with a half-verse for each choir. In the first part, verse 2a is tutti, verse 2b is set to lively homophonic echoes in small note-values culminating in a tutti, verse 3a is again tutti, and so on. The second part, beginning at verse 5, continues from verse 6 with antiphonal repetitions of various lengths culminating in a tutti for verse 7b. More echoes in verse 8a lead into a long tutti for the final half-verse. *In convertendo* has contrasting choirs $(G_2C_2C_3F_3/C_1C_3C_4F_4)$ and much of the choral imitation is transposed or varied (cf. the three versions of 'et lingua nostra exsultatione' at bars 19–25). Those at the same pitch once again recall canonic techniques (bars 76–83). Tuttis function as structural pillars, and are usually approached via overlapped antiphony (e.g. bars 26ff).

The constructional principles in the other three psalms of the 1560s are similar, though antiphonal repetition is somewhat less frequent and usually untransposed, since they are scored for two SATB choirs. The antiphony and succeeding tutti at the close of *Deus misereatur* (Werke 1, vol. 21: 35) are heard twice to crown the structure. Madrigalian word-painting is appropriate to the more concrete imagery of *In convertendo* and *Levavi*. In *Levavi* (ibid.: 71) the rhetorical 'Ecce' which begins verse 4 is set in emphatic multiple echoes and the ensuing revolving canon at 'non dormitabit' utilises the double-choir medium itself in an effective portrayal of the ceaseless activity of the deity (Ex. 24). *Ecce quam bonum* (ibid.: 52) is one of the shortest of psalms (four verses); Lasso does not treat it in a manner substantially different from the others, though it surpasses them in eloquence of expression, notably at the opening, where poetic parallelism is reflected in musical parallelism, the second choir taking up the oscillations of G and F sharp (soprano) and D and E flat (bass), weaving a delicate variation (Ex. 25).

Ex. 24   LASSO, Levavi oculos

Dixit Dominus (ibid.: 27) preserves more of the spirit of liturgical anti-phony, especially in the first three verses, an impression heightened by its emphasis on stereotyped cadence formulae. Antiphony by half-verses is preserved until verse 3b, which is set tutti, and in the first verse Lasso even paraphrases tone 8 in both melodic and cadential outline. Verses 6b, 7b and 8a are given to one choir, whilst 6a and 8b are tutti; the remaining portions inter-sperse antiphonal repetition and tutti in the familiar way. The choirs oppose each other in warlike fashion at moments such as 'implevit ruinas', and the brook ('torrente') flows across the page in Choir 1.

The nine-voice *Miserere*, dated by Boetticher (1958: 660) in the last decade of Lasso's life and known only in manuscript (partial transcr. Carver 1980, vol. 2: 333) is in a different category altogether. Though it lacks the doxology (not unusual with this psalm), the four- and five-part choirs alternate in closed-verse antiphony until the last verse in which Choir 1 joins Choir 2. Even

Ex. 25   Lasso, Ecce quam bonum

here the strictly declamatory texture of the piece is maintained within each
choir, Choir 1 being rhythmically a minim behind Choir 2 most of the way.
The style is like *falsobordone* but no psalm-tone appears to be present; each
choir has its own recurring harmonic scheme, giving an effect like that of an
Anglican double chant. Rich harmonic shifts impart a touch of grandeur to a
simple concept.

Four motets have as their text three or four consecutive verses of a psalm, all
but one setting its opening: *Confitebor tibi* à 8 (Ps. 137: 1–4), *Inclina Domine*
à 9 (Ps. 85: 1–3), *Dixi: custodiam* à 8 (Ps. 38: 1–3) and *Providebam Dominum*
à 7 (Ps. 15: 8–10). *Confitebor* (Werke 1, vol. 21: 56) belongs stylistically with
the early group of psalms; its overall structure pivots around three substantial
tuttis. *Inclina Domine* (ibid.: 106) has a magnificence which Arnold (1978:
176) rightly compares with the political motets. The extra voice in the first
choir makes an extraordinary difference to the sound: the very opening shows
Lasso's skill in free independent five-part writing. The progression of the text
is from prayer to affirmation of the assurance that it will be answered. Thus the
expressive early petitions, divided between the choirs, grow into overlapping

antiphonal repetitions as the text affirms trust in God ('sperantem in te'). The only real tutti and the glory of the piece is the twice stated final section, beginning at 'Laetifica anima'. 'Laetifica' is set as an image of joy in short closely-imitated phrases in short note-values. Throughout this closing passage the choirs emerge wave-like, most strikingly when towards the end the top voices of each choir graphically illustrate the word 'levavi' (Ex. 26).

Ex. 26   LASSO, Inclina, Domine

[Highest voices of each choir]

Psalm 38, *Dixi: custodiam*, is extremely intense and troubled. The portion set by Lasso (Werke 1, vol. 21: 48) ends with the fire burning within, and is thus the more neurotic, lacking the release which comes with the long prayer 'Lord, let me know mine end', which continues to the end of the psalm. Lasso responds with an intensity of expression greater than anything we have yet encountered – the piece might almost be described as mannerist. The opening narrative 'Dixi' followed by direct speech suggests an early switch of choirs, but thereafter the phrases are relatively long, with no text repetition until 'renovatus est' prompts an appropriate double echo. Ex. 27 illustrates Lasso's expressive command of harmony, emphasised by the simplicity of texture; after a remarkable, mysterious shift from G naturals to G sharp in Choir 1, Choir 2's side-stepped G minor is extraordinarily disturbing. Some of the sultry atmosphere of the piece derives from the employment of suspensions

Ex. 27   LASSO, Dixi: custodiam

(sometimes double) and pedal points. In the final tutti, 'exardescet ignis', the fire within rages up and down the texture in a manner no less impressive because we know that such scalic figures are part of the stock-in-trade of Lasso's treatment of tuttis.

The last of the psalm-motets, *Providebam Dominum* (Werke 1, vol. 19: 98), is unusual in that it is in seven parts but is truly polychoral. Four voices were the norm and normal minimum for the composition of a choir in sixteenth-century polychoral writing, though seven-voice double-choir pieces are found occasionally, in Monte for example. Lasso shows on occasions a predilection for the discipline of two- or three-part writing, as we shall see in connection with the *Benedictus Dominus* settings, and of course his *bicinia*, published in the *Magnum opus musicum*, are well-known. In *Providebam* the three-part choir does not contain noticeably more contrapuntal writing than its four-part companion; its texture is more sonorous than might be expected, with care taken to include the third or sixth from the bass in each chord. The text again touches on fear of judgment, though seen in the context of secure faith ('thou wilt not leave my soul in hell'). Lasso's setting has a peculiar tension, derived partly from the top-heavy scoring with its three high treble parts: $G_2G_2C_1/G_2C_2C_3F_3$. The possible downward transposition suggested by these *chiavette* would soften but not eliminate this effect. The pitch difference between the lowest voices of the choirs means that antiphonal repetition involves octave transposition of the bass line. The three G_2 parts interlock in the final tutti so that top Fs, Gs and As are heard almost constantly; this tutti is less contrapuntally textured than many in earlier pieces, and may represent deliberate renunciation of splendour.

Canticles

Lasso's magnificats for double choir are much closer to liturgical practice than his psalms, and they all date from the last two decades of his life. The first two to be published, in the fifth part of his *Patrocinium musices* (1576), show the application of liturgical antiphony in two distinct ways.

The *Magnificat sexti toni* (Werke 2, vol. 14: 94) is in effect a *cantico spez-zato*, if one may coin such a term. The choirs alternate strictly verse-by-verse with the exceptions of verse 6, 'Fecit potentiam', with its warlike antiphony overlapping into tuttis, and the doxology. The odd verses (Choir 1) have the psalm-tone as a *cantus firmus* in slightly longer notes; aware of the danger of tonal monotony which attaches particularly to this tone, Lasso causes the chant to appear on different voices and pitches: tenor on F (verses 1 & 3), bass on B flat, alto on C, soprano on F and finally tenor on F. Whilst the even verses are melodically free they contain cadences which are not inconsistent with the melodic structure of the tone. Greater tonal freedom goes with greater antiphonal interaction of the choirs in Verse 6 with its circle-of-fifths progressions and the doxology, which touches D minor and C minor. It must be said that artifice is not characteristic of Lasso at his best, and that the piece as a whole has a rather formal character. However, in noting that there is little real attempt at portraying the text we should remember that Lasso set the magnificat around one hundred times!

The *Magnificat septimi toni* of 1576 (Werke 2, vol. 14: 112) applies liturgical antiphony in the same way as Scandello's Magnificat discussed in the previous chapter: it is an *alternatim* setting employing eight-part double choir for the even verses only. The source is in choirbook format with the choirs notated on opposite pages of each opening. Verses 6 and 10, for four voices only, are spread across both sides without being assigned to one choir or the other, though the clefs for verse 6 ($G_2C_2C_3F_3$) are the same as for Choir 1. Such a book could obviously not serve for a spaced performance, and indeed such a performance was rarely Lasso's intention.

Like the *sexti toni*, the *septimi toni* makes use of the psalm-tone as a *cantus firmus*, though less consistently. After straight appearances in the tenor of Choir 1 in verses 2 and 4 it disappears from verses 6 and 10, although the overall mode is maintained. In verses 8 and 12 it is hinted at but chromaticised with a C sharp. Each polyphonic half-verse contains tutti writing, usually preceded by a single example of antiphonal repetition in which the psalm-tone, when present, may be imitated or anticipated by the soprano or tenor of the opposite choir, sometimes with its associated bass-line. There is more musical interest in this setting. Cross-choir voice-pairing is employed in multiple-echo fashion to paint the word 'inanes'. The 'Sicut erat' is particularly eloquent, beginning with broad imitation of a descending tetrachord through the lower three voices of each choir and then taken up marvellously by all four voices of Choir 1 (Ex. 28). In the first two phrases the soprano parts hint chromatically at the chant.

The *Magnificat octavi toni* published in 1619 is not known in a manuscript source connected with Lasso, but Boetticher dated it between 1573 and 1579 (transcr. Carver 1980, vol. 2: 367). It is also *alternatim*, with verses 8 and 10 à 4. The psalm-tone is again much in evidence, but the spirit of the piece is very different from the 1576 settings. There is much animated choral imitation of short homophonic phrases in small note-values, contrasting with the broader sweep of the à 4 verses and the tuttis.

Ex. 28   Lasso, Magnificat septimi toni

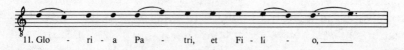

11. Glo - ri - a Pa - tri, et Fi - li - o,____

et Spi - ri - tu - i Sanc - to.____

The Munich Ms. Maier 49 contains a group of three double-choir magnificats, two copied in 1582, the third in 1583. The *quarti toni* (f. 144v; Werke
2, vol. 15: 138) is another *alternatim* setting. Though through-composed, the
septimi toni (f. 130v; Werke 2, vol. 15: 152) is similar in style to the *octavi toni*
of *c*1573–9, with a leisurely opening giving way to lively declamation. The
octavi toni of Ms. 49 (f. 114v; Werke 2, vol. 15: 166) begins with a plainsong
incipit and represents yet another approach to the application of double-choir
writing to a psalm or canticle. The music is continuous, and there is both
antiphonal repetition and tutti writing, but the verses are sharply contrasted in
style and scoring, some being given entirely to one choir or even to a pair
of voices:

verse	1a:	chant	verse	1b:	Choir 1
	2a:	Ch. 2 → 1(↑5th) → 2(↓4th) + Ch. 1		2b:	Ch. 2 → 1(↑5th) + tutti
	3a:	ST of Choir 1		3b:	Choir 1: AB + ST + full
	4:	TB of Choir 2			
	5:	Choir 1			
	6a:	Ch. 2 → 1 (overlapped) + tutti		6b:	Ch. 1 → 2 (overlapped) + tutti
	7:	SA of Choir 1			
	8a:	Choir 2		8b:	Ch. 1 → 2(↓5th) + Ch. 1 → 2(↓4th) + Ch. 2
	9:	Choir 1 (à 3 then à 4)			
	10:	SA of Choir 2			
	11a:	Tutti + SAT of Choir 1		11b:	Choir 1
	12:	Tutti			

The psalm-tone is drawn on freely; at times it is absent altogether, at others
used as a strict *cantus firmus*. Cadences on G occur at the end of each verse
and cadences on C are present at many of the mediants. A beautifully subtle
harmonisation of the tone occurs in verse 9, 'Suscepit Israel' (Ex. 29), notably
the false relation at 'puerum suum' and the deflection of 'misericordiae'
towards A minor. Choral imitation is almost invariably transposed, and in
verse 2a it is sequential.

With the *Magnificat 'Aurora lucis'*, copied *c*1592 (Munich Ms. Maier 51:
f. 99v) and thus one of Lasso's last magnificats, we come across a compositional technique of which Lasso was particularly fond in settings of this canticle as well as in masses. Of the 101 magnificats listed by Boetticher (1958:
963–5) 40 are parodies, the models being chansons, madrigals and motets. The
present example is based, albeit loosely, on Lasso's ten-part setting of the great
Easter hymn for Lauds, published posthumously in 1604 but presumably
dating from between 1582 and 1592 (see note 2). The Magnificat (mod. edn
with the hymn, 1981) is *alternatim*, providing polyphony for the even verses as
in previous examples. The highest voice of the Magnificat is only allotted a C_1
clef as compared with the G_2 clef at the top of Choir 1 of the hymn; it therefore
contains none of the ringing top Gs which are a feature of the hymn.

In actual fact the amount of borrowing of material is small – about fifteen
bars of the hymn out of a total of eighty-nine in Wearing's edition. The open-

Ex. 29 Lasso, Magnificat octavi toni (c1582)

ing phrase (Choir 1) is used several times, always varied. At the beginning of
the Magnificat it is reworked as an imitative point involving the whole ensemble, curiously omitting the B flats. Other borrowings are found in verse 8
(antiphonal exchanges of a static chord from bars 21–2 of the hymn), verse 12,
'Sicut erat' (from the doxological verse of the hymn, extended differently) and
the final Amen, which is elaborated slightly.

Several features set Magnificat and model apart. Virtually uniquely for
Lasso the bass parts in the hymn are spatially conceived, whereas those in the
Magnificat are not. This leads Wearing (1981: 2) to suggest a spacious per-
forming location for the hymn, such as the Frauenkirche, rather than the
Ducal Chapel. The general style of the hymn is dignified and sonorous. The
Magnificat makes conspicuous use of small note-values in two main contexts.
In some antiphonal passages one almost feels Lasso is thinking in *note nere*,
despite the signature, and in verses 6 and 10, which are scored for five voices
only, there are written-out *passaggi*, i.e. decorative figurations, suggesting that
these verses were intended for solo singers. In the à 10 sections the proportion
of tutti to antiphony is much larger in the Magnificat than in the hymn.

The remaining canticles by Lasso for double choir are his three settings of

the Benedictus Dominus from Lauds, found in the same manuscript (Maier 98)
as the *Miserere*. They lack the doxology and may thus have been intended for
Maundy Thursday or the burial service.[6] Like the *Miserere* they alternate
closed verses before joining for the final one, but unlike it they have the
Gregorian tone as a *cantus firmus* in Choir 2, usually in the second tenor but
sometimes in the top part. The *quarti toni* setting in particular is one of the
gems among Lasso's late works (partial transcr. Carver 1980, vol. 2: 393), with
a quiet devotional dignity that is deeply moving. The even verses (except the
last) are given to Choir 2 with the plainchant buried in a sonorous five-part
texture. Choir 1 is heard à 4 (SSAT) in verses 1, 7 and 11 and in beautifully-
textured duets and trios in verses 3 (SS), 5 (SAT) and 9 (SST). The double-
choir setting of verse 12, free of the chant, effectively points the opening word
'Illuminare' in the opening choral imitation by means of a rising fifth landing
on a glowing A major chord. The succeeding tutti takes us to a madrigalian
B flat chord for 'mortis' and back to A for the cadence at the mediant. The
stately antiphonal repetition which follows evokes the steady, gentle steps of
feet guided 'into the way of peace'.

Other liturgical works

Of a different liturgical type, the sequence, yet also utilising closed-verse
antiphony with a double-choir 'finale' is Lasso's *Stabat mater*, published as a
supplement to a collection of four-part motets (1585a). This is surely one of
Lasso's finest works, thoroughly madrigalian in its response to the manifold
agonies depicted in the text (partial transcr. Carver 1980, vol. 2: 401). The discantus and altus partbooks provide a high choir ($C_1C_1C_3C_4$) which alternates
two stanzas (six lines) at a time with a low choir ($C_3C_4C_4F_4$) found in the tenor
and bassus books. The final two stanzas are à 8. The four-part sections employ
Lasso's most eloquent type of declamatory polyphony, never academic and
rarely completely homophonic, wringing the utmost expression from the most
basic of materials: descending scalic motifs, dissonant suspensions, carefully-
placed accidentals and melodic semitones. The tutti which opens stanza 19
leads to a glorious shock: Choir 1 is left alone singing an E major chord on the
word 'morte' immediately after a G major chord. When Lasso next uses an
E major chord at 'Fac ut animae' (Ex. 30) it is the beginning of a stately
progress in sequential antiphony round the circle of fifths to its polar opposite,
B flat, reached in time for the word 'Paradisi'; it will be noticed that with the
exception of the second half of bar 7 and the first half of bar 8 of Ex. 30 the
harmony consists entirely of major triads evoking eternal bliss. At first sight
Lasso would seem to have inverted the usual symbolism of B flat = death; yet
he seems to me to have deepened it. The E major death is the death of Christ
by which he conquered death: therefore for the believer death (B flat) has
become the gate of Paradise.

    The two litanies in manuscript[7] are of little interest, being made up entirely
of block chords chords in *falsobordone* manner. The same is true of the nine-

Ex. 30   Lasso, Stabat mater

Ex. 30 (*cont.*)

voice Litany in the *Thesaurus litaniarum* (1596[(2)]: no. 41). That collection also
contains a through-composed Litany for double choir by Lasso, one of a
group of settings (the named composers are Stabile, Monte, Porta, Lasso,
Victoria, Aichinger, Cavaccio and Klingenstein) which seem to reflect a traditional approach to works of this kind. Lasso's setting (no. 34) is a mixture of
antiphonal treatment, where the choirs alternate complete invocations and
petitions, and responsorial, where one choir sings an invocation, the other the
accompanying petition. More rapid exchanges occur during the last seven
petitions of the second part where antiphonal repetitions of 'Regina' are
superimposed on the prevailing responsorial treatment.

The hymn *Aurora lucis* (mod. edn, 1981) has already been mentioned in
connection with the parody Magnificat based on it. It is a through-composed
setting in motet fashion, highly sectionalised from the point of view of the
number of interchanges between the choirs and the number of tuttis. The
latter are short-lived, none exceeding five bars in length except the final one,
and even that is interrupted. Antiphonal repetition of short phrases is used
sparingly. The overall impression of majesty and awe is not disrupted by the

dignified *tripla* (or *sesquialtera*?) section at 'in hoc pascha gaudio'. In the doxological stanza Lasso uses a resource comparatively rare in his output: a sudden tutti after a rest, the dramatic effect of which is heightened harmonically
by its entering on a B flat chord following the previous D major.

There remain two Marian antiphon settings, *Alma redemptoris mater* and
Salve regina, which of course have no particular ritual structure though a
definite place in the liturgy as devotions to Mary at the end of compline.
Lasso treats them as through-composed double-choir motets. *Alma* (Werke 1,
vol. 21: 14), thought by Boetticher to be some twenty years earlier than *Salve*,
relates to the grand manner of Lasso's earlier polychoral works particularly in
its large amount of tutti writing, occupying two-thirds of the total length of
the piece, so that the antiphony seems almost incidental. *Salve* (ibid.: 18), on
the other hand, belongs to the intimate devotional style of Lasso's later years.
The texture is heavy with suspensions and melting cadences, the choirs succeeding each other in quiet ecstasy without textual repetition for the most
part. The double-choir medium seems particularly suited to this kind of
adoration: the two choirs add to each other's rapture until a tutti releases the
tension. This is seen most beautifully in the final exclamations where the three
vocative adjectives 'O clemens, o pia, o dulcis' overlap into the final tutti
(Ex. 31).

Ex. 31   Lasso, Salve regina

Ex. 31 *(cont.)*

Motets: secular

The only political motet apart from the dialogues which is consistently polychoral is *Ergo rex vivat* (Werke 1, vol. 19: 129), addressed to Emperor Rudolf.
Its bright confidence admits of plenty of tutti writing, amounting to over half
its length. There is an especially interesting piece of choral imitation near the
beginning (bars 4–7) where the bass is transposed up a tone. The thematic
material is conspicuously triadic, especially in the final tutti.

Two other Latin pieces stand by themselves. They are irreverent drinking
songs dating from Lasso's more worldly days. *Jam lucis orto* (Werke 1, vol. 21:
84) borrows its first line from a hymn for prime. It is very chanson-like in the
homophony and clear-cut cadences of the single-choir sections, though the
tuttis generate a certain pomp. The text proceeds very largely in rhymed
couplets which are for the most part split antiphonally with some use of musical rhyme. Occasional tuttis reinforce a line or two. Quick antiphony provides
obvious word-painting as the choirs re-double their efforts at 'bibamus et
rebibamus'.

Vinum bonum et suave (Werke 1, vol. 21: 91) takes for its text a travesty of
the sequence *Verbum bonum*. It contains some animated antiphony, but for
the most part it is superficially more dignified and motet-like in texture. Once

again the poetic structure determines the antiphony, especially at the beginning:

Vinum bonum et suave	Choir 2
Nunquam bibi vinum tale	Choir 1
Vinum cor laetificat	tutti
Vinum purum et germanum	Choir 1
Morbos pellit reddens sanum	Choir 2
Corpus quod rectificat	tutti

The final section, heard twice, includes a change to triple rhythm in the form of major prolation notated by coloration. In the coda the customary plagal cadence is turned into a series of extraordinary fanfare-like repeated chords (Ex. 32).

Ex. 32   LASSO, Vinum bonum et suave

Motets: sacred

There remain seven sacred Latin pieces for double choir. The texts of all except *Bone Jesu* can be traced to liturgical sources:

Laudabit usque:	Ecclesiasticus 51: 8–12
Tui sunt caeli:	Psalm 88: 12 & 15 (Offertory, Nativity)
Benedic, Domine:	dedication of a building
Osculetur me osculo:	Song of Songs 1: 1–3
Omnia tempus habent:	Ecclesiastes 3: 1–8
Omnes de Saba:	Isaiah 60: 6, expanded (Epiphany)

The first two and *Bone Jesu* are assigned by Boetticher to *c*1565. They are sophisticated in their handling of antiphony but less responsive to the text than those of the 1580s. All three attach particular importance to the tutti, but are also particularly deft in their handling of antiphonal repetition.

Most unusually *Bone Jesu* (Werke 1, vol. 19: 154) begins with a twelve-bar tutti doubtless motivated by the words 'splendor paternae gloriae'. The remaining three tuttis are each preceded by three antiphonal repetitions which progressively overlap – the classic constructional device of polychoral music. *Laudabit usque* (Werke 1, vol. 21: 41) is more complex, though it contains a central tutti which divides it into two sections, each opening with longish single-choir passages. Lasso's treatment of antiphonal repetition in this piece is particularly striking; that which leads into the central tutti provides four statements of a bass progression tracing the circle of fifths from G to B flat (Ex. 33). This produces a strong motion towards the tutti which is Venetian in effect. Also Venetian is the enormous pitch range ($G_2C_1C_3C_4/C_3C_4C_4F_5$), the pitch domains of the choirs barely overlapping; this results in some choral

Ex. 33   Lasso, *Laudabit usque*

imitation at the octave. *Tui sunt caeli* (Werke 1, vol. 21: 5) is richer-textured, with no long phrases for single choirs after the opening. The opening uses the pitch contrast, albeit less extreme than in *Laudabit*, to symbolise heaven and earth; the ensuing antiphonal repetition and tutti are repeated in varied form, beginning breathtakingly on a chord of E flat instead of C.

In Lasso's later polychoral music the musical weight given to tutti sections diminishes. Their function is now more to portray or emphasise a phrase of text and to provide the musical punctuation, not to display Lasso's skill in providing conventional splendour. The almost conversational type of alternation of the choirs with each adding a new idea to the flow that we have already seen in *Salve regina* becomes more common, encouraged in some cases by the structure of the text. The overall musical result can still be impressive, but in a different way, and Lasso tends to emphasise the madrigalian possibilities of the text at the expense of purely polychoral interest.

This is already apparent in *Benedic, Domine* (Werke 1, vol. 19: 160), if indeed it dates from c1570. There is an unusually thorough imitative opening for Choir 1, but in the main body of the piece the qualities which it is hoped will reside within the walls of the building being dedicated ('sanitas, humilitas, sanctitas' etc.) are alternated strictly between the choirs, with the exception of 'victoria', which calls forth multiple fanfare-like choral imitation. Most of these qualities are too abstract for obvious musical symbolism, but Lasso gives to each a memorable and distinct musical idea. Only the final eighteen-bar tutti reminds us of his political-style perorations.

The remaining motets under discussion all seem fairly certainly to date from the 1580s. The text of *Omnia tempus habent* (Werke 1, vol. 21: 77) is also, apart from the opening parallelism, made up of a series of contrasting ideas, in this case pairs of opposites. In the *prima pars* the choirs alternate strictly, the higher Choir 1 singing the positive ideas, the lower Choir 2 the negative. A pivotal tutti at 'quod plantatum est' allows Choir 2 to take over as the leader where the positive–negative order reverses in the text. The final couplet is set tutti. In this part the verbal ideas often suggest, and receive, pictorial musical imagery, notably the 'weep–laugh' and 'mourn–dance' juxtapositions. In the *secunda pars* the choirs interact more freely with antiphonal repetition and tuttis, and sometimes a whole couplet is given to one choir. The final one, 'war–peace', is treated in more extended fashion: first a tutti in battle-piece style and then calm antiphonal repetition and a tranquil cadence.

Osculetur me osculo (Anthology no. 10a) takes its text from that most sensual of biblical poems, the Song of Songs, and Lasso makes the most of the voluptuousness. It is ironic in the light of the drinking songs that twice in this text the Beloved is rated above wine! It is a concise setting with only two real tuttis (the final one merely a plagal cadence) and a carefully controlled amount of antiphonal repetition. Much of the latter is at the unison – both choirs are SATB – and indeed is almost canonic. Revolving canonic repetition at 'Trahe me: post te' is a symbolic application of this conventional device –

one choir 'draws' the other after it; this is the central image of the motet, an embodiment of the mutuality of the lovers' responses to each other. The theological allegory is drawn at the end, where similar canonic writing for 'recti diligunt te' depicts the daughters of Jerusalem being drawn after the Beloved.

Omnes de Saba (Werke 1, vol. 21: 1), a motet for the Epiphany, may well be the last of Lasso's polychoral motets, appearing in print in Lindner's *Corollarium cantionum sacrarum* (1590[(5)]). It shares both the festive spirit of *Aurora lucis* and the lively rhythmic style of the *Aurora* Magnificat. Indeed, it is in some ways the most Baroque in purely musical terms of the pieces by Lasso that we have analysed. Tutti writing occupies a large proportion of its length, not concentrated in one or two long passages but distributed throughout so that it punctuates the often multiple antiphonal repetition. The latter often involves subtle shifts of tonality between areas separated by a second or third as well as the usual fourth or fifth. There are three statements of 'de Saba veniunt', for instance, each ending on the dominant of, respectively, B flat, G minor and D minor. In place of a sustained tutti the closing 'Alleluia' is set to a complex pattern of choral imitations which is repeated with the choirs exchanged (Ex. 34). The striking modernity of this passage is due to the cadential pattern in the top parts and the strategic, not strictly sequential layout of the key areas.

Ex. 34   LASSO, Omnes de Saba

Masses

Lasso left three masses for eight voices, all parodies. Somewhat blasphemous in view of its text is the choice of *Vinum bonum* as the model for a Mass published in 1577 (Werke 2, vol. 5: 105). The late *Osculetur me osculo* is the subject of a Mass discovered comparatively recently in the library of the University of Ljubljana (Werke 2, vol. 10: 187; Kyrie: Anthology no. 10b).[8] The *Missa super 'Bell'Amfitrit'altera'* (Werke 2, vol. 8: 55) is not consistent in its division of the ensemble. There is a remarkably high proportion of eight-part writing, contrasting with various three-, four- and five-part groups. The model is so far undiscovered, but it is clear that the Mass does not borrow from it very extensively.

The two truly polychoral masses make a fascinating comparison as examples of parody in the context of double-choir writing; the proportion of borrowed material to more distantly related and free material is significantly different in each case. The *Vinum* Mass draws on about two-thirds of the model (not counting the repeat of the latter's final section), whereas scarcely a bar of *Osculetur* is not heard in the Mass in some form. As is common in parody masses Kyries I and II depend in both cases almost entirely on the model. The Sanctus of the *Vinum* Mass uses much more of the model than that of the *Osculetur* Mass, whilst both have a rather perfunctory single invocation of Agnus Dei developing ideas from the model. The sections for fewer voices (Christe, Crucifixus, Benedictus) are free in *Vinum* but develop ideas from the model in *Osculetur*. The longer movements of parody masses usually draw much less on their models, and this is the case with *Vinum*, though there is a fair amount of literal quotation in the first portion of the Credo. The fully-scored sections of the Gloria and Credo of the *Osculetur* Mass on the other hand contain an astonishing amount of both literal quotation and more distant derivation of material. Indeed, despite the fact that these sections are longer than their counterparts in the *Vinum* Mass they actually contain less 'free' music. Any suspicion that Lasso was here cobbling together a Mass in a great hurry is banished when we realise the sheer skill with which the various portions of the motet are juxtaposed, joined and varied. The motet is certainly a rich quarry for material, and it might be argued that the Mass does justice to ideas which are perforce passed over quickly in the motet.

This is not the place to discuss parody technique in all its aspects, so let us concentrate on areas which concern double-choir writing particularly. Both models and both masses are scored for equal choirs (*chiavette* in the case of *Vinum bonum*), so there is generally little significance to be attached to which choir in a mass borrows from which choir in the model. Both masses predictably employ the opening and close of their model more frequently than internal passages, usually for the opening and close respectively of major sections. In *Vinum* the close of the motet (Ex. 32) with its series of C and G chords hammering home a plagal cadence is used in the Mass as follows: Kyrie II (bars 42–end, with *x* omitted), *Qui tollis* (bars 63–end, with a perfect cadence inserted before a much extended treatment of the scalic idea *y* over a plagal cadence), *Et iterum* (bars 110–end, beginning on a D major chord and omitting *y* in the cadence, and Agnus Dei (bars 11–end, expanded to accommodate the word 'miserere').

Further examples from the *Vinum* Mass will illustrate Lasso's facility in varying or expanding his material. For bars 15–25 of the Credo he borrows bars 50–8 of the model, a piece of choral imitation followed by a tutti, but inserts a new piece of antiphonal repetition before the tutti. At bars 7–8 of the Gloria he derives an antiphonal exchange from the first few notes only of a longer single-choir passage in the model. The same snippet is used in the Credo joined to antiphonal repetition from later in the motet. This dovetailing of one borrowed idea into another occurs again at the beginning of the Agnus Dei, where a condensed version of the opening of the motet is imitated antiphonally and then slips neatly into antiphonal repetition taken from bars 39–40 of the model. In the Gloria of the *Osculetur* Mass (bars 49–58) antiphonal repetition from bars 55–9 of the motet is telescoped into the tutti from its close (bars 64–7).

Both masses contain examples of two fascinating techniques: the splitting between the choirs of a passage previously assigned to one choir, and the opposite, i.e. the condensation for one choir of material previously employing two. One example of the former in the *Osculetur* Mass is the fairly straightfor-

ward division between the choirs of bars 8–14 of the model with minor variants to form bars 9–14 of the Credo. Later in the same movement at 'Et incarnatus est' there is a remarkable adaption of the same passage in quasi-canonic
manner: compare Ex. 35 with bars 8–14 of the motet (Anthology no. 10a). In
the Credo of the *Vinum* Mass short antiphonal phrases are derived from the
opening of the motet (Ex. 36). In the Qui tollis section of the Gloria the whole
of the opening two phrases of the motet (Ex. 36a) is telescoped in a passage
for Choir 1 (Ex. 37). The most fascinating example of this 'condensation' technique is the Christe of the *Osculetur* Mass, where a substantial portion of the
motet (bars 14–24) is reduced for a single choir – see the Anthology. It will be
seen that the bass part follows the original most closely and that the last five
bars are a free extension making use of the ♩. ♫ ♩ figure.

The *Osculetur* Mass contains a number of instances where material stated
only once in the motet is repeated antiphonally either in its original or in some
varied form. There are many felicitous examples of subtle embellishment or
alteration of borrowed material. In the motet the canonic cadences at 'Trahe
me: post te' are all in G dorian, but when they are used in Kyrie II they shift
magically into B flat (see Anthology). A further variant of this material at bars
75–7 of the Gloria incorporates a delightfully syncopated response in the
soprano of Choir 1.

Ex. 35   Lasso, *Missa super Osculetur me osculo*

Ex. 35 (*cont.*)

Ex. 36(a)   LASSO, Vinum bonum

Ex. 36(a) (*cont.*)

Ex. 36(b)   Lasso, Missa super Vinum bonum

Ex. 37 LASSO, Missa super Vinum bonum

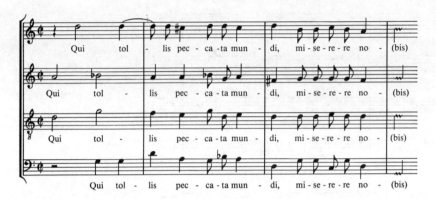

Summing-up

To sum up Lasso's contribution to the development of polychoral writing is a
daunting task. He was able to draw on the experience of the pioneers – the
early psalmists, Phinot and the Habsburg group – transcending their achieve-
ment in a manner befitting one of the century's consummate masters. It is
worthy of note that, with the exceptions of *Aurora lucis* and the final verse of
the *Miserere*, Lasso's concept of double-choir writing does not seem to have
been a spatial one. Doubtless the Ducal Chapel was not large enough to permit
spacing of the choirs. In this matter, though far from consistent in their application of the theorists' recommendations, the Venetians seem to be following
a different tradition, which may have influenced Lasso in the case of *Aurora
lucis*. Yet Lasso remains the first great composer to realise the compositional,
as distinct from liturgical, possibilities of polychoral writing.

6

POLYCHORAL MUSIC IN ROME AND SPAIN

Giovanni Animuccia

It is not yet possible to be certain when polychoral music was first heard in Rome. With the sole exception of Festa's tripartite canonic setting of *Inviolata* (see Chapter 3), evidence of it appears to begin around 1570. In that year, nearing the end of his life, Giovanni Animuccia published his *Secondo libro delle laudi*, which contains several pieces for eight voices and was, like the *Primo libro* of 1563, compiled for Filippo Neri's oratory.[1] His aim, set out in the preface (quoted in *NGr* vol. 1: 437) was to provide music which shunned 'imitations and complexities, in order not to obscure the understanding of the words' but which, to hold the interest of the 'most important gentlemen' who frequented the oratory, made use of other methods of contrast, chiefly differing numbers and combinations of voices.

Sometimes, as in *Jubilate Deo* and *Pater noster*, Animuccia employs various voice-groupings without favouring a particular choral division, a technique familiar to us from the 1568 *Novus thesaurus* repertory. In the third *Salve regina* setting two four-part choirs alternate with closed 'verses', some of which are scored à 6 by means of *divisi*; thus although when both choirs combine briefly in the final section the writing is à 8, at least twelve singers would have been required for a true double-choir performance. Two complete psalm-settings (without doxology) and the laude *Signore dolce mia vita* also proceed largely in verse-by-verse alternation of four-part choirs until the final verse, which contains antiphony between the choirs, mingling of some voices from each, and tutti. The final section of *Deus misereatur* makes use of canonic imitation between the choirs, and in *Beatus vir* we find tutti reiteration of a single-choir idea. The psalms veer between *falsobordone*-like block chords and more decorative cadential phrases, though neither seems to utilise a psalm-tone. The second choir of *Beatus vir* is *a voce mutata*, the clefs being $G_2C_2C_3C_4/C_2C_2C_3C_4$.

In general, these pieces, though direct in expression and undoubtedly fitting for their purpose, are cautious, indeed primitive, in polychoral technique in comparison with the motets of Phinot and works by Lasso and others published in the 1560s.

Polychoral music seems to have caught on rapidly in Rome during the 1570s.

The first eight-voice motets of Animuccia's younger contemporary Palestrina and the still younger Victoria were published in 1572, and in the following year occurred the well-known performance of Victoria's double-choir setting of *Super flumina Babylonis* (see below, p. 118). Both masters left a substantial quantity of polychoral music, and significant contributions were made by Zoilo, Marenzio, the Naninos, the Anerios, Soriano, Giovanelli and others. As Noel O'Regan (1985 and forthcoming) and Graham Dixon (1981) have shown, music for two or three choirs was regularly performed on feast-days in the wealthier Roman churches, especially those associated with particular confraternities. In the seventeenth century Roman polychoral music developed into the unprecedented pomposity and lavishness of what has come to be known as the 'Colossal Baroque'.

Giovanni Pierluigi da Palestrina

Only relatively little of Palestrina's multi-voiced music was actually published before modern times. This is a little surprising, for while it can be argued that there was little demand for music requiring such lavish forces, such an argument seems to carry more weight when applied to music for three or more choirs; many composers of the time did manage to get complete collections of double-choir music published. In Palestrina's case the bulk of it has come down to us in manuscript. Four motets appeared in his *Motettorum liber secundus* (1572), six in his *Motettorum liber tertius* (1575), and four double-choir masses based on his own motets were printed posthumously in the *Missae quattuor octonis vocibus* (1601) of which one, that on *Confitebor tibi*, had previously appeared in 1585[5] with a four-part Mass by Bartolomeo Roy. No other chronological ordering can yet be attempted, but there are many stylistic and formal traits which it is fruitful to explore.

There are grounds for thinking that the motets published in 1572, all settings of psalms or psalm-like texts, represent Palestrina's earliest essays for eight voices. Although they all make extensive use of antiphonal contrast between different groups of voices, these do not crystallise into consistent polychoral divisions. It is therefore very striking that the 1575 motets are all unequivocably polychoral; moreover, the parody Masses which Palestrina came to base on 1572 models are truly polychoral (see below). In fact all of Palestrina's music for eight and twelve voices outside the 1572 volume is polychoral, and in all cases (with very few anomalies) he composes the bass parts in a truly spatial manner as recommended by Zarlino and Vicentino. A change seems to have occurred in Roman perceptions of polychoral music at this time, perhaps indicating a desire for performances with spaced choirs. The same manuscripts which contain modified 'spatial' versions of Lasso's early psalm-motets also contain similar, consistently spatial rewritings of Animuccia's *Pater noster* and Palestrina's 1572 *Laudate Dominum*, neither of which is even consistently polychoral in its original form (O'Regan 1984).

Despite the small amount he published, polychoral music occupies a significant proportion of Palestrina's output – some seventy of his 375 motets, plus four masses, seven litanies, one magnificat and one hymn.

Marian antiphons, sequences and litanies

Three of the 1575 pieces may be described as motets, one is a Marian antiphon, and the remaining two set sequence texts. It will be convenient to use the last three as a lead-in to a discussion of pieces whose texts might of their nature have some bearing on Palestrina's formal procedure.[2] Marian antiphons, beginning with Animuccia, seem to have been singled out quite often by Roman composers for polychoral treament (O'Regan, forthcoming). Palestrina published a double-choir *Ave regina* in 1575 (Opere vol. 8: 196) and in manuscript there are two settings of *Alma redemptoris mater* (Werke vol. 6: 159 & vol. 7: 73), one further *Ave regina* (Werke vol. 7: 124), two settings of *Regina coeli* (Werke vol. 6: 165 & vol. 30: 175) and two of *Salve regina* (Werke vol. 6: 153 & vol. 26: 211), the second of which is à 12. These settings have much in common. All make use of the associated chant melodies, in many cases paraphrasing it extensively, especially in the single-choir sections. Also, with the exception of the eight-voice *Salve regina*, which is through-composed, they all begin with two or three closed versets for alternate choirs. The final portion of the piece then proceeds to a tutti via antiphonal repetitions. One of the *Alma redemptoris* settings (Werke vol. 7: 73) has its 'tutti' in four parts only, in the English *cantoris–decani* manner. The three-choir layout of the twelve-voice *Salve regina* leads to still further sectionalisation, with a verset for each choir in turn, one à 8 for Choirs 1 and 2 in canonic style, and finally antiphonal repetition leading to a twelve-part tutti.[3]

Palestrina's settings of sequence texts also make an interesting group. Of the two eight-part settings of *Lauda Sion*, that published in 1575 (Opere vol. 8: 180) is in motet style, setting only the first two and last two stanzas. It does, however, employ the chant, and Palestrina respects the integrity of the poetic line so that there is no quick antiphony. The other setting (Werke vol. 7: 91) is a different matter; it sets all the stanzas as given in the *Liber usualis* (pp. 945–9, except no. 18) for alternate choirs in triple time, adhering strictly to the chant until the last two stanzas. Where in the chant the same melody is repeated for a subsequent stanza, Palestrina gives the answering choir the same music. The pattern is only broken in the final stanza where line-by-line alternation leads to a tutti for 'Amen. Alleluia'.

The two settings of *Veni sancte Spiritus* form a similar pair, though both set the complete text. In the 1575 version (Opere vol. 8: 186) the chant is subjected to much variation and transposition, and in the other setting (Werke vol. 7: 117) the antiphony is closed until stanzas 9 and 10. Of the three manuscript settings of *Victimae paschali* (Werke vol. 7: 105, 112 & 194)[4] only the first has a clear reference to the chant, but all three begin with closed vers-

ets for each choir in turn. The point at which through-composition begins is
different in each case, but none introduces antiphonal interaction or tutti writing until the final stanza. They thus resemble in form the Marian antiphon settings. *Ave mundi spes, Maria* (Werke vol. 6: 111) has a sequence-style text and
begins with a stanza for each choir in turn. Thereafter the integrity of the
poetic line is respected, although it is sometimes treated in overlapped choral
imitation or tutti.

I have reserved the *Stabat mater* settings until last because one of them, the
eight-part (Opere vol. 33: 43), is one of Palestrina's most famous works and
certainly his most celebrated for double-choir. Once again he allows the poetic
line to remain the smallest unit; the exception is stanza 4, where alternations
by the half-line are suggested by the rhymes: 'Quae maerebat / et dolebat / et
tremebat / cum videbat'. In stanzas 1, 5 and 6 the *aab* rhyme scheme is
reflected in a similar musical pattern. The three-choir format of the twelve-
part setting (Werke vol. 7: 130) offers the most obvious way of splitting up the
three-line stanzas, though as in the eight-part setting complete stanzas are
sometimes given to one choir, or a particular line may be set tutti for emphasis
and contrast. Antiphonal repetition is rarely used, doubtless because of the
length of the text; there is more in the twelve-part setting. Both pieces reveal
a severe homophonic approach, expressive in a rather detached way but,
although careful in their word-setting in terms of verbal accent, lacking direct
portrayal of the emotional content, in spite of a higher than average (for Palestrina) incidence of accidentals. Almost uniquely after the 1572 pieces the
eight-part setting mixes voices from both choirs in stanzas 14–17 to give
heightened register contrast, this despite the spatial treatment of the bass lines
elsewhere in the piece.

Palestrina's double-choir litanies (all in Opere vol. 20) include one à 6 for
two consistently-defined three-part choirs, the remainder being à 8. His normal procedure, as in other double-choir litanies of the period (e.g. those of
Lasso, Porta and Giovanni Gabrieli), is not to adopt a wholly antiphonal or
responsorial approach but to mix the two and inject further variety by means
of tuttis and antiphonal repetitions. Re-use of music for two or more successive invocations and/or petitions sometimes occurs. Interestingly, the Marian
and Jesus litanies all seem to begin with a variant of the same musical
material.

Antiphonal techniques in Palestrina's music

Non-repetitive antiphony, prominent in the pieces by Palestrina so far discussed, brings to mind psalmodic antiphony and its possible employment of a
Gregorian cadence alternation. There are few vestiges of this in Palestrina.
The twelve-part pseudo-psalm *Laudate Dominum in tympanis* (Opere vol. 32:
28) begins with strict verse-by-verse antiphony. The *Nunc dimittis* à 12 (ibid.:
15) in the same manuscript not only has a plainchant incipit, but for much of

the time preserves the cadential structure of tone 3a. The eight-part setting of the same canticle (Werke vol. 7: 181), on the other hand, sets the incipit in polyphony and shows no sign of a Gregorian formula. The only polychoral Magnificat by Palestrina, the *primi toni* for double choir (Opere vol. 16: 323), also contains evidence of an alternating cadence structure (tone 1 transposed). In none of these canticles is there straightforward verse-by-verse antiphony.

Palestrina does not seem to have used double-choir canon, though there are many brief instances of canonic overlap of the choirs. In *Magnus sanctus Paulus* (Werke vol. 7: 171) this results in a brief ostinato (Ex. 38). Note the wonderful upward transposition of 'vere digne est' in Choir 1, followed by a resumption of imitation at the unison. In general, Palestrina's use of antiphonal repetition is marked by delightful variation in the re-statement. He makes sparing use of the imitation of short phrases, and his polychoral music therefore has a restraint and dignity in keeping with his overall approach to church music. This should not blind us to the fact that considerable subtlety is to be found in his antiphonal technique. Rarely does one choir imitate another note for note. The transposition and variation of material by the answering choir is something we have noted from Phinot onwards. It is interesting to compare the opening of Palestrina's *O pretiosum et admirandum convivium* (Werke vol. 7: 10) with Phinot's *O sacrum convivium* (Opera vol. 4: 138). Both composers transpose the phrase, Phinot (using equal choirs) up a tone and Palestrina (with a lower Choir 2) down a fourth (Ex. 39). Moreover, despite Palestrina's richer harmony, there is a general similarity of expression. Later in his motet Palestrina is generally less homorhythmic in the single-choir sections than Phinot, except, as commonly with his generation, in the brief triple-time section.

In Palestrina such subtlety and flexibility is applied also in the varied re-statement of larger paragraphs. Examples are to be found in *Expurgate vetus fermentum* (Werke vol. 6: 144), *Videntes stellam magi* (Anthology no. 11), *Apparuit gratia* (Werke vol. 7: 153), *Haec est dies praeclara* (ibid.: 163), *Laudate Dominum de coelis* (Werke vol. 30: 170), and *Tria sunt munera* (Werke vol. 7: 76). Such pieces represent Palestrina's polychoral style at its most subtly developed; we shall explore as an example *Videntes stellam magi*. It begins with a concise imitative statement for Choir 1; Choir 2 then initiates the next phrase of text homophonically. This procedure occurs time and again when Palestrina and many other composers give new text to the second choir to enter; it may be traced back to Santacroce (see p. 27 above). In this case the second choir is interrupted by an echo of 'gavisi sunt' from Choir 1. Choir 2's music is now (bars 13–17) given to Choir 1; Choir 2 predictably enters with 'gavisi sunt' but then carries on, giving a brief eight-part texture. The two succeeding phrases are stated by Choir 1, then varied by Choir 2: 'et intrantes domum' is transposed up a third, from a minor mode to a major one, with some alterations to the inner voices; 'invenerunt puerum cum Maria' is varied in details with a more expressive 7–6 cadence at bar 27. Choir 1 adds the

Ex. 38   PALESTRINA, Magnus sanctus Paulus

Ex. 39(a)   PHINOT, O sacrum convivium

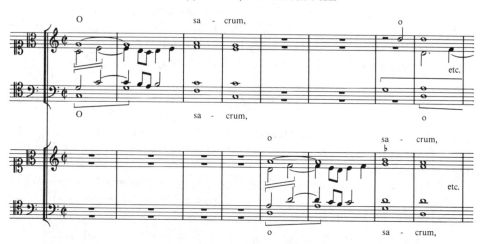

Ex. 39(b)   PALESTRINA, O pretiosum et admirandum convivium

remaining words of the phrase, 'matre eius'. Imitation of a triadic figure on 'et procidentes' leads to the longest eight-part passage so far (bars 39–43), enhancing the words 'adoraverunt eum' with a circle of fifths movement from E flat to C. This neatly punctuates the piece, since the text, following Matthew 2: 11, now turns to the gifts brought by the Magi. The giving of the gifts is divided between the choirs thus:

obtulerunt ei munera	Choir 1; ends in C
obtulerunt ei munera	Choir 2, varied; ends in F
aurum	Choir 1
thus	Choir 2
et myrrham	Choir 1

Palestrina then gives the first 'obtulerunt' phrase to Choir 2, leading us to expect a re-statement with minor variants. Choir 1, instead of taking up the answering repeat, moves straight to the enumeration of the gifts, listing all three in triple time. This 'new' phrase is shown by Choir 2 (bars 70–2) to be a variant of the earlier 'et myrrham' (bars 61–3); it generates a series of antiphonal cadences which home on F before the brief final tutti. *Videntes stellam* is thus a small-scale, intimate piece with delightful surprises.

Other stylistic trends

The varied re-statement of substantial paragraphs seems to be a formal procedure of particular significance to Palestrina. Other devices we have already met. His polychoral style is in general more restrained than the Venetian idiom. *Spiritus sanctus replevit* (Opere vol. 33: 72) represents his closest rapprochement to the Gabrielian manner, with its concisely-imitative opening, homophonic entry of the second choir, occasional use of *note nere* declamation, notably at 'variis linguis', which also employs sequential antiphonal repetition, and an excursion into triple time with a return to duple for the final melismatic 'Alleluia'. *Omnes gentes* (Werke vol. 7: 186) is in many ways the acme of Palestrina's festive style with its tutti opening, trumpet-style triadic figures, high tessitura, and, once again, homophonic declamation in *note nere* and the incursion of triple time at 'psallite sapientes'. The use of quick, homophonic, syllabic word-setting is not common; homophony itself is not unusual, and is often enlivened with melismata on key words.

The additive structures we find in the Gabrielis (see Chapter 7) are not found; if Palestrina repeats a phrase antiphonally, he usually does it once and then passes on to the next. Sequential modulating antiphony, a Gabrielian fingerprint, is very rare; another example occurs in *Jubilate Deo* (Opere vol. 8: 208), bars 24–8, which cadences successively in C, G and D dorian. Alleluia refrains are also rare – *Disciplinam et sapientiam* (Werke vol. 6: 129) is an example. There are a few instances of the 'responsorial' form aBcB, such as *Magnus sanctus Paulus*. The freer attitude to dissonance sometimes encountered in the Gabrielis is hardly ever found in Palestrina. *Jesus junxit se* (Opere vol. 33: 28) stands out for its cadential clash (bar 61) and certain madrigalian harmonic features, including use of the augmented triad.

Tutti writing in Palestrina

Palestrina's concern in tuttis remains the creation of singable vocal lines and consonant harmony. We have already noted the almost total lack of cadential clashes harsher than the standard 4–3 suspension. That being said, his handling of passing notes can produce the most gorgeously rich textures, as at the close of *Dies sanctificatus* (Werke vol. 7: 158), quoted in Ex. 40. The melismatic 'Alleluia' at the end of *Congratulamini* (ibid.: 167) is another example.

Ex. 40 PALESTRINA, Dies sanctificatus

O Domine Jesu Christe

A piece illustrating a very different use of the tutti is *O Domine Jesu Christe* (Werke vol. 6: 140) – plainer, not homophonic but certainly more declamatory, enhancing the adoration of the text. This piece, though its text is slightly longer, invites comparison with Giovanni Gabrieli's famous motet (Anthology no. 15; see Chapter 7). Palestrina uses less chromaticism, though his setting of 'in cruce vulneratum' for three voices of each choir in turn in *fauxbourdon* style is undeniably effective. A certain quickening of rhythm at 'sint remedium animae meae' parallels Gabrieli's setting, but whereas the latter goes on to contrast this in a dynamic way with slower material, Palestrina passes on to his next line of text. Palestrina's final tutti does contain some unusually lively syncopation in the inner parts of Choir 1 of which Gabrieli might have approved.

Parody masses

Parody remains one of the most absorbing fields in Renaissance music for analytical study, as we have already seen with Lasso. Palestrina's double-choir parody masses are on the whole less rich than Lasso's *Missa 'Osculetur me osculo'*, but nevertheless merit a brief discussion. In general contrapuntal elaboration is much more in evidence in the masses, regardless of the degree of homophony in the models. For example, the first Kyrie of the *Laudate Dominum Mass* (motet, Opere vol. 7: 219; mass, vol. 30: 1) takes an imitative point originally à 4 and develops it through all eight voices, without disrupting the choral division. The Mass on *Hodie Christus natus est* (motet, Opere vol. 8: 203; mass, vol. 30: 59), an extremely homophonic motet, shows the polyphonic expansion still more strikingly, in the second Kyrie, for instance, and especially the Sanctus, which opens with a complete transformation of the opening phrase in each choir, omitting the 'Noe' material. Such passages contrast effectively with the many instances where the homophonic character of the model is retained.

The four masses differ in their approach to the borrowing of material. In that on *Laudate Dominum* the Kyrie leans most on the model, the Gloria and Credo least, a very conventional situation. With *Hodie Christus* there is far more borrowing in internal sections of the Gloria and Credo. In the Mass on *Fratres ego enim accepi* (motet, Werke vol. 6: 4; mass, Opere vol. 30: 110) Palestrina is very selective, making striking use in Gloria, Credo and Osanna II of the penultimate phrase of the motet. Selection is still more necessary in the Mass on *Confitebor tibi* (motet, Opere vol. 7: 176; mass, vol. 30: 163), a long bipartite motet whose text is not a psalm but Isaiah 12. Almost every phrase is new material, though often triadic in outline. In the Mass there is conspicuous contrapuntal development extending far beyond anything in the model; thus Palestrina avoids any feeling of short-windedness. Even a homophonic tripletime passage is expanded imitatively in Agnus Dei II. On the whole, however, there is relatively little in these masses which is startling in terms of polychoral technique. An exception, shedding light on Palestrina's changing attitude to multi-voiced composition after 1572, occurs in the Credo of the *Confitebor* Mass, when he clarifies antiphonal repetition which is hidden in the texture of the only partly polychoral model (Ex. 41).

Ex. 41(a)   PALESTRINA, Confitebor tibi (secunda pars)

Ex. 41(b)   PALESTRINA, Missa 'Confitebor tibi'

Ex. 41(b) *(cont.)*

Tomás Luis de Victoria

Motets

Despite his relative youth, Victoria's multi-voiced music began to appear at
almost exactly the same time as that of Palestrina. His eight-part *Ave maria*
(Opera vol. 1: 146) appeared in his motet collection of 1572, but like Palestrina's pieces of the same year it is not consistently polychoral. *Super flumina
Babylonis* (Opera vol. 7: 53), performed in 1573, is a double-choir psalm-
motet setting the first five verses of Ps. 136, though the bass parts are not
always treated in spatial manner. The first version, printed in 1576, was cast in
four sections, the middle two for one choir only. By the time it appeared in
1585, Victoria had merged the last three sections into a *secunda pars*, though
with no alteration to the substance except for the end of what had been the
third section: repetition by Choir 2 at the same pitch of the triple-time phrase
'de canticis Sion' is replaced by an answer from Choir 1 which modulates to
the dominant, thus preparing more satisfactorily for the dramatic tutti which
follows and which had originally opened the fourth section (Ex. 42). This
move towards a more through-composed structure contrasts interestingly with
Victoria's highly sectional approach to complete psalms and canticles.

There is only one other polychoral motet by Victoria – *O Ildephonse*, published in 1600 (Opera vol. 1: 153). This is a concise and conspicuously
homophonic piece, with little adornment beyond the odd decorated cadence
or melisma in tuttis. Sequential antiphonal repetition occurs at 'angelicis

' Ex. 42(a) Victoria, Super flumina Babylonis (1576)

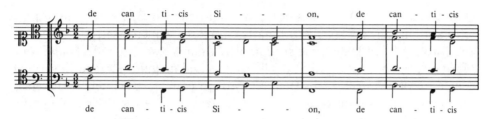

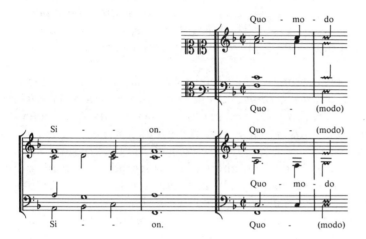

Ex. 42(b) Victoria, Super flumina Babylonis (1585)

manibus', with cadences on, successively, g, C, F and B flat; this progression is
used again in the triple-time portion of the closing 'Alleluia' in such a way as to
lend unity to the piece.

Psalms and magnificats

Unlike Palestrina's, Victoria's polychoral music is mostly found amongst his settings of liturgical texts: five ordinaries and three sequence settings for Mass, and for vespers and compline six complete psalms, two magnificats and four Marian antiphons, plus a litany. The psalms and magnificats tend in varying degrees towards a sectional structure; through-composed sequences of verses set polychorally are contrasted with individual verses set for all or some voices of one choir only or for three or four voices drawn from both choirs. Victoria does usually, however, treat his bass parts spatially. *Ecce nunc benedicite* (1600), the last of the psalms to be published, is rather exceptional in proceeding largely in quasi-canonic antiphony with no verses for reduced forces (Opera vol. 7: 63).

The influence of the psalm-tone varies; definite melodic references, paraphrased or in the form of a *cantus firmus* occur in *Dixit Dominus* (tone 1), *Nisi Dominus* and *Laudate Pueri* (both tone 6), and both magnificats, designated *primi. . .* and *sexti toni. Laetatus sum* and *Ecce nunc* may also be assigned to mode 6, though seeming to bear no reference to the psalm-tone. In *Dixit Dominus* (Opera vol. 7: 1) an alternating cadential pattern (d, g) derived from tone 1 transposed is very obvious, and the large number of cadences on F in *Laudate pueri* is clearly related to tone 6.

The two magnificats are each related to a vesper psalm not only by their common relationship to a psalm-tone, but also by the use of the same music in the doxology. The doxologies of *Dixit Dominus* and the *Magnificat primi toni* (Anthology no. 12) correspond exactly save for one extra phrase at the beginning in the case of the psalm. The doxology of the *Magnificat sexti toni* (Opera vol. 3: 95) appears to be a tightened-up reworking of that of *Laetatus sum* (Opera vol. 7: 27), both works being for three choirs. The 'Gloria Patri' is much shortened, only the last phrase corresponding exactly, and in the 'Sicut erat' the rhythmic patterns are compressed, 'in principio' changing from 𝅗𝅥. 𝅘𝅥 𝅘𝅥 𝅘𝅥 𝅗𝅥 to 𝅘𝅥 𝅘𝅥 𝅘𝅥 𝅗𝅥 𝅗𝅥 . In addition to these borrowings, almost all the doxologies of the psalms and magnificats share a common formal pattern which may be summarised as follows:

> Gloria: antiphony, with or without tutti, triple time
> Sicut erat: antiphony leading to tutti, duple time

The two magnificats appeared in 1600 whereas the two psalms with which they are connected had first appeared in 1581a and 1583 respectively, so presumably the magnificat doxologies were consciously lifted from the psalms. Victoria's publishing activity, certainly as regards his polychoral music, was a curious cumulative process, with new works gradually introduced alongside reprints of older ones. The works added in 1600 (four of the masses, the two magnificats, *Ecce nunc, O Ildephonse* and two of the sequences) share characteristics which may belong to a late style of Victoria: almost total polarisation of homophony with antiphonal sections and imitative polyphony with reduced-voice sections, dramatic use of declamation in small note-values, and in some cases almost excessive use of the 'cheerful' 'F major' mode 6.

In addition, the magnificats are completely sectionalised into verses with contrasts of scoring which look forward to the *concertato alla Romana* style of the seventeenth century.[5] The *primi toni* (Anthology no. 12) opens with a verse in imitative style for each choir in turn with traces of chant paraphrase. Verse 3 is set to homophonic antiphony. Another pair of imitative verses follows, with a choice of two versions of verse 5: à 4 (imitative) or à 3 (canon à 2 with a free voice). Dramatic antiphony with tutti in verses 6 and 8 alternates with two verses (7 and 9) for Choir 2, one homophonic, the other imitative. Triple time provides additional contrast in verses 6, 7 and 10 (the latter for Choir 1) as well as in the doxology, which was outlined earlier. The whole piece seems designed to maximise variety and dramatise contrast in a way which does not happen in the pre-1600 psalms. The extraordinary thing is that Victoria borrowed not only the doxology from the 1581 *Dixit* but also several verses from two *alternatim* settings, one with polyphony for the odd verses, the other for the even verses, published in 1576 (Opera vol. 3: 1 & 6). These make up the à 4 imitative verses 1, 4, 5 and 9 of the double-choir setting. His adherence to the mode and sometimes the melodic outline of tone 1 makes such a procedure possible in spite of the extreme stylistic contrasts we have noted. The twelve-part *Magnificat sexti toni* (Opera vol. 3: 95) not only shares generally structural and stylistic characteristics with the *primi toni* but has a similar relationship with *alternatim* settings in 1581a (Opera vol. 3: 52 & 57).

Sequences

In two of the sequences, *Lauda Sion* (Opera vol. 7: 135) and *Veni sancte Spiritus* (ibid.: 141), Victoria allows the poetic and musical structure of the chant to influence the formal design of his polyphonic settings, though only at the beginning of *Lauda Sion* is there any appreciable reference to the chant melody itself, and only selected stanzas are set. As with Palestrina's motet-style settings of the same texts Victoria respects the integrity of the poetic line, so that while there may be antiphonal repetition, the antiphony is in long-breathed phrases. Both pieces are for equal choirs (SATB) and Victoria tends to swap them when giving the same music to successive stanzas, as at the beginning of *Lauda Sion*:

> 1a: Choir 1 b: Choir 2 c: canonic antiphony + tutti
> 2a: Choir 2 b: Choir 1 c: canonic antiphony + tutti

A different, more subtle parallelism occurs at the beginning of *Veni sancte Spiritus*:

> 1a, b, c: Choir 1
> 2a, b: Choir 2 (variation) c: Choir 1 → 2 (overlapped antiphonal repetition)

Dic nobis Maria (1600; Opera vol. 7: 147) sets only verses 4–8 of the sequence *Victimae paschali*, focussing on the dialogue between Mary and the disciples. Victoria characterises Mary with the slightly higher choir ($G_2G_2C_1C_3$ – the other is $G_2C_1C_3C_4$), and the disciples with double-choir writing. Verse 4, the disciples' question, is repeated after verse 5, eliciting further information as it were. The whole piece is extremely homophonic, with much use of triple time, and there is no trace of the chant save its mode (1, transposed).

Marian antiphons

Victoria's settings of the four Marian antiphons are further contributions to the tradition to which Noel O'Regan has drawn attention (forthcoming). *Regina coeli* and *Salve regina* were printed in 1576, the remaining two in 1581a. *Salve* (Opera vol. 7: 120) is highly sectional, with no less than five of the seven sections in imitative style for one of the choirs. The second paragraph ('illos tuos') of the first double-choir section (beginning 'Eja, ergo') is subjected to varied re-statement, the same materials being re-assembled with a different pattern of antiphony and different tonal relationships. The final section, with its affective fervour combined with majestic, slow-moving harmony, invites comparison with Lasso's *Stabat mater*, especially near the beginning where in the first tutti Victoria employs an extended circle-of-fifths progression: A–D–G–C–F–B flat; a cadence in B flat follows, and the subsequent Choir 2 phrase includes an E flat chord.

Regina coeli (Opera vol. 7: 95) is treated by Victoria as an aBcB form, which it is textually but not in the plainchant melody. The 'Alleluia' refrain is in triple time, a device of which the Venetians hold no monopoly. *Alma redemptoris mater* (ibid.: 73) and *Ave regina coelorum* (ibid.: 85) are both through-composed and of similar dignified character with no quick antiphony and with dovetailed choral interchanges.

Masses

Victoria's polychoral masses are all parodies – four for double choir, of which three are on his own Marian antiphons and the fourth on Jannequin's *La guerre*, and one for three choirs on his psalm-setting *Laetatus sum*. They are all more selective in their use of borrowed material than one would expect and do not employ consistent head-motifs, though major cadential sections are more often borrowed, especially in *Laetatus* (Opera vol. 6: 59). In those based on the Marian antiphons (Opera vol. 4: 72, 99; vol. 6: 1) the borrowing tends to be more common in fewer-voiced sections, which often develop and extend the material differently from the model. The models contain little homophony, and the declamatory homophony pervading Gloria and Credo is not usually borrowed. Three of the 1600 masses (i.e. all except *Salve*) share 'F major' tonality and have much in common stylistically, though only the *Missa pro victoria*

(*Opera* vol. 6: 26) of course has the rapid battle rhythms on one chord derived from the chanson.

Organ parts

A peculiarity of Victoria's 1600 publication is that it supplies an organ part – one was even added to the reprint of *Ave Maria*. It is always associated with Choir 1, whose voice-parts are doubled with occasional simplification. In view of the particular fondness for instrumental participation in church music in some Spanish cathedrals (Stevenson 1961: 32, 139, 144, 166–7) it seems likely that in Spain (and probably also in Roman confraternities) the second (and third) choirs of Victoria's polychoral works would have been doubled by instruments. The Spanish were fond of the more raucous shawms in addition to the cornetti and sackbuts which were preferred in Italy, though it is hard to imagine the use of the former in more reflective, polyphonically-constructed music. In Rome, though forbidden in the Sistine Chapel, wind instruments were used in the Cappella Giulia from at least as early as 1599, and it seems that an organ was positioned with each choir for polychoral performances (Fischer 1979: 115–16). One organ part, that for the *Missa 'Salve'* (*Opera* vol. 4: 72), provides evidence for the downward transposition of pieces notated in high clefs or *chiavette*. The clefs of the Mass are $G_2G_2C_2C_4/G_2C_2C_3F_3$, representing mode 1 transposed, and the organist is directed to play 'ad quartam inferiorem'.

Most aspects of Victoria's polychoral technique have been touched on in our discussion. It is clear that his structural approach differs from that of Palestrina chiefly in his greater tendency towards an almost Baroque sectionalisation, though it should be borne in mind that this occurs in psalms and canticles, genres of less significance in Palestrina's polychoral output. Varied restatement in the Palestrina mould is found rarely – the 'Eja, ergo' section of *Salve regina* is an example. Victoria's later works show an uninhibited brashness of homophonic declamation which we do not find in the older master. This is not necessarily evidence of Venetian influence, but it shows a 'concerto'-like style to have been cultivated in the medium by more progressive composers in the Roman sphere of influence.

Later Roman composers

Roman composers of the generation after Palestrina, such as Felice Anerio, Giovanni Maria Nanino, Ruggiero Giovanelli and Francesco Soriano, showed an ever-growing interest in polychoral music. Marian antiphon settings were prominent, and increasingly motets and psalms (Fischer 1979: 332ff). Such works were still being copied into Cappella Giulia and Cappella Sistina manuscripts well into the seventeenth century (Llorens 1960, 1971). It is significant that when, so it seems, the Compagnia dei Musici di Roma wished to pay tribute to Palestrina, in assembling a joint composition by Palestrina, Dragoni, Giovanelli, Stabile, Soriano, Mancini and Santini, the medium they chose was a Mass for three choirs, based on Palestrina's *Cantantibus organis* à 5 of 1575 (Summers 1982: 14).

In psalms, verse-by-verse antiphony was sometimes employed by earlier composers such as Zoilo and Nanino (Fischer 1979: 315, 317) but later examples are almost always through-composed in motet style. Even so, some composers still pay heed to the cadential pattern of the psalm-tone – e.g. Marino in his *Cum invocarem* of 1596 and Cifra in his *Beatus vir* of 1610 (ibid.: 78–9).

There is a vast amount of Roman polychoral music from the late sixteenth and early seventeenth centuries to be studied,[6] but a number of stylistic developments can at least be signposted. Two trends we observed in the later music of Victoria are paralleled in the music of others that we have seen. The simplification of texture resulting from the greater use of strictly homophonic declamation can be observed in, for example, Nanino (see Schuler 1963) and Giovanelli. The latter's psalm-motet *Laudate Dominum in sanctis*, first published in 1593, is particularly striking in this respect, in tuttis as well as in single-choir phrases (Ex. 43). This extremely pompous idiom, projected onto a grander scale, employing greater and greater numbers of SATB choirs, was the basis of the so-called 'Colossal Baroque' style of occasional music which flourished in Rome from the 1620s onwards (Dixon 1981: 295ff). The other trend, that towards sectionalism with contrasts of scoring, led to increasing diversification of forces in which double-choir passages are set alongside not only sections for smaller numbers of voices in the traditional polyphonic manner, but also true solos, duets etc. made possible by the introduction of the continuo, a step not taken by Victoria, though doubtless encouraged by the

Ex. 43   GIOVANELLI, Laudate Dominum in sanctis

use he and others made of organ parts. This style became known as the *concertato alla Romana* (ibid.: 257, 266ff), and it has a through-composed equivalent in which the scoring changes freely throughout. The latter, especially popular in Northern Italy, has been christened the 'textural' style (Roche 1984: 90ff). Such conceptions of form and scoring clearly belong to the Baroque.

Polychoral music in Spain

It is unlikely that Victoria was responsible single-handed for what seems to have been a real and lasting vogue for polychoral church music on the Iberian peninsula – it is more likely that in his 1600 publication he was helping to satisfy a demand. Francisco Guerrero (1528–99), employed at Seville Cathedral from 1549 until his death, left a few polychoral pieces. The earliest is a rather stolid double-choir *Ave Maria* published in 1570 which proceeds largely in free canonic fashion; the later pieces in his second book of motets of 1589 are more refined.

Philippe Rogier

More interesting is the music of Philippe Rogier (*b* c1561, *d* 1596), a musician of Flemish origin who went to the court of Philip II in Madrid as a boy soprano in 1572. He remained until his death, and for the last ten years of his life was chapelmaster. Probably only one-fifth of his music has survived (Wagner in preface to Opera, vol. 1: xii), but polychoral music forms an important part of it. Following the completion of the extraordinary palace-monastery of El Escorial by 1584 and the completion of the organs by 1590, Rogier wrote music for three choirs and three organs (ibid.: x).

Laudate Dominum in sanctis (Opera vol. 2: 201), surviving in two different

manuscripts in Valencia, is a conventional psalm-motet, mostly homophonic
after an imitative opening for the first choir. Rogier's only printed collection of
motets (Naples, 1595) contains an eight-part *Regina coeli* (Opera vol. 3: 106)
with a number of interesting points. It is very sectional, with a fermata after
each 'Alleluia'. After the first two sections in fairly broad imitative style (with
hints of the chant), 'Resurrexit sicut dixit' comes as a shock in *note nere* with
dotted rhythms, though Choir 1 reintroduces white notes. The 'Alleluia' which
follows is most original; after varied antiphonal repetitions in *note nere*,
Choir 1 reintroduces the broad style, finishing on its own à 4 after an interrup-
tion from Choir 2 in small notes (Ex. 44). The same material is used again in
the final 'Alleluia' in triple time and finally leads to a duple-time tutti.

   A motet for three four-part choirs (SSAT/SATB/SATB), *Verbum caro factum est* (Opera vol. 2: 186), survives in manuscript at El Escorial (Ms. Pluteo

Ex. 44   ROGIER, Regina coeli

56). There is a separate *basso seguente* part for each choir, each with an F_4 clef; that for the high first choir is designated 'arpa', the others 'organo'. In addition there is a kind of 'master' bass part called a *guion* for the guidance of the conductor. The writing for the bass parts is spatial. Once again we encounter very strong contrast between 'black' and 'white' note-values, this time notated under the *note nere* time signature. Much use is made of lively antiphonal repetitions of short phrases. The words 'gloriam ejus' are passed twice around all the choirs in turn before a tutti, with a logical and interesting closed tonal scheme:

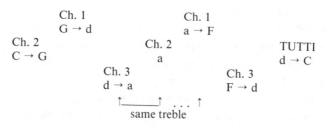

The *Missa Domine in virtute tua* (Opera vol. 2: 111) is based on Palestrina's inconsistently polychoral motet of 1572; Rogier's Mass is spatially conceived – indeed the bass parts sometimes move in unison. The material borrowed from Palestrina falls into two categories: (1) four-part music which is treated antiphonally and (2) tutti ideas which are reworked extensively to end sections. No antiphonal material is borrowed as such. The metamorphosis which the opening motto undergoes as the Mass proceeds is worthy of Lasso.

The ground plans of several movements of the *Missa Domine Dominus noster* are similar in many respects to the *Missa Domine in virtute tua*, but the work as a whole is much more flamboyant with more contrast of harmonic rhythm and more extensive use of lively imitation between the choirs. Its style invites the label 'Baroque', and there is some unconventional dissonance. Rogier's approach to antiphonal repetition is very free and refreshing; homophonic phrases are usually imitated in rhythm only – the tonality and/ or the vertical arrangement of voices is almost always altered. The Mass is probably based on a motet of Rogier's formerly in the library of John IV of Portugal. It has come down to us in two versions: one for double choir ($G_2C_2?F_3/G_2C_2C_3F_3$) with one voice lost (Opera vol. 2: 1, from El Escorial Ms. 79–10), the other for three choirs ($G_2C_2C_3F_3/G_2G_2C_2C_3/G_2C_2C_3C_4$) (ibid.: 42, from El Escorial Ms. 83–3), which is presumably an arrangement of the two-choir version. The inequality of the choirs in the three-choir version means that there cannot be straightforward sharing-out of material without adjustments at least to the vertical ordering of the voices. The two settings make a fascinating comparison, which reveals the following processes:

(1) Antiphonal sections are shared among the choirs with some (but surprisingly little) additional repetition. On occasion, material is even omitted or tightened up.

(2) Tuttis are rewritten using the same ideas and the same harmonic sequence but with different voice-leading.

(3) Two passages in the Credo are completely recomposed for single choir à 4.

(4) Because of the different composition of the choirs, vocal lines are often transposed and/or exchanged in the three-choir version. There is no question of one version being inferior; the three-choir version is a skilful adaption.

Both masses, like *Verbum caro*, have a *basso seguente* part for each choir (always 'organo') with an additional *guion*. In the tuttis of the three-choir setting, the vocal parts of Choir 2 are harmonically incomplete, producing numerous 6/4 chords. The organ line therefore does not double the lowest voice-part in such passages. Choirs 1 and 3 are spatially conceived, so that the effect is rather like adding harmonically self-sufficient organ-parts to Giovanni Gabrieli's normal three-choir arrangement (see Chapter 7). Of considerable interest is the fact that the organ-parts and *guion* in the three-choir version are notated a fourth lower than the vocal parts would require. The editor of the complete works, Lavern Wagner, suggests that the organs must sound a fourth higher; it is surely more likely (cf. the slightly different case of Victoria's *Salve* Mass) that the *chiavette* used in the vocal parts indicate downward transposition. Wagner does not suggest a date for these El Escorial manuscripts, and without seeing them one wonders whether they might represent early to middle seventeenth-century practice; it is known that Rogier's music was performed in Toledo Cathedral as late as 1669 (Opera vol. 1: xi).

From Iberia to the New World

As in Italy, so in Spain the volume of polychoral music composed toward the close of the sixteenth century and into the seventeenth was enormous. Spanish contemporaries of Victoria who cultivated it included Alonso Lobo (*b* c1555, *d* 1617) and Bernardo de Peralta Escudero (also *d* 1617). Their successors included Sebastián Aguilera de Heredia (*b* c1565, *d* 1627), Juan Bautista Comes (1582–1643), Sebastián López de Velasco (late sixteenth century – c1650), Carlos Patiño (*d* 1675), the Netherlands-born Mateo Romero (1575 or 1576 – 1647) and the Portuguese Duarte Lobo (?1565–1646). It is perhaps not surprising that, along with triumphalist Baroque architecture, Counter-reformation Europe also exported its musical complement, the polychoral style, to Central and South America. As Robert Stevenson has shown (1954, 1970), sources in the New World contain a considerable amount of multi-voiced music by Spanish composers, including most of those mentioned above.

VENICE: THE GRAND CLIMAX

Andrea Gabrieli: founder of the Venetian style

It may seem strange to credit Andrea Gabrieli (*b c*1533, *d* 1585)[1] with the foundation of the Venetian style, an honour usually bestowed on Willaert. I have no wish to deprive Willaert of his deserved reputation: he is a front-rank composer whose work is crucial to the development of the Italian madrigal and to the evolution of pan-Italian church music in the later sixteenth century. Clearly too his love of sonority and predilection for clear, syllabic declamation within each voice are part of the background to the Venetian style. However, his music does not yet typify the Venetian idiom as it is popularly understood – rich sonority, colourful harmony and lively interplay of forces; that style is quintessentially represented by the music of the Gabrielis, and nowhere more than in their polychoral music.

Now that we know that Willaert's psalms are not *salmi spezzati* in quite the sense that we once thought (Bryant 1981a), it is even more apparent that there is a large stylistic gap between Willaert's quietly liturgical psalms and Andrea's extrovert multi-voiced motets. Although clearly due in large measure to functional considerations, the difference lies also in the two composers' perceptions of the polychoral medium and its possibilities; Willaert, of course, left no other works for double choir. There is an apparent discontinuity in our knowledge of the history of *cori spezzati* in Venice, partly owing to the absence of sixteenth-century sources in the Biblioteca Marciana representing the repertoire in St Mark's in the middle decades of the century. Rore, who occupied the post of *maestro di cappella* at St Mark's between Willaert and Zarlino, does not seem to have composed polychoral motets.

It is our contention that Andrea, who was appointed to the first organ in 1566, four years after Willaert's death, was more of an innovator than he has been given credit for. Some part may have been played by Annibale Padovano, organist at St Mark's from 1552 to 1565, and Claudio Merulo, organist from 1557 to 1584. Not much polychoral music has survived by Annibale, though it includes his astonishing twenty-four-part Mass composed in or before 1568, discussed in Chapter 4. Merulo's sacred works survive in printed collections of 1594 and (posthumously) 1609, for which we possess no chronology (Debes 1964).

There is no documentary evidence now linking Andrea with Willaert,[2] though he must surely have known Willaert's music. At least as important to his development as a musician was the fact that he spent some of the earlier part of his career outside the *Serenissima*. In 1562 he was amongst the retinue of musicians under Lasso which accompanied Albrecht V of Bavaria to the crowning of Emperor Maximilian II at Frankfurt am Main; Albrecht is the dedicatee of Andrea's book of five-part motets published three years later. He formed connections (later maintained by Giovanni) with the Fugger family of Augsburg and with Archduke Karl at Graz. Andrea's first book of masses (1572) is dedicated to the latter.

Earliest multi-voiced works

It seems likely, then, that Andrea would have got to know Lasso's early poly-choral music, which began to be printed from 1564 onwards. The Austrian connection also demands attention, above all because Giovanelli's *Novus thesaurus musicus* ($1568^{(2-6)}$), printed in Venice but containing mainly music by composers in Habsburg employ, includes the first two multi-voiced motets by Andrea to be published: *Lucide ceu fulvo* à 8 ($1568^{(6)}$: cantus p. 453) and *Deus misereatur nostri* à 12 (ibid.: 457). *Lucide* (mod. edn, Dunning 1974: 217), 'in praise of the Most Serene Prince Ferdinand, Archduke of Austria', is a fair imitation of the Viennese style, a kaleidoscope of everchanging four- and five-voice combinations interspersed with tuttis and employing emphatic syllabic word-setting. It is an idiom to which Andrea returned later in, for example, *Deus qui beatum Marcum* and *O crux splendidior*.[3]

Deus misereatur (mod. edns, 1941: 71 and Dunning 1974: 243) is a setting of the whole of Psalm 66, though without doxology. It is a rare early example of three-choir writing. The use of more than two choirs allows an increased range of tone colour (in some situations involving instrumental as well as vocal colours), more complex interaction between choirs and the possibility of semi-tuttis involving fewer choirs than the full tutti, though at the expense of the natural symmetry and balance of the double-choir medium. A danger, which Andrea avoids, is over-use of antiphonal repetition with insufficient variation. Andrea's search for colour here goes further than the primary contrast between the choirs ($G_2C_2C_3C_4/C_1C_3C_4F_4/C_4C_4C_4F_4$), set out at the beginning when he gives a half-verse to each in turn before a tutti: the first half of verse 4 is set twice in triple time for à 6 antiphonal groups which draw two voices from each choir.

In verses 3, 5 and 6 the psalmist supplies partial verbal repetition, which stimulates Andrea to a dissective process representing in embryo a technique he was later to develop with great subtlety without such textual prompting. In verse 3, for example, the text admits of a truncated repetition by Choir 1 and then Choir 2 of a phrase first heard in Choir 2 and varied harmonically by Choir 3:

[Phrases in brackets are additional repetitions introduced by the composer]
verse 3a: Confiteantur tibi populi Deus: Choir 2
        (Confiteantur tibi populi Deus:)   Choir 3
verse 3b: Confiteantur tibi   Choir 1
        (Confiteantur tibi)   Choir 2
        populi omnes.   à 9 (Choir 3 + $C_4C_4F_4$ of Choir 1 + C_1F_4 of Choir 2)

The general texture is not unreminiscent of the early psalmists – a little stiff and at times completely homophonic. In the tuttis there are also pompous repeated notes and fanfare-like writing. An interesting revision occurs in the 1587 edition which is similar in intent to those later re-workings in Roman manuscripts of Lasso's early psalm-motets. The pseudo-imitation at the beginning of Choir 3's first phrase is virtually eliminated, so that it is shortened by one breve in the original note-values and a more block-like interface between the choirs results.

The *Concerti* volume

Almost all Andrea's remaining multi-voiced sacred works,[4] including all the polychoral ones, are to be found in the *Concerti* of 1587, edited after his death by Giovanni. Evidence of Andrea's continuing reputation in Germany (and perhaps already a vogue there for *cori spezzati*) is to be found in the rapidity with which Nuremberg anthologists reprinted many of them soon after 1587. Listed below are the sacred works for eight or more voices by Andrea in *Concerti* together with the earliest of these concordances, which occur chiefly in Lindner's collections; it will be seen that the German reprints favour joyful rather than introspective pieces:

[Details of the publications are given in the Bibliography]

20.	Benedictus Dominus	à 8,	2 choirs	1590[5] no. 65
21.	Expurgate vetus fermentum	à 8,	2 choirs	1588[2] no. 12
22.	Egredimini et videte	à 8,	2 choirs	1590[5] no. 66
23.	Beati immaculati	à 8,	2 choirs	
24.	Congratulamini	à 8,		1588[2] no. 11
25.	O salutaris hostia	à 8,	2 choirs	
26.	Exsurgat Deus	à 8,	2 choirs	1588[2] no. 47
27.	Quem vidistis, pastores?	à 8,	2 choirs	1588[2] no. 2
28.	Deus in nomine tuo	à 8,	2 choirs	
29.	O crux splendidior	à 8,		1590[5] no. 21
30.	Deus, qui beatum Marcum	à 8		
31.	Jubilate Deo	à 8,	2 choirs	1588[2] no. 53
32.	Ave regina	à 8,	2 choirs	
34.	Deus, Deus meus respice	à 10		
35.	Laudate Dominum	à 10,	2 choirs	1588[2] no. 43
36.	Exsultate justi	à 10,	2 choirs	1588[2] no. 42
38.	Benedicam Dominum	à 12,	3 choirs	1588[2] no. 50
39.	Deus misereatur nostri	à 12,	3 choirs	1588[2] no. 51
41.	Kyrie eleison	à 12,	3 choirs	
42.	Et in terra	à 16,	4 choirs	

43.	Sanctus	à 12, 3 choirs
44.	Magnificat	à 12, 3 choirs 1600[1]

[Nos. 33, 37 and 40 are by Giovanni]

Chronology

The problem of the chronology of Andrea's multi-voiced motets in *Concerti* has until recently seemed insoluble. Those of Lasso survive in prints and manuscripts from throughout his career, yielding a rough chronology for the majority and hence a tentative stylistic yardstick for those which were published posthumously. With Andrea the posthumous *Concerti* volume is our primary source for nearly all the pieces. The musical sources tell us only that *Deus misereatur* and *Lucide ceu fulvo* date from Andrea's German travels earlier in his career or else from very soon after his return to Venice; all that can be said about the remainder is that they all probably date from after his return to Venice in 1566.

There has always been a strong case for connecting the Mass Movements, nos. 41–3, with the visit of the Japanese ambassadors in 1585, when on 29 June mass was sung with four choirs (Sansovino 1663: 457–8). Neither of the Gabrielis was prolific in the provision of music for the ordinary of the mass and Andrea's Gloria is the only mass movement by either which is scored for four choirs. If this music was written specially it may represent the composer's swan-song. Andrea died two months later and had already been ill for three months (Morell 1983: 110). The texts of two motets connect so strongly with the Turkish campaigns of 1569–73 that it seems highly likely that they were composed at that time. *O salutaris hostia*, though taken from the liturgy (a hymn in honour of the Blessed Sacrament), is singularly appropriate as a prayer before battle:

> Bella premunt hostilia,
> Da robur, fer auxilium.
>
> (Our enemies prepare for war;
> Give us strength, come to our aid.)

Benedictus Dominus, a freely-compiled text, is clearly a celebration of some great military victory like that of Lepanto in 1571:

Pugnavit Samson, pugnavit Gedeon, vicit Samson, vicit Gedeon.
Pugnaverunt nostri in nomine Domini; pugnavit Dominus pro nobis, et vicit Dominus inimicos ejus.

(Samson fought, Gideon fought, Samson was victorious, Gideon was victorious.
Ours [i.e. our troops] fought in the name of the Lord; the Lord fought for us, and the Lord was victorious over his enemies.)

It is doubtful whether stylistic analysis is of much help in dating the *Concerti* pieces. Andrea seems to have developed his particular brand of large-scale ceremonial music, using as models Lasso and the Viennese composers, after settling back in Venice. *Deus misereatur* does strike one as primitive in some respects, but the same cannot be said of any other piece. On the other hand, the massive blocks of sound created in the Magnificat seem to belong to the same world as the Mass movements and would suggest that it too is a late work. Since these *concerti* were intended to impress, Andrea may have deliberately sought variety. As a madrigalist, of course, his response to the text, though by no means extreme for the time, could result in a stylistic and formal range wide enough to transcend questions of chronology. In other words, stylistic development may be easy to chart when we have the chronology, but it is a minefield when we have not.

In a thorough study of the Venetian archives, David Bryant (1979, 1981b) has shed a great deal of light on the function of this repertory. The clear distinction between large-scale occasional music and (usually) more modest liturgical music which is clearly seen in Andrea's output is borne out by the archives, and there is evidence that the Venetian usage of the terms *concerti* and *motetti* respectively refers to this distinction. Unfortunately the archival sources nowhere name specific pieces. In an attempt to grapple with the chronological problem, Bryant assumes that when Andrea was required to compose a *concerto* for a particular occasion in the politico-religious life of the Republic the text was generally taken from the proper of the day in question but was also capable of a double interpretation. This assumption enables him to assign virtually all the pieces in the sacred portion of the *Concerti* volume either to one-off ceremonies or to liturgical feasts known to have been celebrated with particular pomp. As an example, he assigns *O crux splendidior* to 3 May 1577, the foundation ceremony for the Church of the *Redentore*. The feast was the Discovery of the Holy Cross and mass was celebrated in the presence of the Doge in the Chiesa di Santa Croce on the Giudecca. The building of the *Redentore* was in fulfilment of a vow concerning the lifting of the plague of 1575–7, and the text of *O crux splendidior* (an antiphon at the Magnificat for both the *Inventio* and *Exaltatio S. Crucis*), with its concentration on Christ's bearing of our sins on the Cross, becomes an allegory for the mercy of God in bringing about a cessation of the plague.

It is not necessary to elaborate further on Dr Bryant's argument, and the interested reader is referred to his thesis (1981b). The neatness with which the circumstantial evidence that he has assembled accounts for the pieces in *Concerti* leads him to some startling conclusions (1981b: 81–3): that almost all the Venetian occasional *concerti* in the period 1566–85 were composed by Andrea Gabrieli and that almost all have been preserved in the 1587 print. We might add that the highly political as well as religious function of these works, despite their apparently liturgical texts, shows how appropriate it was that Andrea should have modelled them to some extent on that great corpus of state music by Habsburg composers. Bryant has attached firm dates to some pieces, more tentative ones to others, and some remain unassigned, mainly

those associated with the great church festivals of Christmas and Easter, or
with the Blessed Virgin (1981b: especially 72–9). Further progress may be
made along these lines, but for the moment it seems safer to base our discussion of Andrea's sacred polychoral music on areas of structural interest largely
irrespective of chronology.

The Lepanto motets

If indeed they are contemporaneous, *Benedictus Dominus* and *O salutaris
hostia* could hardly be more strongly contrasted in both text and music.
Benedictus (transcr. Carver 1980, vol. 2: 410) is extrovert, revelling in the
savage declamation of 'Pugnavit Samson' etc. (Ex. 45). It relies on sweeping

Ex. 45   A. GABRIELI, Benedictus Dominus

gestures and lively syncopated textures rather than subtlety of phrase structure, with plenty of tuttis and a longer-than-usual concluding triple-time
section for 'Laetamini et exsultate'. By using more restrained technical means
O salutaris hostia (transcr. Carver 1980, vol. 2: 435) effectively presents the
opposite emotions: doubt, fear, solemn invocation. Dignified block-like
antiphony alternates with distinctly subdued tuttis which become symbols of
the communal cry for help. It was doubtless by Andrea's restraint in a medium
in which he knew so well how to exult that his original listeners would have
sensed crisis reflected in the music. The expressive effect of the chordal writing
is a long way from the psalm-tone regulated declamation of, say, Santacroce.
The harmony is controlled with deep insight. Persistent *tierce de picardie*
cadences in G and D dorian, occasionally with a phrygian inflection, have a
cumulative effect of restlessness (Ex. 46). The insecurity of *O salutaris hostia*
does not approach the near neurosis of some late works by Giovanni, and the
structural equilibrium of the classic polychoral style is retained.

Ex. 46 A. GABRIELI, O salutaris hostia

Spatial writing in Andrea Gabrieli's polychoral music

To some extent of course the idea of a 'classic' polychoral style is an abstraction whose definition is by no means strictly applicable even to some Venetian polychoral music. We found in the *Novus thesaurus musicus* that thoroughgoing polychoral pieces were rare. Although by comparison Andrea tends towards strict polychoralism, we still find works ostensibly for two or even three choirs which, to a greater or lesser extent, mix voices from different choirs outside tuttis. This happens on occasion in *Expurgate, Exsurgat, Quem vidistis, Deus in nomine tuo, Jubilate Deo, Deus misereatur*, and, especially, *Beati immaculati*. Not surprisingly the theorists' recommendations about bass parts in tuttis are not observed in these cases. The only pieces which qualify in this sense as spatial polychoral works, avoiding 6/4 chords within each choir, are *Egredimini, Ave regina, Laudate Dominum, Benedicam Dominum* and the Magnificat. In the Mass movements the rules are consistently observed only in the lowest two choirs in Kyrie II, Gloria and Sanctus. This is not due to carelessness: with the possible exception of *Quem vidistis* Andrea's attitude appears consistent within each piece.

In St Mark's, of course, the organ galleries from which double-choir motets (as opposed to *Salmi spezzati*) were performed (Bryant 1981a: 180–6) are not very far apart and the organisation of the bass parts not so crucial from an acoustical point of view. On the other hand, if two organs were used, each organist would presumably need a harmonically viable bass to work from. It is tempting to suggest, and perhaps future research will shed light on the matter, that when spaced performance was envisaged and a sufficient number of organs was available, the bass parts were composed spatially; that when there was room to split the choir but not to space the groups appreciably (as at Munich, for example) and perhaps only one or no organ was available, only one of the lowest parts functioned as a bass in tuttis; and that when there was not sufficient room to split the choir at all, polychoral writing was not attempted. In any case, rapid antiphonal exchanges would be difficult to manage at a great distance, as would some of the rhythmically complex tuttis in *note nere* style, which are by no means restricted to pieces notated with a $\mathbb{c}$ signature nor excluded from those with a seemingly spatial approach to the bass parts.

Cadential dissonance

Andrea, like Ruffino and Willaert, quite often allows clashes between the cadential suspension and the leading note itself, the latter either sharpened or, as in one form of the so-called English cadence, flattened. These 'clash' cadences seem to arise as one solution to the problem of cadential part-writing in eight or more parts. (Composers like Palestrina and Lasso avoid doubling the leading note in these situations.) The clashes take on an archaic, mannered, yet somehow peculiarly Venetian sound in Andrea's music. The clash with the unraised leading note is the more common, occurring at cadences in G and D modes where the seventh of the mode is a tone below the final. Most of the smaller numbers of clashes with the sharpened leading note occur in the C, F and B flat modes, though a small number are found in D and A modes where an accidental is supplied. Whereas in Ruffino there is a possibility that clashes with the unraised leading note are signals to the singer with the suspension not to apply *musica ficta* to his cadential phrase, it seems likely that Andrea intends an oblique false relation in such cases: the unraised leading note is always quitted before the cadential voice resolves its suspension. Certainty is not possible, however, since the normal convention in the *Concerti* volume is not to supply sharps or naturals at cadential suspensions.

The dissonant effect of these cadential clashes is in most cases mitigated in that the notes which clash are placed in different choirs, though notable exceptions occur, particularly in the Magnificat (1941: 48), where at bar 55 the clashing voices are a semitone apart in the same choir. Such clashes, though seeming to be archaisms, do not in fact point to an earlier date for the pieces in which they occur. If anything, their concentration in the pieces one suspects of being late works for other reasons (the Mass movements and the Magnificat) rather suggests the reverse.

Psalm-motets and Magnificat

It is instructive at this point to look back at what we considered to be the primary impulses to polychoral writing: dialogic, liturgical and purely musical. Straight away we can say that all Andrea's pieces fall into the third category (unless we admit also a possible 'environmental' factor hinted at above); yet the influence of liturgical antiphony may still be discerned in a few cases. One text, that of *Quem vidistis, pastores?,* is actually a dialogue, but unlike Bonardo, Andrea does not treat it as such (Anthology nos. 5 & 13). Eight pieces take their texts from the psalms, in three cases setting a complete psalm, though without the doxology of liturgical usage:

Beati immaculati	Psalm 118: 1–5
Exsurgat Deus	Psalm 67: 1–3
Deus, in nomine tuo	Psalm 53: 1–4
Jubilate Deo	Psalm 99: complete (5 verses)
Laudate Dominum	Psalm 150: complete (5 verses)
Exsultate justi	Psalm 32: 1–5
Benedicam Dominum	Psalm 33: 1–5
Deus misereatur	Psalm 66: complete (6 verses)

Laudate Dominum for two five-part choirs (transcr. Carver 1980, vol. 2: 465) sticks closest to liturgical antiphony. The first four verses are set for alternate choirs, each mediant and ending marked by a clear-cut cadence, though without any sign of adherence to a Gregorian formula. The texture throughout is polyphonically-enlivened homophony in the tradition of Willaert, though with less imitation and with occasional emphatic declamation. Antiphonal repetition does not appear until verse 5a in stately triple time, and the piece is crowned with a twice-stated tutti back in ¢ . *Jubilate Deo* (mod. edn, 1965: 15) is decidedly more complex. It begins with three verses sung by alternate choirs, but with much variety of declamation and some text repetition. Thereafter tuttis alternate with antiphonal repetition until a final *concertato*-style tutti which is heard twice with the cadence prolonged the second time as an effective close to the piece. As we have already seen, *Deus misereatur* does not conform to liturgical antiphony, though it shares the simple homophonic textures of the early *salmo spezzato* repertory.

The five pieces setting portions of psalms are demonstrably farther removed from any concept of liturgical psalmody. None begins with any semblance of verse-by-verse antiphony. *Beati immaculati* (transcr. Carver 1980, vol. 2: 427) perhaps comes closest to a ritual structure by reflecting half-verse divisions in changing voice-combinations. This highly unconventional piece has virtually no antiphonal repetition until the final section; up until then preoccupation with various five-, six- and seven-part textures (though these almost always include all the voices of one choir or the other) takes precedence over antiphony. The treatment of the last verse to be set is worth mentioning. Beginning à 4 with Choir 1 only, Gabrieli writes in a *crescendo* by number of voices (à 3, à 4, à 5), leading to a tutti re-statement of the first half of the verse which unleashes syncopated *concertato* imitation which contrasts markedly with the dignified style of earlier portions of the piece. This is climax by contrast, of which the Gabrielis were masters. The remaining four psalm-motets all begin non-ritual fashion with antiphonal repetition.

On turning to the Magnificat for three choirs (mod. edn, D'Alessi 1941: 48) it seems at the outset as if Andrea has returned to the realm of liturgical antiphony, and indeed the piece must have been intended for liturgical per-

formance at vespers in St Mark's on a great feast-day. The doxology is set, and
the incipit is left in chant for the only time in these works (other than the
Gloria). Moreover, the outline of tone 8 may be discerned in verse 1b (Choir 2)
and verse 2 (Choir 3), and the alternation of G and C cadences appropriate to
the tone continues to the end of verse 3. The second half of that verse breaks
into demonstrative antiphonal imitation leading to a devastating tutti for
'omnes generationes' which nonetheless cadences on G with a suspicion of a
paraphrase of the chant in the tenor of Choir 2. There, however, we leave the
world of liturgical antiphony again; the remainder of the piece proceeds in a
highly sectionalised manner with modulations to new tonal areas and many
cadences. Andrea's approach to the text is at times highly dramatic. Choir 2
demonstrates the Lord's strength with battle-music (Ex. 47). The phrase

Ex. 47   A. GABRIELI, Magnificat

'Dispersit superbos mente cordis sui' is then dissected by all three choirs. The
exaltation of the humble is portrayed by antiphonal imitation which passes
from low to high through each choir in turn. The emptiness of the departing
rich is revealed when their sumptuous tutti tails off in a mere (!) eight parts.
The sudden, unanimously-attacked tutti is an important formal device in this
piece, occurring no less than five times, four of them in the doxology, where its
cumulative effect creates a thrilling conclusion. This is the most sectional,
block-like, spatially-aware piece we have yet analysed.

Mature antiphonal technique

Awareness of space is certainly a new feature which we find at times in Andrea
but not really in, say, Phinot or Lasso. It seems to me, though, that what really

distinguishes Andrea's work in its most mature manifestations is the even more sophisticated way in which he handles the interaction between choirs. He is as subtle as Phinot and Lasso in his ability to inject variety into the antiphony, avoiding straightforward repetition. Indeed, hardly ever is his antiphonal repetition even at the same pitch, except significantly in *Egredimini et videte*, which is, uniquely for him, scored for two equal choirs (mod. edn, 1965: 9). Where he surpasses both Phinot and Lasso in polychoral technique is in his ability to build initial statements via imitation and dissection into longer musical paragraphs which, although mosaic-like in construction, exhibit a sense of growth and expansion.

In order to illustrate this we shall look in some detail at one piece for two choirs, *Quem vidistis, pastores?*, and one for three, *Benedicam Dominum*. *Quem vidistis* (Anthology no. 13) is not, as we have seen, treated by Andrea as a dialogue. He translates the tension and expectancy of the situation portrayed in the text into purely musical terms. His compositional technique could not have been so subtle if he had employed a strict dialogic division of the ensemble and deprived himself of double-choir interaction until perhaps the closing 'Alleluia'. Instead, he characterises each phrase of the opening question and answer, forging the contribution of each group of protagonists into a little tableau.

The impatience of the anonymous questioners is expressed by means of a number of musical images. After the opening phrase (Choir 1, reiterated tutti) has ended on a D major chord in bar 7, Choir 2 initiates 'dicite' on an unexpected B flat chord. This word is then alternated between the choirs, the bass parts clearly showing the underlying circle-of-fifths progression leading back to D. Despite many I–V–I bass progressions there is no formal syncopated cadence until that in the dominant in Choir 1 at bars 21–2, the last statement of 'annunciate nobis'. The texture builds to eight parts three times, the last two involving revolving imitation of 'annunciate nobis', vividly portraying the haste of the questioners enquiring one after another. A new syncopated homophonic phrase ('in terris quis apparuit') is echoed with a subtle tonal modification (bars 22–5) and the paragraph ends with a résumé of the material from 'dicite'; 'annunciate nobis' is heard in diminution and 'quis apparuit' in augmentation with a drawn-out cadence in C.

The shepherds now sing their reply, in which Andrea discerns three images and gives each a distinct musical equivalent (bars 30–7):

Natum vidimus	Ch. 1 sustained, mainly à 3, awestruck
et choros Angelorum	Ch. 1 homophonic, syncopated, excited
collaudantes Dominum	Ch. 2 homophonic, unsyncopated triple time

With three simple strokes he thus depicts the awe and wonder of the shepherds' contemplation of the manger, their excitement at seeing heavenly beings and the dignity of the latter's praise of God (in 'Trinitarian' triple time). In isolation this exposition is musically disjointed, but Andrea now takes these fragments and expands them through varied repetition to produce a para-

graph comparable in weight with that allotted to the opening question. The
sophisticated use of harmonic progression and tonality already seen in the
opening paragraph is continued in the shepherds' music:

bar

30	Natum vidimus	Ch. 1 cadence: perfect, g
33	et choros Angelorum	Ch. 1 cadence: imperfect, d
35	collaudantes Dominum	Ch. 2 begins on B flat triad after previous A major; cadence: perfect, g, ♮3rd
38	Natum vidimus	Ch. 1 begins as before, but cadence sidestepped as Ch. 2 enters a 5th lower; section ends (Ch. 1 only) with imperfect cadence, g
47	et choros Angelorum	Ch. 1 as before
49	collaudantes Dominum	Ch. 1 A–B flat shift retained but phrase now cadences in B flat
52	et choros Angelorum	Ch. 2 mediant progression B flat to G major, the remainder a 5th lower than Ch. 1 at 33 & 47
54	collaudantes Dominum	Tutti cadencing in g, ♮3rd
58	collaudantes Dominum	Ch. 2 g → B flat
61	collaudantes Dominum	Ch. 1 B flat → g
65	collaudantes Dominum	Tutti B flat → d, ♯3rd

Characterisation does not exclude thematic unity – 'Quem vidistis' (bars 1–4),
'annunciate nobis' (11–12) and 'Natum vidimus' (31–2) all use the descending
tetrachord from the dominant and at other pitches. The closing 'Alleluia'
begins with three antiphonal statements of a plagal close on D, leading into a
concertato-like imitative phrase in *note nere* which resolves in a perfect
cadence in G dorian. This process is repeated and capped with a broad plagal
cadence. Such is the method Andrea employs (and Giovanni after him) in
putting across the essence of the text in terms of syllable pattern, imagery and
emotional content without sacrificing coherent and satisfying musical
structure.

Andrea's mosaic-like method, especially when allied to a consistent and
spatially-handled choral division, results in music which is far removed in style
from the Flemish idiom in which lie its roots. This is especially apparent in
Andrea's mature three-choir works, including the Magnificat and *Benedicam
Dominum*, and the extra choir can make the choral interaction still more
complex. The opening of *Benedicam* (Anthology no. 14) shows how extreme
contrasts of material can become. Choir 2's spacious opening phrase is varied
by Choir 3, but when Choir 1 enters with 'Semper laus ejus in ore meo' it is to
lively syncopated homophony in *note nere* of a type normally reserved for
later in a piece; indeed, Andrea does not at this point integrate the two rhythmic layers: Choir 2 and Choir 3 proceed with new material but still in spacious
vein. The long-range manipulation of these two rhythmic layers is an example
of the importance of harmonic rhythm as a compositional parameter in
Venetian music.

The paragraphs of *Benedicam* are built either on one phrase allied to one
musical idea, or on a longer phrase divided into two distinct ideas. Thus
at bar 29, after a tutti, the words 'et laetentur' are stated by Choir 1 in a
syncopated homophonic phrase which is taken up in sequential modulations

by Choirs 2 and 3, concluding with a semi-tutti version for Choirs 1 and 3. Choir 2 (bar 32) then introduces a homophonic setting (*x*) in longer note-values of verse 3a, 'Magnificat Dominum mecum'. This is taken up a third higher in tonal level by Choir 1 which adds verse 3b, 'et exaltemus nomen ejus in idipsum', in contrasting small note-values (*y*). Choir 3 (bar 40) takes up both ideas, but is pre-empted by Choir 2 in close imitation of the second phrase (*y*):

	Choir 1		
	x+y		
	B flat → d		
Choir 2		Choir 2	
x		*y*	
g → B flat			
		Choir 3	Choir 3
		x	*y*
		d → F	F → g

Each choir sings each phrase of the text once, but the statements interact in a quite sophisticated manner. The tonal scheme is self-contained and carefully structured: we leave the tonic via modulations in rising thirds and return to it at bar 45.

In the remainder of the piece spacious choral imitation of single phrases and sonorous tuttis progress excitingly into looser *concertato* with lively small note-values, as at bars 65ff ('et illuminamini') and 72ff ('non confundentur'). There is always a feeling of logical development, as for instance in the close thematic relationship between the 'Accedite' and 'et illuminamini' phrases (bars 62, 65), redolent of Andrea's experience of instrumental music. As so often, the final section is repeated (from 'et facies vestrae') and crowned with a plagal cadence. It may be that the agitated imitative textures of 'non confundentur' express the possibility of being confounded amidst a welter of notes!

The Mass movements

Andrea's most ambitious sacred composition was the Gloria for four choirs, in all probability intended as a companion piece to the three-choir Kyrie and Sanctus movements which flank it in *Concerti* (mod. edn of all three, 1941: 1). The print is rather ambiguous on this point: these are the only Mass movements, but it is worth pointing out that in order to keep them together the printer (or Giovanni?) disrupted the predominant ordering system, which is by number of voices. The interval of the minor third, ascending then descending, with or without an intervening note, binds the movements together thematically in the manner of a head-motif (Ex. 48).

The mode of the resulting 'Mass' remains an anomaly. Kyrie I and Gloria are in untransposed dorian with a D final, whereas Christe, Kyrie II and Sanctus are in transposed dorian, G final with a one-flat signature. Whatever may have happened when the music was performed, it was usual in the sixteenth century

Ex. 48   A. GABRIELI, Mass movements

(a) Kyrie I, altus, bar 1

(b) Christe, Ch. 2, sextus, bar 1

(c) Christe, Ch. 2, cantus III, bar 13

(d) Kyrie II, Ch. 1, altus, bar 1

(e) Gloria, Ch. 3, cantus, bar 1

(f) Gloria, Ch. 1, cantus, bar 81

(g) Sanctus, Ch. 1, altus, bar 1

(h) Sanctus, Ch. 2, cantus II, bar 8

for the movements of a mass to have a consistent key signature and modal final.[5] Possible light is shed on the problem if we examine the choir labelled 'Capella de Cantori' in Kyrie II, Gloria and Sanctus. In the Gloria this choir, as we would expect from Praetorius's remarks (1619: 114), has the standard SATB clef combination with an overall range E–c″. In Kyrie II and Sanctus it has *chiavette*, $G_2C_2C_3F_3$, a combination normally assigned to treble instruments with tenor voice, amongst other possibilities (ibid.: 153). The ranges here are respectively G–f″ and B flat–g″, i.e. around a fourth higher than in the Gloria. It is tempting to conclude that, whatever pitch level was chosen for the Gloria,[6] if the same *ripieno* choir was used as the 'Capella' throughout, Kyrie II (and Christe?) and Sanctus may have been sung a fourth lower relatively than notated, giving aural if not notational consistency of final. If this was the case, it remains a mystery why the notation in the print is inconsistent.[7]

The Mass movements stand apart from the other polychoral works in some respects. Though they share especially with the Magnificat total polarisation of the forces into separate choirs and a love of massive tuttis, they are lacking in pictorial characterisation and in the exciting *concertato* textures of, say, *Benedicam Dominum*. They are extraordinarily dignified and ceremonial in character. In St Mark's the ordinary of the mass itself does not seem to have been adorned very frequently with music of such solemnity, so the Japanese ambassadors were highly honoured. Imitation by voices, often in Venetian polychoral music a perfunctory gesture designed to get the piece under way, is at greater length than usual. The opening Kyrie à 5 is entirely in the imitative note-against-note idiom of the post-Willaert generation; the Christe begins with an imitative paragraph for Choir 2 but as Choir 1 enters the texture becomes homophonic, remaining so in wave-like antiphony which overlaps into a tutti which is more polyphonic in texture. Kyrie II and Sanctus expand this scheme to suit their three-choir medium.

The Gloria differs in its approach. It is homophonic from the beginning, a reflection doubtless of the length of its text. It surpasses in architectural splendour even the Magnificat. The addition of the fourth choir would, in liturgical sequence, complete a crescendo of sonority begun in the Kyrie. It is a virtuoso piece of composition, employing a bewildering variety of combinations of the four choirs in antiphonal imitation, overlapping amplification, semi-tuttis and tuttis. There is no melodic development, no obvious repetition or recapitulation except at 'Cum sancto spiritu', which is felt as both a return to the tonic (D dorian) and a clear variant of the opening (see Ex. 48, *e* & *f*). Many of the normal stylistic and formal characteristics of sixteenth-century music are lacking. Even antiphonal repetition, though employed from time to time, does not assume the constructional importance that it usually does in polychoral music at this time – i.e. an importance corresponding to that of imitation by voices in music à 4 or à 5. What then are the chief compositional parameters in this Gloria? They would seem to be scoring and tonality. The interaction between the choirs grafted onto the harmonic framework forms a skeleton which needs the flesh of colourful vocal and instrumental scoring to bring it to life, about which more below.

Andrea's tonal orbit is not exceptionally wide, but his strategic use of subsidiary tonal areas is clearly focussed and to that extent forward-looking. Lest it be thought that the text is tacked on to the outside of the music, it must be emphasised that the positioning of climactic tuttis with their obvious utility in articulating the structure is generally synchronised with the syntax and emphasis of the text. Thus the overlapping of two eight-part groups (Choirs 2 and 4 with 1 and 3) in a sixteen-voice sound at 'Gratias' caps the ascending curve of exultation begun at 'Laudamus'. During the course of this paragraph the tonal centre shifts from D dorian to C ionian ('Adoramus'), back to D dorian ('Glorificamus'), then to F (ionian?) ('Gratias') and on to A aeolian ('propter magnam. . .'), in which there is an extended twelve-part cadence. The subsequent sixteen-part tuttis appropriately stress the glory of Christ ('Jesu Christe' and 'Tu solus altissimus'), whereas human weakness ('miserere nobis') calls forth dispersed imitation by choirs.

I believe Andrea to have been unjustly overshadowed by Giovanni. He was of course a many-sided composer, but in the field of ceremonial, and especially polychoral, music his rôle as an innovator was crucial to the way in which Giovanni's music was to develop.[8] More than that, the best of his multi-voiced music stands comparison with the best of Giovanni's 'classic' phase, for which it served as the model.

Giovanni Gabrieli

The music of Giovanni Gabrieli embraces the peak of the polychoral style, and it naturally occupies the central place in this study. In many respects his career ran parallel to that of his uncle. Like the latter he worked as an organist in Munich, from 1575 or before until at least 1579 (Arnold 1979: 9, 15). He was a full member of the Bavarian ducal household and maintained the German connections begun by Andrea, such as those with the Fugger family. Back in Venice he formed close friendships with the composer Hans Leo Hassler and the merchant Georg Gruber. In time the stimulus Giovanni undoubtedly received from Lasso and his circle bore fruit, and in turn Giovanni had a profound influence on German musicians. He taught, amongst others, Tadei, Aichinger and Schütz, and there was widespread cultivation of polychoral music in the classic Venetian manner in both Catholic and Protestant centres of German-speaking lands.

Whilst Andrea's ceremonial music as preserved in *Concerti* represents only a portion of his output for the church (which included also penitential psalms, masses and small-scale motets), almost all Giovanni's sacred works seem to fall into the occasional or ceremonial category; this can be seen not only in the lavish forces required but also to a great extent in the choice of texts (Bryant 1981b: 143–60, 171–8). These are heavily weighted in the direction of commemorations of specific politico-religious significance to the Venetian state and of purely liturgical commemorations which were celebrated before the Doge with especial pomp. The only piece for as few as five voices is the Kyrie I from the 1615 *Symphoniae sacrae. . .liber secundus*. The largest single group of pieces is for eight voices, and there are nearly twice as many pieces for more than eight voices as there are for fewer.[9]

Motets in *Concerti*

Giovanni included five motets of his own in *Concerti*, for six, seven, eight, ten and twelve voices (Opera vol. 1). The first two are for undivided choir, but the last three show that the polychoral style of what we might term his 'classic' phase was already substantially formed by 1587, and clearly modelled on Andrea's mature polychoral idiom. All are for two choirs of contrasted range; indeed, *Deus, Deus meus* à 10 and *Angelus ad pastores ait* à 12 have the low bass combined with high treble parts which Andrea pioneered. The structure of *Deus, Deus meus* (ibid.: 18) is a classic polychoral statement, and may be summarised as

Ch. 2 – Ch. 1 – Ch. 2 – Ch. 1 – tuttis + antiphony – tutti,

a satisfying musical shape articulating also the shape of the text from its barren opening to more joyful conclusion. In view of later developments we may note also the triple-time 'Alleluias' in the two Nativity pieces, *O magnum mysterium* à 8 and *Angelus ad pastores*.

The *Sacrae symphoniae* (1597)

The core of Giovanni's polychoral output is found in the *Sacrae symphoniae* of 1597 (Opera vols. 1 & 2). Since none of its contents can be precisely dated (see note 10) I shall build up a stylistic picture of the volume as a whole, or rather of its vocal contents, since it also includes fourteen canzonas and two sonatas for eight or more instruments (mod. edn, Benvenuti 1931–2, vol. 2). The simplest statistics can be revealing, as the following list shows:

39 motets:	4 à 6, 4 à 7
	18 à 8 (4 for 1 choir, 14 for 2)
	8 à 10 (all for 2 choirs)
	3 à 12 (2 for 2 choirs, 1 for 3)
	1 à 15 (3 choirs)
	1 à 16 (4 choirs)
miscellaneous liturgical items:	2 magnificats (à 8, 2 choirs; à 12, 3 choirs)
	Nunc dimittis à 14 (3 choirs)
	Kyrie à 8, 8, 12 (2, 2, 3 choirs)
	Gloria à 12 (3 choirs)
	Sanctus à 12 (3 choirs)

Of this substantial large-scale repertory the only non-polychoral works are those for six and seven voices and four of the eight-part ones. Thus the tendency towards pure polychorality (and away from the Viennese style) shown in Andrea's large-scale music is fulfilled in Giovanni's. Moreover, the mixing outside tuttis of voices from different choirs found even in ostensibly polychoral pieces by Andrea is almost non-existent in Giovanni's 1587/1597 phase.

Voice ranges

With regard to the contrast between choirs, looked at for the moment purely from the point of view of clefs, the situation is similar: like his uncle, Giovanni rarely combines equal choirs, and exhibits great variety in the shades of contrast employed. Thus some pieces such as *O Domine Jesu Christe* à 8 remain overall within the normal SATB range (in this case $C_1C_2C_3C_4/C_3C_4C_4F_4$), whilst at the other extreme Giovanni extends the overall range even further than Andrea by employing a low B_1 flat in for instance the Magnificat à 12 and Nunc dimittis à 14, and a high c''' in the extraordinary *Maria virgo* à 10 (Opera vol. 2: 66), whose two choirs ($G_1G_2C_1C_2C_3/C_4F_4F_4F_4F_5$) hardly overlap in range at all. In this and other instances unusually wide intervals occur between the choirs when they imitate each other – an octave in *Benedicam Dominum* à 10 and an astonishing eleventh or twelfth in *Maria virgo*, the only piece, by the way, to employ the G_1 clef. In considering such extreme cases we might be tempted to overlook the more subtle shades of sonority; although certain patterns emerge, the number of different clef combinations is large. Whilst Giovanni does use high choirs, the centre of gravity tends to be low. Only three pieces (*Benedicam* and *Maria virgo* already cited, and the three-choir Jubilate à 15) employ more than one clef as high as G_2 or higher, and a bottom choir containing three F clefs is not uncommon. Almost unique, however, is the deep sonority of *Virtute magna* à 12 ($C_1C_2C_3C_4F_3F_4/C_1C_3F_3F_4F_4F_4$).[10]

Performance practice

Consideration of contrast between the choirs in terms of relative pitch is of course only part of the story. It is scarcely possible to rule out entirely vocal performance somewhere in Europe at this time,[11] but certainly in St Mark's, some other churches in Northern Italy, and of course in Germany the Venetian style would have been understood as embracing not just the interplay of contrasting choral groups but an even more colourful layout of forces, including also solo voices and instruments. The choir of St Mark's was by no means large; the *maestro di cappella*, Donato, in 1597 listed three sopranos, five altos, five tenors and four basses (Anthon 1943: 216), and it was precisely to permit the performance of large-scale ceremonial *concerti* (quite possibly in imitation of the sound of the vocal/instrumental ensembles of Munich and other court establishments in the Empire) that St Mark's began to employ instrumentalists. Since *concerti* were primarily occasional pieces, at first only a rather loose arrangement was made in 1568 with one Hieronimo of Udine, who was granted seventy-five ducats annually to provide

with wind instruments and with two of his brothers and other musicians, the *concerti* in the organ lofts which usually take place every year to the honour of the church of St Mark, when the Most Serene Signory comes to church at the time of the solemn festivals of Christmas and Easter, and other festivals throughout the year. . .   (Arnold 1979: 129)

Hieronimo thus assembled whatever ensemble was required, within his resources. In 1576 Giovanni Bassano was appointed as a permanent cornetto player, and in 1582 the situation was stabilised by the establishment of a salaried group of six players, to which others could be added when necessary (Arnold 1979: 138–9).

Giovanni's instrumental music, together with those vocal pieces published in 1615 which have precise instrumentation, gives us a good idea of what instruments were employed along with voices in the earlier 1587/1597 repertory: cornetti of various sizes, trombones in larger numbers, and occasionally a reed, capped-reed or stringed instrument. However, whilst there was probably a customary way of scoring *concerti* in the Basilica, the 1587 and 1597 publications leave the matter in the hands of the *maestro di cappella*. Despite the presence of canzonas for instruments alongside the vocal items in 1597 the latter are laid out to all appearances like ordinary motets with all the parts texted. Virtually the only hint as regards scoring is the presence of the word 'cappella' in a few pieces for three or four choirs, indicating that the choir concerned is a ripieno choir of 'normal' vocal range (usually $C_1C_3C_4F_4$ or $C_2C_3C_4F_4$).

Provided we interpret it with caution, the most detailed source of information concerning the scoring of this classic polychoral music is the third part of Michael Praetorius's *Syntagma musicum* (1619) (see Chapter 8). Praetorius's encyclopaedic interest in instruments naturally led him to attempt to accommodate as many as possible (and perhaps German practice at his time of writing was more colourful in its deployment of forces), but when he mentions instruments, such as cornetti and trombones, which we know to have been in use at St Mark's, then his remarks may have some validity. He was familiar with the music of the Gabrielis, and his suggestions for scoring deal specifically with polychoral music. In addition to the *cappella* concept we glean from Praetorius other general principles of scoring which may be safely applied to the music of Andrea and Giovanni Gabrieli. High choirs may be scored with cornetti and/or violins, the lowest part being sung. Such a practice is entirely consistent with the seeming lack of sopranos in the St Mark's choir. Those high-flown soprano parts are for the brilliant cornettini. Similarly, low choirs may consist of trombones or trombones and bassoons with the top part sung. These possibilities emerge also in the very varied scorings gleaned by Howard Mayer Brown from the descriptions of the Florentine *intermedii* (1973: 62 and *passim*).

We found comparatively few pieces by Andrea in which all the choirs are harmonically self-sufficient, and attempted to explain why this might have been so (see above, pp. 135–6). Not surprisingly, the same is true of Giovanni. In 1587 and 1597 the only double-choir pieces having two such choirs are *Ego sum* à 8, *Domine exaudi* à 10, *Deus qui beatum Marcum* à 10, *Virtute magna* à 12 and *Regina coeli* à 12, and even in these there may be momentary inconsistencies. *Virtute magna* contains instances of a trend which assumes more prominence in the 1615 collections, the *bassus generalis*, with identical writing in the bass of both choirs. In the works for three or four choirs in 1597 Giovanni usually follows Andrea's practice in making the highest choir harmonically dependent on the others in tuttis and semi-tuttis. (Exceptions are the Gloria, unusually for three SATB choirs, and *Jubilate Deo* à 15, which has two equally high choirs, neither harmonically self-sufficient.) This may have something to do with the scoring. Whilst a solo singer might function adequately as the bass of the high choir in single-choir or antiphonal phrases, he is hardly likely to make much contribution to the foundation of a tutti, and Giovanni probably baulked at this date at the idea of having him sing in parallel octaves with the bass of another choir.

Giovanni Gabrieli and his predecessors

A detailed treatment of Giovanni's music piece by piece would require more space than is available here; I shall therefore pick out what seem to me important stylistic and formal traits, beginning with a few comparisons with Giovanni's predecessors other than Andrea. Giovanni's debt to his uncle is undoubtedly enormous, but the influence of Lasso must have been in part direct as well as through Andrea. Though Lasso applied chromaticism sparingly outside those daring early pieces, the *Prophetiae Sibyllarum* and *Timor et tremor*, his use of accidentals, often producing unexpected major triads or a whole series of them – the closing section of the *Stabat mater* is a good example – is reflected in Giovanni's harmonic language. Whilst in general Lasso did not explore extremes of range, there are rare occasions when his use of a choir *a voce mutata* combined with rich harmony points towards Giovanni, as in the lower choir of, again, the *Stabat mater*. Lasso also cultivated scrupulous attention to textual declamation in each part; this too set a standard for Giovanni, who cultivates pure homophony more frequently than Lasso. There is, moreover, the Gabrielian tutti which, whether in Andrea or Giovanni, owes much of its technique to the example of Lasso.

Giovanni might have come across the work of Phinot, and certainly the flexibility of his antiphonal technique suggests as much. The most obvious place to look for influence of the older master is in *Jam non dicam* (Phinot: Opera vol. 4: 154; Gabrieli: Opera vol. 1: 136); Phinot set this text with three 'Alleluia' sections all using the same music, but oddly in view of Giovanni's liking for this idea, the latter's two 'Alleluia' sections are set to different music, the second, incidentally, containing most un-Phinot-like written-out embellishments (bars 37–40). In one instance, though, *Ego sum* (Opera vol. 2: 22), Giovanni recalls a phrase that Phinot used prominently in both the Lamentations and *Sancta Trinitas* – compare Ex. 49 with bars 15–22, 49–54 and 82–7 of the latter (Anthology no. 4). The deliberate diatonicism on Giovanni's part seems deliberately calculated.

We have already postulated the influence, through Andrea, of the Habsburg composers. One direct comparison seems tempting – the à 8 settings by Utendal and Giovanni Gabrieli of *Jubilate Deo* (Utendal: Anthology no. 6; Gabrieli: Opera vol. 1: 105). There are differences of treatment: Utendal's choirs are equal (2×SATB), Gabrieli's contrasting but with unusually high clefs ($G_2G_2C_2C_3/C_2C_3C_4F_3$). Also, Gabrieli's albeit brief insertion of triple

Ex. 49   G. GABRIELI, Ego sum qui sum

time at 'Laudate nomen ejus' gives a different structural feel. Utendal does not attempt anything like the intricate *note nere* imitation of Gabrieli at 'et generationem'. Many general features are similar, however: the short-winded imitative opening for one choir, the subsequent close imitation of downward scalic figures (Gabrieli at 'omnis terra', Utendal at 'in laetitia') and emphatic, often syncopated single-choir or antiphonal declamation used by both composers for phrases such as 'in exsultatione' and 'ipse fecit nos' – compare Ex. 50 with bars 17–20 and 28–9 of the Utendal (Anthology no. 6).

Homophony, polyphony and antiphony

Venetian music, and Giovanni Gabrieli's in particular, is often thought of as homophonic. Homophony allows the polychoral dialogue to emerge as the prime compositional parameter. Sometimes, as in *Beati omnes* and *Domine,*

Ex. 50   G. GABRIELI, Jubilate Deo

Ex. 50 (*cont.*)

Dominus noster (Opera vol. 1: 143 & 151), both à 8, homophony dominates
even in some of the tuttis, though usually with at least one dissenting voice
injecting interest by means of cross-rhythms (e.g. *Beati omnes*, 38–41).
Homophony is especially prominent in triple-time sections (e.g. ibid., 49ff);
such passages are ordinarily used to contrast with rhythmically more elaborate
duple-time music.

Exceptions like *Beati omnes* apart, Gabrieli's habitual procedure is essentially that of Phinot: to employ homophony for single-choir sections and
antiphonal exchanges, and polyphony for tuttis. In single-choir music the
exceptions to this, apart from passing decorative syncopations, are normally
to be found at the beginning of a piece where, almost as a formality, Giovanni
may employ imitation by voices briefly, with close overlapped entries which
often retain only the rhythmic outline. The opening of *Domine exaudi* à 8
(Opera vol. 1: 99) is little more than enlivened homophony; on the other hand,
that of *Jubilate Deo* almost promises an à 4 imitative motet in its comparative
expansiveness (ibid.: 105). In fact, there is little doubt that Giovanni possessed
a contrapuntal gift should he have wished to exercise it: he did not turn to
homophony as an easy option but as a conscious compositional choice. When
his tuttis flower polyphonically he displays a consummate grasp of his craft.
As in Andrea this may be manifest in a maze of *concertato*-like entries of small
motifs, as for example near the close of *O Jesu mi dulcissime* (1597; Opera
vol. 1: 167) (Ex. 51). More often, though, his skill is unobtrusive, residing in
independent but informal voice-leading in tuttis, and in the astonishing
variety of sonorous decoration found in cadential passages for both single
choir and tutti.

Giovanni makes quite frequent use of the 'clash' cadence as we defined it in
connection with Andrea. In contrast to the latter, he is particularly fond of
clashing the suspension with the sharpened leading note; indeed, the form of
the cadence at bar 55 of *O Domine Jesu Christe* (Anthology no. 15), with its
rising scalic figure, is one of Giovanni's fingerprints.

Ex. 51   G. GABRIELI, O Jesu mi dulcissime (1597)

We do not instinctively think of Giovanni as one of music's melodists, though many of his canzonas are catchy enough in that respect: he relies on clichés of his period, making especially prominent use for example of the *nota cambiata* figure. The very plainness of the melodic surface of his music, as with the homophonic tendency, throws the weight of musical argument onto other parameters: polychoral interaction, tonality, harmonic colour and harmonic rhythm.

We have already outlined a typical polychoral formal shape as exemplified by *Deus, Deus meus* (1587), and we shall return to broad formal principles later. It is much harder to convey the sheer variety of Giovanni's handling of detail in his antiphony. Although he quite often begins with long, unrelated phrases for each choir in turn, antiphonal imitation shading into or confronted by a tutti is the primary technique, as we would by now expect. The answering choir is rarely at the unison (though it may be at the octave in some or all voices); even when the phrase is relatively unaltered, transposition by a fourth or fifth often produces decidedly tonal implications, such as the modulation to the dominant at bars 12–13 of *Laudate nomen Domini* (Opera vol. 1: 128). Whilst this sort of thing is not entirely new, it assumes greater importance in Giovanni's music, especially when extended into a series of sequential echoes, typically moving round the circle of fifths. *Jam non dicam* for equal choirs (Opera vol. 1: 136), as well as employing some antiphonal repetition at the unison, contains instructive examples of how such chains of echoes can, depending on accidentals, be made either to confirm or to change an existing key centre. In Ex. 52 the first paragraph (bars 20–5) contains no accidentals and cadences where it began, in C. The second (bars 25–30), after a momentary shift to the flat side, proceeds via the same series of bass notes but modulates to A minor. Such uses of portions of the circle of fifths are in principle no different from the practice of, say, Vivaldi, Bach and Haydn.

In reality, it is impossible to discuss Giovanni's antiphonal technique without touching on his concept of tonality, since the two are so closely connected. Without attempting here a full-scale study of the latter we shall simply observe that Giovanni's music is a fascinating amalgam of the church modes with incidental chromatic alteration and procedures which, in this analytical minefield, it is difficult not to label as pointers to the emergence of tonality in the Baroque sense. An examination of key signatures and finals appears to reveal a conventional enough range of the church mode-derived tonalities of the later sixteenth century.[12] However, any feeling of modality is frequently modified not only by the sharpening of leading notes (both at cadences and in modulatory sequences), but also by the raising of the thirds of what should be minor chords in other contexts also, to produce a rich or bright sound, or to enhance the word-setting.[13] Thus the B naturals near the beginning of *O magnum mysterium* (Opera vol. 1: 10) are there to impart a feeling of mystery; their occurrence is strange so early in an ostensibly G dorian piece. The first type of chromaticism, as we saw with the second half of Ex. 52, is

Ex. 52   G. GABRIELI, Jam non dicam

bound to seem to us with hindsight to point towards tonality. The second type, irrespective of whether or not it is related to the expression of the text, is no more relevant to tonality in the modern sense than similar or more extreme examples in the Italian madrigal repertory. Indeed, it introduces a potential element of instability which is taken to greater lengths in Giovanni's later work. The unraised leading note in bars 2, 6 and 11 of *O magnum mysterium* suggests a mixing of modes, leaving us wondering whether the mode is indeed dorian transposed, or whether it is mixolydian. It is equally futile to seize on the perfect tonal balance of the opening (with Choir 1's opening magically modified by Choir 2 to cadence, phrygian fashion, on the dominant, the tonic being re-affirmed by the tutti enrichment of Choir 1's opening phrase) as an example of a new concept of tonality. After all, the concept of musical structure as being governed by a hierarchy of subsidiary cadential finals around the principal final was fundamental to sixteenth-century music – it was defined by Vicentino in *L'antica musica* (Berger 1980, especially pp. 103ff). It is a question of emphasis. Giovanni's declamatory opening and largely harmonic approach to texture throw the tonal structure into relief in a way that a linearly-governed modal opening might not. To some extent, therefore, it is the polychoral medium itself which leads Giovanni to compose in a manner which we would call tonal. We have already seen how the sequential use of echoes, carried further than in Andrea, can seem remarkably prophetic in this respect. Imitation by choirs at the fourth or fifth often arises from the difference in range between the choirs; when allied to the sharpening of leading notes it can set up tonic/dominant or tonic/subdominant polarities.

The beginning of *O magnum mysterium* also exemplifies the subtle variation in antiphonal repetition which may be introduced by the answering choir, though this should not surprise us in any piece from Phinot onwards. A motet which, most exceptionally in Giovanni's output, makes curiously little use of antiphonal repetition is the 1597 setting of *O Jesu mi dulcissime* (Opera vol. 1: 167). It begins like *O Domine Jesu Christe* (see below), but when the high choir enters it is with new text (a parallel couplet) to new music. This procedure, alternating with declamatory tuttis, predominates until the lively closing section (Ex. 51).

Rhythm

As with Andrea, rhythm is an important parameter in Giovanni, both in terms of the single line, where its contours are matched to verbal stresses, and in terms of harmonic rhythm. In the former case there is the same tendency as in Andrea to contrast longer 'church-style' note values with madrigalian *note nere*. In the opening phrase of *Misericordias Domini* (ibid.: 114) Giovanni sees an antithesis: after the almost Josquin-like phrygian opening for Choir 2 (low), Choir 1 enters with lively syncopation. More typically, the smaller note-values are introduced later in a piece, as part of a general quickening of musical pace. In *Misericordias* the rhythmic antithesis recurs throughout. This type of multithematicism seems to tie in with structural techniques found in Giovanni's ensemble canzonas (Selfridge-Field 1975: 96–7).

In much sixteenth-century music harmonic rhythm is of only incidental importance, insignificant in polyphony whose guiding principle is the combination of linear curves, subservient in homophony to effective harmonisation of the leading voice. In the madrigal repertory and in motets by madrigal-conscious composers, instances may be found of the manipulation of harmonic rhythm for the purpose of portraying a textual image. In much, and especially in Venetian, polychoral music harmonic rhythm assumes prime structural importance. We have already noted two general tendencies: for spacious openings to give way later to lively *note nere*, or for interplay between two rhythmic layers to persist throughout. There is also a relationship between harmonic rhythm and the number of choirs which are singing, for whilst single-choir passages and antiphonal exchanges may be of varied pace, there is a natural tendency for harmonic rhythm to slow majestically in tuttis. The opening of *Maria virgo* (Opera vol. 2: 66) illustrates these points (Table 3).

Table 3

bars		text		harmonic units
1–5		Maria virgo, regina		𝅝 (𝅗𝅥)
5–11	Ch. 2	de radice Jesse, virgo ante partum		𝅗𝅥 (𝅗𝅥)
11–13		virgo in partu, virgo post partum		𝅗𝅥 (𝅘𝅥𝅮)
13–15		incontaminata		𝅗𝅥 (𝅗𝅥)
15–17		Mater Domini		(𝅝) 𝅗𝅥
17–19	Ch. 1	inventrix gratiae		𝅗𝅥
19–21		genetrix vitae		𝅗𝅥
21–23	Ch. 2	aurea porta		𝅗𝅥 (𝅗𝅥)
23–24		gratia plena	antiphonal	𝅗𝅥
24–25	Ch. 1	aurea porta	repetition	𝅗𝅥 (𝅗𝅥)
26–27		gratia plena		𝅗𝅥
27–29	Tutti	benedicta		𝅝·· +𝅗𝅥

Choir 2's opening phrase increases in rate of chord change, decreasing again as Choir 1's entry approaches. Choir 1 repeats this process on a smaller scale. The quickening of harmonic rhythm suggested in statement and repetition of 'aurea porta gratia plena' is impressively contradicted by the spacious tutti on 'benedicta'.

Wider formal procedures

Maria virgo is structurally interesting in other ways, and leads us conveniently into a discussion of some examples of the variety to be found in Giovanni's formal procedures. The material of 'genetrix vitae' (Choir 1), a descending dotted pattern syncopated against itself, is reworked as a tutti at 'venter Christum tuum' (bars 35–7), with another brief reference at the 'ubera' cadence (bar 41). It is then developed at greater length in the third (tutti) phrase of the concluding 'Alleluia' (bars 63–5), and it also has clear affinities with the descending tetrachord underlying the first 'Alleluia' phrase (bars 58–9). When the whole 'Alleluia' section is repeated the third phrase is expanded into an impressive final climax which has the effect of crowning the piece thematically as well as in sheer sonority (bars 73–end).

The re-use of material here does not constitute ritornello or refrain – it is more a form of thematic development. The more obvious use of 'Alleluia' refrains in a small number of pieces was one of Giovanni's most influential formal devices, anticipated though it was by Phinot in his *Jam non dicam*. Five pieces in 1597 have such refrains: *Surrexit pastor bonus* à 10, *Quis est iste* à 10, *Hodie Christus natus est* à 10, *Plaudite* à 12 and *Regina caeli* à 12. Only in the case of the last are the repeats of the word 'Alleluia' present in the liturgical text (though not set to the same music in the chant version). Of the others, *Plaudite* is a centonised text, and the remaining three have texts obtained by combining two liturgical items (Bryant 1981b: 158–9); it is distinctly possible, therefore, that the 'Alleluias' were arranged with the idea of a musical refrain in mind. Although none of these pieces begins with an 'Alleluia', in principle the device is similar to Monteverdi's usual concept of a ritornello – a passage which recurs at the same pitch, rather than at different pitches as in the later Baroque. Only in *Surrexit pastor bonus* (Opera vol. 2: 80) is the refrain subjected to variation, quite substantially in the fourth and final statement, which ends the piece. Duple time is chosen because there is a short passage of triple time immediately before the first 'Alleluia', but in the other four motets the 'Alleluia' refrain is in triple time, the close being clinched by a short coda in ¢, preceded in *Hodie* and *Regina caeli* by a double statement of the refrain. In the fifteen pieces in 1587 and 1597 which contain the word 'Alleluia' Giovanni sets it to a limited number of motifs which almost form a refrain across his output. He is particularly fond of a rhythmically 'straight' phrase, with or without dot, e.g. ¾ ♩. ♪♩ | ♩ or ¢ ♩♩♩♩ | ♩ , often succeeded by syncopation, e.g. ¾ ♩. ♪♩ | ♪♩ ♪♩ | ♩. .

Hodie Christus natus est (Opera vol. 2: 102) is an interesting structure for another reason. Like *Exsultet jam angelica,* published in the 1615 *Reliquiae,* it is an extremely rare exception to Gabrieli's normal practice of putting the choirs on an equal footing in the polychoral dialogue. The high choir takes part only in the refrains until after the fourth, when 'Gloria in excelsis Deo' is set twice to a massive tutti and is succeeded by conventional double-choir writing to the end (including the final refrain). This device is clearly intended to enhance the setting of the text, and has structural affinities with Schütz's conception of *cappella* (see Chapter 8).

The use of three or four choirs

The reader will have gathered that in my view the addition of a third or fourth choir does not necessarily mean an increase in musical subtlety, as opposed to sonority. After all, in conversation there is no substitute for a lively one-to-one debate! Perhaps this is why in two of the twelve-part pieces, *Virtute magna* and *Regina caeli*, Giovanni preferred to retain a double-choir format. In many ways Giovanni's works for more than two choirs in 1597 do not mark any significant advance in their handling of polychoral interaction over Andrea's Magnificat, Mass movements and especially his *Benedicam Dominum*. Giovanni in *Plaudite, Jubilate Deo* and *Omnes gentes* (Opera vol. 2: 111, 219, 232) makes a joyful noise but is less subtle than in many of the double-choir pieces. Those for more than two choirs are primarily exercises in the contrasting of pitch and dynamics, the latter achieved in terms of the number of choirs singing. It is instructive in this respect to compare the famous *Sonata pian' e forte*, one of the instrumental works in 1597, whose 'Pian' and 'Forte' marks are, with one exception (bars 59–60), applied to respectively single-choir and tutti phrases (see *HAM* vol. 1: 200); the markings draw attention to a terraced conception of dynamics.

Omnes gentes, the only piece by Giovanni in 1587 or 1597 for four choirs, makes a particularly splendid effect. It opens predictably with a tutti, but one approached through a written-out *crescendo* as choirs enter successively on a D minor chord. The brief triple-time section 'plaudite manibus' illustrates a technique used throughout the piece – the pairing of choirs (in this case Choirs 2 & 4, then 1 & 3) contrasted with the full tutti. The tuttis often serve to amplify only a single word or two (e.g. 'quoniam', 'populus nobis'). Overlapped choral imitations frequently give rise to tutti textures, notably from 'ascendit Deus' (bars 43ff) and the words 'et Dominus in voce tubae' are given short-lived but virtuoso treatment as a sixteen-part polyphonic tutti with exuberant trumpet figurations of various kinds in all voices. The closing 'Alleluia' features an extended written-out *crescendo* (Ch. 2, Ch. 2+Ch. 4, Ch. 1+Ch. 3, Ch. 2+Ch. 3+Ch. 4, Tutti) which is heard twice. This section cadences on a D major chord, from whence the inevitable crowning plagal cadence is approached via a mediant shift to a B flat chord. By such simple *al fresco* strokes Giovanni achieves some of his most stunning effects.

It is natural to assume that the Mass movements in 1597 – Kyrie, Gloria and Sanctus, all for three choirs (Opera vol. 2: 141, 152, 168) – were modelled on those of Andrea. There are similarities, but there are also differences apart from the obvious one that Andrea's Gloria is for four choirs. Whereas Andrea went out of his way to provide pitch contrast between the choirs, Giovanni uses two standard SATB choirs, one marked 'Cappella', to which is added in Kyrie and Sanctus a choir Vicentino would have described as *a voce mutata* ($C_3C_4F_3F_4$); in the Gloria all three choirs are SATB. The similarities between uncle and nephew are very obvious in the structures of Kyrie and Sanctus, where long imitative or freely polyphonic paragraphs for single choirs precede more rapid interchanges involving antiphonal repetition. In the Gloria (linked to the Kyrie by a rising-fifth head-motif) we have the clear punctuating use of tuttis as in Andrea, and triple time for 'In gloria Dei Patris'. It has to be said, however, that these pieces are rather unadventurous in comparison with the monumental grandeur of Andrea's, and markedly so in harmony and tonality. The twelve-part Magnificat (Opera vol. 2: 177) is grander than the Mass movements, but not as dramatic as Andrea's and with less word-painting; the most exciting music comes in the doxology. Perhaps Giovanni's interest was not aroused by the most commonly sung liturgical texts.

Words and music

Our discussion so far has been to a considerable extent music-centred. It is undeniable that in the pieces for grand festivals, as Denis Arnold said, 'shades of meaning are of lesser importance. . .Indeed, these texts are virtually interchangeable' (1979: 178). If we wish to see Giovanni's sensitivity to the text allied at the highest level to coherent musical construction, then it is to be found in settings of more penitential texts, which usually express some sort of antithesis, or a progression from darkness to light. The building of musical paragraphs tends to be more subtle also when Giovanni is dealing with shorter texts and has time to expand with varied repetition and development. In settings of longer texts his standard technique is similar to that of many other composers: each phrase is set concisely, perhaps echoed complete or in part or reworked with different scoring, and then he passes on to the next. Some sections thus constructed may be repeated in their entirety, especially if they occur near the end of a piece. A good example of a long text is that of *Beati immaculati* (Opera vol. 1: 121). Unlike Andrea, Giovanni writes unequivocally here for double choir with some antiphonal repetition, but each phrase is passed over with perhaps a single echo or overlap of the choirs.

   Some settings of the quieter, subtler type which come to mind are *O magnum mysterium, O Jesu mi dulcissime* and *O Domine Jesu Christe*. We shall examine the last-named (Anthology no. 15). Its text meditates on the Passion:[14]

> O Lord Jesus Christ,
> wounded on the Cross,
> drinking gall and vinegar:

I pray thee that thy wounding
might be the healing of my soul.

There are two basic ideas: adoration of Christ on the Cross, and the joyful realisation that the Christian soul is redeemed through Christ's suffering. The text thus falls into two halves, but Giovanni joins them musically and psychologically by making 'deprecor te' the climax of 'et aceto potatum', i.e. a response to the contemplation of Christ's Passion.

The opening adoring vocative is set (Choir 2, the lower of the two) characteristically to a very slow-moving motif (note the affective falling fifth in bars 5–6). The harmonic rhythm quickens for the more fervent, sequentially rising 'adoro te' figure only to be pulled back by the slow syncopated descending scale of 'in cruce vulneratum'. The melodic interest here is mainly in the top line, the lower parts supporting it with sensuous, sonorous harmony embodying many descending passing notes and some seventh chords, duly prepared (bars 9, beat 3 and 10, beat 3; cf. the 7–6 suspensions in bars 3 and 5). The way in which Giovanni develops and amplifies this material may be compared with Andrea's techniques in *Quem vidistis*. Choir 1 now takes over the opening material a fourth higher, but at 'adoro te' the tension is heightened by the transposition of the music up a further tone and the introduction of a single overlapping statement in Choir 2. 'In cruce' (Choir 1) is overlapped by Choir 2's entering at the original pitch. This time, in contrast to the cadence in C at bars 11–12, the section closes with an affective phrygian cadence ending on an A major chord. In this opening we see both portrayal of the text and musical symmetry of extreme beauty and subtlety. The word 'felle' is isolated in a 'bitter' A minor cadence involving an augmented triad. 'Et aceto potatum' is built from sequential imitation of Giovanni's favourite *cambiata* figure, traversing the same segment of the circle of fifths as the second statement of 'adoro te' (C–G–d–a–e). 'Deprecor te' not only receives its impulse from the preceding phrase, as noted already, but its syncopated descending figure is closely related to that of 'in cruce vulneratum'. Thus the join between the two sections is seamless and they are also thematically related.

Whereas the first section is in soft, dark colours with predominantly slow harmonic rhythm and subtle dovetailing between the choirs, the second embodies the progression from darkness to light. The slow-moving 'deprecor te' music is confronted with and supplanted by the dancing rhythms and forthright *spezzato* exchanges to which the joyful realisation of redemption is set. As in the first section the repetition of material involves changes of choir and pitch level. Finally in the closing tutti the threads are drawn together musically when the 'deprecor te' motif, now set to 'animae meae', is brought into the cantus parts, heralding the final sonorous plagal cadences with their ecstatic scalar and triadic voice-leading. Giovanni usually achieved a final climax by repeating the last section, adding a coda in duple time if it was in triple. Here he achieves it with a thematic summing-up which carries also the desired message that the sinner should enter into Christ's sufferings himself.

Giovanni's later style

It is Giovanni's 1597 pieces which lie at the peak of the polychoral style. The richness of the music published posthumously in the *Symphoniae sacrae. . . liber secundus* and the *Reliquiae sacrarum concentuum*, both of 1615, lies in its diversification. The use of solo voices, partial or total specification of the instrumental scoring and an interest in mannerist expressionism all served to weaken Giovanni's interest in pure polychoral dialogue. The straightforwardly polychoral pieces printed in 1615 may indeed have been composed earlier. In any event, if the 1597 collection places Giovanni among the greatest of late Renaissance composers, then some 1615 works proclaim him a pioneer of early Baroque styles. Few if any 1615 pieces are completely unaffected by some aspect of stylistic change, if only by the use of *bassus generalis* or sporadic insertion of ornamentation.

Mannerism

The obvious comparison is often made between the early and late settings of *O Jesu mi dulcissime* (Opera vol. 1: 167 & vol. 3: 30). The later setting differs mainly in textural detail – matters of written-in ornamentation and the short-winded imitative motifs that were one of Gabrieli's legacies to Schütz. A piece which goes further in the direction of mannerism, particularly in its disjointed syntax, is *Hodie completi sunt* (Anthology no. 16), likewise scored for two equal choirs. The opening line of the text is divided into three segments: 'Hodie', the choirs overlapping with sustained F major chords in duple time; 'completi sunt', triple time with homophonic antiphony incorporating the familiar sequential modulations; and 'dies pentecostes', a brief, jerky à 8 imitative section. None of this material recurs, and it is succeeded by an 'Alleluia' of strangely languid character, triple time then duple. 'Hodie Spiritus Sanctus' is given only to Choir 1, upsetting previous symmetries, and once again shunting from triple to duple time. Note also the fearlessly tritonal C sharp in the top part at bar 25. Only from this point does forward momentum begin to build up, with conspicuous use of sequence, both antiphonal (e.g. 'discipulis' and 'in universum', the latter varied for 'et baptizatus') and within one choir as at 'charismatum' and 'salvus'. The extraordinary emphasis given to single words here is of course also a mannerist trait. The piece is rounded off by a repeat of that languid 'Alleluia', now extended by a striking coda featuring a slow-moving bass line supporting dissonant sequences in quavers and a recurring motif in longer notes.

Exaudi me, Domine à 16 for four choirs (Opera vol. 5: 134), two SATB and two ATTB, is a superb example of mannerist expression belonging to the same world as the six-part *Timor et tremor* but achieved without sacrificing structural clarity. As a four-choir piece its antiphonal interactions are conventionally organised. The mannerism lies in the extraordinary characterisation of a few key images, in particular the phrase 'movendi sunt', set first with what can only be called hockets between the voices of a single choir (Ex. 53a), which later, most terrifyingly, become hockets between choirs in an extended sequential pattern (Ex. 53b).

Ex. 53   G. GABRIELI, Exaudi me Domine

Ex. 53 (*cont.*)

Thematic unity

Pieces like *Hodie completi sunt* are not lacking in 'integrating' as opposed to 'disintegrating' devices – witness the repeat of the 'Alleluia' music, and the re-use of the long-note 'praedicare' figure (top parts from bar 45) for 'salvus erit' (bar 56, tenor of Choir 1, etc.). It is not surprising therefore to find in works like the *Jubilate Deo* à 10 and *In ecclesiis* (Opera vol. 3: 163 & vol. 5: 32) the refrain-principle taken still further than it was in 1597, whilst *Cantate Domino* à 8 (Opera vol. 3: 87) has a clear ABA structure. Among examples of Gabrieli's predilection for thematic unity one piece stands by itself: the re-latively conventional *Litaniae Beatae Mariae Virginis* (ibid.: 109). Like Porta and Lasso Gabrieli approaches the text with a mixture of antiphonal and responsorial techniques. In the opening Trinitarian petitions (bars 11–19) 'miserere nobis' is set to a recurrent phrase transposed to various pitches. Subsequently a four-note *cambiata*-like figure binds together the many utterances of 'ora pro nobis'. Rapid antiphony used for its own sake produces a climax at 'Regina sanctorum omnium'.

The three Magnificats in 1615 are interesting works, more so than those in 1597,[15] particularly from the point of view of structural unity. Those à 12 and à 14 are most unusual in Gabrieli in their utilisation of the chant. The twelve-part (Opera vol. 4: 133) begins with a setting of the incipit for Choir 3 with the chant (tone 6) in the top part. The answering phrase is hidden in the bass of Choir 1 though partially anticipated in the top part of Choir 2. A modern trait is the persistence of triple time from bar 5 until the doxology, though Gabrieli's antiphonal treatment is conventional enough. The most surprising stroke is at 'Sicut locutus est. . .in saecula' (bars 130–48) where the chant is paraphrased very obviously in the top part of Choir 2, almost like a *cantus firmus*. The use of the chant is less obvious but more frequent (tone 1 transposed) in the Magnificat à 14 (Opera vol. 5: 56), which is again otherwise in a classic polychoral style. The Magnificat à 17 (ibid.: 158) is a fine example of four-choir writing, but with effective isolation of the *cappella* at 'Fecit potentiam. . .' and for an even longer passage at 'Sicut locutus est. . .'.

Polychoral writing in the later works

Whilst some 1615 pieces are clearly in the older polychoral style,[16] others show a diminished interest in polychoral dialogue even when ostensibly laid out for double choir; in such cases the choral contrast is perhaps seen as more colouristic than structural. In *Benedictus es Dominus* (Opera vol. 3: 97), for example, although the choral division ($G_2C_1C_2C_4/C_3C_4C_4F_5$) is intermittently apparent aurally from the beginning, it is only in the brief triple-time 'Alleluia' section that polychoral dialogue comes into clear focus, incorporating Gabrieli's favourite sequential imitation.

The rôle of the bass line

One element which affects to a greater or lesser extent most pieces in the second *Symphoniae sacrae* volume is the provision of an organ part. This was no novelty, as such parts had been present in Italian sources as early as the 1590s.[17] In most of Giovanni's late works it is simply, as Denis Arnold pointed out (Opera vol. 3: iii), a *basso seguente*, following the lowest sounding voice at any moment. However, in two cases the organ's rôle is that of a true continuo: *Quem vidistis* and *In ecclesiis* (Opera vol. 5: 1 & 32) both have substantial solo sections with independent, harmonically essential organ bass lines.

There is evidence elsewhere too of Gabrieli's changing attitude to the bass

line which goes beyond what might have been his posthumous editor's deci-
sion to include an organ part for all the pieces. The proportion of works in
1615 with spatially-organised bass lines is much greater than before. In some
cases Gabrieli utilises in tuttis the old technique of moving the basses by
octaves and unisons in contrary motion with occasional thirds: this is true of
O Jesu mi dulcissime, O quam suavis, Cantate Domino, the Litany, *Exaudi
Deus* (lower two choirs only), *Misericordia tua* (ditto), Kyrie II and Sanctus
(ditto), *Confitebor tibi*, Magnificat à 14, and from *Reliquiae: Hodie Christus
natus est* and *Exsultet jam* (lower two choirs). Of the remaining works with
any semblance of a polychoral layout only *Hodie completi sunt, Benedictus
es Dominus, Vox domini* and Christe are non-spatial. All the others employ
for at least some of their length a technique recommended by later theorists
(e.g. Artusi 1589: 47) – that of giving all bass lines the same notes when
combining choirs. Examples of this may be seen in *Exaudi me* (Opera vol. 5:
134). Where a high choir is involved, as in the twelve-part Magnificat already
cited, this may mean that choir's bass moving one or even two octaves higher,
something which was eschewed in 1597.

Pieces with specified scoring

It is of course the pieces which embody fully specified scoring (soloist[s],
chorus and instruments) which represent Giovanni's claim to be considered an
early Baroque composer. In the main they are not polychoral, and to that
extent fall outside the scope of this book. They may indeed suggest a different
performing location from St Mark's. The combinations of solo voices and instruments in, for instance, *Jubilate Deo* à 10 (Opera vol. 3: 163) – minimum
forces 2 cornetti, 5 trombones, bassoon, 2 voices and organ – and *Surrexit
Christus* (Opera vol. 3: 193) à 11 – 2 cornetti, 2 violins, 4 trombones, 3 voices
and organ – belong perhaps to the slightly more intimate surroundings of the
Scuola Grande di San Rocco.

One of these works commands our attention for quite other reasons: *Quem
vidistis* à 14 (Opera vol. 5: 1). Despite the differences of scoring and the longer,
centonised text of Giovanni's piece, it seems to be in part a parody of Andrea's
double-choir setting (Anthology no. 13), an act of homage perhaps. 'Parody'
may be too strong a term – thematic quotation is what it amounts to, as Ex. 54
shows.

Ex. 54(a)   A. GABRIELI, Quem vidistis, pastores?

Ex. 54(b)   G. GABRIELI, Quem vidistis, pastores? (1615)

bars 23–32

Ex. 54(c)   A. GABRIELI, Quem vidistis, pastores? (1615)

bars 33–4

bars 35–8

Ex. 54(d)   G. GABRIELI, Quem vidistis, pastores? (1615)

bars 42–47

With *In ecclesiis* (ibid.: 32; also *HAM* vol. 1: no. 157) the polychoral idea takes on the substance of orchestration. Polychoral dialogue is supplanted by a systematic contrasting of various combinations of soloists, six-part instrumental ensemble and ripieno choir, the whole held together texturally by organ continuo and structurally by an 'Alleluia' refrain which itself reflects the various possibilities of deploying the forces. Polychorality is effectively confined to a suggestion of double-choir dialogue retained through the differently-scored statements of the refrain.

Implied scoring

Whilst in these cases we see the full flowering of the vocal/instrumental *concertato*, it would be a mistake to assume a sudden change of style on Giovanni's part, and undoubtedly we can cautiously project some tendencies which are partly codified in 1615 back to 1597 works. 1615 practices tend to confirm Praetorius's suggestions as we applied them to earlier pieces: relatively large numbers of trombones, smaller numbers of cornetti and occasional use of strings or 'fagotto'. The entrusting of the bottom line of a high choir and the top line of a low choir each to a solo singer sometimes seems implicit in the musical dialogue. A significant amount of the argument in the Magnificat à 14, for example, is generated by imitation between two such C_4 parts (Opera vol. 5: 56).

In other cases an ostensibly conventional polychoral piece may reveal a more complex character. *Salvator noster* (ibid.: 84), for example, is for three virtually unspecified choirs (two inner parts of the middle one are marked 'voce'), and for almost all its length the choirs are manipulated in the usual way, though with much incidental ornamentation of lines. Then in the final 'Alleluia', after a conventional triple-time section, a sudden, unexpected pairing of voice-parts suggests a duet for two cornetti, perhaps answered by two solo voices (Ex. 55). Kyrie I from the otherwise unremarkable and indeed rather conservative Mass movements (Opera vol. 4: 97) contains an example of quasi-improvised ornamentation at its final cadence which must be intended for a solo voice or instrument. All the voices have some ornamental figures earlier in the movement, which also features forward-looking use of dynamic markings.

Contrapuntal writing

One aspect of Giovanni's technique which does not diminish in importance is his contrapuntal gift; in some pieces it assumes a greater rôle as the polychoral element recedes. Although he now permits octave and unison doublings frequently enough, his polyphonic textures still dazzle, however briefly, as in *Salvator noster*, bars 35–7 (Opera vol. 5: 112). It is noticeable that this passage, which is not untypical, begins to approach a typically Baroque patterned figuration.

Renaissance or Baroque?

In one sense, all polychoral music might be termed 'Baroque' with an appropriateness proportional to its monumentality or exploitation of space, rather as the madrigal could be said to be 'mannerist' in some cases at least as early as Rore. Such labels are often misleading, especially with a great composer like Giovanni Gabrieli who inconveniently straddles two of our accustomed style periods. That being said, it seems to me helpful to regard the pure, classic polychoral idiom of 1597 and earlier as being essentially a late Renaissance phenomenon; we may then observe how in 1615 it is displaced or transformed by elements which belong undeniably to a new age.

Ex. 55   G. GABRIELI, Salvator noster

Ex. 55 (*cont.*)

Venetian contemporaries of the Gabrielis

We shall deal here with four composers, three of whom made substantial contributions to Venetian polychoral music. By chance, two were near contemporaries of Andrea Gabrieli, two of Giovanni.

Claudio Merulo

Merulo (1533–1604) was a contemporary of Andrea Gabrieli, though he lived nearly twenty years longer. His polychoral music, contained in a collection of motets and miscellaneous liturgical items of 1594 and a posthumous print of a pair of masses of 1609, lies stylistically somewhere between the two Gabrielis, though with individual traits. They are probably not all Venetian products: Merulo left the employ of St Mark's in 1584 after twenty-seven years' service as organist, and subsequently worked in Parma until his death. At his funeral the Mass was sung with double choir, 'one placed near the organ, the other on the opposite side', as Alessandro Volpino recorded in a letter (quoted by Bastian, 1967: 67).

The *Sacrorum concentuum* (1594) contains 18 motets (14 à 8 (4 for undivided choir), 3 à 10, 1 à 12), 4 magnificats (3 à 8, 1 à 12), a *Regina coeli* à 8, and a group of Kyrie and Sanctus settings. As with Andrea Gabrieli, German anthologists provide us with evidence of the vogue for this type of Venetian music north of the Alps: nine of Merulo's eight-part motets were printed there between 1590 and 1613, mostly in Nuremberg (Opera vol. 5: xiii). Merulo's formal designs are somewhat simpler and less varied than those of Giovanni Gabrieli. *Ave gratia plena* (Opera vol. 5: 42) is a fine dialogue, with Gabriel and Mary characterised respectively by low ($C_3C_4C_4F_4$) and high ($C_1C_2C_3F_3$) choirs. Many pieces conform to a kind of norm which may be summarised as

$$\frac{\text{non-repetitive}}{\text{antiphony}} - \text{tutti} - \frac{\text{antiphonal}}{\text{repetition}} - \text{tutti}$$

There may or may not be antiphonal repetition of a phrase leading into the first tutti. This scheme may be extended in various ways: by an extra tutti near the beginning (*Hodie Christus natus est*, Opera vol. 6: 47); by further non-repetitive antiphony after the first tutti (*Haec est dies*, Opera vol. 5: 61); or by the addition of an 'Alleluia' section (*O rosa incorruptibilis*, ibid.: 55). A change to *tripla* sometime during the second part of the piece is common, as is repetition of the final section. In two cases there is no tutti until the end (*Laudate Dominum* and *Vias tuas, Domine*, Opera vol. 5: 101 and vol. 6: 61). In *Homo Dei* (Opera vol. 5: 90) there is no antiphonal repetition and the two tuttis are identical, giving the responsory form *aBcB*. The only piece with an 'Alleluia' refrain is *Regina coeli* (Opera vol. 6: 179), but it has little formal interest, save possibly in anticipating the *cantilena* style of Croce: all the text is sung by Choir 1, and Choir 2 joins it only for the triple-time refrain.

A fine, concise example is *Deus noster refugium* (Opera vol. 5: 129). The text is Psalm 45: 1–3, and the three verses generate three clear-cut paragraphs. The first two verses are each given to a single choir, beginning with the higher Choir 1 – Merulo always numbers his choirs according to their order of entry, not their range. The expressive opening reminds one of Lasso with its semitone inflections each balanced in imitation by its inversion. Homophony soon supervenes, and Choir 2 enters as a block with verse 2, loosening into close imitation after the mediant. Choir 1 introduces the first half of verse 3, which is then dissected and developed in a manner approaching that of Andrea Gabrieli: the first two phrases are each echoed, the first at the upper octave after a tonally-adjusted first chord, the second merging into a tutti. The seething of the waters is illustrated in madrigalian fashion by the bass of Choir 1, and the tutti is another portrayal of the same image, expressing turbulence in a choppy, pseudo-imitative maze of *note nere* in the manner of Andrea. In the final half-verse, after antiphonal repetition, the final tutti with its predominantly crotchet movement expresses the strength of the mountains. Like Andrea, Merulo likes to play with the rhythmic contrast between 'normal' and shorter note-values under the signature. *Deus noster* also affords an example of Merulo's two veins of tutti writing: the richly sonorous and the intricately interwoven. Merulo's tuttis are amongst the finest portions of these works. They show him to have been no mean polyphonist. Indeed, his use of imitation seems less perfunctory at times than that of the Gabrielis.

The magnificats form a consistent stylistic group. They retain the plainsong incipit, and the verse divisions are generally clearly articulated. Whole or half-verses are often given to a single choir, with antiphonal repetition and tuttis providing both contrast and obvious word-painting. The cadential alternation of the chant is sometimes present but more often ignored in favour of contrasting key areas. The twelve-part *primi toni* is a fine example of three-choir writing, its antiphonal repetition of shorter phrases and massive tuttis the more effective because the greater part of the piece is given over to longer phrases for single choirs. Even when seeking to maintain an antiphonal balance, Merulo's manipulation of tonality prevents the music from becoming predictable (Ex. 56). Merulo is fond of simultaneously-attacked tuttis, though sometimes, as in the doxology of this Magnificat, he brings in two of the choirs before superimposing the third.

The 1594 collection contains several isolated Kyrie and Sanctus movements which are problematical as regards how they should be combined for performance (Opera vol. 6: 132–78). The two *sexti toni* Kyries, respectively à 8 and à 12, require a Christe (plainchant?) to make a liturgical unit. It is rather clearer that the two *sexti toni* Sanctus movements belong together, since the first (à 8) sets only the word 'Sanctus' and the second (à 12) passes over that word quickly in a way totally alien to the custom of the period. The resulting composite Kyrie and Sanctus movements probably belong together because of their mode and a resemblance between their openings. There is also a four-

Ex. 56   MERULO, Magnificat primi toni

choir, sixteen-part setting of the whole Sanctus text and, *quinti toni*, two Kyries and a Christe. Since mode 5 is also an F mode, it is possible that the latter are meant to combine in some way with the *sexti toni* Kyries.

The posthumous collection of 1609 contains, in addition to the two masses, a litany (Opera vol. 2: 140). The latter is conventional, indeed restrained in that Merulo treats each petition as a unit, sometimes amplifying it with tutti writing but never splitting it between the choirs. The first Mass is for eight-part double choir on Wert's *Cara la vita mea*. The model's ever-changing voice combinations make it suitable for metamorphosis into polychoral textures (Bastian 1967: 277–9). There are some shortish examples of antiphonal repetition, but polychoral dialogue does not seem to be the primary impulse. The texture is a mixture of the simple homophony opening most movements, close, densely-woven imitation, with one or two startling eruptions of shorter notes which might suggest a late date for the work (e.g. Gloria, bars 108–11), and broadly sonorous tuttis. The three-choir *Missa Benedicam Dominum*, on the motet by Andrea Gabrieli (Opera vol. 2: 44 (mass); Anthology no. 14 (model)) is finer still, a superb work well worthy of revival. Merulo retains Andrea's interest in rhythmic contrast, though the actual borrowing is rather sporadic. The nature of the mass texts prevents Merulo utilising the same subtlety of antiphonal structure, but there are by way of compensation many glorious tuttis; that closing Kyrie II, for example, begins in intricate *note nere* fashion but broadens out majestically into 'normal' note-values.

Oddly, the mass has a narrower range and consequently less contrast between the choirs than the motet:

$$\text{Gabrieli: } C_1C_2C_3F_3/C_1C_4F_3F_4/C_3F_3F_4F_5$$
$$\text{Merulo: } C_1C_2C_3F_3/C_1C_3C_4F_4/C_1C_3C_4F_4$$

It is true that, whilst total ranges of G_2 to F_5 do occur in Merulo's music, he generally stays within 'normal' bounds more than the Gabrielis do, though he does like a pitch contrast between the choirs. Only rarely (in the litany and *Regina coeli*) does he treat the basses spatially in double-choir pieces; in those for three or four choirs, two of the basses are spatial (though with some anomalies), the other one or two choirs having frequent 6/4 chords. The 1609 publication announces on its title page an organ part which has been lost. Merulo is better known to posterity as a composer of organ music; on the strength of his polychoral works it is time for a re-assessment of his vocal church music.

Baldassare Donato (*b* c1525–30, *d* 1603)

Donato worked all his life for St Mark's, Venice, and eventually succeeded Zarlino as *maestro di cappella* in 1590. If Merulo is more famous for his organ music, then Donato is justly so for his secular music. His surviving sacred works are all to be found in a retrospective motet collection of 1599. Of the forty-nine pieces it contains (including second parts), only the last four are for eight-part double choir. Two large-scale psalm settings, *Dixit Dominus* à 16 and *Beatus vir* à 12, are unfortunately incomplete in a Vienna choir-book (Nationalbibliothek Ms. 16708: ff. 36v & 44v). Of the 1599 pieces, one, *Virgo decus* (no. 49) is a punning echo motet on the same text as Croce's (1594). The others are conventional double-choir motets in a mainly homophonic idiom, the bass parts essentially non-spatial. There is little to characterise them as specifically Venetian in style.

Giovanni Croce

Croce (1557–1609), like Bassano, was a very near contemporary of Giovanni Gabrieli. He lived all his life in Venice, and served the churches of St Mark and S. Maria Formosa. Like Andrea Gabrieli's, his output for the church contains works for modest as well as lavish resources, but in some respects it is more varied than that of either of the Gabrielis. It may also have been more popular; collections of psalms and motets were reprinted in their entirety, and individual pieces are to be found in anthologies up to nearly twenty years after Croce's death. He published a wide range of polychoral music between 1591 and 1597, all of it for eight voices: psalms, canticles, Marian antiphons, motets and parody masses. According to the editor of the posthumous *Sacre cantilene* (1610) he also composed psalms for three choirs (Arnold 1953: 39), but these seem not to have survived. However, one of the magnificent sets of choir-books in Vienna (Nationalbibliothek Ms. 16702, f. 2v) contains a Mass for four choirs ascribed to 'Joan de Croce'.

Croce's provision of music for the office is comprehensive; as well as vespers he catered for the increasingly popular service of compline and even for terce. His compline service appeared first, in 1591, and it affords a complete setting of that office. A double-choir *spezzato* setting of each psalm is provided, with *falsobordone* to cater for other tones, and the collection is rounded off with double-choir settings of all four Marian antiphons. The overriding impression in the psalms is of adherence to the Willaert tradition (Croce was a protégé of Zarlino), especially in the texture and the utilisation of the cadential structure of the psalm tone. Some verses are given entirely to one choir, but choirs are sometimes exchanged at the half-verse and sparing use is made of antiphonal repetition and tutti where it is appropriate to the text. Three of the antiphons are set in through-composed motet style, but *Regina caeli* is more sectionalised and has a triple-time *Alleluia* refrain.

The 1596b collection contains, in addition to the three portions of Ps. 118 for terce, the Te Deum for matins, Benedictus Dominus for lauds and a setting of the Miserere. The psalm portions are treated in the liturgy like three separate psalms, each with doxology. Croce bases them all on tone 3, and consequently is able to set each doxology to the same music. The style is even more strictly homophonic than in the compline psalms, and more verses are allotted to a single choir, except in the doxology. The Benedictus proceeds in strict verse-by-verse alternation until the second half of the last verse, when overlapping antiphonal repetition leads to a tutti, but it is not clear whether it is based on the chant; it is in mode 6, and the restricted ambit of the top parts at times suggests tone 6. The Miserere is mainly in *falsobordone* with double-choir settings of two of the verses, including the last, and the Te Deum is through-composed for double choir.

The vespers collection of 1597 is larger, because of course there is variation in the occurrence of psalms for vespers where there is not for terce and compline. There are twenty-one settings of seventeen different psalms, and one Magnificat. Like the earlier psalms, most have a small pitch difference between the top parts of each choir, but some have the scoring found in Willaert where one choir has both highest and lowest voices. Exceptional is the extreme contrast between the two choirs of the *Laudate pueri tertii toni* ($G_2G_2C_1C_3/C_3C_3C_3F_3$). In general the psalms are similar in structure to those for compline and terce, but a touch more elaborate, with slightly more polyphonic voice-leading and slightly more non-versal antiphony. The long psalm *Domine probasti me* contains, like Willaert's setting, verses for two voices drawn from a single choir (mod. edn, Bryant 1981b: 422). The Magnificat is much more animated, with a *note nere* signature. It contains much recitational homophony but also some intricate interlocking of voices in the Andrea Gabrieli manner. Antiphonal repetition and tuttis are used more frequently, and some of the latter are homorhythmic.

This livelier, one might almost say 'lighter' style is much to the fore in Croce's eight-part motets, published in two volumes in 1594 and 1595. Taken overall, half have the *note nere* signature. It is used to powerful effect in two expressions of Venetian warmongering, *Percussit Saul* and *Benedictus Dominus* (1594: 9 & 10). The former opens with concise and lively imitation leading to battle-music for 'et David decem millia' with rapid repeated notes (Ex. 57). It is natural to compare *Benedictus Dominus* with Andrea Gabrieli's setting of the same text, on which it could have been modelled. Whether it was or not, there are many striking similarities of form, syntax and style. The placing of tuttis and antiphonal repetition is analogous, and at times the music is quite similar, as for instance in the opening Choir 2 phrase and its cadence, and in Ex. 58, which may be compared with Ex. 45 above. In most of the piece Croce's textures tend to be simpler and more clear-cut than Gabrieli's. Croce also knew a quieter motet style, as *Anima mea liquefacta est* (1594: 13) shows. As a setting of Song of Songs (5: 6–8) it is not particularly sensuous, but it is more expansive. The imitation at the opening passes through both choirs with substantial overlapping at the interchange, and its motif recurs inconspicuously in the final tutti on the words 'quia amore'. A textual parallelism

> Quaesivi et non inveni illum;
> vocavi et non respondit mihi

Ex. 57 CROCE, Percussit Saul

Ex. 57 (*cont.*)

Ex. 58 CROCE, Benedictus Dominus

shows Croce to have had a fine ear for tonal contrast; the first line, set in
A minor, is broken into phrases each repeated antiphonally (with some adjustments of scoring and harmony). The second is set to a variation of the same
music in C major extended into a tutti returning to A as key centre (Ex. 59). As
with Andrea, his tonal orbit is not normally wide, and indeed sometimes he is
guilty of tonal monotony.

Ex. 59 CROCE, Anima mea liquefacta est

Another 'quieter' piece, *O Jesu mi dulcissime* (1595: 12), invites comparison with Giovanni Gabrieli's settings of 1597 and 1615. As elsewhere, Croce is more concise, though he makes more use of antiphonal repetition than Gabrieli in 1597. Other factors suggest that one of the pieces might have been modelled on the other: the division of the opening text (Choir 2 – Choir 1 – Tutti), the placing of tuttis generally, the use of punctuating rests in single-choir music and identical rhythm with similar harmony at 'te colimus'. Although Croce does not approach Giovanni's late style as exemplified in the 1615 setting, his opening brings in the voices in exactly the same order and the final section, 'ut veneretur', is in triple time, as in Gabrieli's 1615 but not 1597 setting. There is a certain Gabrielian nervousness also in Croce's setting in the opening phrase of the word 'Jesu' to two semiminims and in the 'patter' declamation, imitatively treated, of the first 'adoro te'.

Croce's liking for the clear-cut leads him naturally to use refrain structures. *Incipite Domino* (1595: 9; mod. edn, Torchi 1897, vol. 2: 335) has a triple-time refrain on the words 'Cantate Domino in cimbalis'. This is a typical festive piece concocted from Ps. 150-type imagery, as is *Buccinate* (1595: 13; mod. edn, Torchi: 323) with its florid or imitative textures emphasising key words; of its three 'Alleluia' passages the second and third use the same music.

Croce's volume of masses of 1596 contains three parody masses for double choir, two on his own motets (1594) and one on Janequin's *La guerre*. The last named and that on *Percussit Saul* are in the battle idiom, though the Sanctus and Agnus Dei of the *Percussit* Mass are in a deliberately more dignified vein, with a modified version of the concisely imitated head-motif prevalent in the first three movements. Oddly enough, 'clash' cadences, which Croce seems to avoid elsewhere, are found in this Mass.

The only work by Croce for more than two choirs which seems to have survived is a *Missa Jubilate Deo* à 16 for four choirs in a Vienna manuscript cited above. I have not discovered its model. It is in a really massive style, recalling Andrea Gabrieli's Gloria in the same mode (D dorian), with which Croce can hardly fail to have been familiar. There is the same preoccupation with sonority and the same reliance on the placing of tuttis to articulate the structure and on colour contrasts to give life. In the Gloria, for instance, Croce begins with a tutti, then pairs the choirs (1+2, 3+4) for some 8/8 voiced antiphony interspersed with tuttis. Some single-choir phrases and some different pairings are found later, but the initial pairing of choirs remains the norm. Kyrie I and Christe are both à 8, for respectively Choirs 3 and 4, 1 and 2. The scoring must have been very similar to Andrea's; indeed after the Kyrie, when there is a change of clefs in Choir 3, three of the choirs are notated in precisely the same clefs:

Gabrieli: $G_2C_1C_2C_4/C_1C_3C_4F_3/C_1C_3C_4F_4/C_2C_4F_3F_5$
'Capella'
Croce:　$G_2C_1C_2C_4/C_1C_3C_4F_3/C_3C_4F_3F_4/C_2C_4F_3F_5$
　　　* 'Capella' *　　　*

The Vienna scribe hints at possible scoring by selective texting: the 'Capella' (Choir 1 in his non-pitch-related numbering) is fully texted, but in the other choirs only the asterisked voice is. This seems to be partial confirmation of Praetorius's suggested scorings for high and low choirs, respectively three high instruments plus tenor voice and tenor or alto voice plus three low instruments. It is difficult to determine if and where Croce might have intended 'clash' cadences – the manuscript is liberally if not exhaustively supplied with sharp signs which eliminate most of the possibilities, even at the risk of creating melodic augmented seconds, as in Ex. 60 from the Gloria, which will also serve as an example of the general style of the work.

Ex. 60   CROCE, Missa 'Jubilate Deo'

Ex. 60 (*cont.*)

The sixteen-part Mass is predominantly a conservative work, and only in one way does it hint at Croce's later style. In the Credo, conventionally enough, the *Crucifixus* section is given to Choir 4 alone. It is preceded by an *Et incarnatus* for just two tenors – treated in the old-fashioned *a cappella* imitative manner, it is true, but contrasting profoundly with the idiom of the rest of the work. Solo–tutti contrast is the mainspring of the formal organisation of the works published posthumously in the *Sacre cantilene* (1610). The difference is that these are highly sectionalised pieces in the new *concertato* manner, held together by a continuo part. Croce had published organ parts for his polychoral music, but these were simply *bassi seguenti* following the lowest sounding note at any point. Although his treatment of the bass parts is always spatial his practice varied between supplying a single organ part to sound with both choirs (e.g. the 1597 vesper psalms) and a part for each choir (e.g. the 1594 motets).[18] The main procedure in the 1610 pieces is the alternation of soloists, singly or in various combinations, with a four-part ripieno group. Stylistically both solo and ripieno sections, though often highly contrasted, are rooted in the predominant homophony of Croce's earlier style, with no sign of the influence of Florentine monody. Sometimes the return of the ripieno takes on the substance of a refrain, again not a new device. The only remaining polychoral element is the suggestion, in the editor's remarks (Arnold 1953: 39), that the ripieno parts may be answered by one or two additional choirs; thus polychorality becomes an optional extra rather than a primary formal device, as indeed it was also, though in a rather different sense, in one or two later works of Schütz.

Giovanni Bassano

Croce's contemporary Bassano (*b* c1558, *d* 1617) is known to music historians as a codifier of the practice of improvised embellishment commonly applied in the late sixteenth century by both singers and instrumentalists. He was himself a cornetto player in the ensemble at St Mark's, of which he became head in 1601. His purely compositional output is small but of considerable quality. His church music was published in two volumes, the *Motetti per concerti ecclesiastici* of 1598 and the *Concerti ecclesiastici, libro secondo* of 1599. These are *concerti* in the functional sense in which Venetians seem to have used the word: stylistically they do not differ substantially from the motets of Croce. Bassano shows the Gabrielian predilection for larger forces: there are only a handful of pieces à 5, 6 or 7, and the bulk are for eight-part double choir. Four out of the five seven-part pieces are also for two choirs – e.g. *Hodie Christus natus est* (1599: cantus p. 9; mod. edn, Arnold 1980: 39). A single organ-bass was published for each collection in 1599; it follows the lowest-sounding voice. As regards the choral bass-lines, Bassano is rather inconsistent; they are partly spatial but with some 6/4 chords in the higher choir.

Bassano's idiom is perhaps the most obviously attractive of all the Venetian composers of this period. It plumbs no depths, but is lively and tuneful, delighting in bright sonorities. The clefs of the lower choirs never descend below F_4, though trombones could still have been used. Lively, often dance-like, homophony in the single-choir sections contrasts very effectively with sonorous tuttis. The latter sometimes betray Bassano's instrumental attitude in slightly odd word-setting. The tonality is extremely clear, with explicit accidentals and modulations to a small number of closely-related keys.

Bassano is most at home in lively *note nere* declamation, though nearly all the pieces in the first volume and half those in the second are notated under the ¢ signature. Inasmuch as the choice of signature is consistent, Bassano seems normally to employ ℂ where the piece actually begins with semiminim declamation. He could still write a piece almost entirely in old-fashioned 'white' notes, like *O Domine Jesu Christe* (1598: cantus p. 19). The three-choir *Ave regina coelorum* (ibid.: 21) proceeds majestically in white notes until a dignified central triple-time section, after which, on the return to duple metre, a limited amount of *note nere* declamation appears. The piece thus neatly zones the three types of metre at Bassano's disposal.

Benedicam Dominum à 8 (1599: cantus p. 11) shares with Andrea Gabrieli's three-choir setting (Anthology no. 14) an early shift from longer to shorter note values (Ex. 61) for the second phrase of text, and indeed the openings are

Ex. 61   BASSANO, *Benedicam Dominum*

musically not dissimilar. The difference lies in the subsequent manipulation of the two rhythmic layers. Gabrieli uses the crotchet (in transcription) as the normal unit, with quaver declamation as a lively contrast to play off against it. In Bassano it is the other way round; despite the time signature most of the piece is in *note nere*. His generation was obviously beginning to prefer uncomplicated rhythmic liveliness to dignified solemnity, as Croce's motets also suggest. In his final 'non confundentur' section Andrea breaks up the homorhythm of his choirs sufficiently to produce a rhythmically complex texture which might momentarily 'confound' the listener. At the same point Bassano continues his homorhythmic choral dialogue, relaxing it only in the tutti cadence leading, as in Andrea, into a slower-moving coda (Ex. 62).

Bassano's formal procedures, from examples I have seen, are simpler than those of the Gabrielis. A comparison of Bassano's and Andrea's settings of *Quem vidistis* is instructive (Bassano, 1598: cantus p. 9; Gabrieli: Anthology no. 13). There are superficial similarities (Bassano's opening is a near-quotation), such as the twice-stated final 'Alleluia', but despite the clear-cut, block-like structure of his music, Bassano cannot match the dissective technique or the sharp characterisation of Andrea. In the passage where the shepherds tell of their experience, Andrea states three contrasting ideas and then builds a longer paragraph from them (see above, pp. 139–40). Bassano also gives these three phrases of text contrasting music, but only two are stated at the outset: 'Natum vidimus' (rather bland triple time) and 'et choros Angelorum' (jerky duple, with *note nere*). In various guises these are built into a para-

Ex. 62   BASSANO, Benedicam Dominum

Ex. 62 (*cont.*)

graph, but the third idea, 'collaudantes Dominum', is a self-contained tutti. All this is musically quite effective, but lacks the subtlety of Andrea. The same general conclusion may be drawn from a comparison of Bassano's *O Domine Jesu Christe* (1598: cantus p. 19) with Giovanni Gabrieli's setting of a closely-related text (Anthology no. 15). The two pieces are similar in length, but Bassano's text is somewhat longer so that his setting is in reality more concise. In place of that wonderful varied re-statement of the opening we find in Gabrieli, the same text is set by Bassano just once, save for a repeat of the tutti 'adoro te':

O Domine Jesu Christe,	Ch. 1
adoro te	Tutti (twice)
in cruce vulneratum	Ch. 2

The final section is a conventional series of ideas the whole of which is repeated unaltered without the feeling of growth engendered by Gabrieli's complex treatment of the tonality and the antiphonal relationship. It may be that the extra phrases of text prevented Bassano from achieving something similar – Gabrieli's text concentrates so marvellously on the heart of the matter:

Gabrieli: deprecor te, ut vulnera tua sint remedium animae meae.
Bassano: deprecor maiestatem tuam, ut crux vulnera morsque tua sit remedium animae meae.

Polychoral music in Northern Italy outside Venice, 1570–1600

The earlier tradition of double-choir psalms and canticles continued, both in Venice and elsewhere in Northern Italy, with more and more appearing in print from the 1570s on. Vespers received the most emphasis, usually in the form of collections of psalms for principal feasts, often concluding with one or more magnificats (e.g. Asola 1574 and 1587, Colombano 1587). Occasionally psalms were published without magnificat (e.g. Chamaterò 1573), or double-choir magnificats were added to *alternatim* psalm settings (e.g. Massaino 1576). There was also a tendency for magnificats to be published in separate collections (e.g. Chamaterò 1575, Colombano 1583). Polychoral compline music began to be printed also (e.g. Asola 1585, Colombano 1593), and even music for terce (e.g. Lambardi 1594).

A trickle of polychoral mass settings was published, mostly single examples with others for fewer voices (e.g. Vinci 1575, Antegnati 1578), occasionally complete collections for double choir (e.g. Asola 1588). As time went on polychoral masses were frequently printed in mixed collections with magnificats, other liturgical items and/or motets. The Gabrieli *Concerti* of 1587 is an early example, though unique in containing madrigals also. Double-choir motets appeared more and more frequently after 1580, sometimes in the form of a few examples at the end of a volume for fewer voices, but increasingly forming complete collections with perhaps the odd piece for three choirs.

Costanzo Porta

Clear links with the generation of Willaert and their psalm-compositions may be discerned through Costanzo Porta and Ippolito Chamaterò di Negri. Porta (1528 or 1529 – 1601) was in fact a pupil of Willaert. His career took him to Osimo Cathedral (1552–65), St Antony's at Padua (1565–7 and 1595–1601), Ravenna Cathedral (1567–74), the Santa Casa at Loreto (1574–80) and Padua Cathedral (1589–95). His psalms and magnificats survive partly in manuscript at Ravenna, Modena, Bologna and Padua (see Opera vol. 17: i), partly in the posthumous *Psalmodia vespertina* of 1605. The majority of Porta's psalms consist of non-repetitive antiphony with exchange of choirs at the end of a verse and sometimes at the mediant also. Antiphonal repetition and tutti writing occurs at times without disturbing this basic principle. At times hints of the psalm-tone are found, but Porta is rarely very concerned to retain an alternating cadence structure. Paradoxically, the *Laudate pueri quarti toni* (Opera vol. 17: 88), exceptional in being composed throughout in motet style with frequent interaction of the choirs, nevertheless has more melodic links with the psalm-tone than usual. Duets occur in one of Porta's settings of the matins psalm *Exaudiat te Dominus* (ibid.: 124), and the other (ibid.: 131) is in closed-verse polyphony with an à 8 conclusion. The magnificats are decidedly more lively, with free alternation and combination of the choirs throughout after a restrained opening in some instances. Some are *alternatim* with double-choir polyphonic verses as in Scandello and Lasso. The magnificats for respectively three and four choirs (Opera vol. 11: 98 & 115) are a little disappointing in their extreme concision. The four-choir piece in particular goes in for massive, almost completely homophonic tuttis.

The form and style of motets and similar pieces by Porta lie as close to Palestrina as they do to Venice, particularly in his use of imitation and stately antiphony; a good example is *Magnum haereditatis misterium* (Opera vol. 18: 112). The first two phrases of text are given to a single choir, each in fairly polyphonic, pseudo-imitative vein. The third phrase is stated by the lower choir, then repeated by the higher choir with considerable harmonic variation. A tutti for 'omnes gentes venient dicentes' follows. The last part of the piece (repeated) is in homophonic triple time, the choirs alternating and then over-lapping into a tutti. In some pieces, though, more progressive and lively textures involving the use of *note nere* and syncopation lean towards the Venetians. *Ad Dominum cum tribularer* (Opera vol. 5: 143), for example, veers almost manneristically between long and short notes. As befits a pupil of Willaert, Porta usually writes spatial bass-parts though there are exceptions, notably in seven-voice pieces set out for double choir.

Ippolito Chamaterò di Negri

Although not as great a composer as Porta, Chamaterò is an interesting figure, not least for his two collections of polychoral vespers music, the *Salmi corista* of 1573 and *Li magnificat* of 1575. The first of the magnificats is to be found in a Treviso manuscript (Ms. 12: f. 64v), and although he was born in Rome (c1535–40), Chamaterò seems to have spent most of his working life in cities in Northern Italy, in some of which we know polychoral music to have been culti-vated in the earlier part of the century – especially Padua, where he was *maes-tro di cappella* at the Cathedral in the early 1560s, and Bergamo, where he was working in 1580. He was *maestro* at Udine Cathedral from 1569 to 1575. The dedications of the above-mentioned volumes contain interesting informa-tion.[19] The psalms are said to conform to the ideals of the Council of Trent with regard to the intelligibility of the text, 'notwithstanding [the fact that] they are for eight voices, in the new manner'. In the magnificats the words may also be heard 'even though [the music] may be sung with eight and more voices, and concerted with all sorts of Musical instruments'. Chamaterò sug-gests rather immodestly that 'this manner of composition. . .has been prac-tised by no one else up till now'. The magnificats are dedicated to Nicolò Sfondrato, Bishop of Cremona, and they were composed when Chamaterò was *maestro della Musica* there – perhaps in the later 1560s.

The first thing to be said is that neither psalms nor magnificats are com-pletely homophonic, and it is rather hard to see what the composer meant by the 'new manner'. They seem to fit perfectly well into the tradition discussed in

Chapter 2. That being said, a considerable stylistic range is to be found within the eight psalms. Only two – *Laudate pueri* and *Laudate Dominum* – are assigned to a psalm-tone, tone 6 in both cases. In *Dixit Dominus* he goes in for massive structural alternations of the choirs with some tuttis but no antiphonal repetition or interaction between the choirs at all. The single-choir sections are occasionally enlivened by brief imitation. The harmonic rhythm slows down very noticeably in the tuttis, which are consequently very sonorous though rather stolid in their voice-leading; as in all the pieces by Chamaterò I have transcribed, the bass-parts are treated non-spatially. There is no systematic cadential layout in this mode 1 setting.

The shortest and longest psalms in the collection – *Laudate Dominum* and *In exitu* – provide an interesting contrast. After the incipit *Laudate Dominum* begins tutti, and verse 1b is immediately repeated with antiphonal repetition and a further tutti. The single-choir sections are conspicuously homophonic, and there is far more interaction between the choirs than in *Dixit*. The doxology begins in triple time with a canonic tutti. *In exitu*, despite the difficulties created by its length, seems a very successful piece. The main reason for this is its rhythmic and textual variety. It is the only piece notated under the *note nere* signature. Chamaterò begins in *note bianche* so that the introduction of smaller note-values with closely-wrought imitation at the beginning of verse 3 can represent the fleeing of the sea. There is some exceptionally lively declamation both in single-choir sections and tuttis, as Ex. 63 shows. Such music may perhaps with justice be referred to as the 'new manner' – it seems to point to the Roman style of psalm-composition of some twenty years later. Antiphonal repetition usually leads to a closely-worked tutti, and tuttis are also used to mark a new verse or half-verse or to reiterate and emphasise a phrase just stated by one choir. Some tuttis are homophonic, and all are more or less syllabic. Occasionally a rather heavy texture is created by the occurrence of low thirds in one of the bass-parts.

The magnificats seem to be in an altogether more gracious style than the psalms. The first of the six eight-part settings (p. 3), the one with the Treviso concordance, makes considerable use of antiphonal repetition and much less use of tuttis. Its opening gambit is a very unusual one – Choir 2 enters with new text to a variation of Choir 1's opening phrase. The nine-part (p. 12) is another forward-looking piece with a *note nere* signature, ostensibly laid out for the unusual combination of three three-part choirs, but these are only partially defined, with four- and five-part groups crossing the primary division. The texture is very full and rhythmically animated, voices overlapping each other in a manner perhaps pointing to the *concertato* style. The twelve-part setting (p. 14) is a fine and relatively early example of three-choir writing. It is not just an adaption of the double-choir style – the interaction of the choirs is more complex. Antiphonal repetition may involve all choirs or only two, and two choirs are often superimposed or overlapped to give eight-part textures. The mediant of the verse is often elided in motet fashion. Of particular note

Ex. 63   CHAMATERÒ DI NEGRI, In exitu Israel

are the impressive tuttis which are often of considerable length and more polyphonic in their voice-leading than those in the eight-part works. Three of them
end with written-in *diminuendi* – i.e. voices drop out before the final cadence –
though only in one case, verse 8b ('et divites dimisit inanes'), does this seem to
be connected with word-painting. Once again the shadow of Phinot hovers in
Choir 2's first phrase – strongly reminiscent of that F major cadential idea
from his *Sancta Trinitas*.

Giammateo Asola

One of the most prolific composers of sacred music in the second half of the
sixteenth century was Asola (?1532–1609). He was born in Verona and died in
Venice, with most of his career spent between those two cities, excepting a very
brief spell in Treviso (1577) followed by a few years in Vicenza. He was a pupil
of Ruffo, and his music breathes a sincere liturgical spirit. His output for the
office (vespers, compline, terce and of the dead) was enormous, much of it
alternatim or with closed-verse antiphony. It includes several collections of
polychoral music – 1574 (vespers), 1585 (compline), 1587 (vespers), 1590
(vespers) and 1602 (hymns for vespers – only two voices survive). There are
also six double-choir masses (1588a and 1588b), a book of motets (1600), and
some polychoral motets scattered amongst other publications.

As with Chamaterò, there is a tangible link between Asola and earlier tradition in the shape of concordances with a Treviso source. Three psalms in the
1574 *Psalmodia ad vespertinas* – *Laetatus sum* (cantus primi chori p. 10),
Nisi dominus (p. 12) and *Lauda Ierusalem* (p. 13) – are found, with minor
differences and without ascription, in Treviso Ms. 12 (at ff. 58v, 60v and 62v).
Asola's handling of the antiphony in the 1574 psalms is similar to Porta's with
regard to the verse divisions – the normal unit in the prevailing non-repetitive
antiphony is the half-verse, with some tuttis and antiphonal repetition, the
latter usually of the first few words of a new phrase. Some psalms begin with
antiphonal repetition of verse 1b (1a is always left in chant), and more occurs
in the doxologies, which are often quite lengthy and impressive with a substantial final tutti. Unlike Porta, however, Asola makes extensive use of the psalm-
tones. He almost always preserves the mediants and endings, usually treating
the last note as a cadential final, occasionally as third or fifth of the chord;
rarely does he cadence at a totally foreign pitch level at such points. Even using
the potentially monotonous tone 6 with, in Asola's transposition in *Laetatus
sum* (p. 10), both mediant and ending cadencing on C, he cadences on the
modal final more frequently than many composers (Table 4).

Only the E cadence at the mediant of verse 3 is incompatible with the psalm-
tone. Asola creates tonal variety by fleeting references to other cadential
pitches during the course of a phrase. Unusually, *De profundis* (p. 18) begins
with an affecting tutti embodying a *cantus firmus* treatment of tone 4. The

Table 4

Verse	Choir	Cadential Pitch	Verse	Choir	Cadential Pitch
1a	chant	C	1b	1	C (tenor c.f.)
2a	2	C	2b	1	C
3a	2	E (phrygian)	3b	1	C
4a	2	C	4b	1	C
5a	2 → 1, 1	F	5b	tutti	C
6a	2	C	6b	1 → 2, 1 → 2, 2	C
7a	tutti, 1	C (tenor c.f.)	7b	2 → 1, 2 → 1, 1	C (tenor c.f.)
8a	2, 1	C	8b	2	C
9a	1	A (phrygian)	9b	2	C (tenor c.f.)
10a	tutti	C	10b	1 → 2	C (tenor c.f. Ch. 1)
11a	1	A	11b	2 → 1, 2 → 1 → 2 → tutti	C (tenor c.f. in tutti)

antiphony which follows sets up the normal half-verse alternation of choirs
and cadential alternation of A and E (Ex. 64). The E of the ending is sometimes harmonised as the fifth of an A chord. Whilst unity is already assured by
the standardisation of cadences, it is increased by the recurrence of longer

Ex. 64   ASOLA, De profundis (1574)

portions of phrases during the course of this psalm. Asola shows himself to be a most modally-conscious composer, and the study of pieces such as these, which include settings of all eight tones, would be of great assistance in understanding how composers translated linear modality into polyphonic terms. The 1574 publication closes with two magnificats, the second *alternatim* with double-choir settings of the even verses.

The *Completorium Romanum* of 1585 provides a very comprehensive double-choir setting of compline – fuller even than Croce's of 1591, including alternative settings of the antiphon and short responsory for use in paschal time, a through-composed setting of all three verses of the hymn *Te lucis*, settings of *Regina caeli* and *Salve regina* and four motets. The style of the psalms, all employing tone 8, is very similar to 1574, but with less use of tutti.

Asola's strict adherence to the psalm-tone is also apparent in his later
double-choir vespers print of 1587, the *Nova vespertina*. Indeed, the only area
where there is any substantial stylistic advance on 1574 is in the area of declamation, which is rather livelier, with some syllables set to semiminims. This is
especially true of the Magnificat, which has judiciously-placed tuttis, some
lively antiphonal repetition and an impressive doxology beginning in triple
time and concluding with a tutti beginning after a rest. The three-choir music
of 1590 seems in the main more dignified, though I have so far had access only
to Choirs 1 and 3.[20] This is a mixed collection, with fifteen vesper psalms, two
magnificats, *Salve regina*, a mass and five motets.

The dignity which characterises much of Asola's polychoral music for the
office is also to be seen in the masses of 1588. Some are parodies, such as the
Missa Cantate Domino (1588a: 1) on his own motet (1585: 14). Others are
named only according to their mode. Curiously moving in its devotional
austerity is the *Missa 3., vel 4. toni* (1588a: 15). Perhaps there is something
about the phrygian mode which encourages this sort of approach – it seems
almost like a calculated demonstration of modal formulae, a throw-back
to the world of Ockeghem and Josquin. The movements with short texts
(Kyrie, Sanctus and Agnus Dei) are mainly in a broad idiom with non-
repetitive antiphony and extensive, richly sonorous tuttis. Imitation both by
voices and by choirs is used very sparingly, the latter even in Gloria and Credo
where phrases are shorter and plainer. At its plainest the style even forgoes
overlapping between the choirs. The work is unified as in a parody mass by a
head-motif and a recurrent plagal cadential formula. Other progressions recur
– notably an A–E–F bass movement in the Gloria and Osanna. As in all
Asola's polychoral music the bass parts, with minor anomalies, are spatially
conceived.

In his motets, however, Asola could when he chose command the most
lively, up-to-date manner. 1588a also contains two motets, one of which,
Decantabat populus (p. 21), is as vibrant as anything by Croce. It begins
in white notes with a concise imitative paragraph on the opening text for
each choir in turn, but thereafter alternates stately triple time with animated
note nere declamation, sometimes cast in the form of rapid antiphonal repetition of short phrases. A three-choir setting of the same text (1590: f. 33v)
seems to be thematically and structurally related. Asola is yet another very fine
composer whose music deserves to be revived alongside that of his greater
contemporaries.

It would be a foolish man who attempted at present an authoritative survey of
the cultivation of polychoral music in Northern Italy in the late sixteenth
century, accounting as it does for the majority of the statistics given already in
Chapter 1. Its cultivation in Venice is thus part of an overall tendency. The
peculiar position occupied by Venetian music is created by the sheer quality
and character of her composers, particularly the Gabrielis, their influence in

German-speaking lands through political, trading and personal links, and by other factors such as the colourful employment of instruments and the connection between some kinds of polychoral music and Venetian state occasions.

Any attempt to chart composers of polychoral music together with the places where they worked is an arduous task. Some composers remained in the employ of one church or monastery for most of their composing lives. Although the records are often incomplete, we can tell that others, including some of the most talented, led a surprisingly nomadic existence, staying only a year in some places. The inescapable conclusion is that polychoral music was heard in most of the places where church music of any artistic quality was to be heard – chiefly cathedrals, but sometimes parish churches in larger cities, convents and of course courts. This fact need not surprise if we admit the possibility of its being sung one-to-a-part, the vast bulk of surviving polychoral music being for two four-part choirs.[21]

Although many institutions employed instrumentalists from time to time and probably used them in the performance of polychoral music, most of the music was still notated as purely vocal, despite what the title page might say. Comparatively rarely before 1600, outside the music of the Gabrielis, does the overall range of the music seem to render instruments indispensable. An interesting exception is Ascanio Trombetti's *Il primo libro de motetti* of 1589, despite its title his only sacred publication and possibly retrospective (he was born in 1544). Trombetti was himself a cornetto player who played in S. Petronio, Bologna, from 1560 until his death, at first on an occasional basis and later regularly (*NGr* 19: 160). The title page of his motet collection carries the description 'accomodati per cantare & far Concerti', and five of the pieces for eight or more voices bear the designation 'Da concerto'. The term 'concerto', to the Venetians a description of function, seems to Trombetti to indicate the use of instruments for, significantly, four of the five pieces singled out have a range greater than that contained within the normal C_1–F_4 clefs, expanding it by the use of G_2 or F_5 or both. The fifth piece, *Multiplicati sunt* (no. 32), is scored for a low Gabrielian combination ($C_2C_4C_4F_4/C_3C_4F_3F_5$). The hand of the instrumentalist is present also in a tendency towards clear-cut structures generated by repetition, and the use of at times quite elaborate sequential scalic patterns doubtless intended for the cornetto.

Finally, then, we have afforded Venetian music a central place in this study which we sought at first to deny. Whilst a huge amount of polychoral music was produced elsewhere, its cultivation in the *Serenissima* has some unique features. It is apparent the more one studies polychoral music that, whilst there is much of quality, Venetian music represented the peak of the style. Perhaps because it was for them an art for special state occasions, the Gabrielis in particular rarely repeat themselves or fall back on formulae. It was the sheer quality of their music that attracted the attention of German publishers and composers and caused them to reprint and emulate it.

8

ACROSS THE ALPS: THE GERMAN CRAZE

Flemish and Italian influence

The great popularity of polychoral music in Germany in the late sixteenth and early seventeenth centuries was one facet of the great enthusiasm for Italian music on the part of patrons and composers in both Catholic and Protestant areas. Once again, though, the beginnings of the cultivation of the idiom are shrouded in mist. It may first have been practised in Germany under Franco-Flemish influence – witness the canons of Kugelmann (1540) and Paminger (1556) discussed in Chapter 3. Johannes Heugel in Kassel produced a double-choir setting of *Consolamini, popule meus* as early as 1539 (*NGr* vol. 8: 540), and in 1544, the year of the composer's death, Resinarius's Te Deum (DDT vol. 34: 183) was published; it proceeds mainly in closed sections alternating between the two four-part choirs. The tuttis are à 4, as in English *cantoris–decani* settings. It seems very likely that Phinot's motets (1548) were influential. They certainly seem to have been popular. We mentioned German reprints of them in Chapter 3, and in the second half of the sixteenth century they were copied into manuscripts in, significantly, several Protestant areas. They are (or were – former Breslau manuscripts, for example, were lost in the Second World War) to be found in libraries in Stuttgart, Nuremberg, Zwickau, Dresden, Brieg and Breslau.[1] Catholic and Protestant composers alike came under the towering influence of Lasso.

Direct Italian, and particularly Venetian, influence came about through personal contact such as that maintained by the Gabrielis with Munich and with the Fugger family of nearby Augsburg. Interestingly, Aichinger, Gumpelz-haimer, Klingenstein and, above all, Hassler, all worked in Augsburg and all composed polychoral music. Many courts employed Italian musicians, not just those closest to Italy such as the Imperial Court and Munich, but also those further off such as that at Dresden, where Antonio Scandello from Bergamo worked from 1549 until his death in 1580, becoming Kapellmeister in 1568. Eventually, budding composers from Germany and even as far away as Denmark began to travel to Italy, and particularly Venice, to experience Italian music at first hand. One of the earliest seems to have been Blasius Ammon, though it is not known with whom he studied. Hans Leo Hassler went from his native Nuremberg to study with Andrea Gabrieli from 1584 to 1585, and Giovanni had the most famous pupil of all in Heinrich Schütz.

The other great channel of Italian influence was the anthology. We have already stressed the importance in the dissemination of polychoral music of the first part of the *Thesaurus musicus* (1564[1]), printed by Montanus and Neuber of Nuremberg. Just over twenty years later, Gerlach's press in the same city brought out the first of eight publications assembled by Friedrich Lindner, Kantor at the church and school of St Egidius, and consisting almost entirely of Italian music. Three of them are motet collections which, from the second on, contain a significant amount of polychoral music:

Table 5

	1585[1]	1588[2]	1590[5]
Up to 7vv. of which	39	36	36
Venetian	9 (Merulo: 8)	8 (A. Gabrieli)	4 (A. Gabrieli)
Other N. Italian	14	14 (Ruffo: 7)	10 (Corfini: 5)
Roman	8 (Palestrina)	6	12 (Palestrina: 8)
German			5
Other	8	8 (Mel: 4)	5 (Mel)
8vv. or more of which	2	20	26
Venetian		11 (A. Gabrieli: 9)	5 (A. Gabrieli: 3)
Other N. Italian	1	5 (Porta: 4)	14 (Ingegneri: 7)
Roman		2	4
German		2 (Hassler)	3 (Klingenstein: 2)
Other	1		

[Spheres of activity rather than of origin – e.g. Lasso is counted as German]

Much more music by Giovanni Gabrieli was available by the time another Nuremberg musician, Hans Leo Hassler's brother Kaspar, began to publish his anthologies in 1598; the bulk of the polychoral music in his *Sacrae symphoniae* volume of that year is by Venetians, whilst that in the 1600 volume is rather more diversified:

Table 6

	1598[2]	1600[2]
Up to 7vv. of which	40	46
Venetian	8	10 (G. Gabrieli: 4)
Other N. Italian	16 (Orazio Vecchi: 6)	19 (Massaino: 5; Orazio Vecchi: 5)
Roman	6 (Palestrina: 4)	4
German	8 (Aichinger: 4)	7
Other	2 (Mel)	6 (Guerrero: 3)

Table 6 (*cont.*)

	1598[2]	1600[2]
8vv. or more	26	33
of which		
Venetian	20 (G. Gabrieli: 10; Merulo: 8)	9 (G. Gabrieli: 5)
Other N. Italian	1	12
Roman		4
German	5 (H. L. Hassler: 3)	7 (H. L. Hassler: 2; Neander: 2)
Other		1

Hassler also published a volume of magnificats (1600[1]) and an expanded reprint of 1598[2] (1613[1]). There was clearly still a demand for Italian, including polychoral, music even after German composers had begun to publish their own in some quantities, as is shown by the later anthologies of Schadaeus and Vincentius (*Promptuarium musicum*, 4 vols.: 1611[1], 1612[3], 1613[2] and 1617[1]), and those of Bodenschatz (*Florilegium Portense*, 2 vols.: 1603[1], enlarged as 1618[1], and 1621[2]). Bodenschatz's first volume contains a substantial amount of music by German composers.

Polychoral music in the Empire

Philippe de Monte

Despite his large output, Monte himself does not seem to have been especially interested in polychoral music, and indeed under him the repertory of the Imperial Chapel seems to have been rather conservative. Of his more than three hundred motets, only a handful are for double choir and one for three choirs. Two of his eight-part masses also contain double-choir writing. Monte shows a preference for linear polyphony and fluid voice-groupings which often override the polychoral divisions. Thus *Benedictio et claritas* (1585: no. 19; mod. edn, Opera 2/A, vol. 5: 141), ostensibly for three four-part choirs (SSAT/SATB/SATB), has frequent five-, six- and seven-part textures, some drawn from all three choirs. This is also true of the two masses – one on Lasso's *Confitebor tibi* (1587: no. 3; mod. edn, Opera 2/B, vol. 2: 79) and the other on Monte's own madrigal *La dolce vista* (Opera 1, vol. 14, from Brussels and Vienna mss.). Where they differ is in their relationship with their respective models. *La dolce vista* in not polychoral, and not much apart from the opening is in fact utilised in the Mass. A rare example of subtle parody technique occurs in the opening antiphonal exchange of Kyrie I, where a reworking of the opening of the madrigal (Choir 1) is wedded to a later passage (Choir 2, from bar 25 of the madrigal) which happens to be a variant of the opening with a faster harmonic rhythm. This Mass retains the declamation in both white and black notes as found in the madrigal. Lasso's *Confitebor tibi* is for double choir, and while borrowing quite extensively (mostly from the first half of the motet), Monte does not always retain Lasso's antiphonal distribution of the material, as for example in Kyrie I:

Lasso   Ch. 1   ab:cd   h
                [v. 1]   [v. 2] } Tutti   g { antiphonal repetition
        Ch. 2   ef: h

Monte   Ch. 1   ab: free extension   e'
                                    mixing } Tutti (free extension)
        Ch. 2   c

From the Credo onwards it is apparent that Monte does not regard the choral division as of paramount significance.

Two of Monte's seven-part motets printed posthumously in Schadaeus's *Promptuarium musicum* are for double choir. *Stellam quam viderant* (1611[(1)]: no. 27; mod. edn, Opera 1, vol. 15: 50) is concise and quite homophonic, but proceeds largely in non-repetitive antiphony until the final phase of the B section of its aBcB form. *Ego sum panis vivus* (1612[(3)]: no. 67; transcr. Oberg 1941, vol. 2: 191) contains some antiphonal repetition but is conservative in its beautifully-wrought dovetailing at choral interchanges. Far more up-to-date are two eight-part psalm-motets. *Laudate Dominum* (Opera 1, vol. 15: 69, from a Berlin ms. of 1599) is a concise, largely homophonic setting of Ps. 150, memorably tuneful and with quite lively interplay between the choirs, the antiphonal repetition often varied and transposed. *Beatus vir* (1617[(1)]: no. 99) (Ps. 1), on the other hand, proceeds mainly in non-repetitive antiphony, the only antiphonal repetition occurring at verse 5a, 'Non sic impii, non sic' (in triple time), and in the final half-verse, where it leads with some rather Andrea Gabrieli-like writing in *note nere* into the closing (and only) tutti. There is much syllabic homophony but also some plastic and expressive polyphonic writing reminding us of the Lasso of the *Stabat mater*.

Jacob Handl

The most prolific writer of polychoral music in the Empire at this time was Handl (1550–91). He sang under Monte in the Imperial Chapel in Vienna but left in 1575. After some years of travel he settled in Moravia in 1579 as choirmaster to the Bishop of Olomouc. By mid-1586 he had become Kantor at St Jan na Brzehu in Prague (*NGr* vol. 8: 141). The nature of his relationship, if any, with the Imperial Chapel, which of course spent much of its time in Prague, is not certain. Between 1586 and the year of his death he published the four books of his *Opus musicum*, a monumental motet collection arranged according to the liturgical year. More than ninety of the total of 445 motets are polychoral, including some for three and four choirs.

General style

There are two seemingly contradictory strands in Handl's compositional personality. The Netherlands idiom, which was much in evidence in the Vienna of his youth, reveals itself in his use of borrowed material and in his delight in canons. We have already referred to the latter in connection with his double-choir *Missa canonica* (see above, p. 49). Most of his polychoral music, however, exemplifies the other side of his personality, the progressive humanistic side, resulting in strict homophony, scrupulous observance of the verbal accent, clear-cut formal structures and clearly-directed, almost tonal harmony. There is no indication that Handl ever visited Italy; as we argued in Chapter 4, this style seems to have emerged in the music of some Habsburg composers in the 1560s, particularly in political motets. Handl did in fact base a double-choir Mass (1580 vol. 1: no. 4; mod. edn, DTÖ 78: 18) on a piece from the *Novus thesaurus musicus*, Christian Hollander's *Casta novenarum*, a motet making use of forthright homophonic antiphony within various, mostly SATB/SATB splits of the ensemble. It is therefore not necessary to assume that Handl knew much if any Venetian music, though he can hardly fail to have been acquainted with the music of Lasso. Like Lasso, he hardly ever conceives his bass-parts spatially, though octaves by contrary motion occur quite frequently, especially at choral interchanges.

Declamation in single-choir phrases

The bulk of the single-choir music in Handl's polychoral works is quite severely homophonic, apart from occasional carefully-controlled melisma (usually to emphasise key words) or syncopation of one voice against the rest. The audibility of the text is thus paramount. Not that there is not variety in the expressive character which the music can bring to the declamation of the text. At times, as in *Quam dilecta tabernacula tua* (DTÖ 40: 83), Handl almost seems to approach the strictness of *musique mesurée* (Ex. 65). At the begin-

Ex. 65   HANDL, Quam dilecta tabernacula tua

ning of *Surge, propera amica mea* (DTÖ 48: 1), on the other hand, he vividly suggests the urgency of the invitation with a mixture of conventional melisma and parlando (Ex. 66). In *Exsultate Deo* (DTÖ 51–2: 218), a catalogue of 'tympanum' imagery, the parlando takes on the character of battle-music. Handl is also capable of extremely expressive declamation, as in *Planxit David* (DTÖ 40: 91), an evocation of David's lament for Absalom. Each of the two *partes* opens with a paragraph for each choir, broken up with rhetorical rests

Ex. 66   HANDL, Surge, propera amica mea

and rendered expressive also by judicious use of chromaticism and suspensions (Ex. 67). Antiphonal interaction between the choirs is restricted to the refrain 'Eheu dolor', with which each *pars* ends, slightly extended the second time.

Ex. 67   HANDL, Planxit David

Tuttis

Handl uses tuttis rather sparingly on the whole, but they do allow a little more floridity and rhythmic variation between different voices. Occasionally, though, he seems determined to demonstrate his Flemish lineage as a composer by indulging in virtuosic eight-part imitative writing. The 'Amen' of the Pater noster (DTÖ 24: 16) recalls the sound of Flemish multi-voiced canons of the first half of the century without being slavishly canonic (Ex. 68). Some tuttis, at the other extreme, are as homophonic as single-choir sections, either in terms of each choir separately, so that the effect is pseudo-canonic, as in *Veni Domine* (DTÖ 12: 14), or in terms of the whole ensemble. The smaller of the two settings of Psalm 150, à 16 for two choirs, has homophony for the primary eight-part groups, splits each of these into two homophonic four-part groups and concludes with à 16 homophony, the final section (in triple time) reiterating just the F major tonic. This manner of setting these 'triumphant' psalms for All Saints' Day may well have been found attractive by later German composers, including Protestants who would have relished the symbol of unity in worship of such massive declamation.

Antiphonal repetition

Despite a clear preference for choirs with equal clefs, (and a preference nearly

Ex. 68   HANDL, Pater noster

as marked for keeping the overall range between C_1 and F_4)[2], Handl's approach to antiphonal repetition is to create variety in the length of phrases reiterated, to vary harmonic and melodic content in the repetition (by imitation at pitch, or transposed and/or harmonically varied). What he rarely does is to change the rhythmic profile significantly – the primacy of the verbal accent is retained. Though we do not come across the sophisticated mosaic-like antiphonal processes found in the music of the Gabrielis, Handl provides plenty of interest in his handling of harmonic variation. At the beginning of *Hodie nobis coelorum rex* (DTÖ 12: 62) the answering choir is identical for one bar, after which each choir reaches the 'relative major' by a different route (Ex. 69).

Ex. 69   HANDL, Hodie nobis coelorum rex

Ex. 69 (*cont.*)

The first choir sidesteps the B flat cadence with a deliciously unexpected G major chord in bar 5, thereafter cadencing in the tonic. The second choir is more emphatic about the B flat tonality (bars 10–11), just touching on the G major chord (bar 12) before cadencing in the dominant. The declamation is also varied in an unusually subtle way. At the beginning of *Salve nos* (DTÖ 24: 21) two much shorter varied 'couplets' are immediately repeated with the choirs exchanged:

> Ch. 1: a   b′   a′ b
> Ch. 2:   a′ b   a   b′

Many other instances of variation technique could be cited, each with its own particular method of re-arranging the material. On the other hand, snatches of canonic writing are quite common, sometimes in the form of a brief revolving ostinato. Sequential antiphonal repetition of the type found in Giovanni Gabrieli is comparatively rare.

Sometimes one feels that Handl falls victim to his own facility, as in the excessive amount of antiphonal repetition at the unison in *Haec est dies* (DTÖ 30: 56), for example. This is especially apparent in five of the six works for three choirs, mostly à 12, and one of those for four choirs. These tend to be rather formulistic, the choirs usually entering in the same order with basically the same material. The fact that it is varied in pitch and harmonic content, effective though this can be in a two-choir context, cannot disguise the predictability of the antiphonal plan.

Psalmody and dialogue

The most successful multi-choired works are psalm-settings: Psalm 80, *Exsultate Deo*, for sixteen voices divided into three choirs 6/5/5 (DTÖ 30: 71) and the identically scored ($G_2G_2C_2C_3C_4F_4 \times 2/C_1C_3C_3C_4F_4F_5/C_1C_3C_4C_4F_4F_5$) twenty-four-part, four-choir settings of the lauds psalms 149 and 150.[2] Ironically, the reason for their success is their eschewing of continual antiphonal repetition in favour of a monumental expansion of double-choir psalmody, with carefully-controlled departures from non-repetitive antiphony. Psalm 149, *Cantate Domino* (DTÖ 51-2: 224), is closest to the old tradition, treating the verse as the basic unit and even adhering to an alternating cadential pattern:

		cadences
v. 1:	Ch. 1	F, d
v. 2:	Ch. 2	F, d
v. 3:	Ch. 3	F, d
v. 4:	Ch. 4	F, d
v. 5a:	Ch. 1 → 2 → 3 → 4	F, A, d, a
5b:	Ch. 1 → 2 → 3 → 4; Tutti	(one chord: d)
v. 6:	Ch. 1	F, d
v. 7:	Ch. 2	F, d
v. 8:	Ch. 3	a, d
v. 9a:	Ch. 3	a
9b:	Ch. 3 → Ch. 1 → Ch. 2+3+4→ Ch. 1 → Ch. 2+3; Tutti	d

Psalm 150, *Laudate Dominum in sanctis* (ibid.: 236), is slightly more complex, though related, in formal outline; it treats the half-verse as the unit and the structural cadences are mostly on d. There are several double-choir psalm-motets which derive their structure at least in part from liturgical antiphony and a couple of pieces which, though not psalm-settings, have texts long enough virtually to require the use of much non-repetitive antiphony.

Three pieces have dialogic elements, including *Quem vidistis* (DTÖ 12: 65) and the *Passio* (DTÖ 24: 123) mentioned in Chapter 1. The third sets a psalm (23) embodying a question-and-answer pattern which is reflected in Handl's antiphony (DTÖ 48: 113). There are also four punning echo-motets which display a predilection for reiterating words and their echoes. Some echoes are linguistically contrived – e.g. 'responsio–sponso' in *Quid mihi crude dolor* (DTÖ 30: 59). Perhaps the most interesting is the Easter piece *Quid plorans mulier* where the 'echoes' are the replies of Mary Magdalen to the Angel (ibid.: 140).

Other formal patterns

In producing so many polychoral motets, some of them rather perfunctory, it is natural that Handl should to some extent rely on well-tried formulae in handling the macro-structure – the aBcB pattern is common (both with and without a division into two *partes*, as is aBB. Most of the pieces not covered in the discussion so far have structures either unique or shared with perhaps one other piece. To the analyst sated by looking at many similar pieces the unique ones always seem of more interest; certainly, limiting oneself to trying to describe a 'typical' motet is bound to result in dull abstraction. One or two pieces may be seen as expansions of the two formulae mentioned. In *Vox clamantis* (DTÖ 12: 16) the repeat of the final tutti links the form to aBB, but there are two sharply differentiated sections preceding it:

$$
\begin{array}{ccc}
a & b & CC \\
\text{antiphonal} - \text{antiphonal} & - & \text{tutti} \\
\mathcent & \mathcent 3 & \mathcent
\end{array}
$$

In *Exsultate iusti* (DTÖ 51–2: 214) there are also three main sections, but the first is re-stated with the choirs exchanged. Structural articulation by means of sharp rhythmic contrast is much in evidence in *Hodie nobis caelorum rex*. After the opening passage quoted in Ex. 69, the declamation of the next phrase is rapid in *note nere* and then an intermediate style is reached, contrasted in turn with triple time. Repetition is only in evidence in the short-term antiphonal sense. Another interesting and unique structure occurs in *Dixerunt discipuli* (DTÖ 48: 121) in which all the material, falling into three sections, is re-stated with the choirs exchanged; the third section is then extended to a tutti cadence after which the second and third sections are further developed:

A	B	C	A′
narration (Ch. 1)+ direct speech (Ch. 2)	– antiphonal repetition	– antiphonal repetition with *note nere*	– (Ch. 1↔2) –

B′	C′	B″	C″
(Ch. 1 ↔ 2) –	(Ch. 1 ↔ 2) extended –	with diminution –	varied & extended

The piece is unusual in that the choirs, far from using equal clefs, have hardly any overlap of range ($G_2C_1C_2C_3/C_3C_4F_3F_4$), and all the swapping of material between the choirs involves octave transposition. Handl seems more concerned with musical structure *per se* rather than characterisation of the dialogue between St Martin and his disciples.

The few pieces with a recurring 'Alleluia' in the text do not employ fully-worked-out refrain structures – the word may recur once to the same music and subsequent statements may be distantly related or unrelated. The only true refrain piece is *O beata Trinitas* (DTÖ 40: 7). This text arises from the conflation of three matins antiphons. The refrain opens and closes the piece and there are four occurrences in all, the first and third antiphonal (Choir 2 imitates Choir 1 at the unison), the second and fourth tutti with altered harmony but the same basic rhythmic outline. The opening phrase is closely related to that of Phinot's *Sancta Trinitas* (Anthology no. 4), though Handl's subsequent style is rather more homophonic and with more antiphonal repetition of short phrases than we find in Phinot.

Masses

We shall not dwell at length on Handl's masses. As well as the *Missa canonica*, there are five parody masses for eight-part double choir, of which three are based on double-choir pieces by Handl himself, one on a motet by Hollander and one on Phinot's *Jam non dicam*. The last-named (DTÖ 94–5: 95) survives, as does one of the others, in the form of just Kyrie and Gloria and was perhaps copied for Lutheran use. It surely represents a tribute to Phinot, whose motets, so popular in German-speaking lands, may well have served, in addition to the Habsburg political motets, as models for Handl's polychoral writing. Even Handl's six-part *Jam non dicam* (DTÖ 30: 156) refers to Phinot's setting.

Handl emerges as a resourceful and many-sided composer who in all probability arrived at his brand of polychoral writing with little or no knowledge of Venetian developments, building on Phinot, Lasso and the political style. His subsequent influence on later German masters is harder to evaluate, though his triumphant psalms seem to have appealed to them.

Large-scale music in Graz

If conservative taste at the Imperial Court itself seems to have restricted the amount of polychoral music heard there, the opposite was true at the Graz court, under both Archduke Karl II (1564–90) and Archduke Ferdinand II (1595–1619). Some of the repertory from the beginning of the seventeenth century has been preserved in large choirbooks in the Nationalbibliothek in Vienna which have already been referred to in Chapter 4 in connection with Annibale Padovano's twenty-four-part Mass. An inventory of the most

important polychoral sources will be found in Appendix 2. We have also
mentioned Croce's large-scale Mass, but analysis of further examples is not
possible at present. The sheer labour involved has inhibited transcription of
these works, let alone their publication, and indeed many survive with one or
more choirs missing. There remains a fruitful field of study here. Nevertheless,
there are some general conclusions which may be drawn.

The composers fall into fairly well-defined groups. The Venetians are well
represented – Annibale Padovano, the Gabrielis, Croce, Merulo, Donato and
Gregorio Zucchini. Uniquely in this group, Annibale left Venice to work in
Austria – he was in the service of Karl II at Graz from 1566 until his death in
1575. Zucchini was a Venetian monk who published a collection of large-scale
polychoral music in 1602. Strikingly, several composers from Northern Italy
moved, like Padovano, to Graz (the years they spent there are given in
brackets): Simone Gatto (from the mid-1570s until his death in 1595); Francesco Rovigo, a pupil of Merulo (1582–90); Francesco Stivori (from about
1602 until his death in 1605); Giovanni Priuli, a pupil of Giovanni Gabrieli
(1614 or 1615 – 19, when he went with Ferdinand to Vienna). Liberale Zanchi,
after a brief stay in Salzburg, served Rudolf II in Prague from 1596 until 1612.
Alessandro Tadei, of Italian extraction, was sent from Graz in 1604 by Ferdinand to study with Giovanni Gabrieli; he returned in 1606, and like Priuli
moved to Vienna in 1619. Large-scale music by some other North Italians was
also collected, some of it presumably, as with the Venetian music, taken from
prints of the time – e.g. by Spontone, Mortaro, Leoni, Antegnati, Varotto. Two
Romans are also represented (Giovanelli and Marenzio), as is Asprilio Pacelli,
an Italian who worked in Warsaw. All this leads to the conclusion that the taste
at Graz was indeed largely for Venetian or Venetian-style polychoral music.
The style was emulated by composers such as Lambert de Sayve, Georg Poss,
who studied in Venice, and Reimundo Ballestra. It seems to me just as valid to
use the term 'Colossal Baroque' to describe some of this music as it is to use it
of Roman polychoral music of the seventeenth century.

Augsburg

Several prominent composers of polychoral music in the late sixteenth and
early seventeenth centuries were associated with Augsburg: Hans Leo Hassler,
Aichinger, Klingenstein and Gumpelzhaimer, a fact which may be connected
with the fact that it was the home of the famous banking family, the Fuggers,
patrons of the Gabrielis. Aichinger and Klingenstein were employed by the
Cathedral, whereas Hassler, although himself a Protestant, wrote most of his
polychoral music for the Catholic rite whilst employed as organist by Octavian
II Fugger. Gumpelzhaimer worked at the Lutheran church and school of
St Anna.

Hans Leo Hassler

The Venetian connection is explicit in the case of Hassler, since he studied in
Venice with Andrea Gabrieli and formed a lifelong friendship with Giovanni.
Although a few were printed earlier in anthologies, the bulk of Hassler's
sacred polychoral works appeared in his motet collections of 1591 and 1601,
the second slightly expanded in a reprint of 1612, and the collection of masses
of 1599 includes one for double choir. By and large, these are works characterised by their sheer exuberance. Hassler has a love of clear-cut phrasing
which even, in 1591, verges on the short-winded. The verbal enunciation is
lively and forceful – even his settings of Latin texts exhibit a rugged Germanic
form of expression. Single phrases may encompass considerable changes of
rhythmic pattern, giving the music an unpredictable, volatile character.
Snappy *note nere* homophony is a characteristic found in common with his
secular and instrumental music, and on occasion it is found even in tuttis. This
is seen in Ex. 70, which illustrates also Hassler's love of quick-fire antiphony

Ex. 70   HASSLER, Jubilate Deo

and sudden changes in the style of the declamation. There are also one or two
psalm-motets in which Hassler is more restrained and retains a certain amount
of verse-by-verse antiphony, though no cadential alternation, as well as two
superb settings of the Miserere with closed verses, one for three choirs
(unusually for three, four and four voices) (1591 no. 46; DDT 2: 153), the other
for two choirs but containing verses à 2 and à 3 as well as à 4 and à 8 (1601
no. 44; DDT 24–5: 174). These last clearly belong to the tradition of Lasso.

Like Giovanni Gabrieli, Hassler had a superb contrapuntal gift. He quite
often begins with an imitative paragraph of considerable breadth, often longer
than in a Venetian composition, though, in the time-honoured manner, it is
usually answered homophonically by the other choir. His tuttis vary from the
basically homophonic to the richly textured. In *Nos autem populus ejus*, the
secunda pars of *Jubilate Deo* (1591 no. 39; DDT 2: 111), we find writing of an
extraordinarily modern cast combining motifs in long and short notes, each
set syllabically (Ex. 71). One of his favourite devices is to begin a sumptuous
tutti after a rest in all the voices and to repeat it immediately.

It is natural that we should seek to compare Hassler and Gabrieli, and there
are various interesting points which come out of such a comparison. The setting of the word 'Alleluia' in *Angelus Domini descendit* (1591 no. 41; DDT 2:
121) employs one of Gabrieli's favourite rhythms: $\frac{3}{2}$ ♩ ♩ ♩ | ♩♩ ♩♩ | ♩ ,
treated homorhythmically by the choirs combined as well as separately, whilst
Hodie Christus natus est (1591 no. 45; ibid.: 147) has an 'Alleluia' refrain, like
Gabrieli's setting of the same text, also for ten voices. In Hassler's *Dum complerentur dies Pentecostes* (1591 no. 42; ibid.: 127) the 'Alleluia' setting, which
occurs twice, employs sequential decorative patterning which is more a feature
of Gabrieli's later style (Ex. 72). Such textures are found from time to time as
a means of emphasising a particular word, but they also suggest instrumental
writing, reminding us that Hassler in his collection of 1601, like Gabrieli in
1597, included pieces for instrumental ensemble. In two general areas of technique Hassler takes a similar line to Gabrieli: he has a fondness for the 'clash'
cadence, and his bass parts are generally spatial in two-choir writing except
where polyphonic voice-leading takes precedence or where one bass part has a
very much higher clef than the other. In three-choir writing there is a spatial
relationship between the lowest two choirs with 6/4 chords allowed in the
highest choir, just as in Gabrieli.

Hassler's setting of *O Domine Jesu Christe* (1601: no. 34; DDT 24–5: 109)
uses the same text as Gabrieli's, and has similarities of detail, notably a syncopated descending scale for 'in cruce vulneratum' and a bitter augmented chord
on the word 'felle' – indeed, Hassler goes one better in terms of word-painting
with bitter suspended ninths on 'et aceto potatum'. Once again though, as we
found in comparing him with Bassano, Gabrieli's formal sense is in a different
class. The recurring antithesis in the second half of Gabrieli's setting is not
matched in the corresponding section of Hassler's piece in which all is dance-
like sweetness and light.

Ex. 71   HASSLER, Nos autem populus ejus

Ex. 72   HASSLER, Dum complerentur dies pentecostes

[each phrase imitated at the unison by Ch. 2]

Occasionally there are hints of the Gabrielian mosaic technique, though only in a very basic form. In *Si bona suscepimus* (1612 no. 39; ibid.: 280) this impression arises at one point through the juxtaposition and variation of two phrases which are strongly contrasted in both rhythm and metre. *A Domino factum est istud* (1601 no. 37; ibid.: 130) is a stranger case. The text consists of two verses taken from the middle of Psalm 117; it is convenient to label the half-verses a, b, c, d and to subdivide the last into d_1, d_2:

> a A Domino factum est istud
> b et est mirabile in oculis nostris.
> c Haec est dies, quam fecit Dominus:
> d_1 exsultemus, d_2 et laetemur in ea.

Hassler progresses through the whole of the text three times. The first time one verse is given to each choir:

> Ch. 2 (high): cd_{1-2-2}
> Ch. 1 (low):   abb

Choir 1 opens in broad style with elements of polyphony; Choir 2's material is more concise and homophonic, changing to triple time for d. Choir 1 now varies Choir 2's material, and then d is expanded, mostly tutti. The second statement is compressed; Choir 2 takes up Choir 1's version of the first verse, beginning an octave higher, but does not repeat the second half of the verse. Choir 1 enters with c, but then we jump straight to the tutti expansion of d, which is, it seems, to act as a refrain. In the third statement the style of sections a and b changes completely, with only the merest suggestion of a thematic resemblance to the first two statements. First a and then b is stated homophonically by Choir 2, to be echoed each time by Choir 1. The word 'mirabile' in section b, formerly emphasised by a melisma, is now treated in sequential repetition. 'Haec est dies. . .' is now set tutti and, as Hassler likes to do, immediately repeated. The section d refrain is heard twice, followed by a final duple-time setting of d_2 by way of a coda. One suspects that what Hassler was really trying to do here was to make a substantial piece out of a relatively short text without resorting to interminable repetitions of each phrase.

One area in which Hassler seems more at home than Gabrieli is that of mass composition. There is only one double-choir Mass in Hassler's 1599 collection, but it is more representative of its composer than the Mass Movements of his Venetian friend. It is unclouded, assured music, characterised particularly in the Gloria and Credo by clear-cut phrasing and rapid antiphonal repetition, often at the unison. There is some polyphonic writing but it is tightly controlled, the most sustained example being the four-part Christe.

The best of Hassler seems to lie in the two exceedingly fine twelve-part, three-choir works in the 1601 collection. Both are grounded solidly in impressive tuttis, but thrive also on an element of unpredictability in the antiphony which was lacking in Handl's multi-choired works. The order in which the choirs sing never becomes formulistic, obvious symmetries are avoided and the ear is constantly teased as to whether the next entry will repeat existing text or bring in a new idea. Semi-tuttis of two choirs are used to increase the textural variety. Hassler's liking for clear-cut sectionalism is shown in the contrasting of successive sections in texture (e.g. amount of melisma) and particularly harmonic rhythm (white notes, black notes, triple metre). In *Domine Dominus noster* (1601 no. 52; DDT 24–5: 242), a setting of the whole of Psalm 8, the sectionalism is emphasised as in late Andrea Gabrieli by important use of rests in all the parts. Near the beginning Hassler perpetrates a most unexpected trick. The first verse, which the psalmist repeats at the end, is set as a triple-time tutti. Choir 1 begins verse 2 in light, tuneful vein, but as soon as it reaches the word 'magnificentia' in verse 2, the other two choirs crash in once more, the tutti lasting until the end of the verse. It is also worth mentioning that at the end of the piece, where Hassler not unexpectedly takes up the opportunity to re-use the opening tutti (twice), he rounds it off with a duple-time coda which, rather than constituting the conventional plagal progression, is actually a rhythmic transformation of the last phrase of the triple-time tutti with an identical pitch sequence in every part. This piece is scored in a characteristically Gabrielian way with high and low choirs embracing the extremes G_2–F_5 flanking an SATB 'Capella'. It ranks with the very best Venetian works.

Some Protestant composers of polychoral music

As we have shown in examining the German anthologies, many Lutheran churches continued to use music with Latin text, and very often by Catholic composers, providing of course that the text was doctrinally 'sound'. (The Lutheran rite itself retained considerable use of Latin.) This facilitated the spread of the polychoral idiom, which must in fact by the late sixteenth century have been absorbed from several different sources: from Venice or elsewhere in Northern Italy, from composers within the Empire such as Handl, and from nearer home, following the example of Lasso and perhaps ultimately Phinot. With church music in the vernacular, in addition to the simple adoption of the motet style for German words, we find also the application of polychoral techniques to chorale settings; the resulting structures are different from any others we have encountered.

Nothing more graphically illustrates the conquest of German music by the polychoral style than its cultivation in the far North and North-East, by composers such as Dulichius in Stettin and Hieronymus Praetorius in Hamburg. Their concept of polychoral music may have come from Lasso and/or Handl, since neither usually writes spatial bass parts. Dulichius (1562–1631) left a not inconsiderable quantity of music for eight-part double choir, most of it published in the four volumes of his *Centuriae harmonias sacras* (1607, 1608, 1610 and 1612). Most of the texts are Latin; the style is conservative but highly accomplished, and some pieces attain considerable liveliness in a Hassler-like manner. Praetorius's music is of more importance and merits consideration at greater length.

Hieronymus Praetorius

Praetorius (1560–1629) represents the finest of Lutheran composers writing polychoral music almost entirely to Latin words. Some fifty of his motets are polychoral (just over half) and there are also nine magnificats and three masses for double choir. His music began to appear in 1599, and between 1616 and 1625 most of it was assembled in the five volumes of the *Opus musicum*. It is possible to see, as with Handl, a Flemish side to Praetorius's technique, but it is less extreme and better integrated. Contrapuntal writing occurs more frequently than in Handl, but imitation is always very close and concise. A certain delight in small-scale contrapuntal 'tricks' can be observed in the 1599 *Cantiones sacrae*.

Praetorius's approach to antiphonal repetition is similar to Handl's: variation without appreciable alteration of the rhythmic structure is the norm. Exact repetition is more common in triple-time sections. One idea new to us is the practice of presenting the answering phrase in diminution, used occasionally by Hieronymus but far more frequently by Michael Praetorius. In the second section of the Nunc dimittis (1599; mod. edn, 1974a: 16), the single word 'Lumen' is set successively to minims, crotchets and quavers in a way suggesting a developmental progression. In three- and four-choir works, Praetorius occasionally employs antiphonal repetition in the formulistic manner we censured in Handl; however the colour contrasts provided by the instruments Praetorius would have expected in performance would do something to counteract the predictability.

Though they may at times be homorhythmic, Praetorius's tuttis frequently arise from quasi-canonic overlapping of the choirs. When the latter are each operating as homorhythmic groups, the result can be rhythmically very lively; we have observed similar textures in contemporary Italian music. In *Angelus ad pastores ait* (1618a; 1974b: 43) revolving canonic imitation is distributed between all three choirs. As with many composers the treatment of the bass parts is often spatial at such points, but Praetorius is not concerned to eliminate 6/4 harmony from individual choirs in his other tuttis. Few write more thrilling tuttis than Hieronymus Praetorius, and they may be quite richly polyphonic. One of his favourite devices when the choirs as a whole are not in a canonic relationship is to concentrate on interweaving the highest parts of each choir. A good example of this technique is the closing tutti of the first section of *Ecce Dominus veniet* (1599; 1974a: 1) – Ex. 73 isolates the voices

Ex. 73   H. Praetorius, Ecce Dominus veniet
[top parts only shown]

concerned. His most magnificent tutti, that closing the four-choir, twenty-part *Decantabat populus Israel* (1618a; DDT 23: 107) applies this technique to an ecstatic rising scale embracing a ninth in the highest voices of Choirs 2 and 4. The most startling is probably a passage in *Jubilate Deo* (1607; 1974b: 1) where the word 'date' is set to a little four-note figure which appears in free ostinato fashion in all twelve voices (bars 26–30). Like Hassler, Praetorius very often adopts the Gabrielian 'clash' cadence in his tutti cadences – i.e. the sounding of the suspended leading note against its resolution. We have to go back a long way, however, perhaps to Ruffino, to find a parallel to the suspension of the dominant chord in one choir against the tonic in the other, as happens in *Quam pulchra es* (1618a; see Gable 1966: 76).

Syncopation is a feature of Praetorius's style even in single-choir sections, and on occasions he uses chains of syncopations in a rather abstract, almost 'instrumental' manner, as in the Nunc dimittis already cited ('quia viderunt', bars 54, 57–60). Indeed, more frequently than Hassler, Praetorius makes use of sequential, often figurate writing and also conventional decorative flourishes. Although the top parts are favoured for the latter, there is no suggestion, as in Giovanni Gabrieli, of soloistic writing. However, such passages do have a recognisably Baroque sound, a foretaste of metrical figural counterpoint. More than that, they proclaim irresistibly their suitability for instruments. *Tota pulchra es* (1618a; 1974b: 62) contains triadic and scalic writing which almost suggests trumpet ensemble style, though the harmony is not sufficiently restricted to enable the actual use of trumpets. Praetorius apparently drew on the services of the Hamburg town musicians, as well as augmenting the church choir with schoolteachers and older pupils, for feasts on which the performance of polyphony was permitted at St Jacob's. Certainly there are some pieces with the expanded Gabrielian compass which demand instruments. *Herr Gott dich loben wir* (1618a; Gable 1966, vol. 2: 427), the German Te Deum, is a case in point ($G_2C_2C_3F_4/G_2C_2C_4F_4/G_2C_2C_4F_4/G_2C_3C_4F_5$). We know that this was performed at the dedication in 1607 of St Gertrude's Chapel, Hamburg, and an account of the instrumentation used has been preserved (Gable in 1974a x; see also Gable 1987). Choir 1 had voices only, whilst the remaining three included respectively cornetti and sackbuts, viols and regal, and organ. The distribution of singers in Choirs 2, 3 and 4 is not recorded. One strange case is *Angelus ad pastores ait*, already cited, which has one closely spaced choir and two with high G_2 parts sounding at times more than an octave above the next voices down, strongly suggesting the use of cornetti ($C_1C_2C_3F_3/G_2C_3C_4F_4/G_2C_3C_4F_4$).

This is not to suggest that Praetorius was indifferent to the texts he was setting. On balance, most of his polychoral works are festive in spirit, and in terms of word-painting, they employ many of the conventional images of the period. Praetorius's full expressive powers are shown in a work like *Videns Dominus* (1599; DDT 23: 60), which depicts vividly the raising of Lazarus. Each phrase of the text is giving a telling musical equivalent. The opening expressive polyphony for each choir in turn is restless but strongly tonal in its harmony with notated F, C, G, and even D sharps. Subsequently Praetorius uses both antiphony and tutti to consummately expressive effect: a brief, slightly decorated tutti for 'ad monumentum', melting antiphonal phrases for 'lachrymatus est' as Jesus weeps. Then he is depicted as a man of action. With great urgency the phrase 'et clamavit' is passed between the choirs then rings forth in a multiple triadic ostinato-cum-echo texture. Jesus calls Lazarus's name six times – four mighty tutti statements are punctuated by tender entreaties in Choir 1 where the soprano part anticipates the lower three voices. His urgent command 'veni foras' is heard tutti, then in a series of canonic post-echoes as it were. At the end of the piece, the astonishment of the witnesses seems to break through in the *fusae* which rise imitatively through the texture in all parts except the second bass; once again there is virtually a canon between the two soprano parts.

A few aspects of macro-structure raise echoes of the Gabrielis. *O admirabile commercium* à 10 (1607; Gable 1966, vol. 2: 187) makes long range structural play of the contrast between *note nere* and *note bianche*. The most important connection, though, is probably the small group of psalm-motets which employ a refrain. In two cases, a textual refrain is created where the psalm itself does not have one. Of these, Gable (1966: 119) rightly singles out *Cantate Domino* (1602; 1974a: 34) as representing the 'peak of Praetorius's compositional skills'. Praetorius makes the first verse into a triple-time tutti refrain; it is heard twice at the beginning of the piece and once at the close. Each of the three statements of the refrain is preceded by a florid imitative passage for Choir 1 based on the opening line of text. These florid passages, which include five bars at the very beginning for the top two voices only, are all worked differently. They are not balanced by music for Choir 2 (though there is some normal double-choir interaction in the central portion of the piece), which means that Choir 2 is to some extent being viewed as a *ripieno* group and Choir 1 as a group of *favoriti* in the Schützian sense, perhaps intended to comprise soloists at least some of the time. This, added to the sharply focussed sectionalisation of the piece and the presence of sequential, instrumental-style writing at times, make it one of Praetorius's most forward-looking creations. The two remaining refrain pieces, including *Levavi oculos* (1602; DDT 23: 79), employ a purely musical refrain which recurs, adapted and varied, to different words. All these refrains are entirely or principally in triple time.

Praetorius left nine double-choir settings of the magnificat (1601), all of them *alternatim* with polyphony for the even verses (Gable 1966: 38). The one that is available in modern edition, a *quinti toni* setting (DDT 23: 125), illustrates also Praetorius's use in a small number of pieces of German texts associated with pre-existing melodies, for it is a Christmas setting with two well-known songs appended, *Joseph, lieber Joseph mein* and *In dulci jubilo*; it is surely no accident that both melodies share not only the mode but also the triadic profile of tone 5. The Magnificat itself reminds one rather of Scandello's setting in the reiterated tuttis which end verses 2 and 4. Verse 6 contains conventionl enough imagery in the breathlessly exchanged antiphonal phrases on 'dispersit superbos', but verse 8 verges on the mannerist in the use of rests to isolate tutti statements of the words 'implevit bonis' and more particularly 'dimisit' (Ex. 74). Note the way Praetorius's liking for dialogue between

Ex. 74   H. PRAETORIUS, Magnificat quinti toni

Ex. 74 (*cont.*)

the two highest parts overrides the choral division – in this instance both happen to be in the same choir. *Joseph, lieber* is set without any verbal repetition
after the opening, antiphony being mostly line-by-line with a substantial
amount of tutti. *In dulci jubilo* is set strophically à 8. Praetorius's setting of
the chorale *Ein Kindelein so löbelich* (1618a; 1974a: 48) is more elaborate,
approaching the technique of Samuel Scheidt and Michael Praetorius in their
chorale motets. Most phrases of the chorale are heard twice, and at times the
piece verges on double-choir canon.

Praetorius's polychoral music, then, is at times worthy, like Hassler's, to be
compared with the best Venetian music. Though it lacks the spatial approach
to bass parts (and Praetorius's liking for elaborate syncopation might at times
make undue spacing of the choirs hazardous for that reason), it possesses a
clear formal shape, a lively, even intense, response to the text and a clear, if
unspecific, demand for the participation of instruments. Though Praetorius
stops short of specifying solo voices or instruments, there are several elements
in his style which justify the use of the term Baroque to describe them.

Michael Praetorius

Syntagma musicum

If most composers were content to leave questions concerning performance
practice to the discretion of the *maestro di cappella* or *Kapellmeister*, Michael
Praetorius (1571(?)–1621) was reluctant to do so without providing them with
copious instructions setting out the limits within which their freedom lay.

So prolific was he in instructions, not only in his famous treatise *Syntagma musicum* (1619) but also in the prefatory material to his musical publications, that he has appeared to posterity to be more important as a writer than as a composer, a view which this study would hope to modify, at least from the standpoint of his polychoral output, for dry theorist he was not, and few have more to tell us about the day-to-day music-making of his time. *Syntagma musicum III, Termini musici*, contains recommendations concerning polychoral music, principally its scoring. Though Praetorius was obviously familiar with much Italian, and particularly Venetian, music, there is no evidence that he ever went to Italy, and his remarks probably apply more to German practice, which favoured a heavier instrumental involvement. In what follows, his main points concerning polychoral practice will be summarised. This part of the treatise is further subdivided into three sections, which we shall refer to as Parts 1, 2 and 3.

The numbering of choirs: In Part 2: Chapter 11, three methods are described: (1) numbering from the lowest choir upwards; (2) in order of entry; (3) from the highest choir downwards. Andrea Gabrieli is said to use method 2, Giovanni sometimes method 2 but usually method 3.

Unison and octave doubling: Part 2: Chapter 12. Praetorius defends the use of unison doubling in his *Urania* (see below), especially between cantus and bass parts of the choirs, but also between the inner parts. If the choirs are spaced, the harmony will thereby 'resound more fully and...be more clearly heard throughout the entire church' (Lampl 1957: 157). Reducing the number of real parts removes the necessity for lines to be broken up with rests. (Ex. 60 exemplifies such broken lines.) He justifies in the time-honoured manner the doubling of bass parts in tuttis, quoting a substantial passage from Artusi (1589, part 2: chapter 16). He is more circumspect about octave doubling, preferring to limit it to situations where one part is vocal, the other instrumental – e.g. a low choir may have its top part sung by an alto and played an octave higher by a violin. Alto parts in tuttis may be similarly doubled, though it worries him that consecutive fifths may then result between the doubling part and the existing cantus. Instruments like recorders always sound one or two octaves higher. Octave doubling in general is compared with the registers of an organ. He recommends adding instruments to the bass line at the lower octave in tuttis, stating it to be common Italian practice, and the lowest part or *bassett* of a high choir, usually a tenor singer, may move an octave higher than the bass parts of other choirs even when these are sung. Octaves are not otherwise to be used between voice parts, with the exception of the chorale melody in compositions with congregational participation. There were seemingly in Praetorius's memory musicians who disapproved of octave and unison doubling of the bass parts, but came round to the idea.[3] When a high choir has been composed purely 'by the rules', i.e. without octave doubling by its *bassett* of the true bass, as in Giovanni Gabrieli's *Symphoniae sacrae* [1597], then a foundation part (organ etc. or a bass instruments) may be added to that choir.

Solo voices: Part 3: Chapter 1. After Giacobbi (1609) choirs made up of solo voices are called, *inter alia*, *voci concertate* or *Concertat-Stimmen*. These must be the best singers, competent in the new Italian manner. Praetorius also talks about the *chorus vocalis* without making it clear whether it is a solo or ripieno group, and the *chorus instrumentalis*.

The definition of capella: Part 3: Chapter 2. Three meanings are given:

(1) An additional choir 'extracted from several different choirs' (Lampl 1957: 195), usually sounding only in tuttis. In Praetorius's own compositions *capella* groups may be added where the choirs unite, points he marks 'Omnes' or 'Chorus'. This type of *capella* is a ripieno vocal group with instruments, particularly at sixteen-foot pitch on the bass line. Praetorius associates this practice with Austria and the Empire. Up to three such groups may be disposed around the church, each consisting of a minimum of four singers. Unisons and octaves occur (presumably with voices in the other choirs rather than within the *capella*). Praetorius has seen manuscripts but not prints of music by Giovanni Gabrieli using *capellae* in this manner.

(2) However, Gabrieli's normal use of the term is synonymous with Praetorius's *chorus vocalis*. It is indispensable and is to be distinguished from choirs which are made up of instruments with at least one *Concertat-Stimme*. Viols or violins may be used [presumably doubling the voices].

(3) A non-essential instrumental choir, to be positioned at distance from the vocal choir.[4]

The capella fidicinum: Part 3: Chapter 3. This is a group, usually of stringed instruments (violins, viols, lutes, harps etc.), designed to accompany one, two or three solo singers, to please those Germans who regard such Italianate textures as otherwise too thin. It can even be an ensemble of the English broken consort type.

The scoring of choirs: Part 3: Chapter 7. Praetorius begins his discussion of the way in which various clefs and combinations of clefs suggest the use of various combinations of instruments with suggested scorings for three motets by Lasso: *Laudate pueri* à 7, (which begins antiphonally but does not maintain a consistent division of the voices), *In convertendo* à 8 and *Quo properas* à 10:

Laudate pueri Dominum à 7

1 Chorus C_1 } two transverse flutes or two violins or two cornetti
C_1
C_3 voice

2 Chorus C₃   voice
    C₄
    C₄ } three trombones
    F₄

In convertendo à 8

1 Chorus G₂ } three transverse flutes or three mute cornetti or three violins or one each of
    C₂ } violin, cornetto, transverse flute/recorder
    C₃

    F₃   tenor singer with or without trombone; or trombone or bassoon alone, with a
      choirboy on the discant

2 Chorus C₁
    C₃
    C₄   voices alone or { viols, violins or recorders with voice on C₁ or C₄ or both
    F₄

          bassoon or trombone

Quo properas à 10

		1.	2.	3.
1 Chorus	C₁	cornetto or voice		
	C₃			
	C₄		voices	voices
	C₄			
	F₄	trombones		
2 Chorus	C₁	cornetto or voice	cornetto	
	C₃			
	C₄	trombones		violin family
	C₄		trombones	
	F₄	trombone majore		

		4.	5.	6.
1 Chorus	C₁			
	C₃			
	C₄	voices	violin family	violin family
	C₄			
	F₄			
2 Chorus	C₁	recorders	fiffari	recorders
	C₃			
	C₄	trombones	trombones	trombones
	C₄			
	F₄	bassoon		bassoon

		7.
1 Chorus	C₁	recorders
	C₃	
	C₄	trombones
	C₄	
	F₄	bassoon
2 Chorus	C₁	cornetto
	C₃	
	C₄	trombones
	C₄	
	F₄	

(These suggestions should be read in the light of Praetorius's warning (p. 114) that at least one part in each choir must be sung.) He continues by setting out various types of choir and their possible clef combinations.

The cornetto and violin choir: $G_1G_2C_1C_2{}^5$. Possibilities: cornetti; violins; 1 violin + 2 cornetti; 2 violins + 1 cornetto; 1 violin, 1 cornetto & 1 flute or recorder. One part may also be sung. In this case the *bassett* may be given to a trombone or other instrument. Otherwise the *bassett*, usually notated under C_3, C_4 or F_3, is either sung or simultaneously sung and played by trombone or bassoon. If there is another C_3 part besides the *bassett* it may be given to a trombone (if the player can manage an alto part) with cornetti, or a viola with violins.

Choir of transverse flutes: $C_1C_1C_2C_4$, $C_1C_2C_3F_3$, $C_1C_3C_4F_3$ (sometimes also F_4 or G_2 clefs). Three transverse flutes with bassoon, pommer or trombone. (The flutes sound an octave higher.)

Human voices (both capella and Concertat-Stimmen); choir of recorders; choir of viols; choir of violins: $C_1C_3C_4F_4$; $C_2C_3C_4F_4$. Viols are more usually given the first type of trombone clef combination. (The recorders sound an octave higher.)

Choir of trombones/bassoons: Praetorius gives many possibilities, beginning with two fairly standard four-part combinations, $C_3C_4C_4F_4$ and $C_3C_4C_4F_5$, and continuing with more unusual five-part combinations, all with three or four F clefs, going as low as F_6 in some instances. Trombones, bassoons or pommers, or trombones and bassoons are used. The C_3 part would normally be sung, as might the C_4 part with the best melodic line; in the latter case the alto must not be sung, but played an octave higher on an alto recorder or violin. Any C_1, C_2 or G_2 part would be sung or played on cornetto or violin. Such instruments (i.e. trombones etc.) can also be used with the *capella* clefs if downward transposition by a fourth or fifth is employed.[6]

Choir of lutes: By this is meant not necessarily lutes only, but any available combination of plucked instruments. Praetorius gives an account of a performance of Wert's sacred dialogue à 7 *Egressus Jesus* arranged for two theorbos, three lutes, two citterns, four harpsichords and spinets, seven viols, two transverse flutes, two choirboys, one alto singer and a large bass viol, without organ or regal, so that, because of all the plucked strings, the piece 'crackled through the church'. This is a surprising combination to find in church, though not on stage or in the chamber.

Latin music

Praetorius's music with Latin text falls into two broad categories – the motets and psalms published in 1607e, and the material assembled for the Latin portions of the Lutheran liturgy in the four volumes of 1611 – *Missodia*, *Hymnodia*, *Eulogodia* and *Megalynodia*. The motets and psalms (Werke vol. 10) are mostly polychoral, the largest group for eight-part double choir, including a mass setting. The style is unremarkable, for the most part typical of the Italian polychoral motet style of the late sixteenth century. *Exaudi Deus* (no. 29, p. 103), for instance, is a classic polychoral shape, beginning with a long phrase for each choir, proceeding via antiphonal repetition to a tutti. Later, at 'in saecula sperabo', there is sequential choral imitation of short phrases, and the final tutti is approached through imitative entries in small note-values. Some of the psalm-settings, such as *Laudate pueri* (no. 30, p. 107) contain a high proportion of non-repetitive antiphony. By far the most interesting group of pieces employs the refrain technique. *Confitemini Domino quoniam bonus* seems to relate to the *cantilena* of Croce, though of course this is the one psalm in the book (Vulgate 135) which has a refrain in each verse. Praetorius sets it to an eight-part musical refrain marked 'Chorus vocibus, Instrumentibus et Organo' which alternates with various combinations of voices marked 'Sola Voce'; where the bass is not singing, an independent continuo line is provided. In other pieces, the 'refrain' is expressed solely in terms of scoring, without musical repetition. In the *Canticum trium puerorum*, i.e. the Benedicite, for instance (no. 34, p. 150), the odd verses are given to ever-increasing combinations of voices ('Sola Voce') in imitative style (v. 1 à 2, v. 2 à 3, etc.) with the even verses set homophonically in triple time for voices, instruments (unspecified) and organ divided into two choirs. In pieces of this type polychoral dialogue is either restricted to the 'refrain' sections or disappears altogether. Praetorius's other setting of Ps. 135 on the other hand (no. 52, p. 310) retains a purely polychoral approach with many symmetries in the deployment of its four choirs. The refrains are not set identically, though they are related; some are for a single choir, some for semi-tuttis à 8 and some à 16, the last using the same music. The first halves of the verses are varied not only in scoring (most of them are for single choirs, and the choirs are highly distinct in range) but also in style, with more elaborately conceived word-painting.

The 1611 volumes contain a small amount of polychoral music. The *Missodia* (Werke vol. 11) contains a slightly different version (p. 152) of the Mass previously issued in the *Motectae et psalmi* (cf. Werke vol. 10: 118). The polychoral substance is unaltered, and it is impossible to call many of the changes improvements. In the Kyrie, for example, he often interchanges the soprano and tenor parts of the first choir. Other changes include both the addition and removal of detail in final cadences. The oddest changes concern the substituting of longer note values, as for example in the antiphonal repetition in the Amen of the Credo, which is much more exciting in the earlier version. The two double-choir Latin Magnificats in the *Megalynodia* (Werke vol. 14) are also re-workings of earlier settings. One (p. 79) amounts to a parody, at times close, at times distant, of the German Magnificat in *Musae Sioniae I* (cf. Werke vol. 1: 22), itself based on the *tonus peregrinus*. The other (p. 88) is a revision in the direction of simplification of the Latin setting in *Motectae et psalmi* (cf. Werke vol. 10: 142). Unlike the case of the Mass, the basic structure is changed in places, usually by the omission of antiphonal repetition.

The only polychoral item in the *Eulogodia* is a curiosity announced on the title page as *'Salve Regina, correcta'*, i.e. *Salve Rex noster* (Werke vol. 13: 67). This has references to the chant, which even emerges as a *cantus firmus* in the third *pars*. Chant is very much in evidence in the *Hymnodia* (Werke vol. 12), a comprehensive collection of settings of Latin hymns retained in Lutheran usage. A few hymns have verses set for eight-part double choir.

Chorale settings

Praetorius's approach to the chorale embraced both elaborate motet-style treatment and also the common touch, the desire to involve the congregation. In both areas he employed polychoral techniques. His large-scale chorale motets fall into two categories – the traditional polychoral works making up the bulk of *Musae Sioniae I–IV* and the chorale-concertato settings of the *Polyhymnia* (1619).

The polychoral chorale motets differ from any corpus of music we have so far studied not in the mere fact of their dependence on pre-existing melodic material but in the nature of that material – metrical, divided into lines, strong and rugged in melodic character. It is not surprising to discover considerable consistency of style and procedure in Praetorius's approach. At the beginning the first phrase of the chorale melody usually appears in rather mechanical imitation in the first choir, answered either imitatively or homophonically by the second choir. If the first choir's phrase is homophonic, the second may echo all or only part of it. A particular feature of Praetorius's use of antiphonal repetition is diminution – i.e. reduction of the note-values – and other types of variation as well as transposition may occur. When he has dwelt sufficiently on each line he passes on to the next. 'Sufficient' in some contexts may in fact be just one statement – i.e. he may alternate the choirs line-by-line with no repetition. In addition to the dignified antiphony produced by treating the line as the normal unit, incidental changes of pace for variety are created by antiphonal imitation of short phrases, and climactic tuttis are also introduced, though rather sparingly in most cases. Antiphonal repetition may at times overlap into a tutti, even on occasions in the form of a temporary revolving canon, as in *In dulci jubilo* (*Musae Sioniae II* no. 5; Werke vol. 2: 31). Praetorius quite frequently treats the chorale melody as a *cantus firmus* for a few bars, surprisingly in the bass rather than the tenor, and in long notes with rather Josquin-like imitative writing in the upper parts. Such passages have a curiously retrospective character. Climactic tuttis may also bear the chorale as a *cantus firmus* in the soprano.

Musical relationships between lines of the chorale automatically set up formal patterns in the polyphonic setting, and the same happens in through-composed settings of more than one stanza. The effect of these may be of a chain of variations, as in *Puer natus in Bethlehem* (*Musae Sioniae II* no. 6; *Werke* vol. 2: 36). There is a rare example of psalmodic antiphony in *Musae Sioniae V* – a German setting of Psalm 22 (no. 153; *Werke* vol. 5: 318). This piece is interesting from a tonal point of view. It has a G final and begins and ends with a B flat signature, but successive sections are notated with and without the flat. In the sections with the flat there is evidence of the alternation of cadences in B flat and g.

In parts of the German Te Deum, *Herr Gott dich loben wir* for three choirs (*Musae Sioniae III* no. 1; *Werke* vol. 3: 1), and systematically in the five three-choir chorales which end *Musae Sioniae II*, Praetorius demonstrates for the first time his technique of doubling up top and bottom parts in tuttis so that the chorale melody is duly emphasised and the bass of the harmony firmly anchored. Most of these pieces are rather plain in style and contain little antiphonal repetition. The most elaborate is the last, *In dich hab ich gehoffet, Herr* (no. 30; *Werke* vol. 2: 183). It has a fairly typical ground plan; there are six stanzas, but Praetorius provides music for four, underlaying the words of stanzas 3 and 4 to the same music as 1 and 2. This does not stop him in indulging in some word-painting, which becomes apparent in stanza 3 where the phrase 'hilf mir' is begun on every beat for six successive beats by each choir in turn! Such touches enliven what can at times be a rather detached 'objective' idiom.

In the *Urania* of 1613 Praetorius set a series of chorales in this plain manner for two, three and four choirs. There is no verbal repetition, and the choirs alternate usually line by line, sometimes stanza by stanza, with punctuating tuttis. Most pieces are to be performed strophically, and sometimes different music is provided for at least some of the stanzas. In tuttis soprano and bass parts and even some other parts double up. Praetorius's aim was to show how simple four-part chorales could be arranged, with the minimum of additional counterpoint, for large-scale polychoral performance. The plainness of the music would have been offset by vocal and instrumental colour. In his elaborate preface to this work, Praetorius sets out in an exhaustive series of tables the way he envisages using two, three and four choirs in line-by-line fashion in chorales with stanzas of four, six, seven, eight, nine and twelve lines. He also gives a couple of tables showing verse-by-verse structures. It is clear also from the text that some chorale verses could be sung by all in unison and some verses or lines thereof taken by a soloist or soloists. Thus music which is basically extremely simple could in practice be performed with the most elaborately schematic changes of scoring.

The chorale concertato

The pieces in *Motectae et psalmi* with a sectional structure articulated by the scoring (there is one also at the end of *Musae Sioniae IV*: no. 34, *Dank sagen wir alle Gott* – Werke vol. 4: 175) anticipate at least to some degree the chorale motets or concertos of *Polyhymnia caduceatrix* (1619), but they do not prepare us for the kaleidoscopic richness of the collection. There is still a strong polychoral element, but it functions alongside solo voices treated in an Italianate manner with written-out embellishments, more specifically-conceived 'orchestration' instead of the myriad 'possibilities' of music notated in the old-fashioned vocal-polychoral manner, and an indispensable continuo. The forces still tend to be conceived and assembled as choral blocks, but they are often subdivided in such a way as to produce mixed textures with little or no polychoral dialogue. Solo–tutti contrast and internal contrast between soloists is more important. The florid parts for a single soloist are generally elaborations of the chorale melody, and the unadorned line is given also, as in Monteverdi's *Possente spirto*. Some of the instrumental parts show signs of idiomatic figuration – e.g. no. 21 *Wachet auf* (Werke vol. 17: 192) contains in its third section some violinistic cross-string and repeated-note figuration. Each piece is prefaced with meticulous directions as to how it is to be performed, and the whole work is preceded by an *Ordinantz* full of general performance instructions, detailed examination of which, rewarding though it would be, is beyond the scope of this study.[7]

It is not possible to generalise any longer since each piece is unique in its scoring. The principle of antiphony is absorbed as a function of scoring; thus viols may alternate with lutes, a solo voice with the vocal/instrumental tutti, one pair of voices with another pair, or voices may alternate with instruments. Some pieces are more sectional in form than others. A good example of a fully sectionalised piece is no. 24 (p. 268), *Siehe wie fein und lieblich ist*. It is cast in three sections which may be summarised as follows:

1. Teil
(a) Sinfonia à 4
(b) SS duet with continuo, leading to contrasting of other symmetrical groups: SAT/SAT, SATB/SATB, ATB/ATB
(c) Ripieno 'Lobet den Herren' – instrumental choir and 3 vocal choirs (one brief T solo with instruments)

2. Teil
(d) Solos and duets, concluding à 4
(c₁) Sinfonia à 4 (= first half of c)

3. Teil
(e) Solos, duets etc. with instruments at times leading to tutti+polychoral elements, then duets & trios with instruments
(c) 'Lobet den Herren Repetatur in 1. Teil ad finem'

Rather as with Giovanni Gabrieli, conventional-looking polychoral pieces may not be what they seem. No. 28 (p. 388), *Lob sei dem allmächtigen Gott*, is scored for four four-part choirs and laid out with strict verse-by-verse and line-by-line antiphony in the *Urania* mould. Choir 1 doubles Choir 4 in tuttis and other doublings mean that the polyphony is in a lot less than twelve parts.

However, not only are the choirs colourfully scored (1: voice, flutes and bassoon; 2: two voices and viols; 3: voice and trombones; 4: voice and a mixed group of instruments): contrasts of speed (*Lento–Presto*) and dynamics (*piano–forte*) are indicated.

In no. 29 (p. 404), *Erhalt uns Herr*, the fourth choir, marked 'Chorus pro Capella', is used in one of the ways defined in *Syntagma III* (see above), which we shall find frequently in Schütz: it never sounds on its own and partially doubles lines in the other choirs. Near the beginning Praetorius adds it to the second statement of a tutti, a clear case of terracing the scoring to change the dynamics. No. 34 (p. 566), *In dulci jubilo*, has not only a *capella* but a trumpet ensemble. The latter, consisting of two clarini, principal and *Alter Bass*, is used as a reinforcing group, sometimes sounding with just one other choir. Although Praetorius allows quite a bit of diatonic dissonance with the drones and passing notes of the trumpet choir, a glance at the continuo part reveals the harmonic limitations imposed by using trumpets. In *Ach mein Herre, straf mich doch nicht* (no. 37, p. 644) Praetorius makes use of the fashionable Italian device of echo – not just single but double echoes involving three choirboys in a 'Chorus puerorum' accompanied by a three-part 'Chorus instrumentorum'. Later they are joined by a three-part 'Chorus adultorum' and two *capella* groups, one of instruments and one of voices. Double choir as opposed to solo vocal echo is used in the setting of the alternative, metrical setting of the Lutheran Gloria *Allein Gott in der Höh sei Ehr* which forms part of the *Missa: gantz teudsch* (no. 38, p. 664). The first choir is marked 'forti voce', the second 'Echo Pian, vel submissa voce' with no indication as to whether it is to be distantly spaced. The other, prose setting of the Gloria, *Glory sei Gott* is in a more sumptuous polychoral idiom with solo elements and, towards the end, very florid writing for two solo instruments. The final piece in the collection, a German Magnificat (no. 40, p. 708) is a splendid multi-sectional piece which seems to draw together all the resources – solos, duets, trios, polychoral antiphony, instrumental sinfonias and even echo. One side of Praetorius which is normally unadventurous – his treatment of harmony and tonality – is also slightly more developed in this piece. Of all Praetorius's output, here is music which deserves to be revived, not for profundity of content, but for brilliant effectiveness, a vindication of Praetorius as a supremely practical composer.

Johann Hermann Schein

German music in the years after Praetorius was dominated by the 'three S's' – Schein, Scheidt and Schütz. In the church music of all three we can see a move from polychoral writing to the new concerto style with continuo, some of it on a large scale with polychoral elements, but more often for much smaller forces. Of the three, Schütz paid little attention to the chorale, and only Scheidt employed polychoral techniques to any degree in connection with it.

With the exception of a few occasional pieces, the polychoral music of Schein (1586–1630) is all early, published in his *Cymbalum Sionium* in 1615, a collection generally thought to contain music written over the previous ten years. Part of Schein's education was gained at Schulpforta; although Boden-schatz had just left, it seems likely that Schein would have come into contact with the music Bodenschatz had collected for use at the school and which he published in his *Florilegium* (1603[(1)]), including polychoral music by several Italian composers as well as Germans such as Handl, Hassler and Hieronymus Praetorius. There are a dozen pieces in 1615 for eight or more voices, all but three with Latin text; a couple have inconsistent choral divisions.

Though Schein often writes homophonically, it is clear that, like Giovanni Gabrieli, he possessed a superb contrapuntal gift. He often develops lines of text at length, but rarely utilises straight or even transposed repetition. His antiphonal repetition is constantly varied, by just a few notes, or by compre-hensive re-writing or development. Schein's exceptional formal sense is shown above all in his setting of *Quem vidistis, pastores?* (no. 19; mod. edn, Werke vol. 4: 1). Schein uses the same version of the text as Andrea Gabrieli, and one wonders whether in fact he knew Andrea's setting, which was reprinted by Bodenschatz in 1603[(1)] (no. 53). Certainly no one else uses re-statement and development with a mastery comparable with that of the Venetian. At the beginning, Choir 1 ($C_1C_1C_3C_4$) varies Choir 2 ($C_3C_4F_3F_4$)'s opening phrase with considerable tonal subtlety, roughly a fifth higher. The setting of the opening question ends with a very Gabrielian phrase, echoed at the upper octave. In the shepherds' reply, like Andrea, Schein gives each verbal image a distinct musical equivalent, but it is developed to an even greater degree, to more than three times the length of the question. It is worth giving a tabular analysis, as we did with Andrea:

Table 7

choir	text	cadences	comments
2	Natum vidimus	F, d($\sharp$)	solemn
tutti	et choros ang.	F, g($\natural$)	syncopated, quasi triple time
tutti	collaudantes Dom.	A($\sharp$), g($\natural$)	close imitation of rising scale in dotted rhythm
2	alleluia	F, B$\flat$, d	theme x – homophonic
1	alleluia	d($\sharp$)	theme y – paired imitation of upward moving quavers – $+x$
2	alleluia	F, g($\natural$)	x
1	alleluia	d, g	x
2	alleluia	g	y
tutti	alleluia	g($\natural$)	$y+x$
2	natum vidimus	d($\sharp$) imperf.	compressed, varied
tutti	et choros ang.	F, c($\natural$)	first phrase same, second deflected tonally
2	collaudantes Dom.	g($\natural$)	now in triple time (scalic material retained)
1	alleluia	d($\sharp$) imperf.	x

2	alleluia	a($\sharp$) imperf.	x
1	alleluia	g, g	$x+y+x$
2	alleluia	g($\natural$)	$y+x$
1	natum vidimus	F, g($\natural$)	variant of the first statement
1	et choros ang.	F, d($\sharp$)	new tonal deflection of second phrase
tutti	collaudantes Dom.	g($\natural$), g($\natural$)	still in triple time – polyphonic element less conspicuous
2	alleluia	g($\natural$)	new idea z in crotchets
1	alleluia	g($\natural$)	z
2	alleluia	B♭	x
1	alleluia	g($\natural$)	x
2	alleluia	d($\sharp$)	x
1	alleluia	g	x
tutti	alleluia	g($\natural$)	z', now presented as an augmentation of y
2	et choros ang.	g($\natural$), F	new tonal orientation
tutti	collaudantes Dom.	g($\natural$), g($\natural$)	same as the previous statement
2, 1, tutti	alleluia		repeat of whole of preceding alleluia section, from the introduction of idea z

Thus Schein works through the whole of the shepherds' reply three times, varying the music and its antiphonal distribution. The fourth time he begins with the second phrase. In using three distinct ideas to set the 'Alleluia', he is clearly thinking in abstract structural terms rather than simply of word-setting. He only employs exact repetition at the end of the piece where it creates a fitting climax.

Schein makes conventional use of a refrain in no. 30 (p. 142), *Venite exulte-mus Domino*. The text is Psalm 95: 1–5, and the first verse is heard four times as a triple-time tutti. The 'Alleluia' sections of *A Domine factus est istud* (no. 23, p. 35) form a less conventional partial refrain with a feeling of constant forward development:

$$a - \text{refrain } (x) - b - \text{ref. } (y) - c - \text{ref. } (y' + z) - d - \text{ref. } (z')$$

Two pieces make dramatic use of dialogue elements. In *Ehr sei Gott* (no. 28, p. 91) the shepherds, represented by a six-part SAATTB choir, as it were overhear and react to the song of the angels, sung by a high four-part choir (TrTrSA). The triple-time 'finale' contains remarkable tutti shouts of 'Ehr', 'Macht' and 'Kraft' ('glory', 'might' and 'power') separated by rests. In *Quem quaeris, Magdalena* (no. 29, p. 117) two interlocutors (angels?) represented by two low choirs, question Mary Magdalen (a high choir). After a massive, extended triple-time tutti, the piece becomes a conventional three-choir structure, but demonstrating Schein's superb formal sense. The first tutti is balanced by a stylistically similar one nearer the end of the piece, and both are followed by continuously developing antiphonal 'alleluia' sections. Oddly enough, Schein does not write spatial bass parts, and his handling of dissonance is generally conventional, with no place for the 'clash' cadence.

Samuel Scheidt

Scheidt (1587–1654) published not only a whole volume of eight-part double-choir music (*Cantiones sacrae*, 1620) but also, only two years later, a volume of large-scale *concertato* pieces (*Pars prima concertuum sacrorum*, 1622). Despite designating the latter volume 'the first part', Scheidt published no more music on such a lavish scale. As with Schütz in Dresden, the deprivations of war disrupted musical activity in Halle. It is thought that some of the smaller concertos Scheidt published between 1631 and 1640 may be arrangements of pieces originally conceived for lavish forces like those used in 1622.

The Cantiones sacrae

Scheidt set a higher proportion of German texts than Schein, sometimes making use of the chorale in a double-choir motet idiom as in Michael Praetorius. His music is more rugged and Germanic than that of Schein, and his dissonance treatment rather more akin to that of Giovanni Gabrieli, even extending to unprepared sevenths. He normally takes care to vary the reply in his antiphonal repetition, with the exception of two rather tedious echo pieces which end the 1620 volume (Werke vol. 4); in these the echo choir often repeats whole phrases. His procedure in chorale settings is illustrated by *Nu komm der Heyden Heiland* (Anthology no. 17). Like Praetorius, he develops each line before proceeding to the next. In this case, there are four lines. The first two are developed at length with long-breathed antiphonal phrases (partly imitative) leading to quicker antiphony culminating in a tutti. The third line moves in ever-longer antiphonal phrases to its tutti, whilst the fourth is presented in slightly embellished eight-part homophony.

The most impressive pieces in the 1620 collection are probably the 'free' German pieces. No. 4 (p. 23), *Ich hebe meine Augen auff* (Psalm 121), shares with *Herr wie lang* (nos. 1–3) the maximum register contrast between its choirs ($G_2G_2C_2C_3/C_3C_4F_4F_5$). For one extraordinary piece of word-painting the top two voices of the first choir ('Himmel') are contrasted with the lowest two of the second choir ('Erde'), which clearly rules out these voices all being supplied by instruments, a possibility the clef-combination would otherwise allow. Later, at 'und der dich behütet', the music progresses in sequential antiphonal repetition round a substantial portion of the circle of fifths: A–D–G–C–F–B flat, all major chords, in the manner of Lasso. The best piece of all, certainly the most expressive, is probably *Zion spricht* (no. 33, p. 158), written as a burial song for the composer's father, Conrad Scheidt. (A version of the same text by Samuel's brother Gottfried (no. 35) is a much paler affair.) It begins with a long phrase for each choir in turn, exploring Lasso-like imitation by inversion of a semitonal motif. Both choirs end with just one voice, Choir 2 its lowest, Choir 1 its highest, symbolising the abandonment by God described in the text (Isaiah 49: 14–16a). The soul rants against this in the succeeding tutti and rapid antiphonal declamation on the same text (Ex. 75).

Ex. 75 SCHEIDT, Zion spricht

The choirs mirror each other's grief at 'dass sie sich nicht erbarme' where Choir 1's descending chromatic motif is answered by rising chromaticism in Choir 2.

The Latin works in 1620 are on the whole more conventional, though not without points of interest. Scheidt cannot, any more than Hassler, match the subtlety of Giovanni Gabrieli in his setting of *O Domine Jesu Christe* (no. 6, p. 32). An aspect of Gabrieli's late style which comes out in *Tulerunt Dominum* (nos. 20–1, p. 96) is the counterpointing of *note nere* declamation against longer notes. *Surrexit pastor bonus* (no. 23, p. 107) has a triple-time 'Alleluia' refrain in Gabrielian rhythm. One odd piece has a structure unique in my experience; in *Veni sancte Spiritus* (no. 7, p. 35) the tenor of Choir 1 has a *cantus firmus* in semibreves throughout surrounded by antiphonal repetition between the other three voices of Choir 1 and the four voices of Choir 2.

The Pars prima concertuum sacrorum

Although the others would obviously have been performed with instrumental participation, there is only one piece in 1620 which specifies instruments: *In dulci jubilo* (no. 15, p. 70) has two optional clarini which mostly double two of the vocal parts, adding occasional divisions. With the 1622 collection we see the full flowering of the *concertato* style in Scheidt's music, though applied to Latin and German liturgical texts rather than to chorales. The continuo is now an integral part of the texture, with the bass parts in tuttis doubled up. (Scheidt had sometimes but by no means always written spatially in 1620.) Idiomatic instrumental parts appear, though which instruments are intended is not always specified. Scheidt is particularly fond of the new Italian fashion, duet-writing. Most of these works have multi-sectional structures articulated with the utmost clarity with instrumental sinfonias and tuttis as important structural pillars. As in Praetorius the polychoral content varies from piece to piece, virtually disappearing in some cases. It usually surfaces not as a permanent element but as a structural device dominating a particular section. This includes not only vocal but, taking a cue from the polychoral canzona of Gabrieli and others, purely instrumental sections, like the double-choir sinfonia which opens the *secunda pars* of *Hodie completi sunt* (no. 5; Werke vol. 14: 61). This piece also contains triple-time 'Alleluia' refrain into whose final appearance is interpolated an echo section with the choirs marked 'forte' and 'pian'. One of the two *alternatim* Magnificat settings, the *octavi toni* (no. 9; Werke vol. 15: 37), has a verse ('Sicut locutus est') in which the tenor voices sustain the psalm-tone in long notes against a double-choir sinfonia with florid treble parts – reminding us very much of the use of chant in the larger Magnificat in Monteverdi's 1610 Vespers; it can be seen as an instrumental application of the principle in use in Scheidt's *Veni sancte Spiritus* (1620).

One piece will not only illustrate well the sectional structures Scheidt employs but also gives us unique insight into how a composer relates the old and new styles in his mind. *Angelus ad pastores ait* (1622 no. 13; Werke vol. 14: 83) is an arrangement with continuo and added instrumental sinfonias of a double-choir ($C_1C_3C_4F_4 \times 2$) setting in 1620 (no. 13; Werke vol. 4: 60). The 1620 setting falls into five clearly defined sections:

a.   Imitative opening for Choir 1. Chordal entry of Choir 2 initiates quick antiphony and a chordal tutti.
b.   'annuncio vobis': canonic duet for the C_1 voices.
c.   'gaudium magnum': triple-time homophonic tutti.
d.   Antiphony, some utilising only the top two voices of each choir, leading to tutti.
e.   Triple-time 'Alleluia', homophonic, antiphony + tutti.

In 1622, these are retained with alterations and interpolations as follows:

x.   Sinfonia – takes up material of a. 2 very florid treble parts (cornetti or violins?) + bass instrument + organ.
a.   Virtually unaltered, the instruments sometimes an octave above or below the corresponding voice part.
b'. Duet – but with added continuo and considerable re-working giving closer canonic writing.
c'. Tutti – extended with antiphony.
x.   Sinfonia, as before.
d'. Re-scored, with the two-part antiphony now between SA and TB of Choir 1 until S of Choir 2 becomes involved.
e'. Re-written, with 'pian' and 'forte' effects and a new duple-time climactic cadence.[8]

Heinrich Schütz

A consideration of Schütz, the greatest German composer of the 17th century, forms a fitting final climax to our consideration of the flowering of the polychoral style in Germany. Not only was he the heir of the impressive tradition stemming from Lasso through native German composers – Hassler, Hieronymus Praetorius and others – to Michael Praetorius, but he studied for just over three years with Giovanni Gabrieli, an apprenticeship cut short by the latter's death. He thus absorbed the grand Venetian style first hand (as well as other Italian idioms, such as that of the polyphonic madrigal), just as he was to do some years later with the *seconda prattica* under the guidance of Monteverdi.

The principal fruit of Schütz's preoccupation with the Venetian style was the *Psalmen Davids* collection of 1619, but a few other polychoral pieces date from the intervening years after his return from Venice,[9] initially to Kassel (whence the Landgrave Moritz had sent him to Venice), but soon to move to Dresden to work at the Saxon court of Elector Johann Georg I. These early works are a diverse group. *Jauchzet Dem Herren* (SWV 36a; Werke 2, vol. 28: 61) is a three-choir setting of Psalm 100 laid out in double-echo format. Choir 2 repeats in whole or part the material of Choir 1, with an occasional initial harmonic adjustment, and Choir 3 echoes Choir 2. The style is very homophonic. A two-choir version of the same piece was printed in *Psalmen Davids* (SWV 36; Werke 2, vol. 24: 145). Close canonic writing in the central portion (bars 43–53) breaks the monotony, and the piece is immeasurably enhanced by the addition of a setting of the doxology beginning à 1, then à 2, à 3 etc. *Wo Gott der Herr nicht bei uns hält* (SWV 467; Werke 2, vol. 32: 30) is a rare chorale setting in which the melody is passed between three treble voices each accompanied by their own instrumental group, respectively lutes, viols and trombones. The shadow of Giovanni Gabrieli's late style lies across *Christ ist erstanden*, particularly in its use of augmented chords and in its primary scoring for three voices with a larger complement of instruments (a choir of viols and one of trombones). Two *capella* groups are added in the final section, as the title and organ part make clear, though the voice-parts of these groups are lost (more on Schütz's concept of *capella* below).

In 1618, a year before his own marriage, Schütz composed two polychoral wedding concertos. There seems to have been a long-standing German tradition of polychoral occasional pieces for weddings and other important social events which goes back to the 1580s. *Wohl dem, der ein tugendsam Weib hat* (SWV 20; Werke 1, vol. 14: 111) has a double-choir ritornello interspersed with 'intermedium' sections for voices drawn from Choir 2 only. *Haus und Güter* (SWV 21; vol. 14: 129) is notable for a three-part choir ($C_1C_1F_4$), accompanied by lutes according to the continuo part, which has a modern trio-sonata-like texture.

The Psalmen Davids

This collection, Schütz's most important contribution in the polychoral sphere, has certain features which differentiate it from both the Venetian and German practice of the time. Its full title is *Psalmen Davids sampt etlichen Moteten und Concerten*. The texts are drawn from elsewhere in the Bible as well as from the psalter. Although the doxology is set in many of the psalms, they do not seem intended to be strictly liturgical; only in a couple of instances is pre-existing material present. Schütz's deployment of forces is flexible, yet clearly codified. It hinges on a distinction, sometimes implicit in Gabrieli but not stated, between an 'elite' group of solo singers or singers and instrumentalists, the *coro favorito*, and a reinforcing group or *Capelle* (Schütz's German spelling) which, unlike the Gabrielian use of the term, is normally to be made up of instruments, though it may consist partly or even wholly of voices. In many cases these *Capellen* are dispensable if insufficient forces are available. Schütz probably did not invent this method of scoring: Praetorius's *Erhalt uns Herr* (1619 no. 29; Werke 17: 404) has a fourth choir marked 'Chorus pro Capella' which never sounds on its own and always doubles or partially doubles other voices; see also Praetorius's definitions of *Concertat-Stimmen* and *capella* (above, p. 218). A setting in manuscript of *Nun danket alle Gott* by Scheidt (Werke vol. 16: 41) has three four-part vocal choirs marked 'favorita' at one point, and in addition to a five-part *chorus instrumentalis* there is a six-part *capella* which only sounds in tuttis. A more modest *Warum betrübst du dich* (ibid.: 61) employs double-choir writing interspersed with solo and duet sections; four further voices are added at points cued in the continuo by the word 'omnes'. Schütz may also have been influenced by Viadana, whose *Salmi a quattro chori* came out in Venice in 1612, the year the former returned to Germany. The preface to Viadana's volume, like that of Schütz, gives detailed instructions for the performance of the psalms (full translation given in Roche 1984: 118–19), and despite an important difference of terminology, Viadana's concept is not dissimilar. It may be summarised as follows:

Choir 1 à 5: 5 competent singers, accompanied by the organ.
Choir 2 à 4: the *cappella*; at least 16 singers and possibly some instruments.
Choir 3 à 4: a high choir; violin or cornetto on the top, singers on the next highest part, voices
    and instruments on the lowest two.
Choir 4 à 4: a low choir; voices and instruments.

Viadana's first choir obviously corresponds to Schütz's *favoriti*, but it is Viadana's third and fourth choirs, which may be omitted when necessary, which are the equivalent of Schütz's *Capellen*. Roche (1984: 119) makes the point that in Italy Viadana's idea of an optional ripieno group 'did not become common till around 1630'. Schütz's preface is such an important document that it seems appropriate to give here a full translation of the seven points he makes concerning performance (the original may be seen in facsimile in Werke 2, vol. 23: viii):

1. The *Cori Favoriti* must be well differentiated from the *Capellen*. *Cori Favoriti* I call those choirs and voices which the *Capellmeister* generally favours and [they] should be made up of the best and sweetest [voices], whilst on the contrary the *Capellen* are to be brought in with a strong tone and with magnificence. On account of this then the organist should take care when these terms are found in the *Basso continuo*, and register the organ with discretion, now quietly, now strongly.

2. In the disposition and arrangement of the Capellen for double-choir pieces one can take care that the choirs be placed cross-wise and that *Capella I* is nearest to the other *Coro favorito* and on the contrary *Capella 2* is nearest to the first [*Coro favorito*] so that the *Capellen* will make the desired effect.

3. [The] *psalm* Ich hebe meine Augen auff, [the] *psalm* Der Herr ist mein Hirt, [the] *Concerto* Lobe den Herren meine Seele (here also can be added Nun lob mein Seel, [the] *Canzona*, when one wishes to leave out the instrumental *Capellen* and do it only with eight voices). In those [pieces] listed above [the] *Coro secondo* uses a *Capell* and is thus strongly voiced, whilst *Coro I*, which is a *Coro favorito*, is on the contrary weaker and only of four singers; thus one is free if one wishes to copy from the said *Coro I* after the dash where it says *Capella* whereby another *Capell* will be created specially, so that the choir will be more in proportion.[10]

4. The *Capellen*, which are scored for high voices, are for the most part intended for cornetti and other instruments. However when singers are also available, so much the better and in this case one might copy out from the deep bass parts with the F on the fifth line which are comfortable for large *Violon*, *Quartposaun* [and] *Fagott* other basses with the correct ambitus for the bass singers and with F on the fourth line.

5. Where these same *Instrumental Capellen* with high clefs are found it is easy to judge that on the contrary the *Cori favoriti* must be scored with singers, as for the most part in this whole work up until the *Moteten, Concert &c.* such choirs are meant to be sung. However, several of the psalms, namely: 1. Herr unser Herrscher, 2. Wol dem der nicht wandelt, 3. Wie lieblich, 4. Wol dem der den Herren fürchtet, are not rendered bad when the higher choir is made up of

cornetti/violins, the lower of trombones or other instruments and in each choir a part is sung along with them.

    6. Since I actually set my psalms in *stylo recitativo* (which to date is scarcely known in Germany), as to my mind, for the composition of the psalms, there is scarcely any better manner than that one, then on account of the quantity of text which is to be continuously recited without manifold repetitions, I offer to those who have no knowledge of this method my friendly request [that] they will not in the performance of my said psalms hurry over the beat but hold to a middle way, so that the words of the singers may be recited comprehensibly and might be heard. Failing this an extremely disagreeable harmony will result and nothing but a *Battaglia di Mosche* or battle of the insects, contrary to the intention of the author.

    7. The *Basso continovo* [sic] is intended properly speaking only for the psalms. From the motet Ist nicht Ephraim to the end of this opus painstaking organists will busy themselves with setting down a score, as also they will know (should more than one organ be available) how to extract [additional] bass parts from the psalms.

What exactly Schütz meant by *stylo recitativo* is unclear. There are three devices to which it could conceivably apply, and it could even refer to all three. The most obvious is monodic vocal writing in the Italian style, but most of the solo vocal writing is for two or more voices or combined in a Germanic manner with instruments. There are, however, a few instances of single solo voices accompanied only by continuo, most notably in Psalm 121, *Ich hebe meine Augen auf* (SWV 31; Werke 2, vol. 24: 1), in which all four voices of the *coro favorito* are heard alone, answered in each case by double-choir antiphony. The solo writing is expressive and pictorial, if rather 'instrumental' in its *passaggi* (Ex. 76). Schütz's remarks suggest rather that he is referring to choral writing. His reference to recitation is suggestive of *falsobordone* technique, of which indeed there are some instances. In Psalm 84, *Wie lieblich sind deine Wohnungen* (SWV 29; Werke 2, vol. 23: 155), verses 8–10a are set to three tutti phrases, each beginning with free recitation on a chord and ending with a cadence. The effect is dramatic rather than formulistic, since it serves to heighten the fervent prayer beginning at verse 8, and each phrase outlines a

Ex. 76   SCHÜTZ, Ich hebe meine Augen auf

different tonality; the third phrase begins on an F major chord after the final
D major of the second. It is my belief, however, that Schütz's recitative style is
in fact the almost neutral, homophonic, metrical declamation which forms the
backbone of the psalm-settings in particular, constituting a foil to the vivid
word-painting, polyphonic elaboration of texture and lively antiphony in
which these settings also abound. It is well illustrated in the first piece, Psalm
110, *Der Herr sprach zu meinem Herren* (SWV 22; ibid.: 1), of which the first
half of the second verse is given in Ex. 77. Recitational homophony gives way
to delicate illustration of the word 'senden'.

Ex. 77   Schütz, Der Herr sprach zu meinem Herren

Notwithstanding the flexibility in performance, within certain limits, which Schütz envisaged, it is both possible and helpful to assign the pieces in 1619 to a few easily definable categories.

1. Conventional polychoral works: Most of these are for double choir with no suggestions for instrumentation (SWV 24, 25, 28, 29, 30, 35, 36, 37). One (SWV 42, 'Motette') is scored for ST and three trombones in each choir. Another (SWV 43) is for three choirs scored in the Venetian manner as described by Praetorius: 3 cornetti + baritone voice / SATB / alto voice + three trombones.

2. Works with optional Capellen: In this category there are always two *cori favoriti* with one (SWV 22, 27) or two *Capellen* (SWV 23, 26, 32, 34, 40, 46). The latter have no independent rôle in the presentation of the text and enter to reinforce the tutti or one or other of the *cori favoriti*. The latter are harmonically self-sufficient, and the music is impoverished but still performable without the *Capellen*. Unison, octave and even two-octave doubling is to be found between parts in the *Capellen* and the *cori favoriti*.[11] The *Capellen* often extend the range of the ensemble in both directions – e.g. in SWV 23 with normal SATB clefs in the *cori favoriti* the two *Capellen* have $G_2C_1C_3F_5$. In most cases there are no suggestions for instrumentation, but SWV 46 ('Concert') has two fully-specified *favorito* groups of voices and instruments reinforced by two *Capellen* with no scoring instructions. The same is true of SWV 40 ('Motette'), but the *cori favoriti* become *Capellen* in full sections.

3. Works with indispensable Capellen: To this group belong the three pieces mentioned in point 3 of Schütz's preface (SWV 31, 33, 39). In these, soloists are drawn from a single *coro favorito* which is also used as a unit in double-choir antiphony with a *Capelle*; Schütz suggests that in the latter passages the *coro favorito*'s music be given to a second *Capelle* to forestall balance problems. No instrumentation is suggested. Schütz also suggests that the only chorale-based piece in the collection, *Nun lob, mein Seel* (SWV 41), can be performed as a piece of this type, its single vocal *coro favorito* becoming a *Capelle* when it is required to alternate with the second choir, an indispensable four-part *Capelle*. In its fully-realised format, it also has two fully-specified five-part instrumental *Capellen*. Two other uniquely-scored pieces have an indispensable *Capelle*: *Wohl dem, der den Herrn fürchtet* (SWV 44) has two *favorito* groups, each with one voice and four instruments, a vocal SATB *Capelle* with an independent rôle in the argument, and an optional *Capelle* of unspecified composition, whilst *Danket dem Herren* (SWV 45) has two *cori favoriti* (one vocal SSAT, the other alto voice and three trombones), a five-part *Capelle* and a trumpet part.

4. Works approaching the mixed concertato: The two works in this category

(SWV 38, 47), although scored in choral blocks, have substantial solo episodes which exploit various combinations of solo voices and instruments.

Before we look at some examples from these categories, there are a few general points to be made. Schütz generally followed Gabrieli and perhaps even early Monteverdi in his approach to dissonance, which can be quite startling in tutti sections particularly. He quite often clashes the suspended leading note with its resolution in tutti cadences, the 'clash' cadence of the Gabrielis; some of these are extremely dissonant. In Psalm 6, *Ach Herr* (SWV 24; Werke 2 vol. 23: 53), it is an open question whether the pain expressed in the opening verse or his desire to maintain a canonic relationship between the choirs led him to clash momentarily chords a fifth apart on the last syllable of 'züchtige' (Ex. 78). The closing section of Psalm 137, *An den*

Ex. 78   SCHÜTZ, Ach Herr, straf mich nicht

Wassern zu Babel (SWV 37; Werke 2 vol. 24: 177) makes eloquent use of double suspensions combined with anticipations. Mediant progressions of the kind so beloved by Giovanni Gabrieli are quite common, as at the opening of Psalm 84 where they express sheer wonder at 'How lovely' the dwelling places of God are. There is probably nothing as stunning in Gabrieli as the shift in the middle of a tutti phrase of Psalm 111, *Ich danke dem Herrn* (SWV 34; Werke 2 vol. 24: 87) from a chord of C minor to A major (bar 57). In functional tonal parlance it is a move from the tonic of C minor to the dominant of D major, the jolt arising from the fact that the two chords have no note in common.

Schütz's treatment of the bass parts is usually spatial, with some of the basses doubled when there are more than two choirs. There are momentary anomalies, and in Psalm 8, *Herr, unser Herrscher* (SWV 27; Werke 2 vol. 23: 113), with a large difference in range between the *favorito* groups (SSAT/ATBarB), there are some 6/4 chords in the higher group. The continuo part is usually a *basso seguente*, but may be partially independent in solo sections. Unlike Scheidt, Schütz does not give the instruments passages on their own, with the sole exception of a sinfonia based on Gabrieli's *Lieto godea* which precedes the doxology of Psalm 111. Nor are individual instruments yet characterised, with the exception of the inevitable limitation of the trumpets in SWV 45 to the notes of the harmonic series (c′, e′, g′, c″, d″, e″), though instruments, like solo voices, are sometimes given more florid music than *Capelle* participants. In the *Motette, Die mit Tränen säen* (SWV 42; Werke 2 vol. 25: 135) Schütz splits the choirs, alternating the four voices (two from each choir) with the six trombones (bars 58–70). There is no differentiation in the material here, but at the end of the piece the vocalists are given ornamental figuration whilst the trombones sustain long notes. The primary rôle of the instruments is to provide colour contrast and sonority, though doubtless they would also have furnished idiomatic improvised embellishments.

The most conservative pieces are naturally to be found in the first category – conventional in many respects but of a high artistic quality. Whilst Schütz chose all the texts in the collection for their affective or pictorial qualities, he seems to have used the straight double-choir medium to set those with the most obviously expressive possibilities – the penitential psalms 6, *Ach Herr, straf mich nicht mit deinem Zorn*, 130, *Aus der Tiefe*, and 137, *An den Wassern zu Babel*, the motet *Die mit Tränen säen*. Psalms 6 and 130 are in the phrygian mode, and Psalm 137 is in a deliberately plain style with the emphasis on affective harmony. However, the group also includes the echo piece already discussed, Psalm 100, *Jauchzet dem Herren*, and the vigorous Psalm 98, *Singet dem Herrn ein neues Lied*. As befits a composer whose opus 1 was a collection of Italian madrigals, Schütz's word-painting is particularly vivid, as indeed Psalm 98 shows. Many examples could be given, but one of the best is the portrayal of the wind in Psalm 1, *Wohl dem, der nicht wandelt im Rat der Gottlosen* (SWV 28; Werke 2 vol. 23: 135), which begins as in Ex. 79, blowing from one choir to the other for twenty bars in all, the phrase abbreviated after a while to 'die der Wind'. Word-setting of a rhetorical, as opposed to pictorial, power is exemplified by the opening of Psalm 128 (SWV 30; Werke 2 vol. 23: 178), which is divided between the choirs as follows:

Ch. 1: Wohl dem, wohl dem, der den Herren fürch – tet   *a a b*
Tutti: wohl dem   *a*
Ch. 2: (8ve lower) wohl dem, der den Herren fürch – tet   *a b*

The word 'fürchtet' (fears) has a madrigalian rest between the syllables in three out of the four voices during which the tenor alone sounds the first syllable, giving the effect of fearful hesitation.

The kind of expansion with antiphonal repetition on a phrase which takes Schütz's fancy, illustrated in Ex. 79, is a charming feature of these psalms

Ex. 79   SCHÜTZ, Wohl dem, der nicht wandelt

which offsets the concision of the basic *stylo recitativo*. Some pieces have relatively expansive openings in declamatory or imitative motet style, and when a
psalm ends with a setting of the doxology it is often set as a climactic 'finale'.
A particularly fine example is also to be found in Psalm 1, in which the final
line, 'und von Ewigkeit zu Ewigkeit, Amen', is spun out as a kind of free,
modulating canon for twenty-eight bars. The lower three parts of each choir
outline simple cadential progressions in alternation, but the top parts overlap
them in such a way as to produce five-part textures most of the time. Schütz

evinces a very strong grasp of tonality here; if we begin from the first half of the last verse ('Wie es war im Anfang'), cadential progressions occur at the rate of one to a bar as follows:

g	(plagal)	– 4 cadences
d	(perfect)	– 2 cadences
g	(perfect)	– 5 cadences
C	(perfect)	– 5 cadences
F	(perfect)	– 5 cadences
B flat	(perfect)	– 5 cadences

each new key is initiated by a different choir

At this point Choir 1 pulls us back to G minor with a diminished fourth B flat – F sharp in the bass, leading into the final tutti with its reiterations of I–V–I progressions in that key.

In general it may be said of the pieces in the first two categories that Schütz has little opportunity to utilise the repetition of material which characterised so much concerted music in the early seventeenth century. In the psalms he creates an ebb and flow between the continuum of the recitation and the greater musical interest of polychoral antiphony and tutti. This is especially clear in the first piece, Psalm 110, *Der Herr sprach zu meinem Herren* (SWV 22; Werke 2 vol. 23: 1). Most of the time one of the *cori favoriti* recites the first half of the verse, answered by the other choir, by the tutti or by antiphonal repetition in the second half. Exceptions are verse 4 (tutti, *falsobordone*) and verse 7 (*coro favorito I* alone).

In category 2 and category 3 pieces the *Capellen* may be used throughout, or they may help to articulate the form on a large scale, as well as enhance the text, by being reserved for dramatic or exultant moments. In Psalm 110 the single *Capelle* is brought in in the second half of most verses, in tuttis and otherwise usually but not exclusively in support of *coro favorito II*. It is never of course heard on its own. In the richly-textured Psalm 122 (SWV 26) the *Capellen* are used throughout. In Psalm 2, *Warum toben die Heiden* (SWV 23; Werke 2 vol. 23: 23), the *Capellen* are silent in verses 3–7a, re-entering in verse 7b to emphasise the words of the Lord 'Thou art my son, today have I begotten thee'. In the chorale setting, *Nun lob, mein Seel* (SWV 41; Werke 2 vol. 25: 97), the *Capellen* are used to reinforce a recurring metrical contrast: each line of the paraphrase is developed by the *coro favorito* in duple time in imitative chorale motet style and then re-stated in triple-time antiphony with all three *Capellen*. Because of the doubling or reinforcing rôle of the *Capellen* Schütz's syntax, however many groups are involved, is basically that of double-choir antiphony.

A more overt refrain structure naturally arises in the 'responsorial' Psalm 136, *Danket dem Herren*, which Michael Praetorius set in Latin as *Confitemini Domino*. Schütz set this twice (SWV 32 and 45), and although the settings are distinct, his quantitative treatment of verbal stress is so consistent that the refrains come out in identical rhythm in both cases. SWV 32 (Werke 2 vol. 24: 24) is a category 2 piece with two *favorito* groups of contrasting range and two SATB *Capellen*. It is a beautifully thought-out structure in which the refrain is never allowed to become monotonous. There are five clearly defined sections:

1. vv. 1–5:   1st half: Coro fav. I; response: Coro fav. II + Cap. I (response repeated à 12 after v. 5)
2. vv. 6–9:   1st half: Coro fav. II; response: Coro fav. I + Cap. I (response repeated à 12 after v. 9)
3. vv. 10–15: as section 1 (except v. 13: à 2 with à 2 response – miniature canons with independent continuo; some variation of response, and extended antiphonal treatment of it in v. 15, ending tutti)
4. vv. 16–25: as section 2 (return to 'Ur-form' of response, again with antiphony & tutti closing v. 25)
5. v. 26:   extended tutti with canonic triple-time antiphony (Cap. II enters for the first time in this section)

The response, which by its nature is cadential, forms a kind of modulating ritornello:

verse: 1 2 3 4 5 | 6 7 8 9 | 10 11 12 13 14 15 | 16 17 18 19 20 21 22 23 24 25 | 26
key: d d C G a d | d d F a d | a G A* d d a d | a a a a a G G d F d | a d d
       [* half-close in d; Picardy thirds in final chords are not shown]

The last verse is another superb example of Schütz's handling of tonality. After the close of verse 25 on a D major chord (*tierce de picardie*), verse 26 begins after a rest on a B flat chord with a massive tutti which cadences in C. It is then repeated a tone higher to cadence in the tonic, again with a *tierce de picardie*. The triple-time setting of the response which follows again begins on B flat, but expands on the modulation back to the tonic by using sequential antiphonal repetition to pass through F, C, G majors and D minor before cadencing in A minor. The whole process is then repeated twice, but cadencing in the tonic in *ouvert–clos–clos* manner. The other setting of this text, SWV 45 (Werke 1, vol. 3: 182), is more loosely organised; for its scoring, see category 3 above. The responses in which the trumpets join the ensemble must of course be in C. The obligatory *Capelle* carries some of the responses on its own, and there is a considerable amount of duet writing for voices drawn from the vocal Choir 1.

The two pieces described as *moteti* seem to be so defined because of their texts (SWV 40, *Ist nicht Ephraim mein teurer Sohn* is from Jeremiah 31: 20, whereas SWV 42, *Die mit Tränen* is only part of a psalm, Ps. 126: 5–6) and their relatively conventional polychoral style. *Nun lob, mein Seel* is described as a *canzon* because of its use of a metrical text and its associated chorale melody. In applying the term *concert* to three pieces, Schütz seems to be distinguishing them stylistically from the *moteti*. Again, theirs are not straight psalm texts: SWV 39, *Lobe den Herren*, is taken from Ps. 103: 2–4, SWV 46, *Zion spricht*, has the same text (Isaiah 49: 14–16) as Scheidt's funeral motet, whilst SWV 47, *Jauchzet dem Herren*, is centonised from a number of psalms.

What these pieces have in common is important use of solo voices, sometimes allied to precise instrumentation. It is apparent that Schütz would have used this term also for some other pieces from our categories 3 and 4 if they had not also been settings of complete psalms: Psalm 121 (SWV 31), with its systematic use of solo voices already mentioned above, Psalm 23 (SWV 23), with its extensive use of two-voiced textures, and Psalm 150 (SWV 38).

Lobe den Herren (Werke 2, vol. 25: 65) has a *cantilena* structure with a refrain framing solo sections, one for tenor alone and two for all four *favorito* voices. On the third of its four appearances, the refrain, otherwise triple-time, is reworked in duple. Repetition of material is also employed in the two works I have placed in category 4, sacred concertos on a grand scale. Psalm 150, *Alleluja! Lobet den Herren* (ibid.: 3) begins with a triple-time, mostly tutti 'Alleluia' which is re-worked and extended with antiphonal writing at the end. There are two SATB *cori favoriti* which also become *Capellen*, and two scarcely dispensable instrumental *Capellen*, one scored for three cornetti or violins with one trombone or bassoon, the other for cornetto or recorder, two trombones and one further trombone or else a bassoon. The 'or's are not really alternatives, as we shall see. Apart from the framing 'Alleluia's, the formal procedure is akin to that of Psalm 121, with soloists introducing the text of each verse before it is treated polychorally. The difference here is that the solo sections involve pairs of voices combined with pairs of instruments drawn from across the primary choral division, with continuo: verse 1: 2 soprano voices + 2 bassoons; verse 2: 2 alto voices + 2 cornetti + 2 bassoons or trombones (top and bottom of each *Capelle*); verse 3: 2 tenor voices + 3 trombones (*Capelle II;* 'Lobet ihn mit Posaunen'); verse 4: 2 bass voices + violin + recorder ('Lobet ihn mit Saiten und Pfeifen'); verse 5: 2 soprano and tenor pairs with continuo only; verse 6: tutti, homorhythmic, with one brief phrase for two sopranos. In verses 1–4 Schütz uses the term 'risposta à 2' to describe the imitative, sometimes canonic or echo-like relationship between the voice-parts; verse 5 has 'risposta à 4'.

Jauchzet dem Herren (SWV 47; Werke 1 vol. 3: 239) forms a fitting closing climax to the collection. The words of the shortest psalm, 117, recur as a refrain between the extracts from Pss. 98, 150, 148 and 96 which make up this 'psalm above psalms', as Moser called it (1959: 338). From its more delicate scoring Schütz draws textures of great variety; once again he is able to match some of them with the content of the text: two flutes and solo tenor; solo tenor with lutes ('mit Harfen'); solo soprano and strings with triadic material ('mit Pauken'); the same group ('mit Saiten') in dialogue with the two flutes and solo tenor ('und Pfeifen') and so on. In these last two works, whilst not entirely forsaking the polychoral medium, Schütz embraces decisively the world of the mixed *concertato*.

Schütz's later polychoral music

Schütz did not cease to write polychoral music after the publication of 1619. Two motets date from around 1620, one for double choir (SWV 464) and one, *Veni sancte Spiritus* (SWV 475), for four choirs of which two have the 'trio sonata' make-up of two trebles and bass. The *Resurrection History* of 1623 has a closing chorus for double choir. It is thought that he intended bringing out a companion volume to the *Psalmen Davids*. Five psalms in manuscript at Kassel (Psalm 7, SWV 462; Psalm 15, SWV 466; Psalm 127, SWV 473; Psalm 5, SWV Anhang 7; Psalm 137 (not in SWV)) were copied between 1627 and 1632 (*NGr* 17: 7; all in Werke 2 vols. 27 & 28). They show a continued move away from polychorality in the direction of the mixed *concertato* with polychoral elements, as does Schütz's only Latin psalm-setting, *Domine est terra* (Vulgate 23; SWV 476), the date of composition of which is not known. The disruptive effects of the Thirty Years' War on musical life at Dresden are well-known, and Schütz turned, of necessity, to smaller forces.

He used the polychoral medium in a special way, for two very special occasions. For the Electoral Assembly at Mühlhausen in 1627 he wrote a double-choir piece in which the first choir bears the Latin antiphon *Da pacem, Domine*, the second choir a ceremonial, political text, the two choirs eventually joining in the words of the antiphon.[12] The *Musicalische Exequien* of 1636, written for the funeral of Prince Heinrich Posthumus of Gera, contains, besides a conventional double-choir motet, a remarkable setting of the German Nunc dimittis (Werke 2, vol. 4: 60) in which a five-part choir 'next to the organ' sings the words of the canticle, now loudly, now softly ('fortiter' and 'submisse'), alternating and overlapping with a three-part choir (two soprano 'seraphim' and a baritone 'blessed soul with the seraphim') placed 'in the distance' which sings the words 'Selig sind die Toten' (Rev. 14:13 and Wisdom 3:1), made famous by Brahms in his *A German Requiem*.

Three works of around 1640–50 are only polychoral at all if the *Capellen* are employed. These include Schütz's best known short piece, *Saul, Saul, was verfolgst du mich?*, published in 1650 (SWV 415; *HAM* vol. 2: 33), which, if the two optional *Capellen* are added to the six solo voices, two violins and continuo, surrounds and overwhelms the listener with its vivid evocation of Christ's words to Saul on the road to Damascus. The *Capellen* reinforce dynamic contrasts and splits of texture which are already present in the main ensemble.

That Schütz probably never tired of the purity of the classic double-choir medium is shown in his return to it in old age in his monumental settings of Psalm 119, Psalm 100, and the German Magnificat. All are now available in Werke 2, vol. 39, though sadly two voices of the psalms have had to be reconstructed. Schütz returns to the objective, recitational style of the *Psalmen*

Davids, with occasional elaboration of the texture, especially in the doxology, which is set after each section of Psalm 119. The psalm-sections begin with plainchant, as does the doxology which continues with a *cantus firmus*. Schütz permits himself some extrovert vocal embellishment in Psalm 100. In the Magnificat, in which as in Psalm 100 more antiphonal repetition is admitted, everything is pared to the bare essentials, yet there remains much of the rugged energy Schütz shares with Scheidt. It is a monument to the seemingly endless fascination of double-choir antiphony.

POSTSCRIPT

In tracing the line of polychoral music from Italy, and particularly Venice, to Germany and as far as Schütz, we have explored but one strand of musical history. It was of course entwined with other strands. As the *concertato* style of Michael Praetorius, Scheidt and Schütz demonstrates, German composers were in continuous touch with developments in Italy. The list of composers mentioned by Praetorius in *Syntagma musicum III* is impressive and shows how up-to-date his knowledge was. Having said that, we have been at pains to point out also the German-ness of the music of these composers, which is never submerged by the adoption of Italian idioms.

German composers might have continued to write polychoral music if the Thirty Years' War had not prevented them. In Italy also economic forces helped to make the cultivation of polychoral music in the seventeenth century less widespread than it had been in the peak years at the end of the sixteenth century. There was also a change of taste and compositional style to be reckoned with. Roche points out (1984: 116) that after the death of Giovanni Gabrieli few composers in Northern Italy composed motets for large ensembles. Whatever the forces available, composers came to prefer the new medium of a few solo voices with continuo for motets as not only practical but flexible and admirably suited to word-painting and expression. The large-scale contrasts of polychoral writing remained useful for enhancing the more 'neutral' texts of the psalms for vespers and compline and the mass ordinary.

In these genres some composers continued to write straight eight-part double-choir music, almost as a kind of *prima prattica*, and indeed the habit persisted in Venice even as late as Vivaldi (Arnold, *NGr* vol. 4: 777). A more fashionable trend was to draw soloists from one choir (Viadana 1612) or both choirs (Giacobbi 1609), whilst still retaining a fair amount of double-choir antiphony. In the mixed *concertato*, on the other hand, polychoral elements are only one resource among many in the drive to maximise variety of scoring and texture. This approach was pioneered by Giovanni Gabrieli in his late works, and is clearly seen in the most famous work of the period, Monteverdi's Vespers (1610). Even a piece like *Nisi Dominus* with a consistent double-choir format has no real cut-and-thrust between the choirs – rhythmically fearfully complex tuttis frame single-choir music in which the chief interest lies in lively declamation. In *Ave maris stella* the various groups are completely separated in self-contained verses and ritornellos providing contrasts of scoring but no organic interaction between the forces.

These pieces are conservative examples of Monteverdi's *cantus firmus* techniques in the Vespers. The most progressive movement, the bigger of the two Magnificats, is another sequence of closed verses, each uniquely scored and with no polychoral element to speak of. Except in its systematic employment of *cantus firmus* it is almost an example of what paradoxically became known as the *concertato alla romana*. This highly sectional form became popular in Rome, and sometimes had polychoral elements. It probably has its origin in works like Victoria's polychoral magnificats (1600), and Dixon (1981: 267) cites a setting of *Aeterna Christi munera* by Agazzari (1603) as a rudimentary example contrasting single-choir and tutti verses with one for SSA soloists. This contrasts with the continuously varied scorings within a through-composed piece which Roche defines as the 'textural' technique (1984: 90ff) and which may, on the largest scale, have polychoral passages. Dixon (1981 vol. 2: 179) gives an early Roman example in G. F. Anerio's *Jubilemus in arca Domini Dei* (1611). Solos and duets contrast with tuttis and the piece ends with a double-choir passage, the whole held together by the continuo.

Music for three or four choirs was written by a few composers in Northern Italy after the Gabrielis, such as Zucchini (1602), Pallavicino (posthumous collection of 1605) and Viadana (1612), and perhaps there was more that has not survived – the publication of large quantities of it would clearly not have been economic. It is chiefly from Rome, however, that we have evidence of the continuing cultivation of the multichoral style, what has come to be known as the 'Colossal Baroque', though only a fraction of the music, and not the most lavish, found its way into print. Multichoral performances took place with increasing frequency after about 1620, at a time when the plain double-choir style was giving way in Rome to the mixed *concertato* (Dixon 1981: 273, 295). Only in size was such music in any way extraordinary – one can perhaps see the *prima prattica* surfacing again in the fact that in most cases the forces were made up of SATB choirs.

Polychoral technique lingered on in its pure form, then, as a legacy from the Renaissance, side by side with newer idioms we would regard as indubitably Baroque. Yet in part it was from or through polychoral music that many of those new devices developed. Preoccupations with ensemble problems solved by giving one or more organs an accompanimental rôle and/or by constructing a common bass line in tuttis are part of the background to the emergence of the continuo. The idea of producing contrasts of colour and dynamics by adding and subtracting differently-scored groups led ultimately to the art of orchestration. The idea of contrast between one or other of the choirs with the tutti is a step on the road to the Baroque concerto, particularly when, as in some of the motets of Giovanni Gabrieli and others, use is made of a musical refrain distinct in style from the intervening episodes. Above all, just as we saw the emergence in essence as early as Josquin of some of the principles which govern the construction of polychoral music, so in the seventeenth century we can see even in small-scale concerted music the continued working out of structural patterns originating in polychoral writing. The perception of passing material between voices or voices and instruments as antiphony or musical dialogue rather than as contrapuntal imitation in the *prima prattica* sense says a lot about the stylistic difference between the few-voiced *concertato* and classic Renaissance polyphony. The forces may even alternate and unite in such a way as to suggest that the music was derived from or could convincingly be arranged in a polychoral format.

The study of polychoral music is not at an end. Much music is waiting to be unearthed and studied, and I am acutely aware of the gaps that remain in this book's coverage. Nor it seems are composers tired of exploring spatial effects, though nowadays it is more likely to be done with the help of electronics. It is interesting how composers down the years have turned to polychoral writing for a particular dramatic purpose or just to create excitement – Bach in his St Matthew Passion, Berlioz in his *Roméo et Juliette*, Walton in *Belshazzar's Feast* – or purely as a structure, as in Vaughan Williams's Mass in G minor. In the hands of Lasso, the Gabrielis, Schütz and their contemporaries polychoral music was not only a popular and sophisticated medium, as capable of quiet expressivity as of majesty and pomp; it was a vital force in the transition from the Renaissance to the Baroque.

APPENDIX 1

READINGS FROM VICENTINO, ZARLINO AND TROIANO

Nicola Vicentino, *L'antica musica ridotta alla moderna prattica*, Rome 1555

Cap. XXVIII Ordine di comporre à due chori Psalmi e dialoghi, et altre fantasie.

Nelle chiese, & in altri luoghi spatiosi et larghi, la musica composta à quattro voci fa poco sentire, anchora che siano molti Cantanti per parte, nondimeno & per varietà, & per necessità di far grande intonatione in tali luoghi, si potrà comporre Messe, Psalmi, & Dialoghi, & altre cose da sonare con varij stromenti, mescolati con voci; & per far maggiore intonatione si potrà anchora comporre à tre chori. Et il Compositore prima avvertirà, & eleggerà il tono che vorrà fare sopra le parole, & poi comporrà & osserverà il tono, overo il modo della compositione fatta sopra il canto fermo, o di sua fantasia, ò con fuga, ò senza; & quando il primo choro darà principio, si farà che l'intonatione delle prime voci siano buone da intonare, cioè ò per unisono, ò per quarta, ò per quinta, ò per ottave, ò per decima, ò per duodecima, ò per quintadecima: & quando s'haurà cantato, & che se vorrà pausare, & dar fine alla prima clausula del primo choro, si farà ch'il secondo choro piglierà sopra la metà dell'ultima nota, del choro primo antedetto, ò per unisono, ò per ottava de tutte le parti; (in essempio) come sarebbe ch'il Tenore pigliasse l'unisono con l'altro Tenore, & il Contralto per unisono con l'altro Contralto; et il Soprano a voce mutata, che verrà come un Contralto, pigliasse ò per unisono, ò per consonanza di terza, ò di quinta di sotto a detto Soprano: & il Basso pigliassi ò per unisono de l'altro Basso, ò per ottava, come meglio gli verra piu commodo; & quando un choro non piglera la voce da l'altro choro, o per unisono, ò per ottava, non sara buon da sentire, et il pigliar della voce sara fallace; & questa presa di voce dè esser sempre sopra la meta dell'ultima nota, che sara appresso un sospiro, ò una pausa, & a piu pause, acciò che la voce intonata sia per guida sicura, a l'altra che haura da intonare & mantenere il modo. Et il secondo choro per varieta si comporre il Soprano, che sara a voce mutata, & l'altro a voce piena: & il choro che haura da incominciare doppo le pause, non incomincierà mai quando l'altro haurà finito, ma sopra la metà dell'ultima nota, come disopra ho detto. Et s'avvertirà quando si vorrà far cantare due ò tre chori in un tempo, si farà che i Bassi di ambo due, o di tutti tre i chori s'accordino, & non si farà mai quinta sotto in un Basso con l'altro, quando tutti à un tratto cāteranno, perche l'altro choro haurà la quarta disopra, & discorderà con tutte le sue parti. Perche quelli non sentiranno la quinta sotto, s'il choro sarà alquanto discosto da l'altro choro; & se si vorrà far accordare tutti i Bassi, s'accorderanno sempre in unisono, ò in ottava; & qualche volta in terza maggiore, ma non si riposerà piu di tempo d'una minima, perche detta terza maggiore, sarà debole à sustentare tante voci, & à questo modo le parti non discorderanno; & i chori potranno cantar anchor separati uno da l'altro, che accorderanno nell'ordine sopra detto; & se ancho saranno le parti lontane; poi nelle compositioni de Dialoghi, si farà che tutte le parti canteranno in circulo; allhora si potrà comporre della quinte ne Bassi facendo però stare quelli sempre uno appresso a l'altro, per rispetto che uno de Bassi haurà la quarta di sopra a l'altro, acciò non discordi se fusse lontano dalla parte Bassa: & il medesimo ordine si terrà nel pigliare delle voci, come ho di sopra detto. Et il Compositore si reggerà secondo il suggietto delle parole, & come s'accorderanno i due Bassi; qui noterò molte note unisone, & con l'ottave, & con le terze; acciò il Discepolo possi meglio imparare con gli essempi che con parole.

[Vicentino's example which follows is given as Ex. 1, p. 10.]

Gioseffo Zarlino, *Le istitutioni harmoniche*, Venice 1558

Part of Terza pars: *chapter 66*

[The version given is the first edition; where later editions alter or add to the text substantively, the variants are given in notes at the end.]

Accaderà alle volte di comporre alcuni Salmi in una maniera, che si chiama a Choro spezzato, i quali spesse volte si sogliono cantare in Vinegia nelli Vesperi, & altre hore delle feste solenni; & sono ordinati, & divisi in due Chori, over in tre;[1] ne i quali cantano Quattro[2] voci; & li Chori si cantano hora uno, hora l'altro a vicenda; & alcune volte (secondo il proposito) tutti insieme; massimamente nel fine: il che stà molto bene. Et perche cotali Chori si pongono alquanto lontani l'un dall'altro; però avertirà il Compositore (acciò non si odi dissonanza in alcuno di loro tra le parti) di fare in tal maniera la compositione; che ogni Choro sia consonante: cioè che le parti di un Choro siano ordinate in tal modo, quanto fussero cōposte à Quattro voci semplici, senza considerare gli altri Chori; havendo però riguardo nel porre le parti, che tra loro insieme-mente accordino, & non vi sia alcuna dissonanza: Percioche composti li Chori in cotal maniera, ciascuno da per sè si potrà cantare separato,[3] che non si udirà cosa alcuna, che offendi l'udito. Questo avertimento non è da sprezzare: percioche è di grande commodo; & fu ritrovato dall'Eccellentissimo Adriano. Et benche si rendi alquanto difficile, non si debbo però schivare la fatica: percioche è cosa molto lodevole & virtuosa; & tal difficultà si farà alquanto più facile, quando si haverà essaminato le dotte compositioni di esso Adriano; come sono quelli Salmi, Confitebor tibi domine in toto corde meo in consilio iustorū: Laudate pueri dominum: Lauda Ierusalem dominum: De profundis: Memento domine David, & molti altri; tra i quali[4] è il Cantico della Beata Vergine, Magnificat anima mea Dominum, il quale composi gia molti anni[5] a tre Chori.[6] Queste compositioni vedute, & essaminate, saranno di gran giovamento a tutti coloro, che si dilettaranno di comporre in tal maniera: Conciosia che ritroverà, che li Bassi de i chori si pongono tra loro sempre[7] Unisoni, overo in Ottava; ancora che alcuna volte si ponghino in Terza: ma non si pongono in Quinta:[8] percioche[9] torna molto incommodo; & oltra la difficultà che nasce, è impossibile di far cosa, che torni bene, secondo il proposito.[10] Et questa osservanza viene ad essere molto commodo alli Compositori: percioche lieva a loro la difficultà di far cantare le parti delli Chori, che tra loro non si ritrova dissonanza.[11]

Part of Quarta pars: *chapter 15*

Percioche quando vorra comporre sopra le parole del Cantico evangelico nominato di sopra, che si canta nel Vespero fà dibisogno, che seguiti il Modo[12] & la Intonatione, che si canta ne i Canti fermi[13] il detto Cantico; si come dè fare anco[14] quando componerà sopra le parole di alcuno Salmo, che si canta[15] nel Vespero, overo in altre hore; sia poi tal Salmo composto in maniera, che li suoi Versi si possino cantare con un'altro choro scambievolmente; come hà composto Iachetto, & molti altri; o pur siano tutti interi, si come compose Lupo li Salmi Incon-vertēdo Dominus captivitatem Syon & Beati omnes qui timent Dominum, a Quattro voci sotto 'l Modo ottavo[16] overamente siano composti a due chori; come li Salmi di Adriano Laudate pueri Dominum: Lauda Hierusalem Dominum: & molti altri; che si chiamano a choro spezzato.

Massimo Troiano, *Discorsi delli triomfi, giostre, apparati, é delle cose piu notabile fatte nelle sontuose nozze, dell'illustrissimo & eccellentissimo Signor Duca Guglielmo. . .1568 à 22 di Febraro*, Munich 1568.

p. 102

Fortunio: 'Equi se sonò a dodici, a tre Chori: primo Choro con quattro viola da Gamba, secondo, quattro flauti grossi, e terzo, quattro strumenti varij: Cioe una Dolzaina, na Corna-musa, un Fiffaro, e un corno Muto. . .'

p. 150

Fortunio: 'E tra le altre Musiche, che fatte vi furono, questo bel concerto udivi: opera a 24. Otto viole da Gamba, otto Viole, da braccio, & otto stromenti varij: cio è un Fagoto, una Cornamusa, un Cornetto muto: un Cornetto alto: un Cornetto grosso storto, un Fiffaro, una dolzaina, & un Trombone, grosso: una volta senza voci, prima e seconda parte fu sonato: e dopo compartiti, da Messer Orlando, con otto Sonore voci, unaltra volta fu fatto. . .'

p. 182

Fortunio: 'La Domenica [7 March], fù cantata sollennemente, una Messa à 24. dell'eccellente Messere Anniballe Paduano, Organista, dello Sereniss. Arciduca Carlo, d'Austria. E nel desinare l'eccellente Messere Orlando di Lasso, tra le altre Musiche, che fatto havea: Un Mottetto a quaranta fece cantare e sonare quale fù degno d'ogni honore e laude.'

Marinio: 'Ditemi a che modo furono compartite le parte?'

Fortunio: 'Otto Tromboni, otto Viole da gamba, otto flauti grossi, un strumento da penna, & un Liuto grosso, tutto il restante supplirono le voci, e fù ditto tre volte, con grandissima audienza.'

Marinio: 'E chi fù l'autore di questa superba, & inodita compositione?'

Fortunio: 'Lo Signore Alesandro striggio gintilhuomo Mantuano: quale per il merito delle sue gran virtù, con grandissima provisione, e comodità presso il gran Cosimo, Duca di Firenza, se intertiene.'

SOME CHOIRBOOKS IN THE ÖSTERREICHISCHE NATIONALBIBLIOTHEK, VIENNA: LIST OF CONTENTS

[These manuscripts represent the repertory at the Graz court *c*1600.]

Ms. 16702. Four choirbooks, the music for one choir in each book. Foliation as in the first book.

f. 2v Missa Jubilate Deo à 16. Joan de Croce
f. 21v Missa sup. Audite me à 16. Franciscus Stivorio
f. 39v Missa sine nomine à 16. Franciscus Stivorio
f. 55v Missa à 16. D. Gregorio Zuchinio
f. 75v Missa Dominus regnavit à 16. Lampertus de Saÿve
f. 93v Missa sine nomine à 16. Alexandro Thadei
f. 115v Missa à 16. Georgius Poss
f. 140v Missa à 16. Di Giovan Priuli
f. 161v Missa à 16. Con le trombe. Reimundo Ballestra
f. 182v super Hoc tegitur à 17. Georgius Poss
f. 206v Missa à 26. In ecco. Georgius Poss
f. 240v Missa à 24. Hannibal Patavinus [In books 1–3 only]

Ms. 16703. One choirbook. All the music except f. 2v is à 8, mostly divided into two choirs across the opening. A few pieces are not strictly polychoral.

f. 2v Aspice domine à 4. Anon
f. 7v Laudate dominum omnes gentes. Vincentius Bellaver [Attributed to Faignient in 1585[1], no. 41]
f. 12v Laudate dominum in sanctis eius. Franciscus Rovigo
f. 21v Obsecro vos fratres. Simon Gatto
f. 26v Perfice gressus meos. Annibal Perini
f. 31v Benedicite omnia opera. Bartholomeus Sponton
f. 36v Deus misereatur nostri. Orlando di Lasso
f. 43v Domine a lingua dolosa. Anibal Padovano
f. 50v Duo seraphim. Lucretij Quintiani
f. 55v Si acuero. Ludovici Viadanae
f. 61v Domine exaudi orationem meam. Horatio Vecchio
f. 66v Peccantem me quotidie. Horatius Vecchio
f. 69v Factum es silentium. Constantius Porta
f. 76v Ad dominum cum tribularem. Constantius Porta
f. 82v Ornaverunt faciem templi. Constantius Porta
f. 86v Secunda pars. Omnes gentes plaudite manibus
f. 91v Percussit Saul mille. Joann: de Croce
f. 97v Benedictus dominus deus. Joann: de Croce
f. 104v Audite verbum domini. Joann: de Croce
f. 111v Factum est silentium. Joann de Croce
f. 118v Benedicite omnia opera. Rogerij Joannel
f. 126v Exultate deo. Rogerij Joannelij

f. 133v Laudate dominum in sanctis eius. Rogerius Joannellus
f. 142v Jubilate Deo. Rogerij Joannelli
f. 150v Quare fremuerunt gentes. Asprilius Pacellus
f. 156v Exurgat deus. Asprilius Pacellus
f. 167v Regna terrae. Asprilius Pacellus
f. 176v Cantate domino. Asprilius Pacellus
f. 187v Iubilate deo. Asprilius Pacellus
f. 199v Benedictus dominus deus. Andreas Gabrielis
f. 205v Beati immaculati. Andreas Gabrielis
f. 211v Exurgat deus. Andreas Gabrielis
f. 217v Deus in nomine tuo. Andreas Gabrielis
f. 223v Iubilate deo omnis terra. Andreas Gabrielis
f. 230v Domine exaudi orationem meam. Joan: Gabriel
f. 235v Misericordias domini. Joan: Gabriel
f. 242v Beati immaculati. Joan: Gabriel
f. 248v Domine dominus noster [index: Joannes Gabrielis]
f. 256v Diligam te domine. Joan: Gabriel
f. 261v Hoc tegitur. Joan: Gabriel
f. 268v Ego sum qui sum. Joan: Gabriel
f. 275v In te domine speravi [index: Joannes Gabrielis]

Ms. 16707. Three choirbooks, of which the first is lost. Foliation from the second book.
f. 2r Missa à 12. Andreae Gabrielis [Kyrie, Sanctus]
f. 11r Missa à 12. Joan Gabrielis [Kyrie, Gloria, Sanctus]
f. 22r Missa à 12 super Susanna un giour. Franciscus Rovigo
f. 38v Missa à 12 super Laudate dominum de coelis. Luca Marentio
f. 64v Missa à 12 super Erano i capei d'oro. Anthonio Mortaro
f. 80v Missa à 12 super Ab Austro veniet. Leon Leoni
f. 98v Missa Borromea à 12. Constantius Antegnatus
f. 113v Missa à 12 super Hodie completi sunt. Michalis Varoti
f. 129v Missa à 12 super Benedicam dominum. Claudij Meruli Correȝiensis
f. 151r Missa à 12. Reimundo Pallestra
f. 172v Missa prima à 12. D. Gregorio Zuchino
f. 193v Missa secunda à 12. D. Gregorio Zuchinio
f. 213v Missa à 13. Georgius Poss
f. 247v Missa à 14 super Omnes gentes. Lambertus de Seÿve
f. 266v Missa à 15. Lampertus de Saÿve
f. 288v Missa à 15 [index: Ecco chio lasso il core]. Simon Gatto

Ms. 16708 Apparently three choirbooks, of which at least the third is lost. I have only
   seen the second book, from which this foliation is taken.
f. 2r A.12. Di Antonio Mortaro da Brescia
f. 2v Dixit dominus. Primi toni
f. 6v Confitebor tibi. Octavi toni
f. 11v Beatus vir. Sexti toni
f. 15v Laudate pueri, Secundi toni
f. 18v Laudate Dominum. Quinti toni
f. 20v Laetatus sum. Tertij toni
f. 23v Nisi dominus. Quarti toni
f. 27v Lauda hierusalem. Quinti toni
f. 30v Magnificat: Tirsi io mi parto a Dio. Di Antonio Mortaro da Brescia
f. 36v Dixit dominus à 16. Balthasaro Donato
f. 39v Confitebor à 12. Bartholomeus Sponton
f. 44v Beatus vir à 12. Balthasaro Donato

f. 48v Laudate pueri à 12. Rogerio Joannel
f. 53v Laudate dominum à 12. Bartholomeus Sponton
f. 56v Magnificat à 12. Primi toni. Anthonio Mortaro
f. 62v Magnificat à 12. Andreas Gabrielis
f. 68v Magnificat à 12. Joan Gabrielis
f. 74v Magnificat à 12. Claudio Merulo da Corregio
f. 79v Magnificat à 12. Franciscus Stivorio
f. 85v Magnificat à 12. Georgius Poss
f. 92v Magnificat à 12. Secundi toni. Joannes Cavatius
f. 96v Magnificat à 12. Sexti toni. Joannes Cavatius
f. 100v Magnificat à 12. Organum. Octavi toni. Jacobus de Brouck
f. 106v Magnificat à 12. Innocentius Bernardi
f. 112v Magnificat à 14. Reimundo Pallestra
f. 119v Magnificat à 15. Franciscus Stivorio
f. 126v Magnificat à 16. Liberalis Zanchius
f. 131v Magnificat à 16. Franciscus Stivorio
f. 137v Magnificat à 18. Joan Gabrielis
f. 145v Magnificat à 18. Georgius Poss
f. 153v Magnificat à 20. Con le tronbe. Reimundo Ballestra
f. 159r Magnificat con il Sicut locutus est à 20. In ecco. Joan Gabrielis [The music begins at 'Sicut locutus' in this book]
f. 165v Magnificat à 33. Joan Gabrielis
f. 171r Ad Completorium. A.8. Bartholomeus Sponton
f. 171v Cum invocarem
f. 175v Tertij toni [falsobordone for In te domine speravi]
f. 177v Octavi toni [falsobordone for Qui habitat]
f. 181v Clamabit ad me à 9 [v. 15 of Qui habitat]
f. 189v Ecce nunc benedicite [vv. 1, 3 à 4]
f. 191v Gloria patri à 9
f. 193v Versus secundus Hymni Te lucis ante terminum
f. 195v Nunc dimittis à 12
f. 198v Salve regina à 8. Bartho: Sponton
f. 201v Regina coeli à 8. Bartholo. Sponton
f. 206v Magnificat à 8. Bartholo Sponton
f. 209v Gloria patri à 13 [for f. 206v]
f. 216v Te deum laudamus à 9. Lucae Marenti [f. 216r: à 13]

NOTES

1 The origins and development of *cori spezzati*

1 *Fiffaro*; some kind of flute seems more appropriate with these quiet instruments than a shawm (normally *piffaro*).

2 The early Italian contribution

1 Full inventories with concordances of all these Treviso manuscripts are given in Carver 1980: 35-7, 39-44. Concordances of non-*spezzato* psalms by Jachet also occur in Casale Monferrato (Crawford 1975: 154), Bologna and Stuttgart (Lewis 1979: 501-5).
2 Carver 1980: 35-8. These concordances provide evidence that different sets of odd (or even) verses of a given psalm were interchangeable in pieces of this type. Adherence to the psalm tone and the mode renders credible even the marrying of odd and even sets by different composers, as happens in one or two cases in 1550[1].
3 Based on comparison with the same library's Ms. A17, which is signed and dated 1522 by Passetto.
4 Preserved incomplete in a Castell'Arquato manuscript. See Slim 1962: 37.
5 Chamaterò is possibly the youngest composer of this group. We shall return to his psalms (1573) and magnificats (1575) in Chapter 7.
6 Ascribed to 'Lupus' in the index of the ms, but to Mouton in 1564[1]: no. 3.
7 I.e. those present in both Treviso Ms. 24 and 11b; the author has been hampered in transcribing from Treviso manuscripts by being unable so far to obtain microfilm copies of any save Ms. 11b. Fortunately the concordances and a visit to Treviso have made it possible to score most of the *salmi spezzati* of established authorship which have survived complete. There remains therefore much work to be done on the anonymous pieces.
8 Guainaro's *Exaudiat te Domine* in the later portion of Padua Cathedral Mss. D25 and D26 is probably the product of his second, brief period as *maestro* at the Cathedral in 1576.

3 The Franco-Flemish tradition

1 That conflictingly ascribed to both Gombert and Mouton in Verona Ms. 218 is in fact by Verdelot – see H. Colin Slim in *NGr* vol. 19: 633. The piece has one canonic pair of voices, and before they enter three high voices entering simultaneously are imitated an octave lower after three breves. For Festa's eight-in-four canon on this text see below.
2 'Absque pausis 5 cum pausis 10 vocum', an interesting parallel perhaps to the possibility raised by Gerstenberg (Willaert, Opera vol. 8: x-xi) that in Italian the term *coro spezzato* may refer to the rests in each choir's music.
3 See Haar (1971) for a more general discussion of this interesting area, which concerns music employing what we should term 'imitation' as well as canon.
4 Reese pointed out (1954: 270) that Pierre de la Rue's Mass on this motet is in a different mode with no flats in the signature of the *dux*, or indeed specified accidentals of any kind. See the preface to Feininger's edition (1950). I was also puzzled by this until I realised recently that there is an earlier concordance for the motet, with no ascription, in Brussels, Bibliothèque

Royale de Belgique, Ms. 228, f. 1v. In this source (mod. edn, Picker 1965: 172) there are no flats in the signatures of any of the voices, though some *ficta* B flats are necessary. In this version, the piece works almost entirely as *fuga*.

5 Müller, *NGr* vol. 10: 293, where the à 8 setting is erroneously described as a canon at the fifth.

6 The Mass's head-motif bears a certain resemblance to Phinot's *Sancta trinitas*.

7 *Tulerunt Dominum* is musically the same as the first part of *Lugebat David*; it may be by Gombert – see Noble, *NGr* vol. 9: 735. The former is given in Josquin 1933: 22.

8 An occupational hazard of the study of polychoral music is the time-consuming transcription which is often necessary before a piece reveals its character. Sources do not always indicate polychorality.

9 Interestingly, the sole source of this Mass is a manuscript at Munich used for a performance by Lasso around 1568–70: D-Mbs Ms. Maier 7 (Mus. Ms. 1).

10 Anticipated and possibly inspired in scope if not in layout or style by Striggio's *Ecce beatam lucem*, about which more in Chapter 4.

11 The present analysis is of necessity brief; for a more comprehensive treatment with musical examples see Carver 1980, vol. 1: 126–45.

12 ATB in Bologna (I-Bc); AB8 in Verona (I-VEaf).

13 It also survives incomplete in Munich (D-Mbs) Maier Ms. 132 (Mus. Ms. 1536), discantus f. 121r, with the Agnus Dei.

14 See for instance his 1595 collection of masses, which includes a *Missa 'Hodie completi sunt'* for three choirs.

4 Dissemination and aggrandisement

1 Mod. edn, Dunning 1974: 154, where it is unaccountably not laid out in two choirs.

2 Mod. edn, Dunning 1974: 160, again not printed in double-choir format.

3 The contents are given in Appendix 2.

4 The Nationalbibliothek Mss. 16703, 16707 and 16708; for their contents, see Appendix 2.

5 In the second section the phrase 'Rex caelestis' is re-used instead of 'Agnus Dei', presumably a scribal error.

5 The polychoral works of Orlando di Lasso

1 It used to be thought that *In convertendo, Deus misereatur* and *Levavi oculos* were originally composed c1552–3, when Lasso was in Italy, and revised for publication over ten years later (Boetticher 1955), a theory I accepted without question (Carver 1980, vol. 1: 203). The argument was based on copies made by Santini from Roman manuscripts which Boetticher assumed transmitted Lasso's original versions of these pieces. The sources have now been rediscovered, and it is apparent that the Roman copies are later revisions of the printed versions (O'Regan 1984)! The alterations were made to make the pieces fit in with Roman attitudes to polychoral music in the later sixteenth century; Lasso's dovetailing of voices at choral interchanges is reduced and the bass parts are rendered spatial.

2 The text is taken from the Tridentine Breviary (Hymn at Lauds on Easter Sunday), used at the Bavarian Court from Christmas 1581. See Clive Wearing in Lasso 1981: 2.

3 *Providebam* is not Lasso's only motet à 7, but it is the only one laid out for double choir.

4 E.g. Ms. Maier 132, an enormous collection of multi-voiced works, virtually all concordant with one or other of the big anthologies 1555[(9–11)], 1564[(1)], 1568[(2–6)] or 1578[(1)], or an *Einzeldruck*.

5 None of Castileti's many pieces in the *Novus thesaurus musicus* of 1568 is polychoral.

6 Though we should remember that none of Lasso's thirty-odd complete psalm-settings includes the doxology – see Roche 1982: 14–17.

7 À 9: Munich Ms. Maier 50: f. 138v; à 10: Ms. 100: f. 1v.

8 Ms. La 339, where it is not fully texted; see Hermelink 1968.

6 Polychoral music in Rome and Spain

1 I am very grateful to Noel O'Regan for generously sharing with me his transcriptions from Animuccia 1570.
2 In what follows I have wherever possible cited the more recent Palestrina edition by Casir-miri *et al.* (Opere) with its modern clefs; the old edition begun by Haberl (Werke) is still indispensable for many works.
3 Choir 3, reconstructed in Werke vol. 26, has now been traced in I-Rn Mss. 77–88. I am grateful to Noel O'Regan for this information.
4 A fourth setting of which only one choir survives (Werke vol. 32: 180) is very similar in form.
5 Though of course lacking as yet the continuo. On Victoria's organ parts see below. On the *concertato alla Romana* see Dixon 1981: 266ff.
6 Noel O'Regan's forthcoming dissertation on this subject is eagerly awaited.

7 Venice: the grand climax

1 Revised birth and death dates as given in Morell 1983: 110–11.
2 Morell 1983: 112. If not born until 1533, Andrea could not have sung under Willaert in 1536 as originally stated by Caffi (1854–5, vol. 1: 166).
3 And also in *Benedicam Dominum* and *Exsultate justi*, two eight-part motets found only in late German sources, 1603[(1)] and 1618[(1)].
4 See note 3. Another exception is the fifth penitential psalm, *Domine exaudi* (1583).
5 Unless there were external reasons why this was not possible, like the diverse modes of the chants used by Josquin in his *Missa de Beata Virgine*.
6 And it can hardly have been much different from modern pitch, given the notated range of C–a″ across the four choirs and that the extremes of the range are employed frequently.
7 Perhaps the idea was to facilitate more performances of the Kyrie and Sanctus in situations where bass instruments such as trombones were not available. This would not explain why the five-part Kyrie I was printed at low pitch.
8 Reese's remark (1954: 497) that Andrea's *Deus misereatur* was written under the influence of Giovanni was clearly made without knowledge of the 1568 edition.
9 It is true that in the 1615 publications the relationship between the number of voices and the number of performers is different in some of the specifically scored pieces for solo voices and instruments, which function more like chamber music, despite their apparently lavish number of 'voices'. However, this does not invalidate the general argument.
10 The clefs of the single-choir *Exaudi Deus* à 7 are even more extraordinary: $C_4C_4F_3F_4F_5F_5$. Praetorius (1619: 159) says that these sorts of combinations indicate the use of trombones and perhaps also bassoons.
11 Though extraordinary singers would have been necessary to negotiate the wide overall range sometimes demanded by both Gabrielis. It may be that a piece such as *O Domine Jesu Christe* with its 'normal' overall range was thus scored so that it could be rendered without instruments during Passiontide.
12 Though with decided preferences; those employed in 1587 and 1597, in decreasing order of frequency, are: g (one flat), 14; a, 10; F (one flat), 8; G, 7; d, 5; e, 3; C, 1; d (one flat), 1; a (one flat), 1.
13 This tendency is present also in Andrea's music – see for instance the many *tierce de picardie* cadences in *O salutaris hostia* and also bars 15–22 of *Benedicam Dominum* (Anthology no. 14).
14 Bryant (1981b: 62–3) suggests that it was written for a commemoration of an event which took place originally in 1584 – the reception of some relics, all of which seem to be referred to in some way in this text: a thorn, pieces of the Cross, a piece of the column on which Our Lord was scourged and a piece of the pole on which the sponge was proffered. Bassano published a setting of a related text in 1598.
15 It is a matter for regret that two more settings, à 18 and à 33, are incompletely preserved in Vienna (A-Wn Ms. 16708, f. 137v & 165v).

16 E.g. in the *Symphoniae* volume: *O quam gloriosam* à 16, *Buccinate* à 19, the magnificats and some smaller-scale pieces, and from *Reliquiae*: *Hodie Christus natus est* à 8 (a *contrafactum* of the early madrigal *O che felice giorno*) and *Exsultet jam angelica* à 14.

17 Article 'Continuo' in *NGr*, vol. 4: 685–6.

18 The organ parts of the 1594 and 1597 collections contain instructions for the downward transposition of each piece, ranging from down a tone for the pieces in the lowest clefs to down a fourth or even a fifth for those in *chiavetti*. Some pieces have two suggested transpositions. The precise significance of these indications remains to be investigated, but it seems likely that two factors are involved: the downward transposition of pieces written in higher clefs on account of their mode and the possibility of Venetian organs being at a pitch somewhat higher than was comfortable for the singers.

19 Though I can find no mention in the copy of the psalms I consulted (I-Bc) of improvised vocal counterpoint, as cited in *NGr*, vol. 4: 112.

20 RISM is over-optimistic in suggesting that I-Bc possesses Choirs 1 and 2 – in fact it only has Choir 1. I-MOd has Choirs 1 and 3; I have not seen the copies at Faenza or Assisi.

21 There was of course plenty of four- and five-part music available for more modest establishments, and around 1600 the monodic and few-voiced *concertato* motet began to provide music of comparable artistic standard requiring even fewer performers.

8 Across the Alps: the German craze

1 Stuttgart: Gottwald 1964: 11, 41–2; Nuremberg: Rubsamen 1957: 297–8; Zwickau: Vollhardt 1893–6: 16, 40; Dresden: Steude 1974: 54, 59, 61, 77–8, 93–4; Brieg: Kuhn 1897: 3; Breslau: Bohn 1890: 1, 12–15, 20, 31, 35, 47–9, 52, 57, 63.

2 The G_2 clef occurs in about a quarter of the two-choir pieces, but only those for four choirs have a bass as low as F_5.

3 Hieronymus Praetorius was not using this technique at this time.

4 This comes closest to Schütz's use of the term in 1619, though the latter does not rule out the use of voices also.

5 I have not seen this combination on its own; it lacks a *bassett*, and presumably represents types of clef used to write cornetto and violin parts. Choir 1 of Giovanni Gabrieli's *Maria virgo* (1597) has $G_1G_2C_1C_2C_3$.

6 Giacobbi gives similar scoring for a low choir or *choro grave* in the preface to his psalms of 1609, suggesting viols or similar instruments as alternatives to trombones.

7 *Syntagma musicum III*, Part 3: Chapter 8, also gives information on the performance of these works.

8 The idea of bringing music in an older style up to date and the importance in the minds of early seventeenth-century composers of the refrain structure is illustrated also in Praetorius's reference to 'Alleluia' refrains he supplied for Phinot's *Jam non dicam* and *Sancta trinitas* and to motets by Lasso (*Syntagma III*: 188). Unfortunately these have not survived.

9 The chronology followed here is that given in the worklist accompanying Joshua Rifkin's article on Schütz in *NGr*, vol. 17: 1.

10 The editor of the *Psalmen Davids* in Werke 2 has confused this point by completely separating the *favorito* from its *Capelle* function in the double-choir sections of these pieces.

11 Viadana also advocates octave doubling (Roche 1984: 119).

12 For a detailed analysis of this sophisticated piece and its complex structural symmetries, see Werke 2, vol. 38: xxxvii–xxxviii; the piece itself, ibid.: 75.

Appendix 1 Readings from Vicentino, Zarlino and Troiano

1 1573 and 1589 read 'due o più Chori'.

2 1573 and 1589 insert 'o più'.

3 1589 omits 'separato'.

4 1573 and 1589 read 'tra i quali sono i Salmi; *Dixit Dominus Domino meo: Laudate pueri*

dominum: *Laudate Dominum omnes gentes*: *Lauda anima mea Dominum*: *Laudate Dominum quoniam bonus est Psalmus. Lauda Ierusalem Dominum*; il Cantico. . .'

5 1589 inserts 'fà'.

6 1589 adds 'per uso della Cappella del Famosissimo Tempio di San Marco; della quale da questi Sig. Illustriss. già ventiquattro anni sono, mi fù dato il governo'.

7 1589 inserts 'distanti per'.

8 1589 reads 'ma non si pongono però in Quinta; se non sopra la parte del Tenore'.

9 1589 inserts 'altramente'.

10 1589 adds 'essendo che si odi sempre nel cantare qualche asprezza'.

11 1589 adds 'Lodarei però, ne havrei per inconveniente quello, che molte fiate hò fatto anch'io; che quando si passasse 'l numero de due chori, & anco nell'istessi due chori, che i Bassi d'un Choro cantasse anco la parte dell'altro; percioche ne seguitarebbe, dirò cosi, che la sustentarebbe di maniera, che la farebbe comparere altra tanto; essendoche quella parte che è raddoppiata si viene più à udire; che fa la si cantasse semplicemente da una voce; come ben lo dimostra Aristotele nel Problema 2. della 19 Settione. Oltra di questo il Compositore potrebbe variare l'Harmonia, piu che non si fà; percioche ponendo i Bassi differenti di modulatione, non si può far molta varietà d'Harmonia nelle Compositioni. Et chiunque proverà cotesta cosa, potrà conoscer l'utile, ch'ella potrà apportare. Nè però alcuno si dee conturbar di questo; percioche se'l bisognasse havere cotal rispetto; per dire che canteranno quest'istesso l'una parte che canteranno l'altre parti; non bisognerebbe anco che nelle capelle, ne i chori, non vi fusse altro che una voce per parte, nel cantar le compositioni che ivi si cantano.'

12 1573 and 1589 substitute 'la Salmodia' for 'il Modo'.

13 1589 inserts 'cantandosi'.

14 1573 reads 'il detto Cantico; il che leggiadramente e stato osservato da Morale Spagnolo. Qual medesimo debbe anco osservare, quando componerà. . .'. 1589 reads 'il detto Cantico; il che leggiadramente per dare un'essempio e stato osservato oltra molti altri da Morale Spagnolo. Quel medesimo debbe anco osservare, quando componerà. . .'.

15 1589 inserts 'canoniche'.

16 1573 and 1589 insert 'delle Salmodie'.

REFERENCES AND SELECT
BIBLIOGRAPHY

Musical sources

Checklist of manuscripts

Manuscripts are included here of which the author has first-hand experience. Books or articles containing detailed information, such as description or list of contents, are given at the end of each entry.

BERGAMO, Biblioteca Civica. 1207D, 1208D, 1209D. Jeppesen 1958; Ravizza 1972b; this book: 20.

BOLOGNA, Archivio di San Petronio. A36, A37. Census-Catalogue vol. 1: 84.

MODENA, Archivio del Duomo. 5. Dondi 1896.

MODENA, Biblioteca Estense. Lat. 454 & 455. Bukofzer 1950, Kanazawa 1975.

MUNICH, Bayerische Staatsbibliothek. The first number in each case refers to Maier's catalogue: 7 (Mus. Ms. 1), 18 (Mus. Ms. 46), 23 (Mus. Ms. 64), 29 (Mus. Ms. 56), 45 (Mus. Ms. 15), 49 (Mus. Ms. 23), 50 (Mus. Ms. 21), 51 (Mus. Ms. 14), 98 (Mus. Ms. 49 & 50), 100 (Mus. Ms. 48), 127 (Mus. Ms. 41), 132 (Mus. Ms. 1536), 261 (Mus. Ms. 91). Maier 1879.

PADUA, Biblioteca del Seminario Vescovile. A17, D25, D26. Garbelotto 1952, Carver 1980: 45-7, this book: 20.

ROME, Biblioteca Apostolica Vaticana. Cap. Sist. 20. Llorens 1960.

TREVISO, Archivio del Duomo. 11b, 12, 22, 24. Census-Catalogue vol. 3: 241, 245-7; D'Alessi 1931, 1954; Carver 1980: 34-44; this book: 17-19.

VERONA, Accademia Filarmonica. 218. Turrini 1937, Böker-Heil 1969; this book: 19-20.

VIENNA, Österreichische Nationalbibliothek. 16702, 16703, 16707, 16708. This book: Appendix 2 & passim.

ZWICKAU, Ratsschulbibliothek. 325, 732. Vollhardt 1893-6.

Early prints

Anthologies are listed first; in the case of single composer publications RISM series A numbers are given at the end of each entry. Where reference is made to two distinct publications of the same year by a single composer, they are distinguished as, for example, 1596a, 1596b.

1534[5]. *Liber tertius: viginti musicales quinque, sex, vel octo vocum motetos habet. . .*Paris, P. Attaingnant. Mod. edn, Smijers & Merritt 1934-64: vol. 3.

1535[4]. *Liber duodecimus: XVII. musicales ad virginem Christiparam salutationes habet. . .* Paris, P. Attaingnant. Mod. edn, Smijers & Merritt 1934-64: vol. 12.

1539[8]. *Cantiones quinque vocum selectissimae. . .*Strasbourg, P. Schöffler.

1539[25]. *Musiche fatti nelle nozze dello illustrissimo Duca di Firenze il signor Cosimo de Medici e della illustrissima consorte sua mad. Leonora da Tolleto.* Venice, A. Gardane. Mod. edn, Minor & Mitchell 1968.

1540[7]. *Selectissimae necnon familiarissimae cantiones. . .fugae quoque, ut vocantur. . .von acht Stymmen bis auf zwo.* Augsburg, M. Kriesstein.

1540[8]. See Kugelmann 1540.

1550[1]. *Di Adriano et di Jachet. I salmi appertinenti alli vesperi per tutte le feste dell'anno, parte a versi, et parte spezzadi accomodati da cantari a uno et a duoi chori.* Venice, A. Gardane. Mod. edn, Willaert, Opera vol. 8.

1553[7]. *Liber primus sexdecim musicales modulos continens, ex pluribus vocibus compositos.* Paris, A. Le Roy & R. Ballard.

1554[17]. *I sacri et santi salmi di David profeta. . .composti da. . .Cipriano Rhore, e Iachet da Mantoa. Con li suoi magnificat a uno choro. A verse a quatro voci.* Venice, G. Scotto.

1555[10]. *Secundus tomus Evangeliorum, quatuor, quinque, sex, et plurium vocum. . .de Ascensione Christi. De Missione Spiritus Sancti.* Nuremberg, J. Montanus & U. Neuber.

1555[11]. *Tertius tomus Evangeliorum, quatuor, quinque, sex, et plurium vocum. . . de Trinitate. De Dedicatione Templi. De Coena Dominica.* Nuremberg, J. Montanus & U. Neuber.

1556[29]. *Der fünffte Theil schöner frölicher frischer alter und newer teutscher Liedlein mit fünff Stimmen.* Nuremberg, J. von Berg & U. Neuber.

1564[1]. *Thesaurus musicus continens selectissimas octo, septem, sex, quinque et quatuor vocum Harmonias. . .Tomi primi continentis cantiones octo vocum. . .Nuremberg, J. Montanus & U. Neuber.

1568[2-6]. *Novi thesauri musici liber primus. . .Petri Ioanelli bergomensis de Gandino, summo studio ac labore collectae. Novi atque catholici thesauri musici. Liber secundus [tertius, quartus, quintus & ultimus].* Venice, A. Gardano. Mod. edn of vol. 5: Dunning 1974.

1568[7]. *Cantiones triginta selectissimae: quinque. sex. septem: octo: duodecim et plurium vocum, sub quatuor. . .collectae & in lucem editae, per Clementem Stephani.* Nuremberg, U. Neuber.

1578[1]. *Selectae cantiones octo et septem vocum, in usum Academiae Reipublicae argentoratensis.* Strasbourg, N. Wyriot.

1585[1]. *Sacrae cantiones, cum quinque, sex et pluribus vocibus. . .studio & opera Friderici Lindneri. . .Nuremberg, C. Gerlach.

1585[5]. *Di M. Giovanni Pierluigi da Palestrina una messa a otto voci sopra il suo Confitebor a due cori. Et di M. Bartolomeo lo Roi. . .una messa a quattro. . .Venice, herede di G. Scotto.

1587[16]. *Concerti di Andrea, et di Gio. Gabrieli organisti. . .continenti musica da chiesa, madrigali, & altro, per voci, & stromenti musicali, à 6, 7, 8, 10, 12, & 16. . .Libro primo et secondo.* Venice, A. Gardano.

1588[2]. *Continuatio cantionum sacrarum quatuor, quinque, sex, septem, octo et plurium vocum, de festis praecipuis anni, a praestantissimis Italiae musicis nuperrimè concinnatarum. . .redactae, studio & opera Friderici Lindneri.* Nuremberg, K. Gerlach.

1589[17]. *Thesaurus motetarum. . .in diese breuchige Tabulatur gebracht von Jacobo Paix. . . Strasbourg, B. Jobin.

1590[4]. *Musica per concerti ecclesiastici.* Venice, G. Vincenti.

1590[5]. *Corollarium cantionum sacrarum quinque, sex, septem, octo et plurium vocum, de festis praecipuis anni. . .redactae studio & opera Friderici Lindneri.* Nuremberg, K. Gerlach.

1596[2]. *Thesaurus litaniarum. . .quatuor, quinque, sex, plurium vocum compositae. . .collectae, opera & studio Georgii Victorini.* Munich, A. Berg.

1598[2]. *Sacrae symphoniae. . .quaternis, V. VI. VII. VIII. X. XII. & XVI. vocibus. . .Editae studio & opera Casparis Hasleri. . .Nuremberg, P. Kaufmann.

1600[1]. *Magnificat octo tonorum, diversorum excellentissimorum authorum, quatuor, V. VI. VII. VIII. & XII. vocum.* Nuremberg, P. Kauffmann.

1600[2]. *Sacrarum symphoniarum continuatio. . .quaternis, V. VI. VII. VIII. X. et XII. vocibus. . .Nuremberg, P. Kauffmann.

1603[1]. *Florilegium selectissimarum cantionum . . .4. 5. 6. 7. & 8. vocum. . .ac labore M. Erhardi Bodenschatz. . .Leipzig, A. Lamberg.

1611[1]. *Promptuarii musici. . .V. VI. VII. & VIII. vocum. . .collectore Abrahamo Schadaeo. . . Strasbourg, K. Kieffer.

1612[3]. *Promptuarii musici. . .V. VI. VII. & VIII. vocum. . .pars altera. . .collectore Abrahamo Schadaeo. . .Strasbourg, K. Kieffer.

1613[1].   *Sacrae symphoniae diversorum excellentissimorum autorum: quaternis, 5. 6. 7. 8.*
          *10. 12. & 16. vocibus. . .editae, studio et operâ Casparis Hasleri. . .*Nuremberg, P.
          Kauffmann.

1613[2].   *Promptuarii musici. . .V. VI. VII. & VIII. vocum. . .pars tertia. . .collectore Abrahamo*
          *Schadaeo. . .*Strasbourg, K. Kieffer.

1615[2].   *Reliquiae sacrorum concentuum Giovan Gabrielis, Iohan-Leonis Hasleri. . .VI. VII.*
          VIII. IX. X. XII. XIII. XIV. XVI. XVIII. XIX. vocum, noviter exprontae à Georgio
          Grubero. Nuremberg, P. Kauffmann.

1617[1].   *Promptuarii musici. . .V. VI. VII. et VIII. vocum. . .pars quarta. . .collegit vero. . .*
          *Caspar Vincentius. . .*Strasbourg, A. Bertram.

1618[1].   *Florilegium Portense, continens CXV. selectissimas cantiones 4. 5. 6. 7. 8. vocum. . .*
          *Collectum et editum autore M. Erhardo Bodenschatz. . .*Leipzig, A. Lamberg &
          C. Closemann.

1621[2].   *Florilegii musici Portensis. . .V. VI. VII. VIII. X. vocum. . .pars altera. . .collectore et*
          *editore M. Erhardo Bodenschatzio. . .*Leipzig, A. Lamberg.

Agazzari, Agostino. 1603. *Sacrae laudes de Iesu, B. Virgine, angelis, apostolis. . .liber secundus.*
     Rome, A. Zannetti. A 334.

Anerio, Giovanni Francesco. 1611. *Litaniae deiparae virginis. . .una cum quatuor illis anti-*
     *phonis, quae pro varietate temporum post completorium cani solent. . .*Rome, B. Zannetti.
     A 1099.

Animuccia, Giovanni. 1570. *Il secondo libro delle laudi.* Rome, eredi di A. Blado. A 1238.

Antegnati, Costanzo. 1578. *Liber primus missarum sex et octo vocum.* Venice, A. Gardano.
     A 1260.

Asola, Giammateo. 1574. *Psalmodia ad vespertinas. . .octonis vocibus infractis decantanda. . .*
     Venice, erede di G. Scotto. A 2517.

     1584. *Sacrae cantiones. . .paribus quaternis vocibus decantandae.* Venice, G. Vincenti &
     R. Amadino. A 2555.

     1585. *Completorium romanum duae B. Virginis antiphonae. . .quatuorque alia motetta,*
     musica octonis vocibus infractis decantanda. Venice, erede di G. Scotto. A 2560.

     1587. *Nova vespertina omnium solemnitatum psalmodia, cum cantico Beatae Virginis.*
     Octonis vocibus. Venice, R. Amadino. A 2568.

     1588a. *Missae tres octonis vocibus liber primus.* Venice, R. Amadino. A 2570.

     1588b. *Liber secundus missas tres, duasque sacras cantiones continens. Octonis vocibus.*
     Venice, R. Amadino.

     1590. *Vespertina omnium solemnitatum psalmodia, canticum B. Virginis duplici modula-*
     tione. . .Salve Regina, missa, et quinque divinae laudes. Omnia duodenis vocibus, ternis
     *variata choris. . .*Venice, R. Amadino. A 2581.

     1600. *Sacro sanctae dei laudes, octonis vocibus infractis decantandae.* Venice, R. Amadino.
     A 2605, 1600[3].

     1602. *Hymnodia vespertina in maioribus anni solemnitatibus octonis vocibus infractis. . .*
     Venice, R. Amadino. A 2607.

Bassano, Giovanni. 1598. *Motetti per concerti ecclesiastici a 5, 6, 7, 8, & 12. voci.* Venice,
     G. Vincenti. B 1233.

     1599. *Concerti ecclesiastici a cinque, sei, sette, otto & dodeci voci. . .libro secondo.* Venice,
     G. Vincenti. B 1234.

Bendinelli, Agostino. 1585. *Sacrae modulationes octonis vocibus concinendae. . .liber primus.*
     Verona, S. a Donnis. B 1907.

Cambio, Perissone. 1550. *Il secondo libro di madrigali a cinque voci con tre dialoghi a otto voci*
     & uno a sette voci. Venice, A. Gardano. C 554.

Chamaterò di Negri, Ippolito. 1573. *Salmi corista a otto voci, per le feste di Natale, di Pasqua,*
     & altre feste del anno, secondo l'ordine del concilio di Trento. Venice, herede di G. Scotto.
     C 279.

     1575. *Li magnificat a otto, a nove, & a dodeci voci.* Venice, herede di G. Scotto. C 281.

Cifra, Antonio. 1610. *Vesperae, et motecta, octonis vocibus decantanda. . .*Rome, B. Zannetti. C 2187.

Cleve, Johannes de. 1579. *Cantiones seu harmoniae sacrae. . .quatuor, quinque, sex, septem, octo & decem vocum.* Augsburg, P. Ulhard & A. Reinheckel. C 3205.

Colombano, Orazio. 1583. *Li dilettevoli Magnificat composti sopra li otto toni a nove voci, accommodati per cantar & sonar in concerto: con una a quatuordeci voci, a tre chori.* Venice, G. Vincenti & R. Amadino. C 3423.

1587. *Ad vesperas Davidice modulationes in omnibus totius anni solemnitatibus. . .novem vocibus, cum cantico B. Mariae Virginis.* Venice, G. Vincenti. C 3426.

1593. *Ad completorium, psalmi duplices, primi octonis nonisque vocibus secundi concinendi, cum antiphonis solitis B. Virginis Mariae.* Venice, R. Amadino. C 3428.

Croce, Giovanni. 1591. *Compietta a otto voci.* Venice, G. Vincenti. C 4428.

1594. *Motetti a otto voci. . .*Venice, G. Vincenti. C 4429.

1595. *Motetti a otto voci. . .libro secondo.* Venice, G. Vincenti. C 4436.

1596a. *Messe a otto voci.* Venice, G. Vincenti. C 4441.

1596b. *Salmi che si cantano a Terza, con l'inno Te Deum, & i salmi Benedictus e Miserere a otto voci.* Venice, G. Vincenti. C 4448.

1597. *Vespertina omnium solemnitatum psalmodia octonis vocibus decantanda.* Venice, G. Vincenti. C 4449.

1610. *Sacre cantilene concertate a tre, a cinque et sei voci con i suoi ripieno a quattro, et il basso per l'organo.* Venice, G. Vincenti. C 4463.

Donato, Baldassare. 1599. *Il primo libro de motetti a cinque, a sei, et otto voci.* Venice, A. Gardano. D 3416.

Dulichius, Philipp. 1607. *Prima pars centuriae octonum et septenum vocum harmonias sacras laudibus sanctissimae triados consecratas continentis.* Stettin, the author. D 3688. Mod. edn, DDT 31.

1608. *Secunda pars centuriae. . .*Stettin, the author. D 3689. Mod. edn, DDT 41.

1610. *Tertia pars centuriae. . .*Stettin, the author. D 3690.

1612. *Quarta pars centuriae. . .*Stettin, the author. D 3692.

Festa, Costanzo. 1583. *Litaniae Deiparae Virginis Mariae, ex sacra scriptura collectae.* Munich, A. Berg. F 643. [Actually by Porta, 1575.]

Gabrieli, Andrea. 1565. *Sacrae cantiones. . .quinque vocum. . .liber primus.* Venice, A. Gardano. G 49.

1572. *Primus liber missarum sex vocum.* Venice, li figliuoli di A. Gardano. G 53.

1583. *Psalmi Davidici, qui poenitentiales nuncupantur. . .sex vocum.* Venice, A. Gardano. G 56.

Gabrieli, Andrea and Giovanni. 1587. See 1587[16].

Gabrieli, Giovanni. 1597. *Sacrae symphoniae. . .senis, 7, 8, 10, 12, 14, 15, & 16, tam vocibus, quam instrumentis.* Venice, A. Gardano. G 86. Mod. edn, Opera vols. 1 & 2.

1615. *Symphoniae sacrae. . .liber secundus, senis, 7, 8, 10, 11, 12, 13, 14, 15, 16, 17, & 19, tam vocibus, quam instrumentis.* Venice, Gardano/Magni. G 87. Mod. edn, Opera vols. 3–5.

Giacobbi, Girolamo. 1609. *Prima parte dei salmi concertati a due, e piu chori.* Venice, A. Gardano & fratelli. G 1821.

Goudimel, Claude. 1566. *Septième livre de pseaumes de David, mis en musique à quatre parties en forme de motetz.* Paris, A. Le Roy & R. Ballard. G 3199.

Guerrero, Francisco. 1547. *Motecta. . .quae partim quaternis, partim quinis, alia senis, alia octonis et duodenis concinuntur vocibus.* Venice, G. Vincenti. G 4866.

1555. *Sacrae cantiones, vulgo moteta nuncupata, quatuor et quinque vocum.* [Seville], Martinus a Montesdoca. G 4867.

1570. *Motteta. . .quae partim quaternis, partim quinis, alis senis, alia octonis concinuntur vocibus.* Venice, figliuoli di A. Gardano. G 4871.

1589. *Mottecta. . .quae partim quaternis partim quinis, alia senis, alia octonis concinuntur vocibus, liber secundus.* Venice, G. Vincenti. G 4875.

Handl, Jacob. 1580. *Selectiores quaedam missae. . .Missarum VII. & VIII. vocum, liber I.* Prague, G. Nigrin. H 1976.

1586. *Tomus primus, operis musici, cantionum quatuor, quinque, sex, octo et plurium vocum.* . .Prague, G. Nigrin. H 1980. Mod. edn, DTÖ 12 & 24.

1587a. *Secundus tomus musici operis.* . .Prague, G. Nigrin. H 1981. Mod. edn, DTÖ 24 & 30.

1587b. *Tertius tomus musici operis.* . .Prague, G. Nigrin. H 1982. Mod. edn, DTÖ 40.

1590. *Quartus tomus music operis.* . .Prague, G. Nigrin. H 1985. Mod. edn, DTÖ 48 & 51-2.

Hassler, Hans Leo. 1591. *Cantiones sacrae de festis praecipuis totius anni 4. 5. 6. 7. 8. et plurium vocum.* Augsburg, V. Schönigk. H 2323. Mod. edn, DDT 2.

1597. *Cantiones sacrae.* . .*editio altera, ab ipso autore correcta, & motectis aliquot aucta.* Nuremberg, P. Kauffmann. H 2324. Mod. edn, DDT 2.

1599. *Missae quaternis, V. VI. et VIII. vocibus.* Nuremberg, P. Kauffmann. H 2327. Mod. edn, DDT 7.

1601. *Sacri concentus quatuor, 5, 6, 7, 8, 9, 10 & 12 vocum.* Augsburg, V. Schönigk. H 2328. Mod. edn, DDT 24-5.

1612. *Sacri concentus.* . .*editio altera, correcta, & motectis aliquot aucta.* Nuremberg, P. Kauffmann. H 2329. Mod. edn, DDT 24-5.

Hollander, Christian. 1570. *Newe teutsche geistliche und weltliche Liedlein, mit viern, fünff, sechs, siben und acht Stimmen.* Munich, A. Berg. H 6322.

Kugelmann, Johannes. 1540. *Concentus novi, trium vocum, ecclesiarum usui in Prussia precipue accomodati.* . .*Item etliche Stuck mit acht, sechs, fünf und vier Stymmen hinzugethan.* Augsburg, M. Kriesstein. K 2967, 1540[8]. Mod. edn, 1955.

Lambardi, Girolamo. 1594. *Psalmi ad tertiam, una cum missa.* . .*octonis vocibus.* Venice, R. Amadino. L 365.

Lasso, Orlando di. 1565. *Modulorum.* . .*quaternis, quinis, senis, septenis, octonis et denis vocibus modulatorum secundum volumen.* Paris, A. Le Roy & R. Ballard. L 784.

1566. *Sacrae cantiones (vulgo motecta appellatae) sex et octo vocum.* . .*liber quartus.* Venice, A. Gardano. L 796.

1568. *Selectissimae cantiones.* . .*sex & pluribus vocibus.* Nuremberg, T. Gerlach. L 815.

1570a. *Selectiorum aliquot cantionum sex vocum fasciculus, adiunctus in fine tribus dialogis octo vocum.* Munich, A. Berg. L 833.

1570b. *Mellange.* . .*contenant plusieurs chansons, tant en vers latin qu'en ryme francoyse, à quatre, cinq, six, huit, dix parties.* Paris, A. Le Roy & R. Ballard. L 834.

1573a. *Moduli sex, septem et duodecim vocum.* Paris, A. Le Roy & R. Ballard. L 858.

1573b. *Sex cantiones latinae quatuor adiuncto dialogo octo vocum. Sechs teutsche Lieder mit vier, sampt einem Dialogo mit 8. Stimmen. Six chansons françoises nouvelles a quatre voix, avecq un dialogue a huict. Sei madrigali nuovi a quatro, con un dialogo a otto voci.* . . Munich, A. Berg. L 860.

1576. *Patrocinium musices.* . .*Magnificat aliquot, quatuor, quinque, sex, et octo vocum, quinta pars.* Munich, A. Berg. L 885.

1577a. *Missae variis concentibus ornatae.* . .*cum cantico Beatae Mariae, octo modis musicis variatio.* Paris, A. Le Roy & R. Ballard. L 900.

1577b. *Moduli, quatuor, 5. 6. 7. 8 et novem vocum.* Paris, A. Le Roy & R. Ballard. L 904.

1581. *Libro de villanelle, moresche, et altre canzoni, a 4. 5. 6. et 8. voci.* Paris, A. Le Roy & R. Ballard. L 930.

1582. *Fasciculi aliquot sacrarum cantionum cum quatuor, quinque, sex & octo vocibus.* Nuremberg, T. Gerlach. L 937.

1585a. *Sacrae cantiones.* . .*quatuor vocum.* Munich, A. Berg. L 955.

1585b. *Cantica sacra, recens numeris et modulis musicis ornata.* . .*sex et octo vocibus.* Munich, A. Berg. L 956.

1588. *Moduli quatuor et octo vocum.* Paris, A. Le Roy & R. Ballard. L 985.

1604. *Magnum opus musicum.* . .*complectens omnes cantiones quas motetas vulgo vocant.* . . Munich, N. Heinrich. L 1019.

1619. *Iubilus B. Virginis hoc est centum Magnificat.* Munich, N. Heinrich. L 1031.

Le Jeune, Claude. 1564. *Dix pseaumes de David.* . .*à quatre parties en forme de motets, avec un dialogue à scept.* Paris, A. Le Roy & R. Ballard. L 1672. Mod. edn, Expert 1928.

1585. *Livre de mélanges.* . .Antwerp, C. Plantin. L 1674.

1606. *Pseaumes en vers mesurez mis en musique, à 2. 3. 4. 5. 6. 7. & 8. parties.* Paris, P. Ballard. L 1692. Mod. edn, Expert 1905–6.

Malvezzi, Cristofano. 1591. *Intermedii et concerti, fatti per la commedia rappresentata in Firenze.* Venice, G. Vincenti. M 262, 1591[7]. Mod. edn, Walker 1963.

Marino, Alessandro. 1596. *Completorium ad usum romanum duodenis vocibus concinendum.* Venice, R. Amadino. M 685.

Massaino, Tiburtio. 1576. *Concentus quinque vocum in universos psalmos. . .cum tribus Magnificat, quorum ultimum novem vocum modulatione copulatur.* Venice, A. Gardano. M 1266.

Merulo, Claudio. 1594. *Sacrorum concentuum octonis, denis, duodenis et sexdenis vocibus modulandorum. . .liber primus.* Venice, A. Gardano. M 2365. Mod. edn, Merulo, Musica sacra, vols. 5 & 6.

1609. *Misse due, cum octo, et duodecim vocibus concinende, additeque lytaniae Beatae Mariae Virginis octo vocum.* Venice, A. Gardano & fratelli. M 2367. Mod. edn, Merulo, Musica sacra, vol. 2.

Monte, Philippe de. 1585. *Sacrarum cantionum cum sex & duodecim vocibus. . .liber primus.* Venice, A. Gardano. M. 3319. Mod. edn, Opera 2, series A, vol. 5.

1587. *Liber I. Missarum.* Antwerp, C. Plantin. M 3320. Mod. edn of no. 7, *Missa 'Confitebor tibi':* Opera 2, series B, vol. 2.

Monteverdi, Claudio. 1610. *Sanctissimae Virgini missa senis vocibus ac vesperae pluribus decantandae. . .*Venice, R. Amadino. M 3445. Mod. edn, Opere vol. 14.

Palestrina, Giovanni Pierluigi da. 1572. *Motettorum quae partim quinis, partim senis, partim octonis concinantur, liber secundus.* Venice, G. Scotto. P 705. Mod. edn, Opere vol. 7.

1575. *Motettorum quae partim quinis partim senis, partim octonis vocibus concinantur, liber tertius.* Venice, erede di G. Scotto. P 711. Mod. edn, Opere vol. 8.

1601. *Missae quatuor octonis vocibus concinendae.* Venice, R. Amadino. P 688. Mod. edn, Opere vol. 30.

Pallavicino, Benedetto. 1605. *Sacrae dei laudes, octo, et una duodecim, duae vero sexdecim vocibus concinendae. . .*Venice, R. Amadino. P 771.

Phinot, Dominique. 1548a. *Liber secundus mutetarum, sex, septem, et octo vocum.* Lyons, G. & M. Beringen. P 2017. Mod. edn, Opera vol. 4.

1548b. *Premier livre contenant trente et sept chansons.* Lyons, G. & M. Beringen. P 2018. Mod. edn, Opera vol. 3/1.

1548c. *Second livre contenant vingt et six chansons.* Lyons, G. & M. Beringen. P 2019. Mod. edn, Opera vol. 3/2.

1554. *Liber secundus mutetarum quinque vocum.* Pesaro, B. Cesano. P 2020. Mod. edn, Opera vol. 2.

1555. *Il primo libro di salmi a quatro voci a uno choro, con la gionta di dui Magnificat.* Venice, A. Gardano. P 2022.

Porta, Costanzo. 1575. *Litaniae Deiparae Virginis Mariae cum octo vocibus.* Venice, G. Angelieri. P 5179.

1605. *Psalmodia vespertina omnium solemnitatum octo vocibus decantanda. . .cum quattuor canticis B. Virginis itidem octo vocum, uno tantum excepto bis octo vocibus concinendo.* Venice, A. Gardano. P 5185. Mod. edn, Opera vols. 11 & 17.

Portinaro, Francesco. 1557. *Il terzo libro di madrigali a cinque & a sei voci, con tre dialoghi a sette & uno a otto.* Venice, A. Gardano. P 5226.

1568. *Il secondo libro de motteti a sei, sette et otto voci.* Venice, A. Gardano. P 5222.

1572. *Il terzo libro de motetti a cinque, sei, sette et otto voci.* Venice, gli figliuoli di A. Gardano. P 5223.

Praetorius, Hieronymus. 1599. *Cantiones sacrae de praecipuis festis totius anni 5. 6. 7. & 8. vocum.* Hamburg, Philipp de Ohr. P 5336. [Expanded reprints: 1607, 1622a.]

1602. *Magnificat octo vocum super octo tonos consuetos, cum motetis aliquot 8. et 12. vocum.* Hamburg, Philipp de Ohr. P 5333. [Reprint: 1622b.]

1607. *Cantiones sacrae. . .5. 6. 7. 8. 10. & 12. vocum. . .operum musicorum auctoris tomus primus. . .*Hamburg, Philipp de Ohr. P 5337, 1607[5].

1616. *Liber missarum, qui est operum musicorum tomus tertius, V. VI. VIII. voc.* Hamburg, H. Carstens. P 5329.

1618. *Cantiones variae V. VI. VII. IIX. X. XII. XVI. XX. vocum quae sunt operum musicorum tomus quartus. . .*Hamburg, the author. P 5341.

1622a. *Cantiones sacrae. . .quae sunt operum musicorum tomus primus. . .*Hamburg, the author. P 5338, 1622[8].

1622b. *Canticum B. Mariae Virginis, seu Magnificat. . .quod est operum musicorum tomus secundus. . .motectis aliquot 8. 10. & 12. vocum. . .*Hamburg, the author. P 5334.

1625. *Cantiones novae officiosae V, VI, VII, VIII, X et XV voc., quae sunt operum musicorum tomus quintus. . .*Hamburg, M. Hering. P 5343.

Praetorius, Michael. 1605. *Musae Sioniae. . .mit VIII. Stimmen gesetzt. . .Erster Theil.* Regensburg, the author. P 5348. Mod. edn, Werke vol. 1.

1607a. *Musae Sioniae. . .mit VIII. und XII. Stimmen gesetzet. . .ander Theil.* Jena, the author. P 5349. Mod. edn, Werke vol. 2.

1607b. *Musae Sioniae. . .mit VIII. IX. und XII. Stimmen gesetzet. . .dritter Theil.* Helmstedt, the author. P 5350. Werke vol. 3.

1607c. *Musae Sioniae. . .mit VIII. Stimmen gesetzet. . .vierdter Theil.* Helmstedt, the author. P 5351. Werke vol. 4.

1607d. *Musae Sioniae. . .mit II. III. IV. V. VI. VII. VIII. Stimmen. Fünffter Theil.* Wolfenbüttel, the author. P 5352, 1607[12]. Werke vol. 5.

1607e. *Musarum Sionar: motectae et psalmi latini. . .IV. V. VI. VII. VIII. IX. X. XII. XVI. vocum. . .I pars.* Nuremberg, A. Wagenmann. P 5361. Werke vol. 10.

1611a. *Missodia Sionia. . .2. 3. 4. 5. 6. & 8. vocibus, (chorali cumprimis observata). . .* Wolfenbüttel, the author. P 5362. Werke vol. 9.

1611b. *Hymnodia Sionia. . .3. 4. 5. 6. 7. & 8. vocibus, (chorali cumprimis observata). . .* Wolfenbüttel, the author. P 5363. Werke vol. 12.

1611c. *Eulogodia Sionia. . .2. 3. 4. 5. 6. 7. & 8. vocibus, (chorali cumprimis observata). . .* Wolfenbüttel, the author. P 5364. Werke vol. 13.

1611d. *Megalynodia Sionia. . .5. 6. & 8. voc. . . .*Wolfenbüttel, the author. P 5365. Werke vol. 14.

1613. *Urania oder Urano-Chorodia. Darinnen XVIII der fürnembsten, gebreuchlichsten geistlichen teudtschen Kirchen Gesänge. . .auff 2. 3. und 4. Choren zugebrauchen.* Wolfenbüttel, the author. P 5368. Werke vol. 16.

1619. *Polyhymnia caduceatrix et panegyrica. . .darinnen XL solennische Friedt- und Freudens-Concert: mit 1. 2. 3. 4. 5. 6. 7. 8. 9. 10. 11. 12. 13. 14. 15. 16. 17. 18. 20. 21. und mehr Stimmen, auff II. III. IV. V. und VI. Chor, cum basso generali seu continuo.* Wolfenbüttel, the author. P 5370. Werke vol. 17.

Rogier, Philippe. 1595. *Sacrarum modulationum. . .quae quaternis, quinis, senis, & octonis vocibus concinuntur, liber primus.* Naples, 'Ex Typographia Stelliolae, ad Portam Regalem'. R 1936. Mod. edn, Opera.

Sales, Franz. 1598. *Dialogismus 8. vocum de amore Christi sponsi.* Prague, Georg Nigrinus. S 399.

Scheidt, Samuel. 1620. *Cantiones sacrae, octo vocum.* Hamburg, M. Hering. S 1348, 1620[8]. Mod. edn, Werke vol. 4.

1622. *Pars prima concertuum sacrorum. II. III. IV. VIII. et XII. vocum adiectis symphoniis et choris instrumentalibus, cum basso continuo seu generali pro organo.* Hamburg, M. Hering. S 1350. Werke vols. 14–16.

Schein, Johann Hermann. 1615. *Cymbalum Sionium sive Cantiones sacrae, 5. 6. 8. 9. & 12. vocum.* Leipzig, A. Lamberg. S 1375. Mod. edn, Werke vol. 4.

Schütz, Heinrich. 1619. *Psalmen Davids sampt etlichen Moteten und Concerten mit acht und mehr Stimmen nebenst andern zweyen Capellen, dass dero etliche auff drey und vier Chor nach beliebung gebraucht werden können. Wie auch mit beygefügten Basso continovo vor die Orgel, Lauten, Chitaron, etc.*. Dresden, the author. S 2275. Mod. edn, Werke 2, vols. 23–5; Werke 1, vol. 3.

1623. *Historia der. . .Aufferstehung. . .Jesu Christi. . .*Dresden, G. Bergen. S 2277. Mod. edn, Werke 2, vol. 3.

1636. *Musicalische Exequien. . .mit 6. 8. und mehr Stimmen zu gebrauchen*. Dresden, W. Seyffert. S 2289. Mod. edn, Werke 2, vol. 4.

1650. *Symphoniarum sacrarum tertia pars. . .*Dresden, C. & M. Bergen. S 2295. Mod. edn, Werke 1, vols. 10 & 11.

Tudino, Cesare. 1554. *Li madrigali a note bianche, et negre cromaticho, et napolitane a quatro, con la gionta de dui madrigali a otto voci*. Venice, G. Scotto. T 1334.

Utendal, Alexander. 1573. *Sacrae cantiones sex, et plurium vocum. . .liber secundus*. Nuremberg, T. Gerlach. U 121.

Varotto, Michele. 1563. *Missarum liber primus, cum sex vocibus*. Venice, G. Scotto. V 987.

1595. *Liber primus missarum octonis vocibus, quibus una adiuncta est duodecim vocibus decantanda*. Milan, eredi di F. & S. Tini. V 994.

Viadana, Ludovico. 1602. *Cento concerti ecclesiastici, a una, a due, a tre, & a quattro voci, con il basso continuo per sonar nell'organo*. Venice, G. Vincenti. V 1360.

1612. *Salmi a quattro chori per cantare, e concertare nelle gran solennità di tutto l'anno, con il basso continuo. . .*Venice, G. Vincenti. V 1400.

Victoria, Tomás Luis de. 1572. *Motecta, que partim quaternis, partim quinis, alia senis, alia octonis vocibus concinuntur*. Venice, li figliuoli di A. Gardano. V 1421.

1576. *Liber primus qui missas, psalmos, Magnificat ad Virginem Dei Matrem salutationes, aliaque complectitur*. Venice, A. Gardano. V 1427.

1581a. *Hymnis totius anni. . .qui quattuor concinuntur vocibus, una cum quattuor psalmis, pro praecipuis festivitatibus, qui octo vocibus modulantur*. Rome, F. Zanetti. V 1428.

1581b. *Cantica B. Virginis vulgo Magnificat quatuor vocibus. Una cum quatuor antiphonis Beatae Virginis per annum: quae quidem, partim quinis, partim octonis vocibus concinuntur*. Rome, F. Zanetti. V 1430.

1583. *Motecta, que partim quaternis, partim quinis, alia senis, alia octonis, alia duodenis vocibus concinuntur. . .*Rome, A. Gardano. V 1422.

1585. *Motecta festorum totius anni cum Communi sanctorum, quae partim senis, partim quinis, partim quaternis, alia octonis vocibus concinuntur*. Rome, A. Gardano. V 1433.

1592. *Missae quattuor, quinque, sex et octo vocibus concinendae. . .liber secundus*. Rome, F. Coattino. V 1434.

1600. *Missae, Magnificat, motecta, psalmi, & alia quam plurima, quae partim octonis, alia nonis, alia duodenis vocibus concinuntur, haec omnia sunt in hoc libro ad pulsandum in organis*. Madrid, 'ex typographia regia'. V 1435.

Vinci, Pietro. 1575. *Missarum cum quinque, sex, & octo vocibus, liber primus*. Venice, erede di G. Scotto. V 1659.

Walter, Johann. 1566. *Das christlich Kinderlied D. Martini Lutheri Erhalt uns Herr, etc. Auffs new in sechs Stimmen gesetzt. . .*Wittenberg, J. Schwertel. W 178.

Wert, Giaches de. 1567. *Il quarto libro de madrigali a cinque voci*. Venice, A. Gardano. W 875. Mod. edn, Opera vol. 4.

1581. *Modulationum cum sex vocibus, liber primus*. Venice, erede di G. Scotto. W 852. Opera vol. 16.

Willaert, Adriano. 1550. See 1550[1].

1555. *I sacri e santi salmi, che si cantano a Vespro et Compieta con li suoi himni, responsorii et Benedicamus. . .a uno choro & a quatro voci. . .con la gionta di dui Magnificat, a quatro voci*. Venice, A. Gardane. W 1123.

1559. *Musica nova*. Venice, A. Gardane. W 1126. Mod. edn, Opera vols. 5 & 13.

Zucchini, Gregorio. 1602. *Harmonia sacra in qua motecta VIII. IX. X. XII. XVI. & XX. vocibus, missae autem VIII. XII. & XVI. contextae vocibus continentur. . .*Venice, G. Vincenti. Z 360.

Modern Editions

Alberti, Gasparo. 1983. *Zwei doppelchörige Magnificat*, ed. Victor Ravizza, Wolfenbüttel. Das Chorwerk, 136.

Arnold, Denis (ed.). 1980. *Ten Venetian motets*. London.

Benvenuti, Giacomo (ed.). 1931-2. *Andrea e Giovanni Gabrieli e la Musica Strumentale in San Marco*. Milan. Istituzioni e monumenti dell'arte musicale italiana, 1 & 2.

Brumel, Antoine. *Opera omnia* (CMM 5), ed. Barton Hudson, vol. 3, Rome, 1970.

Commer, Franz (ed.). 1844-58. *Collectio operum musicorum Batavorum saeculi xvi*, 2.

Daser, Ludwig. 1964. *Motetten*, ed. Anton Schneiders. Lippstadt. EDM (1st series) 47.

Dulichius, Philipp. DDT 31. *Prima pars centuriae. . .Stetini 1607*, ed. Rudolf Schwartz, rev. Hans Joachim Moser. Wiesbaden & Graz, 1958.

DDT 41. *Secunda pars centuriae. . .Stetini 1608*, ed. Rudolf Schwartz, rev. Hans Joachim Moser. Wiesbaden & Graz, 1958.

Dunning, Albert (ed.). 1974. *Novus thesaurus musicus vol. 5* (CMM 64). Rome.

Expert, Henry (ed.). 1905-6. *Les Maîtres musiciens de la Renaissance française*, 20-2. Paris. 1928. *Monuments de la musique française au temps de la Renaissance*, 8. Paris.

Gabrieli, Andrea. CM. *Complete Madrigals*, ed. A. Tillman Merritt. Vols. 11 & 12. Madison, 1984. RRMR 51 & 52.

1941. *Musiche di Chiesa*, ed. Giovanni D'Alessi. Milan. I classici musicali italiani, 5.

1965. *Drei Motetten, zu 8 Stimmen*, ed. Denis Arnold. Wolfenbüttel & Zurich. Das Chorwerk, 96.

Gabrieli, Giovanni. *Opera omnia* (CMM 12), ed. Denis Arnold, vols. 1-5, Rome, 1956-68.

Gombert, Nicolas. *Opera omnia* (CMM 6), ed. J. Schmidt-Görg. Rome. Vol. 3, 1963; vol. 9, 1975.

Guerrero, Francisco. 1978. *Duo seraphim à 12*, ed. Bruno Turner. London.

Handl, Jacob. DTÖ 12. *Opus musicum I*, ed. Emil Bezecny & Josef Mantuani. Vienna, 1899 (*R* Graz, 1959).

DTÖ 24. *Opus musicum II*, ed. as above. Vienna, 1905 (*R* Graz, 1959).

DTÖ 30. *Opus musicum III*, ed. as above. Vienna, 1908 (*R* Graz, 1959).

DTÖ 40. *Opus musicum IV*, ed. as above. Vienna, 1913 (*R* Graz, 1959).

DTÖ 48. *Opus musicum V*, ed. as above. Vienna, 1917 (*R* Graz, 1960).

DTÖ 51-2. *Opus musicum VI*, ed. as above. Vienna, 1919 (*R* Graz, 1960).

DTÖ 78. *Sechs Messen*, ed. Paul Fisk. Vienna, 1935 (*R* Graz, 1960).

DTÖ 94-5. *Fünf Messen*, ed. Paul Fisk. Vienna, 1959 (*R* Graz, 1979).

Hassler, Hans Leo. DDT 2. *Cantiones sacrae*, ed. Hermann Gehrmann, rev. C. Russell Crosby. Wiesbaden & Graz, 1961.

DDT 7. *Messen*, ed. Joseph Auer, rev. C. Russell Crosby. Wiesbaden & Graz, 1961.

DDT 24-5. *Sacri concentus*, ed. Joseph Auer, rev. C. Russell Crosby. Wiesbaden & Graz, 1961.

Josquin des Prez. *Werken*. Vol. 3, ed. Albert Smijers, Amsterdam, 1952; supplement, ed. M. Antonowycz & W. Elders, Amsterdam, 1969.

1933. *Drei Evangelien-Motetten*, ed. Friedrich Blume. Wolfenbüttel. Das Chorwerk 23.

Kugelmann, Johannes. 1955. *Concentus novi*, ed. Hans Engel. Kassel & Basel. EDM, Sonderreihe 2.

La Rue, Pierre de. 1950. *Missa Ave sanctissima*, ed. Laurence Feininger. Rome. Documenta polyphoniae liturgicae Sanctae Ecclesiae Romanae, serie 18: 1.

Lasso, Orlando di. Werke 1. *Sämtliche Werke, alte Reihe*, ed. F. X. Haberl & A. Sandberger, Leipzig. Vol. 1, 1894; vol. 10, 1898; vol. 19, 1908; vol. 21, 1926.

Werke 2. *Sämtliche Werke, neue Reihe*, ed. S. Hermelink & J. Erb. Kassel & Basel. Vol. 5, 1965; vol. 8, 1968; vol. 10, 1970; vol. 14, 1986; vol. 15, 1986.

1981. *Aurora lucis rutilat and Magnificat super Aurora lucis rutilat*, ed. Clive Wearing. London.

Liber usualis. Ed. the Benedictines of Solesmes. Tournai & New York, 1962.

Malipiero, G. F. & Fagotto, V. (eds.). 1965. Antonfrancesco Doni, *Dialogo della musica*. Vienna & London. Collana di musiche veneziane inedite e rare 7.

Merulo, Claudio. *Musica sacra*, ed. James Bastian (CMM 51). Vol. 2, 1971; vol. 5, 1982; vol. 6, 1984.

Minor, A. C. and Mitchell, B. 1968. *A Renaissance Entertainment*. Columbia, Missouri.

Monte, Philippe de. Opera 1. *Opera omnia*, ed. C. van den Borren & G. van Doorslaer. Bruges. Vols. 14 & 15, 1930.

    Opera 2. *Philippi de Monte Opera*, ed. R. B. Lenaerts *et al*. Leuven. Series A, vol. 5, 1981; series B, vol. 2, 1979.

Monteverdi, Claudio. *Tutte le opere*, ed. G. F. Malipiero, Asolo 1926–42, rev. edn, 1954, vol. 14.

Mouton, Jean. *Opera omnia* (CMM 43), ed. A. C. Minor. Vol. 4. Rome, 1974.

Palestrina, Giovanni Pierluigi da. *Werke*, ed. F. X. Haberl *et al*. Leipzig, 1862–1903 (*R* 1968). Vols. 6, 7, 26, 30, 32.

    Le opere complete, ed. R. Casimiri *et al*. Rome, 1939– . Vols. 7, 8, 16, 20, 30, 32, 33.

Phinot, Dominique. *Opera omnia* (CMM 59), ed. Janez Höfler & Roger Jacob. Vol. 2, Rome, 1974; vol. 3, Rome, 1979; vol. 4, Neuhausen–Stuttgart, 1982.

Picker, Martin. 1965. *The chanson albums of Marguerite of Austria*. Berkeley and Los Angeles.

Porta, Costanzo. *Opera omnia*, ed. Siro Cisilino. Padua, 1964– . Vols. 5, 11, 17, 18.

Praetorius, Hieronymus. DDT 23. *Ausgewählte Werke*, ed. Hugo Leichtentritt. Wiesbaden, 1905 (*R* Graz, 1959).

    1974a & b. *Polychoral motets*, ed. Frederick K. Gable. Madison. RRMR 18 & 19.

Praetorius, Michael. *Werke*. *Gesamtausgabe der musikalischen Werke*, ed. Friedrich Blume *et al*. Wolfenbüttel, 1928–40, 1960.

Resinarius, Balthasar. DDT 34. *Newe deudsche Gesenge*, ed. Johannes Wolf. Wiesbaden, 1908 (*R* Wiesbaden & Graz, 1958).

Rogier, Philippe. *Opera omnia* (CMM 61), ed. Lavern J. Wagner. Rome, 1974–6.

Scheidt, Samuel. *Werke*, ed. G. Harms & C. Mahrenholz. Hamburg, 1923–62 and Leipzig, 1971– . Vols. 4, 14, 15, 16.

Schein, Johann Hermann. *Sämtliche Werke*, vol. 4, ed. Arthur Prüfer. Leipzig, 1912.

Schering, Arnold. 1931. *Geschichte der Musik in Beispielen*. Leipzig.

Schütz, Heinrich. Werke 1. *Sämtliche Werke*, ed. Philipp Spitta *et al*. Leipzig, 1885–94, 1909, 1927 (*R* 1968–73). Vols. 3 & 14.

    Werke 2. *Sämtliche Werke*, ed. Wilhelm Ehmann *et al*. Kassel, 1951– . Vols. 4, 23, 24, 25, 27, 28, 32, 38, 39.

    1961. *Unser Herr Jesus Christus*, ed. Werner Braun. Kassel.

    1972. *Stehe auf, meine Freundin*, ed. Wolfram Steude. Leipzig.

Sermisy, Claudin de. *Opera omnia* (CMM 52), ed. Gaston Allaire. Vol. 2, Rome, 1972.

Smijers, A. & Merritt, A. T. (eds.). 1934–64. *Treize livres de motets parus chez Pierre Attaingnant en 1534 et 1535*. Paris. Vols. 3 & 12.

Striggio, Alessandro. 1980. *Ecce beatam lucem*, ed. Hugh Keyte. London.

Sweelinck, Jan Pieterszoon. *Werken*, vol. 5, ed. Max Seiffert. Leipzig, 1898.

Tallis, Thomas. 1966. *Spem in alium*, ed. Philip Brett. London.

Taverner, John. 1923. London. Tudor church music 1.

Torchi, Luigi. 1897. *L'arte musicale in Italia* 2. Milan.

Victoria, Tomás Luis de. *Opera omnia*, ed. Felipe Pedrell. Leipzig, 1902–13 (*R* 1965). Vols. 1–4, 6, 7.

Walker, D. P. (ed.). 1963. *Musique des Intermèdes de 'La Pellegrina'*, Paris.

Wert, Giaches de. *Opera omnia* (CMM 24), ed. C. MacClintock & M. Bernstein. Rome, 1961– . Vols. 4 & 16.

Willaert, Adriano. *Opera omnia* (CMM 3), ed. H. Zenck & W. Gerstenberg. Rome, 1950– . Vols. 4, 5, 8, 13.

Books and Articles

Adrio, Adam. 1970. 'Samuel Scheidt's Cantiones sacrae octo vocum von 1620: Beobachtungen und Anmerkungen'. In *Kerygma und Melos: Christhard Mahrenholz 70 Jahre*, ed. Walter Blankenburg *et al*, p. 210. Kassel.

Alfieri, E. 1970. 'La cappella musicale di Loreto – dalle origini a Costanzo Porta (1507–1574)'. *Quadrivium*, 11/ii: 5.

Anthon, Carl. 1943. 'Music and musicians in Northern Italy during the sixteenth century'. Unpublished dissertation, Harvard University.

1946. 'Some aspects of the social status of Italian musicians during the 16th century'. *JRBM*, 1: 111, 222.

Armstrong, James. 1978. 'How to compose a psalm: Ponzio and Cerone compared'. *SM*, 7: 103.

Arnold, Denis. 1953. 'Giovanni Croce and the concertato style'. *MQ*, 39: 37.

1955. 'Instruments in church: some facts and figures'. *Monthly Musical Record*, 85: 32.

1955–6. 'Ceremonial music in Venice at the time of the Gabrielis'. *PRMA*, 82: 47.

1959a. 'Andrea Gabrieli und die Entwicklung der "Cori-spezzati"-Technik'. *Mf*, 12: 259.

1959b. 'Music at the Scuola di San Rocco'. *ML*, 40: 229.

1959c. 'The significance of "cori spezzati"'. *ML*, 40: 4.

1965. 'Music at a Venetian confraternity in the Renaissance'. *AcM*, 37: 62.

1970. 'God, Caesar and Mammon: a study of patronage in Venice 1550–1750'. Inaugural lecture, University of Nottingham.

1972. 'Schütz in Venice'. *Music and Musicians*, 21/1: 30.

1978. 'The grand motets of Orlandus Lassus'. *EM*, 6: 170.

1979. *Giovanni Gabrieli and the music of the Venetian High Renaissance*. London.

1980. 'Cori spezzati'. *NGr*, 4: 776.

Artusi, Giovanni Maria. 1589. *L'arte del contrapunto ridotta in tavola. Seconda parte*. Venice.

Bastian, James George Jr. 1967. 'The sacred music of Claudio Merulo'. Unpublished dissertation, University of Michigan.

Bent, Margaret. 1984. 'Diatonic ficta'. *EMH*, 4: 1.

Berger, Karol. 1980. *Theories of chromatic and enharmonic music in late 16th century Italy*. Ann Arbor.

Boetticher, Wolfgang. 1955. 'Eine Frühfassung doppelchöriger Motetten Orlando di Lassos'. *AMw*, 12: 206.

1958. *Orlando di Lasso und seine Zeit*. Kassel and Basel.

Bohn, Emil. 1890. *Die musikalischen Handschriften des XVI. und XVII. Jahrhunderts in der Stadtbibliothek Breslau*. Breslau.

Böker-Heil, N. 1969. 'Zu einem frühvenezianischen Motetten Repertoire'. In *Helmuth Osthoff zu seinem siebzigsten Geburtstag*, ed. U. Aarburg & P. Caan, p. 59. Tutzing.

Bossuyt, Ignace. 1983. *De componist Alexander Utendal (c.1543/1545–1581)*. Brussels.

Braun, Werner. 1980. 'Kompositionen von Adam Gumpelzhaimer in Florilegium Portense'. *Mf*, 33: 131.

1984. 'Giovanni Gabrieli und Württemberg'. *Analecta Musicologica*, 22: 3.

Brown, Howard Mayer. 1973. *Sixteenth-century instrumentation: the music for the Florentine intermedii*. Rome.

Bryant, David. 1979. 'Liturgia e musica liturgica nella fenomenologia del "Mito di Venezia"'. In *Mitologie: Convivenze de Musica e Mitologia*, ed. G. Morelli, p. 205. Venice.

1981a. 'The *cori spezzati* of St Mark's: myth and reality'. *EMH*, 1: 165.

1981b. 'Liturgy, ceremonial and sacred music in Venice at the time of the Counter-reformation'. Unpublished dissertation, University of London.

Bukofzer, Manfred. 1950. 'The beginnings of choral polyphony'. In his *Studies in Medieval and Renaissance Music*, p. 176. New York.

Bussi, Francesco. 1967. *Piacenza Archivio del Duomo: Catalogo del fondo musicale*. Milan.

Caffi, Francesco. 1854–5. *Storia della musica sacra nella già Cappella ducale di San Marco in Venezia dal 1318 al 1797*. 2 vols., Venice. *R* Milan, 1931.

Carver, Anthony F. 1975. 'The psalms of Willaert and his North Italian contemporaries'. *AcM*, 47: 270.

1980. 'The development of sacred polychoral music to 1580'. Unpublished dissertation, University of Birmingham.

1981. 'Polychoral music: a Venetian phenomenon?'. *PRMA*, 108: 1.

Casimiri, Raffaele. 1935. 'Disciplina Musicae e "Mastri di Capella" dopo il Concilio di Trento nei maggiori Istituti Ecclesiastici di Roma: Seminario Romano'. *NA*, 12: 1, 73.

1941-2. 'Musica e musicisti nella cattedrale di Padova'. *NA*, 18: 1, 101; 19: 49.

Census-Catalogue of manuscript sources of polyphonic music 1400-1550. Vol. 1, 1979. Vol. 3, 1984. American Institute of Musicology.

Collet, Henri. 1914. *Victoria*. Paris.

Crabtree, Phillip D. 1971. 'The vocal works of Gioseffo and Francesco Guami'. Unpublished dissertation, University of Cincinnati.

Crawford, David. 1975. *Sixteenth-century choirbooks in the Archivio Capitolare at Casale Monferrato*. American Institute of Musicology.

D'Alessi, Giovanni. 1931. 'I manoscritti musicale del sec. XVI° del Duomo di Treviso'. *AcM*, 3: 148.

1952. 'Precursors of Adriano Willaert in the practice of Coro Spezzato'. *JAMS*, 5: 187.

1954. *La Cappella Musicale del Duomo di Treviso (1300-1633)*. Treviso.

David, Hans T. & Mendel, Arthur. 1945. *The Bach reader*. New York.

Debes, L. H. 1964. 'Die musikalischen Werke von Claudio Merulo (1533-1604)'. Unpublished dissertation, University of Würzburg.

Dixon, Graham. 1981. 'Liturgical music in Rome (1610-45)'. Unpublished dissertation, University of Durham.

Doe, Paul. 1970. 'Tallis's "Spem in alium" and the Elizabethan respond-motet'. *ML*, 51: 1.

Dondi, Antonio (ed.). 1896. *Notizie storiche ed artistiche del Duomo di Modena*. Modena.

Doni, Antonfrancesco. 1544. *Dialogo della musica*. Venice, G. Scotto. RISM 1544[(22)]. Mod. edn, Malipiero & Fagotto 1965.

Einstein, Alfred. 1949. *The Italian madrigal*. Princeton.

Eitner, Robert. 1877. *Bibliographie der Musik-Sammelwerke des XVI. und XVII. Jahrhunderts* Leipzig.

1899-1904. *Biographisch-bibliographisches Quellenlexikon der Musiker und Musikgelehrten*. Leipzig.

Eitner, Robert & Kade, Otto. 1890. *Katalog der Musik-Sammlung der Kgl. öffentlichen Bibliothek zu Dresden*. Leipzig.

Fay, Robert V. 1946. 'The vocal style of Michael Praetorius'. Unpublished dissertation, Eastman School of Music, Rochester, NY.

Federmann, M. 1932. *Musik und Musikpflege zur Zeit Herzog Albrechts: zur Geschichte der Königsberger Hofkapelle in den Jahren 1525-1578*. Kassel.

Fenlon, Iain & Keyte, Hugh. 1980. 'Memorialls of great skill: a tale of five cities'. *EM*, 8: 329.

Fischer, Klaus. 1979. *Die Psalmkompositionen in Rom um 1600 (ca. 1570-1630)*. Regensburg.

Fouse, Donald. 1960. 'The sacred music of Giammateo Asola'. Unpublished dissertation, University of N. Carolina.

Gable, Frederick K. 1966. 'The polychoral motets of Hieronymus Praetorius (1560-1625)'. Unpublished dissertation, University of Iowa.

1987. 'St Gertrude's Chapel, Hamburg, and the performance of polychoral music'. *EM*, 15: 229.

Gamba, B. 1836. *Ordine delle Nozze dell'Illustrissimo Signor Missier Constantio Sforza. . . 1475*. Venice.

Garbelotto, A. 1952. 'Codici musicali della Biblioteca Capitolare di Padova'. *Rivista Musicale Italiana*, 54: 289.

Gaspari, Gaetano. 1890-1905. *Catalogo della Biblioteca del Liceo Musicale di Bologna*. 4 vols., Bologna (*R* 1961). Vol. 5 ed. U. Sesini, Bologna, 1943 (*R* 1970).

Glixon, Jonathan. 1983. 'A musicians' union in sixteenth-century Venice'. *JAMS*, 36: 392.

Godefroy, T. 1649. *Le Cérémonial français*. Paris.

Gottwald, Clytus. 1964. *Die Handschriften der Württembergischen Landesbibliothek Stuttgart*, Series 1, vol. 1: *Codices musici*, 1. Wiesbaden.

1969. 'Antoine Brumels Messe "Et ecce terrae motus"'. *AMw*, 26: 236.

1974. *Die Musikhandschriften der Staats- und Stadtbibliothek Augsburg*. Wiesbaden.

Haar, James. 1971. 'Zarlino's definition of fugue and imitation'. *JAMS*, 24: 226.

Halm, A. 1902–3. *Katalog über die Musik-Codices des 16. und 17. Jahrhunderts auf der Kgl. Landesbibliothek in Stuttgart*. Leipzig.

Hansen, Peter. 1939. 'The Life and Works of Dominico Phinot (c. 1510–1555)'. Unpublished dissertation, University of N. Carolina, Chapel Hill.

Harran, Don. 1970. 'Towards a definition of the early secular dialogue'. *ML*, 51: 37.

Hermelink, S. 1968. 'Eine neu aufgefundene doppelchörige Messe von Orlando di Lasso'. *Mf*, 21: 202.

Hertzmann, Erich. 1929–30. 'Zur Frage der Mehrchörigkeit in der ersten Hälfte des 16. Jahrhunderts'. *ZMw*, 12: 138.

Höfler, Janez. 1969. 'Dominique Phinot i poceci renesansnog visehorskog pervanja (1548–1568)'. *Zvuk*, 100: 497.

Jarvis, Sister Mary E. 1959. 'The Latin motets of Hans Leo Hassler'. Unpublished dissertation, University of Rochester.

Jeppesen, Knud. 1941. 'Eine musiktheoretische Korrespondenz des frühen Cinquecento'. *AcM*, 13: 38.

1946. *The style of Palestrina and the dissonance*. Revised edition, London 1946 (*R* 1970).

1958. 'A forgotten master of the early 16th century; Gaspar de Albertis'. *MQ*, 44: 311.

Kade, R. 1913–14. 'Antonius Scandellus (1517–1580): ein Beitrag zur Geschichte der Dresdener Hofkantorei'. *Sammelbände der Internationalen Musik-Gesellschaft*, 15: 535.

Kanazawa, Masakata. 1975. 'Two vesper repertories from Verona ca.1500'. *Rivista Italiana di Musicologia*, 10: 155.

Kaufman, Henry W. 1966. *The Life and Works of Nicola Vicentino*. Rome.

Kenton, Egon. 1967. *Giovanni Gabrieli*. Rome.

Kimmel, William B. 1942. 'Polychoral Music and the Venetian School'. Unpublished dissertation, Eastman School of Music, Rochester, NY.

Kinkeldy, O. 1910. *Orgel und Klavier in der Musik des 16. Jahrhunderts*. Leipzig. *R* Hildesheim 1967.

Köchel, L. R. von. 1869. *Die Kaiserliche Hof-Musikkapelle in Wien von 1543 bis 1867*. Vienna.

Kroyer, Theodor. 1909. 'Dialogue und Echo in der alten Chormusik'. *Jahrbuch der Musikbibliothek Peters*, 1909: 13.

Kuhn, Friedrich. 1897. *Bescriebendes Verzeichnis der alten Musikalien. . .des Königlichen Gymnasiums zu Brieg*. Leipzig.

Launay, Denise. 1957. 'Les motets à double choeur en France dans la Iʳᵉ moitié du XVIIᵉ siècle'. *RdM*, 40: 173.

Lenaerts, R. B. M. 1935. 'Notes sur Adrian Willaert, maître de chapelle de Saint-Marc à Venise de 1527 à 1562'. *Bulletin de l'Institut Historique Belge de Rome*, 15: 107.

1938. 'La Chapelle de Saint-Marc à Venise sous Adrian Willaert (1527–1562)'. Bulletin de l'Institut Historique Belge de Rome, 19: 205.

Leuchtmann, H. 1977. *Orlando di Lasso*. Vol. 2: *Briefe*. Wiesbaden.

Lewis, Mary S. 1979. 'Antonio Gardane and his publications of sacred music, 1538–1555'. Unpublished dissertation, Brandeis University.

Lionnet, Jean. 1987. 'Performance practice in the Papal Chapel during the 17th century'. *EM*, 15: 4.

Llorens, Jose. 1960. *Capellae Sixtinae codices musicis notis instructi sive manu scripti sive praelo excussi*. Vatican City.

1971. *Le opere musicali della Cappella Giulia. I. Manoscritti e edizioni fino al '700*. Vatican City.

Long, Joan. 1971. 'The motets, psalms, and hymns of Adrian Willaert and the liturgy of the Basilica di San Marco in Venice'. Unpublished dissertation, Columbia University.

MacClintock, Carol. 1966. *Giaches de Wert (1535–1596): life and works*. American Institute of Musicology.

Mahrenholz, Christhard. 1924. *Samuel Scheidt: sein Leben und sein Werk*. Leipzig. R 1968.

Maier, J. J. 1879. *Die musikalischen Handschriften der Kgl. Hof- und Staatsbibliothek in München*. Munich.

Marco, Guy A. & Palisca, Claude V. 1968. *Gioseffo Zarlino: The art of counterpoint*. New Haven & London.

Mendel, Arthur. 1948. 'Pitch in the 16th and early 17th centuries'. *MQ*, 34: 28, 199, 336, 575.
   1978. 'Pitch in Western music since 1500'. *AcM*, 50: 1, 328.

Moore, James H. 1981a. *Vespers at St Mark's: Music of Alessandro Grandi, Giovanni Rovetta and Francesco Cavalli*. Ann Arbor.
   1981b. 'The *Vespero delle Cinque Laudate* and the role of *Salmi Spezzati* at St Mark's'. *JAMS*, 34: 249.

Morell, Martin. 1983. 'The biographies of Andrea and Giovanni Gabrieli'. *EMH*, 3: 101.

Moser, Hans J. 1959. *Heinrich Schütz: his life and work*. Transl. Carl F. Pfatteicher. St Louis.

Muoni, Damiano. 1883. *Gli Antegnati organari. . .*Milan.

New Oxford History of Music, The. Vol. 4, ed. Gerald Abraham, London 1968.

Nutter, David. 1977. 'The Italian polyphonic dialogue of the sixteenth century'. Unpublished dissertation, University of Nottingham.

Oberg, Paul M. 1944. 'The sacred music of Philippe de Monte'. Unpublished dissertation, Eastman School of Music, Rochester, NY.

O'Regan, Noel. 1984a. 'The early polychoral music of Orlando di Lasso: new light from Roman sources'. *AcM*, 56: 234.
   1985. 'The Archconfraternity of the Most Holy Trinity in Rome and its music, 1550–1600'. Paper read to the Conference on Medieval and Renaissance Music, University of Nottingham, July 1985. [A revised version was read to the Secondo Convegno di Studi Palestriniani, Palestrina, May 1986 and will be published in the conference proceedings.]
   Forthcoming. 'Sacred polychoral music in Rome, 1575–1621'. Unpublished dissertation, University of Oxford.

Osthoff, Helmuth. 1967. *Die Niederländer und das deutsche Lied*. Tutzing.

Peterson, F. E. 1966. 'Johann Hermann Schein's Cymbalum Sionium: a liturgico-musical study'. Unpublished dissertation, Harvard University.

Powers, Harold S. 1980. 'Mode'. *NGr*, 12: 377.
   1981. 'Tonal types and modal categories in Renaissance polyphony'. *JAMS*, 34: 428.

Praetorius, Michael. 1619. *Syntagma Musicum III: Termini musici*. Wolfenbüttel. Transl.: Hans Lampl, unpublished dissertation, University of S. California, Los Angeles, 1957.

Ravizza, Victor. 1972a. 'Frühe Doppelchörigkeit in Bergamo'. *Mf*, 25: 127.
   1972b. 'Gasparo Alberti: ein wenig bekannter Komponist und dessen Portrait'. In his *Festschrift Arnold Geering zum 70. Geburtstag*, p. 72. Bern & Stuttgart.

Reese, Gustave. 1954. *Music in the Renaissance*. London.
   1960. 'The polyphonic magnificat of the Renaissance as a design in tonal centers'. *JAMS*, 13: 68.

Reitter, Lumir. 1937. *Die Doppelchortechnik bei Heinrich Schütz*. Derendingen.

Roche, Jerome L. A. 1968. 'North Italian liturgical music in the early seventeenth century'. Unpublished dissertation, University of Cambridge.
   1982. *Lassus*. London.
   1982–3. '"Musica diversa di Compietà": Compline and its music in 17th-century Italy'. *PRMA*, 109: 60.
   1984. *North Italian church music in the age of Monteverdi*. Oxford.

Roncaglia, Gino. 1957. *La Cappella Musicale del Duomo di Modena*. Florence.

Rubsamen, Walter H. 1949/51. 'Music research in Italian libraries; an anecdotal account of obstacles and discoveries'. *Notes*, 6: 220; 8: 70.

1957. 'The international 'Catholic' repertoire of a Lutheran church in Nürnberg 1574–1597'. *Annales Musicologiques*, 5: 284.

Sandberger, Adolf. 1894/5. *Beiträge zur Geschichte der bayerischen Hofkapelle unter Orlando di Lasso*. 2 vols. (1 & 3), Leipzig.

Sansovino, F. 1663. *Venetia città nobilissima et singolare*. Revised edition, Venice.

Saulnier, V. L. 1959. 'D. Phinot et D. Lupi, musiciens de C. Marot et des marotiques'. *RdM*, 43–4: 61.

Schuler, Richard J. 1963. 'The life and liturgical works of Giovanni Maria Nanino (1545–1607)'. Unpublished dissertation, University of Minnesota.

Selfridge-Field, Eleanor. 1975. *Venetian instrumental music from Gabrieli to Vivaldi*. Oxford.

Senn, Walter. 1954. *Musik und Theater am Hof zu Innsbruck*. Innsbruck.

Silbiger, Alexander. 1977. 'An unknown partbook of early sixteenth-century polyphony'. *SM*, 6: 43.

Skei, Allen B. 1968. 'Jacob Handl's polychoral music'. *Music Review*, 29: 81.

  1981. *Heinrich Schütz, a guide to research*. Garland Press.

Slim, H. Colin. 1962. 'Keyboard music at Castell'Arquato by an early madrigalist'. *JAMS*, 15: 35.

Smallman, Basil. 1985. *The music of Heinrich Schütz*. Leeds.

Smijers, Albert. 1919–21. 'Die Kaiserliche Hofmusikkapelle von 1543–1619'. *Studien zur Musikwissenschaft*, 6: 139; 7: 102; 8: 176.

Smith, Peter. 1978. 'Girolamo Giacobbi and his Salmi Concertati of 1609'. *Studies in Music (Ontario)*, 3: 15.

Smither, Howard E. 1967. 'The Latin dramatic dialogue and the nascent oratorio'. *JAMS*, 20: 403.

Steinhardt, Milton. 1951. *Jacobus Vaet and his motets*. Michigan.

Sternfeld, Frederick W. 1980. 'Aspects of echo music in the Renaissance'. *SM*, 9: 45.

Steude, W. 1974. *Die Musiksammelhandschriften des 16. und 17. Jahrhunderts in der Sächsischen Landesbibliothek zu Dresden*. Wilhelmshaven.

Stevenson, Robert. 1954. 'Sixteenth- and seventeenth-century resources in Mexico. Part I'. *Fontes Artis Musicae*, 1: 69.

  1961. *Spanish Cathedral Music in the Golden Age*. Berkeley & Los Angeles.

  1970. *Renaissance and Baroque musical sources in the Americas*. Washington DC.

Strunk, Oliver. 1950. *Source Readings in Music History*. New York.

Summers, William J. 1982. 'The *Compagnia dei Musici di Roma*, 1584–1604: a preliminary report'. *Current Musicology*, 34: 7.

Tebaldini, Giovanni. 1895. *L'Archivio Musicale della Cappella Antoniana in Padova*. Padua.

Tiozzo, Iginio. 1935. 'Maestri e organisti della Cattedrale di Chioggia fino al XVII secolo'. *NA*, 12: 284.

Troiano, Massimo. 1568. *Discorsi delli trionfi, giostre, apparati, é delle cose più notabile fatte nelle sontuose nozze, dell'illustrissimo & eccellentissimo Signor Duca Guglielmo. . .* Munich.

Turrini, G. 1937. *Catalogo descrittivo dei manoscritti musicali antichi della Società Accademia Filarmonica di Verona*. Verona.

  1941. 'L'Accademia Filarmonica di Verona'. *Atti e Memorie della Accademia Scienza et Lettere di Verona*, serie V, 18: 230.

Vale, Giuseppe. 1930. 'La cappella musicale del Duomo di Udine dal sec. XIII al sec. XIX'. *NA*, 7: 87.

Van den Borren, Charles. 1946. 'La contribution italienne au 'Thesaurus Musicus' de 1564'. *JRBM*, 1: 33.

Van Doorslaer, G. 1921. *La vie et les oeuvres de Philippe de Monte*. Brussels.

Vicentino, Nicola. 1555. *L'antica musica ridotta alla moderna prattica*. Rome.

Vollhardt, Reinhard. 1893–6. *Bibliographie der Musikwerke in der Ratsschulbibliothek zu Zwickau*. Leipzig.

Weaver, Robert. 1961. 'Sixteenth century instrumentation'. *MQ*, 47: 363.

Winter, Paul. 1964. *Der mehrchörige Stil*. Frankfurt.
Zacconi, Ludovico. 1592. *Prattica di musica*. Venice.
Zarlino, Gioseffo. 1558, 1562, 1573, 1589. *Le istitutioni harmoniche*. Venice. 1589 = vol. 1 of *De tutte l'opere del r.m. G. Zarlino*. Eng. transl. of Part 3: Marco & Palisca. 1968.
Zenck, Hermann. 1949. 'Adrian Willaerts "Salmi spezzati" (1550)'. *Mf*, 2: 97.

INDEX